2001
COACH OF THE
YEAR CLINICS

Football Manual

Edited by
Earl Browning

COACHES
CHOICE ™

www.coacheschoiceweb.com

ISBN: 1-8518-485-3

Library of Congress Catalog Card Number (ISSN): 1-534-925-X

Transcription: Tom Cheaney

Book layout and cover design: Paul Lewis

Diagrams: Steve Haag

Photos of Bob Stoops: courtesty Jerry Laziure

Photo of Tom Osborne: courtesy SID department, University of Nebraska

Printer: V.G. Reed and Sons, Inc.

Coaches Choice
P.O. Box 1828
Monterey, CA 93942
www.coacheschoiceweb.com

Contents

Contents

THE ZONE BLOCKING SCHEME

University of Notre Dame

It's a pleasure to be here today. My topic today is about zone blocking. I'm going to talk about our scheme and how we teach it. I really believe this is a great package. It is a package you want to use.

In this scheme there are interchangeable parts. A guard can play tackle. The tight end can play guard, and the tackle can play the tight end. This is a system that is easy to learn and one you can rep out because of a limited amount of time.

Every offense needs an opportunity to stretch the field. You stretch the field with the running game, the pass, and the option game. I am a "Run the ball kind of guy." The older I get and the more places I go, I find myself going back to where I started. If you want to win, you have to have great special teams, be able to run the ball, and play great defense.

At Notre Dame the weather does not corporate some times. You have to be able to run the ball. I am not a pass-happy guy. I have evolved from one pass a game to where I would throw a little more than that, but I want to run the ball.

You have to believe what you believe in and coach it with a passion. It doesn't matter what type of offense it is, believe in what you are doing. Make sure your kids believe that you believe in what you are doing.

I start meetings with this every day. This is what I base my teaching on. *It is difficult for a team to have outstanding morale, confidence and enthusiasm when it cannot look to the offensive line to establish the tempo of the ball game.*

The offensive front establishes the tempo of a game. You have to preach that daily. The offensive line has to be mentally tough, and you have to coach mental toughness.

If the offensive line comes to the huddle with confidence in their eyes, the quarterback will rise. If they come back without confidence, the quarterback will get down, and he will not be able to be the leader he needs to be. To me that is an important concept. Every day I coach that with my players. I am in their face every day. That is the way it is.

When I came to Notre Dame, one of the things I had to do was be a person that would coach the offensive line hard. That is what I do. That is the way it has to be. We have a high character level, great students, and great people, but we have to coach them hard. Our schedule is very demanding. We have to be mentally tough.

This is the last philosophical thing I say before I get on to the business at hand. I have a very simple philosophy of coaching; it hasn't changed since I was in high school. When I was in high school, there was a number of faculty members who felt I was too hard on my kids. The part they didn't understand was I loved my players and they loved me. We as educators, teachers, and coaches have to push our players hard on the field, but when they come off you have to put your arm around them and love them. You love them hard and coach them hard. If you don't love them hard, don't try to coach them hard. Kids will give you everything they have, if they feel you are giving it back to them. That has been the case for that freshman in high school to the first round pick in the NFL.

I am close to my guys at Notre Dame. The come to my house, stay for dinner, and are like part of my family. But when I coach them, I get right in the middle of their chests.

Our philosophy of zone blocking is very simple. It starts with a MATE CONCEPT. That means two people working together. That is what zone blocking is about. When you zone block, you are blocking a play side linebacker. When you combo block, you are blocking a backside Linebacker. There is a common thread. The mate concept takes place in both blocks.

Before I move to specific zone blocks, I need to talk to you about the principles of combinations. Combination blocking is done for a reason. You want to get tremendous movement on the down lineman. The inside zone play is a downhill, kick-you-in-the-face play.

I don't want to insult anyone, but I want to cover the principles of double team and double team to a backer. When you are comfortable with those principles, you are ready to move on to teaching the zone play. I want to coach principles. Principles in a multiple offense I use every day. It is like money in the bank. I can come back to the bank as opposed to a specific thing that can only relate to one kind of play. I want to demonstrate a double team right now. We work on this every single day. The drill we do is called DE-LIVER-TAKE-OVER.

The first thing we want to talk about is how to move the down man. The general principles apply. Both linemen get toe to toe and hip to hip. Both linemen get four eyes on the linebacker. The lineman who is posting on the double team is trying to deliver the ball of his shoulder into the chest of the down defender. The second lineman comes hip to hip with the post blocker, and they squeeze the down defender. They never want to put their outside hand on the defender. If they do, their butts come apart. We want their hips together as they walk the defender back.

The deliver-take-over skills are used for the finish in the block. Both linemen are watching the linebacker. They are waiting for him to scrape one way or the other. When the linebacker takes his side, the lineman to that side delivers the down defender to the other lineman. He full extends his arm and pushes the down defender toward the other offensive lineman. The post lineman takes over and works to get his face across and squares up on the defender.

The lineman never wants to turn his shoulders toward the sideline. If he does, he forces the running back into an entry point. We don't want to force the back anywhere on a zone concept. We want the back to be able to pick his hole.

What we just did is not a zone block, it is a generic drill to teach double team and take over. We work on this every day, although we don't spend much time doing it. But remember the average SAT score at Notre Dame is 1380. They pick up coaching pretty fast.

I'm going to give you some evolution of the zone block. I don't want to bore you, but I think it is important to understand why we zone block. Football blocking used to be man-on-man blocking. But fifty defenses starting slanting the front one way or the other. The guard is supposed to block the linebacker. The defensive tackle slants into the guard and picks him off his block. The offensive tackle is chasing the slanting tackle down, and the linebacker is running free. Because of that, man schemes were no good any more.

The thing that hurts running plays is penetration. Penetration creates negative plays. The offensive is off schedule and can't produce an efficient run. The offense ends up punting the ball on fourth down, because they can't effectively run the ball.

Zone blocking allows the offensive linemen to rip off the ball without the threat of defensive movement. It also gives you two bodies on one body at the point of attack.

The next thing is the numbering system. How do you know who blocks who? It is a very simple rules system to tell you who has whom. The tight end has playside gap number three. The frontside tackle has playside gap number two. The frontside guard has playside gap number one. The center has zero. The backside guard has playside gap number one and the backside tackle has playside gap number two. I'll come back to all this in a minute.

In our terminology, PSG means playside gap. In zone blocking, the lineman steps with his playside foot into his playside gap, and blocks his responsibility. I'm not very sharp, but if I was the playside tackle, I could remember that rule.

To locate our block responsibilities, we have a count system. The center know anyone aligned on him or over him is zero. The center starts the count. After that, everyone simply counts one, two, and three. The smartest guy has to be the center. He has to know when he is covered. When we have a stack, we put the smaller number on the bottom. In a tackle-linebacker stack, the tackle would have the low number.

Let's look at some examples of our counting system. The first defense is a 50 defense. The nose guard is zero. The linebackers are 1 to the tight end side and 1 to the back side. The defensive ends are 2's, and the outside linebackers are 3's.

50 DEFENSE

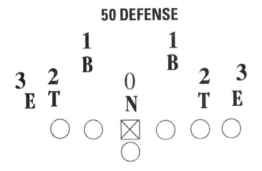

The next defense is an Eagle G defense. Notice the center has no one over him. The numbering starts with the right guard.

EAGLE G

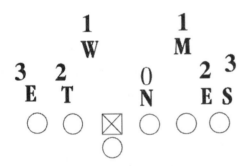

The last example is what we call a Load. It is an over defense with a stack in the strongside B-Gap and backside A-Gap.

LOAD

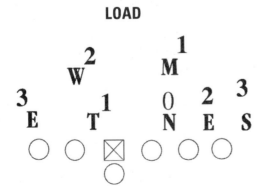

I need to go back to some zone principles. Your kids need to understand whether it is an inside zone play or outside zone play. If the play is an inside zone play, we are talking about vertical movement. If it is an outside zone play, we are not concerned with movement as much as we are getting the bounce. We want to secure the box.

We want to step with the playside foot. The second thing we have to do is run off the ball. We get hip to hip with our mate. The next thing is to get four eyes on the linebacker. The next principle is whether you are covered or uncovered. I'll tell you about this in a minute. It is a key principle.

If a man is head up or an inside shade, it means the same thing to me. There is a threat of an inside move. The other thing is outside. From an outside shade, there is no inside threat. If you are uncovered, you need to know where the defender is aligned on the covered man. We need to know if he is shaded toward you or away from you. The uncovered lineman makes the call in zone blocking.

It doesn't matter whether it is a tight end and a tackle, a tackle and a guard, or a center and a guard, the technique is the same for everyone. For the clinic talk, lets suppose the defense is a 50 defense. The offensive tackle has a 5-technique defensive tackle on him. The guard has a 30 technique linebacker aligned on him. The tackle is covered with an outside shade. The guard is uncovered. He makes the zone block call to the tackle. You have to make up your own terminology. If the tackle's name is Jessie, that could be your zone call.

The center has a nose guard on him. The center calls zero. The guard is uncovered and has number 1. The tackle is covered and has number 2. The tackle knows he can rip off the ball and not worry about inside movement.

Let's get to the technique. The covered man is the tackle. His aiming point is the playside outside number of the defender. His footwork is what I call a wedge step. On the inside zone play, we want movement. You can't step backwards and get movement down the field. He never uses a crossover step or loses his base on the inside zone play. He steps with a ninety-degree step outside and squares up on the block.

If he gets an inside move by the tackle, he is halving the block with the uncovered man. The uncovered man is looking at the shade of the tackle on the offensive tackle. The shade is away from him. His pre-snap read tells him he is going up on the linebacker. He takes a wedge step at the offensive tackle, keying the inside shoulder of the defensive tackle. He takes one step at the defensive tackle.

If he reads the tackle coming down, he drives on the tackle. The offensive tackle has two hands on the tackle, and we are taking him foot-to-foot and hip-to-hip back. We have four eyes on the linebacker. When the linebacker scrapes outside, the tackle comes off and takes over the linebacker.

OUTSIDE SHADE

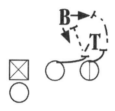

If the shade on the covered lineman is head up to the inside, the pre-snap read is a slant inside. The covered man's target is the outside number of the man over him. Since the shade is head up, the outside number is right in front of the covered man. He takes a wedge step into the outside number of the defensive tackle. If the defensive tackle plays straight, the offensive tackle walls off the outside number waiting for the take-over block of the guard. If he slants, he knows he is going to be on the double team with the guard who takes over the block on the defensive tackle.

The uncovered lineman's pre-snap key tells him he is going to double team with the tackle and take over the block on the down man. He is keying the inside shoulder of the defensive tackle. If the shoulder stays or comes inside, the guard and tackle are doubling team. If the shoulder goes away, he is up on the linebacker.

INSIDE SHADE

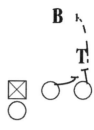

To the backside, it is the same deal. The defense is an Eagle defense. There is a strongside shade on the center with a 5-technique for the defensive tackle and end to the strongside. To the weakside, the guard has a 3-technique on him. The tackle has a 5-technique on him. The tackle does not worry about the defensive end because the playside is opposite him. We are not blocking the backside 5-technique. The play is going to the strongside. The backside linemen are stepping with their playside feet. The guard is covered. The man on him has an inside shade to the tackle. The guard takes an up-and-down step and walls off the inside number of the 3-technique. If the shade on the center is trying to get backside, the guard is protecting against that move or is up on the backside linebacker.

The tackle takes a wedge step, chases down on the tackle, and blows up to the Will linebacker. On the backside, we are ripping and cutting. I love to cut the defenders. They don't like it. We are harassing them, just like they do us. We are flat running on the backside.

We do the same thing to the frontside or backside. The blocks have the same configurations and concepts. The techniques are generic by looks and positions. You, as a football coach, have an opportunity to come out every day, take one concept, and drill the heck out of it. Every day that your players get better at this scheme, you are putting money in the bank. It will pay dividends.

Next, we are going to the outside zone. I am going to make this overly simple. On the outside zone and zone option, the basic principle is clog the box. I am not looking for movement. The aiming point for the blocks is wider. The footwork and steps are wider. The step is deeper and wider, because penetration is not necessarily an enemy.

If the alignment on the covered lineman is head up, he is thinking over take by the inside lineman. His aiming point on the block is the outside biceps of the defender. This footwork is a tough step and a rip through to the linebacker. He has to stay on track. The key coaching point is to keep his outside arm free and based on the alignment of the defender. He should almost have no contact with the defender unless the defender is working outside.

The uncovered man's technique is as follows. His aiming point is to get his face across the defender. His footwork is a big reach step with his playside foot. He steps like he is pulling. The coaching point is important. Because the shade is toward the uncovered man, there are two indicators to take over the block. If the defender widens, he has to stay on his path and over push the defender's shoulder. The object is to seal the front rather than to get movement.

OUTSIDE ZONE HEAD UP

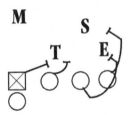

If the covered man has an outside shade on him, he is still aiming for the biceps. His footwork is a wide wedge step with his playside foot. He might have to use a circle reach. The coaching point is to bring both hands with no fear of inside movement by the defender. He should knock back the outside biceps of the defender. He needs to keep his shoulders as square as possible.

The uncovered lineman's aiming point is to get across the face of the defender. His footwork is a wide wedge step with his playside foot. It is a big reach step. Because the shade of the defender is

away from the uncovered lineman, he has one indicator. Unlike the inside zone play, if the shoulder does not come to him, he continues to press for the shoulder. He doesn't go up on the linebacker. He wants to seal the front and take over the block. If at all possible, he wants to cut down the defender.

OUTSIDE SHADE

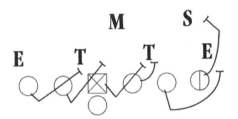

Here is the other phase I really like about the inside zone play. You can get multiple in your formations. You can keep one blocking scheme for any formation you want to use. In any offense, your fullback should be like the tight end. There are similarities in those positions. We run out of two backs and one tight end.

When we run the inside zone, it is a split zone. The tight end is going to wedge step and block the playside number of the defender in the 9-technique. The tackle is uncovered. He makes a call to the tight end for the zone block. He keys the inside shoulder of the 9-technique. If the shoulder doesn't come toward him, he is driving on the linebacker. If the shoulder comes toward the tackle, the tight end and tackle have the 9-technique and the linebacker.

The guard is thinking he has playside gap alone. He is blocking, and he knows his technique. The center is uncovered and has to decide who he is going to work with. If the 3-technique to the playside is a spiker, we will work him that way. If he does not move around, we send the center to work with the backside guard. That will stop the penetration off the backside. The center has zero to one. He is driving the zero, and making the zone call with the guard. The backside guard has 1, and the backside tackle has 2. The tackle is uncovered and is zone blocking with the guard. They have 1 and 2 to the backside.

The fullback is blocking the backside and becomes the tight end to that side. He is blocking number 3. He is driving at the outside hip of the backside tackle, and he is going to cut the defensive end.

We are a drop-step team on the weakside zone. The tailback drop steps, and receives the ball from the quarterback. His aiming point is the butt of the guard. He is running downhill at the butt of the guard. He is reading the first down lineman to the playside. That lineman is going to dictate where the tailback is going to hit. If the first down lineman stretches, the tailback goes inside of him. If there is something inside, he moves backside further. He continues until he finds his entry point through the line of scrimmage.

INSIDE ZONE

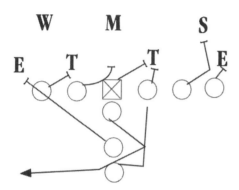

For this play to work, we have to do an unbelievable job of coaching the back. If you are going to run the zone play, all of your coaches have to be on the same page. I don't want to hear anyone talk about running to daylight. How we want to teach it is to get the back downhill at the butt of the offensive guard. We want him to read number one and press the heels of the offensive lineman. Our concept for the back is SLOW-TO-FAST-THROUGH. If the back cuts on air, the linebacker will start to flow, fake the tackle, come back over the top, and beat the tackle.

When that happens, I am running on the field to get in the back's face. The back is accountable for the backside linebacker. I hold the lineman accountable for the penetration. I hold the back accountable for pressing the heels of the offensive linemen to hold the backside linebacker. That is critical, and everyone has to coach it the same way. The quarterback is going to fake the naked bootleg. He is going to hold any blitz by the corner or any end for whom we might not have a replacement. He has to sprint on his bootleg fake. If he doesn't bootleg like he has the ball, I'm going to be in his face. Everybody has a job to do. We

are counting on everybody if the play is to be successful. You have to be consistent and coach them all the same way.

To stop the zone play, the defense wants to get the fourth man down. They want four defenders to each side. You have to block the fourth man with a fullback going strong or bring someone in motion from the outside.

You need to account for that extra man in the box. People have gone so far to say that when the fourth man comes into the box, the only solution is to throw the ball. There is not much good that happens when you throw the ball. If you are ahead by three and have to move the ball, you have to have a way besides throwing the ball. What ever it takes, get someone on the fourth defender. The best way is to recruit a back that makes the defenders miss.

You don't need big linemen to run a zone play. You can get a double team. Two is better than one any day. Get as many double teams as you can get, and you have a shot at moving the ball. Be as uncomplicated as you can get, and you have a shot at winning.

When you come to these clinics, it is not about X's and O's. I heard John Robinson talk at the national convention. There must have been a thousand coaches there. He said that every coach should have been a high school teacher and coach. That is where the fundamentals are taught. Coach fundamentals that are sound. Build a great foundation. I have nothing to say to you that is rocket science. I am here to tell you that it is not about the pen. It doesn't matter what the coach knows, it is what his kids can do.

When you come to clinics, learn how to be a great teacher of techniques and concepts. Coaching is motivation of kids. Coaching is fundamentals. If you build a great foundation, you can put any framework you want on it, and it will stand forever. Don't build a good framework with a crappy foundation. The foundation will crack, and everything will crash. That is why I like the zone play. It is technique sound and simple to understand.

If you give your students a test and they all fail it, whose fault is it? It's your fault. Take responsibility for what you teach. If they don't understand, it is our job to educate them. Coaches are teachers. Fellows, I'm out of time.

RUNNING BACK TECHNIQUES AND DRILLS

Cincinnati Bengals

I would like to give you some background about myself. I am from Harrisburg, Pennsylvania. I went to a high school called John Harris High School. In ten years, we lost four games. We were a pretty good football team. Jan White, Jimmy Jones, and Dennis Green, the head coach at Minnesota, were on the team on which I played. From there, I went to Taft Junior College in California. Next, I went to Cal Western in San Diego.

I graduated from Cal Western, where I received my teaching certificate. I taught at Morris High School in San Diego. I left Morris High School and went to Scottsdale Junior College. From there, I went to Nevada-Las Vegas on the way to SMU. From SMU, I then went to Stanford and finally to the Cincinnati Bengals where I've been for the last seventeen seasons. I am starting my eighteenth year. I am very fortunate to be in one NFL city for this length of time.

After I got the job with the Bengals, I saw Frank Kush. I've known Coach Kush for a long time. He used to recruit Pennsylvania. He told me something I never forgot: "Don't stop coaching." A lot of times people think when a guy becomes a pro, he knows everything. That is not so. What you have to do is break down what they know and build up what you are trying to do, so they can fit into your system. If a player can't execute the concepts of what you are trying to do offensively, you don't have a chance, especially in our league. I'm going to talk to you this evening about an old concept of our 15 and 16 play, which is our number one running play. Also, I will go over what we are doing today on 26 and 27 and the counter action off that play.

I am going to show you how we link all this together. Defensive people are looking at our plays and trying to figure out ways to detect the plays we are running by watching our footwork and angles that the backs are taking. What we are trying to do is have our techniques so similar that it will throw the linebackers off. Years ago, we ran 16 and 17, which is the inside zone play. We still run the play today, but we do it a little differently.

What we want to deal with is the footwork that goes with this play. The most important thing in this footwork is the stance. People don't understand that because I am talking about the stance of an I-back. If you have players who get their legs too wide, they can't get in the sync of what you want them to do with their footwork.

We want a relaxed stance, with their feet about shoulder width apart. It is important to bend your knees. To move from your stance, the first thing you have to do is sink your hips. If you don't bend your knees, you can't sink your hips.

The first step the running back has to take is the *drop-open* step. The next thing he has to do is take his left leg, since we were going to the right, and throw it over his right leg in a crossover step. You really have to stretch with the left leg. The next thing is to turn downhill. By that time, his shoulders are square. His aiming point is the inside leg or butt of the tackle.

The running back is aiming at the butt of the offensive tackle, but he is keying the defensive end, who is playing over the offensive tackle. He presses the line of scrimmage and makes his break. He cannot cut back until he gets to the heels of the offensive linemen, and the nose tackle has crossed his face.

James Brooks, Icky Woods, and Harold Green all ran this play. They all had exceptional feet and we had a lot of success running this play. You press the ball to the heels of your offensive linemen. At that point, there were three things they could do with the ball.

They could *cram* the ball, which meant they could take it straight ahead. They could *bounce* the ball, which meant take it outside, or they could *cut back*.

Against the 3-4 defense that most pro teams ran with a nose tackle, this was a good play. The tackle and tight end reached outside on their men. The guard went up on the Mike linebacker. The center and backside guard combo the nose tackle and backside linebacker. The backside tackle and fullback took care of the defensive end and outside linebacker.

The back had three choices depending on what his front side read told him. If the defense played straight, he could cram the ball straight ahead. If they slanted inside, he could bounce the ball outside. If they slanted outside, he could cut the ball back.

16 VS STRAIGHT 3-4

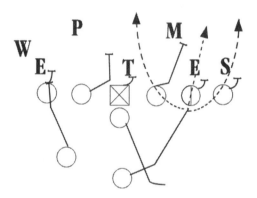

The whole concept with the zone play was to get the defenders to move. We wanted them to flow with the back. We ran this play with a lot of success.

Eventually however, the defenses started to adjust. They deduced to the backside with the end and outside linebacker. They shaded the nose tackle to the tight end side. The defense told us they were going to stretch with our movement, but they weren't going to let us cut the ball back.

When the guard, tackle, and tight end reached, the defenders flowed like they had always done. But the defense put a guy like Refrigerator Perry on the center, and he couldn't block him. The center was aiming for an outside head position on his block, but he couldn't get that position. The only thing you could do was to cram the ball or cut it back. If you cut the ball back, the nose tackle was sitting right there. To get the cut back, you had to go on the other side of the nose tackle and we couldn't get it that far.

16 VS REDUCTION

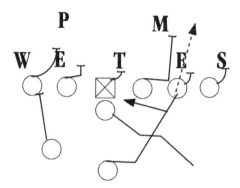

We had the 18-19, the outside zone, to compliment that play, but we needed something else. Some teams still run this play just like I showed you. Some teams predetermine to bounce the ball outside when everything comes down.

The old way we ran 16-17 wasn't giving us the production it had in the past. We had to make a change.

Our footwork changed. We still took the drop-open step, but instead of crossing over with the left leg, we shoot it toward the hole. We are going forward with the left leg. Instead of being square to the line of scrimmage, we are chasing the tackle at an angle. Everyone is on a tilt, which looked like the old outside zone play except on a tighter course.

The running back is aiming for the outside number of the offensive tackle. When the linemen are taking their drop steps, the back is doing the same thing. It is like a dance with everyone taking the same steps. The running back is chasing the inside leg of the tackle. Everyone is blocking just like the old 16-17 play.

If the defensive end goes outside, the back can cram the ball just like the old play. The tackle is working for an outside head position on the defensive end, and the end is trying to stay outside. The next move is called *take it*. If the Sam linebacker, the outside linebacker, comes down inside, the running back takes the ball to the outside.

The next thing he can do is *cut it up*. This is not a cut back. It looks like it, but it is not. I don't know any backs that can chase the leg of the tackle and see what is going on backside. That is the concept. The key to the whole play is to get width and make the defense move and create seams.

NEW 16-17 VS REDUCTION

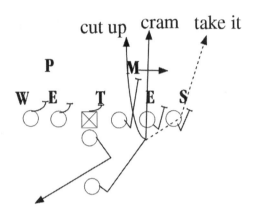

I use a phrase that describes what we are doing. The phrase is SLOW-TO-FAST-THROUGH. When you do that, you have to have tempo. It is not slow motion. It is patience. The back takes his drop-shoot step and takes off for the hole. If the offensive lineman doesn't blow the defender off the ball, the running back has to be patient. He has to keep his head up and his feet alive. If he drops his head, he can't see. If he loses his feet, he can't make a cut. That is what this play is all about. The back has to make the sudden cut and still maintain the body control to make a play. The back is still going to the heels of the offensive line.

If the offensive lineman is having trouble getting movement out of the defender, I tell the back to tease the defender with a fake move. If the defender moves, he goes the other way. You have to have body control to make that fake and move. To tease with the head and shoulders, they have to be up. If the back drops his head, he is not going to make a move.

If there is a log jam at the hole, the back has to make a move, but he has to remember to get up the field. We want to finish the run up the field. If we ran the ball every play and got zero yards, I'll take that, as long as we didn't get minus yards

If the back takes it outside, at some point he has to plant, get up the field, and finish the run. The finish on the backside is extremely important in this running play. I can't emphasize enough how important that is.

When you are zone blocking people, you don't have to knock them down. But, you have to stay on the block. If we can prevent the backside from coming off the edges of our blocks, we have a play.

As soon as the back breaks the line of scrimmage, he will make a move. They know the concept, footwork, and tempo, but at some point his athleticism has to take over. These are the things we as coaches can't coach. Don't put a back in the situation where he becomes a robot. Football is not like that. The runner has to run with his eyes. He is going to see things you don't see. You have to trust the running back that he is going to make the right read. He obviously is not going to make the right reads all the time. If somebody lets a block go on what I call a no-touch, the back can't control that. He has to forget about it and get back on track for the next snap. He is human. Don't make him a robot. Let him run with his eyes.

Let's talk about drilling these techniques. The footwork is not as easy as it sounds. I use two bags aligned with an aiming point. The tailback gets in his stance, drop-shoots, and runs through the bags. This is something they probably haven't done previously, and they get the feel for what we want doing this drill.

FOOTWORK/BAG DRILL

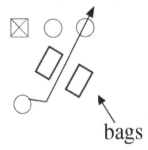

bags

The next drill we use helps the running backs with their reads. We put three bags over the offensive blockers. The middle bag is the focus point for the back. We give the bag holders a direction. If we give them the inside direction, the back takes it outside. The next time we may have the two inside bags go down and the outside bag go out. The back has to read that and cram it inside. The next time, the two outside bags go outside, and the inside bag goes inside, the back cuts it up. We work these drills both right and left. Believe it or not, this drill becomes fun for the running backs.

OUTSIDE READ

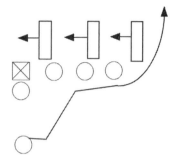

CRAM READ

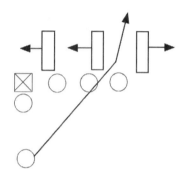

CUT UP READ

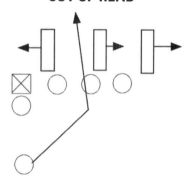

Once the backs get through the line, they have to do something at the second level. At our level, we have to do two things at once. We don't have enough individual time to do all of these drills separately. We may have only ten to fifteen minutes of individual time to work on both the passing and running game. I have to be selective with what I do. I take two drills and put them in one period.

I use the old gauntlet while I'm working on their footwork. I put a second bag behind the gauntlet and have them make a move off that bag. They come out of their stance, do the footwork, chase to the line, bust through the bags, and do a spin off the second bag. The next thing time through instead of spinning, we make him miss by using a flash move. The next time through, we use the balance drill. That is left hand down to the ground with the ball in the right arm. The next step is right hand down with the ball switched to the left arm. The next step is back to the left hand down and the ball switched back to the right arm.

GAUNTLET DRILL

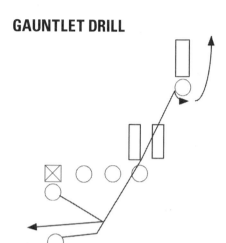

We have worked stance, footwork, aiming point, and what we can do at the second level. This is our bread and butter. We would rather run this play then any other.

As I said before the backside blocking is tremendously important. I work a drill called end-wind seal. This is the zip-lock for the back side. This is the backside blocking for the 16 zone play. We run the play with two tight ends and two backs. If we call 16-17 Mike, that tells the wide receiver he has to block the force on the play. The back to the backside has the Wind linebacker's (the outside linebacker's), area. The tackle is coming up the field. If the defensive end is going outside, he continues up for the Wind linebacker. He is not blocking a man, he is blocking an area. The back takes the area outside the offensive tackle. He is doing the same thing. He is blocking the area and taking either the end or the Wind linebacker.

BACKSIDE SEAL

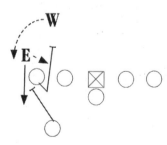

If we run this play to the backside, we call it 16-17 Wind. We like to run it from the I formation. You can run it from the off set, but we prefer the I formation. The tackle is taking his open step and locking on the defensive end with an outside head position. We don't want the back to go straight for the linebacker. If he does, the linebacker will fill, and we don't want that. We want the linebacker to flow. We want him to go outside with his head in an outside position to make the linebacker move outside. The footwork and angle are the same.

What it creates is a huge seam to cram the ball into. If the linebacker doesn't widen, we have a great opportunity to get outside. The block of the fullback is one of the hardest things we have to teach. He wants to turn and make an aggressive block. This is not an isolation play. When we run this play from an off set position, I tell the fullback to cheat inside.

16-17 - WIND

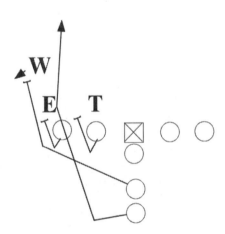

If we get a loaded look, which involves a defensive tackle and end over your guard and tackle, with the outside linebacker aligned on the line of scrimmage, we make an adjustment. When the linebacker is on the line of scrimmage, he is generally coming hard. If we are in the I formation, we shift out into an off-set position with the fullback. It is an unfair advantage for our fullback. We don't want to shorten our fullback's neck by making him take on a linebacker blitzing hard from that position. We want to shorten the distance. If we have a second tight end in the game, we don't have that problem.

If we run the stretch play, we don't have to block the zip area. The zip area is the backside tackle box.

The defensive ends and linebacker can run you down from behind from that area on the inside zone play.

Players are going to make plays, but they have to follow the road map. The back has to chase the defense outside. As soon as the back gets his head and shoulders back inside, the linebackers freeze. You don't have the flow, and you don't create the seam for your offensive linemen. The offensive linemen are expecting the back to chase outside. If the back stops and comes back, it makes the offensive lineman look like he didn't do the job, when actually it was the back who made the mistake. We want the linebacker to flow over the top of the play. The back has to create an illusion that he is running the outside zone. Our 16-17 is a play between our old play and the stretch play.

The next play is called 26-27, which is the outside zone play. It used to be called 18-19. Some teams still run this play. On the 18-19 play, we could run it from the one-back set. The tailback took a short control step and ran for the outside hip of the tight end. He keyed the block of the end man on the line of scrimmage. He had to feel the block on the next inside defender. This is not a cut-back play, it was a cut-up play. The back either went outside, or he cut the play up. People have seen Corey Dillon cut the play back. He is an athlete and made something happen. He did everything we wanted him to do, but at some point he made a play.

If you play a great backside defender and ran this play, we would have to block him. The front side defense would force you to cut the ball up. If that happens the backside end or linebacker pursuing down the line can make the play.

We no longer run 18-19, but it doesn't mean we are not going to do it next year. The play we are running now is 26-27. We run the play out of the I formation. It is an outside stretch play, but it is a tight stretch play. We are running at the inside leg of the tight end. It is very important that the back run at the inside leg or the butt of the tight end. It is easier for a back to go inside out, then to go outside in.

We like the play versus the reduction front. If the defensive tackle is in a 3-technique, we block down on him with the offensive tackle. The fullback has the B-gap to the linebacker to the safety. If the linebacker fills the B-gap, the fullback blocks him right now. The guard is pulling for the force on the play. We want the drop-open step from 16 and the short control step from 26 to look the same to the linebackers. It is very important for the back to take a short control step. The fullback and tailback can't take off at the same time. If they do, you have congestion. You have to give the fullback a chance to get out in front.

The fullback is working for an outside head position on his block. The pulling guard is also looking for an outside head position. With the outside head position, we are trying to wall off the inside. The thing we don't want to do is get our butts in the hole and create a traffic jam. We want to dip and rip right through the outside of the defender. I tell them when they think they have good position, take one more step. If they do that they can dip and rip and get all the shoulder surface on the defender they want. If they drop their heads, they are going down. If the end widens, the back will cut the ball up.

26-27 - OUTSIDE ZONE

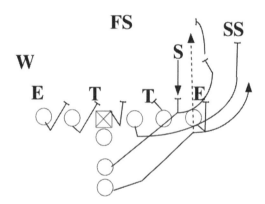

If the defense covers the guard and tackle and walks the Sam linebacker up on the tight end, we have options. We go to our loaded scheme. We block the tackle and tight end down, pull the guard, who kicks out or logs the Sam linebacker. The center will try to block the Mike linebacker. If he can't get him, the fullback has him. If we lose the fullback on the block on the Mike linebacker, the tailback has to make the secondary defender miss. If the center can get the Mike linebacker, the fullback is going all the way to the safety.

26-27 - OVERSHIFT

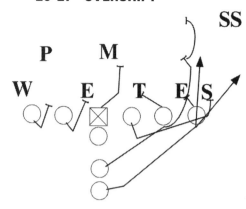

We drill the 26-27 just like the 16-17. We use bags to teach reads and angles. We work on our footwork and stance during these drills.

Before we even start talking about footwork, I take some cones and do this drill. I call this drill in and out. I set up five cones. I have a line of backs. I call the hike sequence and hand the ball to the back who runs to the cones. He runs into the first gap of cones, and back pedals out. He then attacks the second gap and back pedals out, does the same thing through all the cones, and finishes with a hard run after the last cone. His feet are really alive in this drill. How many times have you seen a back you thought was going to be tackled, and all of a sudden he back pedaled out of the tackle and continued down field? That is what this drill teaches. This is a great warm-up drill that teaches the things you want taught. The players have to keep their feet alive and run with their head up.

IN AND OUT DRILL

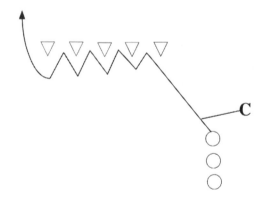

The play we put in is a compliment to both the inside and outside zone plays. We call it 34-35 Twin. It is a counter play. We like to run this play to the weakside. We call it Twin, which stands for Tackle on Wind linebacker. We only like to run this play against a weakside reduction. The whole key is getting linebackers to react and move. It is a big thing in our league, because the linebackers are being coached to look at a back's angles.

A lot of times when backs run counters, they counter step, but their shoulders never change. When that happens the linebacker know what they are doing. We like to assimilate the action of the inside zone play. This is a modified inside zone play. Instead of running at the inside leg of the tackle, we are running at the butt of the guard. The back does his drop-open step. His second step is normal, but his third step is a redirect step under control. On his third step, he is coming downhill toward the line of scrimmage.

When we run this play, I tell our tailbacks to cheat back in their alignment. We are normally six and half to seven yards off the line. When our tailback gets the ball, we want him to be on the strongside of the middle. It is the quarterback's job to stay out of the running back's way. We want him to be tight to the B-gap.

This play is a tackle trap for us. The playside tackle has to take the defensive end up the field. The tight end is blocking down on the defensive end. The fullback is blocking on the Sam linebacker. The right guard steps out at the defensive end to keep him from coming down inside and goes up on the Mike linebacker. The center and onside guard block the defensive tackles. The backside tackle pulls, turns up in the hole, and blocks the Wind linebacker.

34-35 TWIN

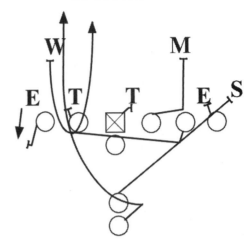

If the onside guard has a 3-technique on him, there is a strong chance the pull will go inside the guard. The back should see that on alignment. If everyone were to slant down, the ball and all pulls would go outside. If we run the play to the strongside, we would tag the play 34-35 TOM. That stands for Tackle On Mike.

All three of these plays give the defense essentially the same look. They have been good for us. We are commited to running the football. Let's watch some film of what I've talked about. I hope that showed you what we are trying to do. We are a real good football team and are really close to proving it. If we can get our quarterback in line and doing the things we think he can, we will be a team to be dealt with in the future. We have a good scheme, and it is a good attack. Remember, however, that players make plays. Thank you very much.

OFFENSIVE LINE TECHNIQUES AND DRILLS

The Ohio State University

It is good to be here. I appreciate high school football coaches. I coached at LSU for five years. When someone uses the term "COACH" regardless of where you are, it means something special. Where ever you are and you have that "Coach" tag, you are something special to those young kids. I have been able to see this all through the years.

I am going to talk about offensive line play and how I teach the offensive linemen. I think the progression in which you teach is very important. This is true if you are a line coach or a linebacker coach. It is important to believe what you teach. These kids can spot a phony a mile away. If you are not sold on what you are teaching, the players will know it. They will have a little doubt in their mind.

Another important point in coaching offensive lineman is that you talk the same language. When you talk to the players and they answer you, it has to be in the same language. I started coaching at Marshall University in 1965, and I have been at several schools since that time. In all of those years, I have never let the kids say "probably, or I think." When you ask them a question, they need to give you the answer in terms that both of you understand. The worst thing for an offensive lineman is to come to the line of scrimmage and have doubt in his mind about what he is to do. We want them to be able to go to the line of scrimmage and carry out their assignment without having to think what they are doing. It has to be like they are walking and chewing bubble gum. They do not have to think about what they are doing, they just do it out of habit. If you have the players prepared to carry out their assignment, they develop the attitude they can't wait to get after the defensive man.

The thing I like about offensive lineman is toughness. The first day of practice at Ohio State, we talk about toughness. You have to explain to the offensive line what toughness is. Some players think

toughness is pushing around a pile, or that toughness is a cheap shot. Some players think toughness is running off at the jaws. To me, toughness is sticking your nose in the block. It is getting a clean block and getting after the defender. Even when things are not going well, you must stay after the defender. By the time the fourth quarter comes around, you will own the defender. You have to tell the kids what toughness is.

I want to talk about some requirements for a good blocker. The first point we talk about is strength: In the running game, the lineman must be strong enough to move a defender of equal size by brute force. In the passing game, the lineman must be strong enough to stop the defender's charge at the LOS and maintain that position.

The second point is mobility. I am talking about initial quickness, feet, agility, coordination, body balance and control. In the running game, the lineman must be quick enough to meet defenders on his side of the LOS and mobile enough to stay on the block when the defender is trying to escape. In the passing game, they must have enough mobility to slide, mirror and maintain the inside position on a pass rusher—giving ground grudgingly until the ball is thrown.

The blocker has four advantages. I want to list these advantages.

FOUR ADVANTAGES A BLOCKER HAS:

- Knowing the snap count
- Direction of the ball
- Proper use of leverage
- Proper alignment

I want to touch on the proper use of leverage. Leverage is when the blocker strikes his initial blow at a point. The blocker must be low enough to create a lifting force on the defender. He must be close enough to neutralize his charge. The force must be continued to get the defender on his heels so he is unable to make a counter move.

We want to teach the blocker to "hit up and through the defender."

Line of force is that 45-degree angle up and through the defender in which we channel all our force.

Let me get to the teaching progression for the base block. We believe the base block is the most important block of an offensive lineman. This block is used when blocking at the point of attack. The objective is to get movement, option blocking the defender the way he wishes to go. You must maintain contact.

Following is the sequence of how we teach this drive block. First we teach stance and start, and then sequences are taught in reverse order to ensure the athlete experiences the perfect block.

FIRST PHASE – STANCE / STARTS

We start off with a good base. We want a base at least armpit width but never wider than your shoulders. We want a staggered stance with the toes in and the heels out. We want the feet lined up in a toe-to-instep or toe-to-heel relationship. If you are a right handed player, we like to put the right foot back. The right toe will be on the instep of the left foot, or possibly to the heel. That is the way we want them to line up. Some of the kids you get may be a little different. Some kids may be 6'6", and some kids will be 5'10". You may have to be lenient with those type players. You want them to feel comfortable. The players are the ones that have to play, so they need to be comfortable. The players are the ones that have to feel comfortable. If they have to get into a different stance in order to feel comfortable, that is fine.

We have had a lot of fun with this over the years. We tell the players that all of us are either from the country or the city. I ask them how many of them are from the country. They raise their hands. I ask those country players if they ever took a crap in the woods. "Yes, I did coach." They look pretty good from that point. Then, we get the city players up front. I ask them to squat down like they are going to take a dump in the woods. I tell them to look at their heels. "You are going to get "do-do" on your heels." Tell them to get down and get the butt out of the way.

The thing about offensive lineman is the fact they play from an uncomfortable position. In the off-season, we start them off by having them squat down just like they are going to take a crap in the woods. Have them squat for 30 seconds and then have them stand up. We keep doing that, but we add a few seconds each time until they can stay in the squat position for one minute. Then, we have them do a quarter-eagle squat. We put a line on a wall where they can put their hands on the wall in that squat position. Then, we have them walk down the line in that squat position with their hands flat on the line as they move down the line. They have to be low. It is an unnatural position for the linemen. They have to learn to play that way.

Their weight is on the inside balls of the feet. Their knees are in and over their ankles. We want a "Z" in their knees. The power-producing angles are created by the bend in the ankles and knee joints.

We have them put their down hand slightly inside their rear foot. Their weight is extended comfortably from their shoulder. We want them to reach out far enough to create a balanced stance with 60 percent of their weight forward and 40 percent of their weight back. We still like to use the tripod with the fingers of the down hand on the ground.

We want the head cocked back slightly. We tell them to get into a "bull" neck position. We want them to have some peripheral vision so they can see the feet of the defender. We like to use the phrase "look through the eyebrows."

The next point is the off hand. We take the off hand and put the wrist on the left knee. When they take that first step, we want the off hand and everything else to be going in the same direction.

It is important in teaching stance to have a system and to be consistent with the way you teach it. The way we like to teach this is by having all of the offensive lineman together. We give them commands – "feet shoulder-width apart, stagger the stance, squat down, right hand down, left hand on the knee." Then, we get them up and start again. When I clap my hands, I want them to clap their hands and then take two steps and get down in their stance. "Ready break." We call set – and they get down in their stance. We keep them down in that stance. They have to be comfortable. We walk around as they sit in their stance. Make them sit in that stance until they are comfortable.

Our initial movement must be forward—not upward. It is like a sprinter going out of the starting blocks. If the defender is over the offensive lineman, we want the blocker to drive off the up foot and step with the rear foot. If the defender is to either side, the blocker must step with the foot nearest him.

Here are the coaching points for the rear foot lead. Mentally shift the weight to the push foot and step with the near foot. I will show you a tape of the drill we use to teach this. It is our one step drill.

ONE STEP DRILL

- The first step should be a 3-inch step out and slightly up, attacking the line of scrimmage.

- The knee of the up foot should point toward the ground (it should roll over the toe of the up foot).

- Arm action should be like a sprinter coming out of the starting blocks.

- The back should be flat, and the chest should be on the thigh.

- The blocker should bull the neck and sight the target.

- The blocker should follow up quickly with his third step.

- The blocker should stay down low and maintain his lift leverage.

Next, we work on the up foot lead. We want to mentally shift the weight to the push foot and step with the up foot. Then, we do the one step drill. The first step should be a 3-inch step out and slightly up attacking the line of scrimmage.

SECOND PHASE – FIT POSITION

The purpose of this phase is to show the blocker ideal blocking position utilizing power-producing angles. We must put the defender in a challenge position and have the offensive blocker fit into him.

- The offensive blocker is in a good position.

- Feet parallel—"toes in—heels out."

- Good bend in the knees—create power producing angles.

- Knees in over the ankles.

- Butt down.

- Back arched.

- Good bull neck.

- Eyes in the solar plexus of the defender.

- Arms are in a blocking position; fists of the hands at the bottom of the defender's breast plate, forming a triangle with the hairline and both fists.

- The defender is in a challenge position.

- The defender's feet are slightly staggered – up foot at the edge of the board.

- The defender holds the blocker under his arm.

- The defender gives resistance.

THIRD PHASE – FOLLOW THROUGH

The purpose of this phase is to have the player experience an ideal block (i.e., to teach the proper use of leverage, the hip roll, the acceleration of the feet and the maintenance of a block).

The offensive blocker will align in a fit position, his toes at the end of the board. The defender will be in a challenge position holding the blocker in place.

Walking down the board. The blocker will walk the defender down the board with a "bulled" neck, power-producing angles and, feeling pressure at the small of his back, he should never raise up. The defender must give steady resistance.

Hip roll:

- The blocker will roll his hips and accelerate his feet. When executing a block, he will make contact and have a stalemate.

- In order to get movement, the blocker must roll his hips and accelerate to dominate a defender.

- The hip roll is the underneath action — the snapping of his knees straight out and the shooting of his hips through.

- His feet should be underneath his shoulder pads to guard against over extension.

Hold:

- Half way down the board on the command "hold," the blockers will stop.

- The position of the blocker should be checked.

Finish:

- On command, the blocker stays locked on and sustains.

FOURTH PHASE – CONTACT

The purpose of this phase is to teach the contact phase of the drive-block technique. We want to emphasize the use of his arms and the timing of the pop.

The offensive blocker in a down position situates himself one step from the defender. The defensive man will assume a challenge position. The defender should be in a good two-point stance bending his knees as much as possible with his chest out and his head tucked. He will catch the blocker rather than deliver a lick.

The offensive blocker takes only one step — jolting the defender backwards. He should concentrate on ripping his arms and taking a short, powerful step.

FIFTH PHASE – HIT AND DRIVE

The purpose of this phase is to put all aspects of the drive block together. The offensive blocker is aligned in a 3-point stance, a foot away from the defender, his toes at the end of the board. To start, the defender will be in a 2-point stance. As the drill progresses, he will move to a 3-point stance without boards.

The offensive blocker will explode out of his stance and drive the defender down the board. Employing a good base and acceleration of the feet are emphasized. The defender will make a good collision, and then allow the blocker to drive him down the board while giving ground slowly. As the drill progresses, the distance is varied between the blocker and the defender to aid in the development of a rhythm of blocking at defender at varied distances away.

The two whistle drill can be used in this phase. The first whistle is to check body position; the second whistle is to release the athletes from the drill.

SIXTH PHASE – SECOND EFFORT

The purpose of this phase is to teach the blocker to maintain contact when the defender is spinning out or disengaging the blocker.

The coach will give the defender a direction spin. When the defender reaches the end of the board, he will spin out of the block in direction indicated by the coach. The blocker must step with his near foot in the direction of the spin, aggressively attacking the defender. The blocker should never cross his feet or kick his heels together. He should maintain a good base.

SEVENTH PHASE – VS. SHADE ALIGNMENTS

The purpose of this phase is to teach the drive on opponents who are aligned in shaded or off-set alignments.

This phase is the same as the hit and drive phase except that the blocker and the defender start from a position with their inside foot on the outside of the board. The blocker's first step must be perfect in order to get to the solar plexus of the defender. His second step must be up field, while maintaining his base. Practice inside to outside shades of the offensive blocker.

The second block we teach is the lead block. This is an aggressive block that is used to prevent a defender from pursuing the ball. Our teaching sequence for this block is as follows:

FIRST PHASE – STANCE AND START

The stance is exactly the same as for the drive block. In the start, the first step will depend on the defender's alignment (45% - head up, 30% shade, etc.) During the first step, the blocker's shoulders will turn and the chest will be kept on the thigh.

SECOND PHASE – POINT OF AIM

All linemen and tight ends should use the armpit for their point of aim vs. a down lineman. They should drive to the play side, their hand to the defender's outside hip.

THIRD PHASE – THREE-STEP DRILL

The coach should use a slow count (i.e., 1 – 2 – 3) to exaggerate each step of lead block. The blocker's first step must be at an appropriate angle, his chest on his thigh while turning his shoulders.

His second step is a power step, driving it down the crotch of the defender. He rips his backside arm as he steps. He should not let his step hang; he must get it down quickly.

His third step is up field, trying to square his shoulders. He should get to the point of his aim. A sled can be used to work various aiming points of aim of the lead block.

After each pass is thrown, all offensive linemen must run quickly to their assigned coverage area and locate the ball. If the pass is completed they must sprint down field and block for the receiver. If the pass is intercepted, they must sprint to the ball and surround the interceptor.

SETS - PASS

Pass Protection Techniques

Stance: Proper stance for offensive linemen was discussed previously, but it must be emphasized that a blocker must always use the same stance. Any ad-

justment in stance that gives away our intention to pass gives the advantage to the defense. However, the blocker should mentally shift his weight to his push foot so he is prepared to make his initial step when getting set.

Getting Set: A pass blockers success depends upon his ability to move from his stance to his set position. He should move into position as quickly as possible. The concept of "sets" is designed to tell the blocker the initial movement he should take on the snap to put himself in the best position to block his man. His set position prior to contact must be in direct line between the defender and the quarterback.

Footwork: The blocker's footwork (set) is based on a rusher's alignment.

Vs. Head-up alignment: The blocker should drop step four inches with his outside foot. He should keep square with the defender. His inside foot always remains in front of his outside foot. He should pull back his hips, with his butt still slightly up, and squat thrusting his head and shoulders back.

Vs. Outside alignment: The blocker should kick-step with his outside foot (30 degrees) to where his foot now is aligned within step of the defender's outside foot. He should keep his shoulders square, and move his inside foot to keep his balance, always keeping inside foot up.

Vs. Inside alignment: The blocker should slide his inside foot to gain a head-up position. His outside foot is again on the in-step of the defender's outside foot. He should keep his inside foot up.

Body position:

- Head – thrown back with the chin up and the eyes focused on the bottom of the numbers of the defender.

- Back – straight or flat, but never rounder.

- Feet – shoulder-width apart.

- Knees – bent in power-producing angles, but never straightened.

- Butt – down and tucked to keep his center of gravity low.

- Hands and elbows – the hands are at eye level, armpit-width apart; the thumbs are up; the elbows are near the body.

- Shoulders – always square to the line of scrimmage.

Teaching Sequence – Pass

General information:

- Two men work together.

- We teach the four phases in reverse order.

- We show each player the ideal position (set and fit) for pass protection.

Fit position (1st Phase): We put the defender in a pass rush position and have the offensive blocker "fit" into him.

Offensive blocker "fit":

- Head is back with shoulders square.

- Butt is tucked with knees bent.

- Back is straight; lower back is arched.

- Feet are shoulders-width apart with toes pointing straight ahead. Inside foot is always up.

- Open hands are placed in armpit area.

- Arms are extended but slightly bent.

- Eyes are focused on base of defender's numbers.

Pressure (2nd Phase):

- From fit position, defender moves in either direction laterally.

- Blocker will slide and apply pressure by locking arm and pushing to the direction the defender is moving. The blocker should not allow his opposite arm to become lazy and lose contact with the defender.

- Always maintain a shoulder width base. Keep your head and shoulders back and stride with the knees bent. Do not get over extended.

- Four-way pressure can be practiced by allowing the defender to pull rush or pull the blockers, as well as move laterally.

Pop (3rd Phase):

- Blocker is in a "ready" position.

- As the defender approaches, the blocker will thrust or pop his arms forward and at the same time, replace a foot. This foot replacement ensures a strong, solid base.

- Contact is made with the heel of his palms to control and stop charge of the defender. The defender's shoulders should snap backwards.

- The timing of the pop should be emphasized (i.e., arms thrusting forward and replacing a foot). The timing of the pop on the defender should be practiced by approaching from different angles and utilizing the pop in shuffle drill.

Full go (4th Phase):

- The offensive blocker is now in a three-point stance.

- The defender will rush from a three-point stance.

- We now combine all teaching phases of pass protection.

You have to work every single day to drive block and angle linemen. This comes in the individual period. You have to constantly work on the first step and where the defender is angling. The blocker's second step has to go in the direction the defender is going. You have to work on this everyday. I also think you have to work on the combination blocks every single day. If you do a lot of gap blocking or step blocking, I think you have to work on those blocks everyday. If you do not work on them everyday, it will get sloppy.

If I could say something on the gap block, it may help. I will explain what we do on the gap block. We can look at the center blocking back on the 2-technique man. The center does not know if the 2-technique man is going to plow into him, or go up field and read the block. This could be a tackle blocking down on a 3-technique, a guard blocking down on a 1-technique, or the center blocking on the backside. The key to the block is the first step. The step must be really flat. It is a short, flat, quick step. It is really quick. The second step is the adjustment step. If the man plays into the blocker, the second step is into the defender and the contact point is the near armpit and the near number. The next step is to get the near foot in the center of the defender and get the head into the man and knock him out of the hole.

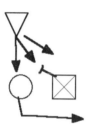

The next block is the combination block. It does not matter which two linemen we are talking about. It could be a center and a guard, a guard and a tackle, or a tackle and the tight end. We are working on a combo block on the linebacker.

In the diagram here, we have a defender in the shade technique on the offensive player on the left. We use the terms THICK and THIN. It means who is going to hit thick and who is going to hit thin. The inside man is going to hit the down man thick with his near foot. The step is almost straight up field. He is going to the near number of the down defender.

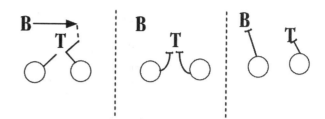

The step of the outside blocker is up field where he will slide in inside slightly. He is the outside man, and he steps with his inside foot. His second step is very important. That step must be parallel to his first step to keep his shoulders squared. You have to rep, rep, rep this in practice. The outside blocker is going to combo block on the linebacker inside. He makes contact with the down lineman on his near number. The footwork becomes a little different. His shoulders must be square to the LOS. If the linebacker comes over the top, we tell the outside man not to come off the block on the down man until the linebacker comes to his near ear hole. At that point, the outside blocker starts working off his man. He keeps his inside shoulder low and runs through the defender to the linebacker. The big mistake the outside blocker often makes is to get too loose with his hips, thereby opening a gap between him and the inside man. That allows the down defender to come up field where the inside blocker can not control him.

If the second step of that outside man is not parallel with his first step, his shoulders get turned and the linebacker comes over the top. The outside blocker then has a hard time getting squared up to make that block on the linebacker.

This block is used on cutback plays. You want to get the linebackers moving on those plays. This is how we want to come off the block and square up on the linebacker.

If the linebacker hangs in the same position, we stay in our double-team block. We want good movement on the play. If the linebacker runs a blitz, the inside man can make contact on the line of scrimmage.

I wanted to get into the 3-Step pass protection out of the one-back set and a 5-Step pass protection out of the two-back set. The rules for the offensive linemen are almost the same for all three positions. I do not have time to get into that now.

I really enjoy talking about the offensive line. When you break it down and show the kids what you want them to do, you have the opportunity to work with them even though they may not have as much athletic ability as some of the other players on the field. They are fun kids to work with and fun kids to coach. Hopefully, you have gotten something out of this that you can take back and use in your program. Thank you very much.

EFFECTIVE USE OF HIGH SCHOOL BOOSTER CLUBS

ROD BAKER
Wyandotte Roosevelt High School
Alumni Football Club

I would like to thank the NIKE people and Don Lessner for inviting me to speak. It is also a great pleasure to talk about our organization today. That is the Wyandotte Alumni Football Club which was started in 1985 by three gentlemen: Jim Johnson, Mason Grahl, and Hank Chlebek. Hank is here. Please raise your hand. Hank was the head coach in Wyandotte at that time, and he was instrumental in getting us going. It is a dynamic organization that is one of a kind.

Our mission statement is simple: "To preserve the football at Roosevelt High School; to promote and enhance the growth of our high school football program; to provide partial scholarships to deserving Roosevelt football participants as determined by the Board of Directors; to establish and maintain the Roosevelt Football Hall of Fame." I want to discuss each point and tell you how we accomplish our mission.

Currently, the club has about 250 members, but that fluctuates. It can be as high as 350 to 400. We have a ten-man Board of Directors, and a seven-man Advisory Board, made up of former Bear players, coaches, and volunteers.

First I want to talk about what we do. These are things the Alumni Football Club provides for our football team. I have a partial list today. This is definitely not everything we do, but it is a good portion of it. There are some things I feel are very important to our football program that have become traditional, and we do these things all the time. All of this is paid for by our Alumni Football Club.

The first avenue of support involves team meals. Every Friday during the season, we have a team meal right after school. The Alumni Club pays for this, while the kitchen staff at the school cooks the meals. The coach provides the menu. The team meal keeps our team together after school until we play that night.

You are in the same boat we are. You don't have a lot of kids who have two parents who are not working. They may not be home. I like to know that my players are not having a bag of burritos and a ding-dong for dinner before they go out and play. This way, we can keep them together. It is a big help for our seniors too, because they talk at each one of these meals. Our seniors take leadership and ownership of the football team.

One of the other guys big in some of the things we do is Bart Estola, who is now the head coach at Shelby High School. He is in the crowd today. A lot of the things came in with him when he was the head coach at Wyandotte in the nineties. We have tried to add onto some of the things Bart did, and we have evolved from there.

We pay for five extra coaches. We have coaches from each level—varsity, JV, freshman, and seventh and eighth grade—paid for by the Alumni Club. That is huge. When you have fifty kids out for freshmen football and only have two coaches provided by the school system, one more guy really helps a lot.

All of our video stuff comes from U.S. Sports Video. It is quality equipment, and all of our levels at the high school get a chance to use it. We have cameras for game tapes, and extra video cameras for scouting, practice, and projection screens. Our projection screen will show expanded images, plus we have extra VCR's and TV's that we use for different teams. The JV and freshmen can watch film on the same day as we play. All of this comes with a price, and it is not cheap. Without the Alumni Football Club, we could not afford this.

Let me go back to our mission statement. In the 1980's, Wyandotte athletics were not very good. The condition of all the athletic programs was not great. When they started the club, the purpose was to support football. But by taking football fund raising out of the school's hands and putting it into this club, more money became available for every other sport at the school. Since then, our female athletic programs have gotten better and the other boy's programs have got better. Now, I think we are competitive in Class A all across the board.

We have an editing system with four VCR's and a computer with it so we can make copies of game tapes or cut ups of the games. We have a highlight tape for each one of our players, and we send their tapes out at the college level. That is big for our kids. We have quality game tape that really helps us with evaluation in our assessment process. And it really helps college coaches get a good look at our kids. One of the things I think is extremely important is our showcase of plaques and memorabilia from Wyandotte football which sits right outside the high school gym. It has pictures of all of our Hall of Fame members, plus memorabilia from the forties and fifties. We go back in football to 1898. Two years ago, we had our "100 Year Celebration". It makes football a little different sport when kids see some of those older folks and what was going on before.

Since 1985, we have given partial scholarships to over 135 former players. Each scholarship is usually right around $1,000. By the end of this year, we will have spent over $135,000 that we raised to give kids a chance to go on to school. They don't have to play football, and they do not have to go to a major university. They can go to trade school, a junior college, or a community college. Our purpose is to give kids a start, give them a boost, and try to help them out. The only criteria is to play varsity football at Wyandotte. Any senior can apply for this scholarship.

The last thing is our Hall of Fame Banquet where we honor our inductees and interzone board winners who serve Wyandotte youth. At the banquet one year, we had the members of the 1943 team that were undefeated and untied. They all get together as a group and drink a lot beer, and tell how great they were. You would be surprised how good people get 25 years later. It is a chance for all of us to get together. It is an excellent night for us to celebrate some of our players from the past. We get a lot of former people who volunteer just to help our kids.

I do want to mention our *Parents Handbook*. I have a guy in the Alumni Club who puts out a *Parents Handbook*. The book has such things as the rules we use in school, and maps of different places we play in the league. We meet with the parents and give them a copy of the book. We try to include anything a parent would want to talk about during the season. We try to get this taken care of before the season starts. We have a parents meeting, and the booklets are handed out to all parents of players from grades 9 though 12.

The organization is large and we have support. But without the ten guys on the Board of Directors, we would not be doing any of this. Our Board of Directors make sure we have a quality program and everyone of our football players has a quality experience when they leave Wyandotte.

Hank Chlebek made the comment to me the other day, "Who the hell thought this thing would have gotten this big?" We thought we were doing great the third year of the club when we made $4,000. We now make that now off one raffle. bingo was huge for us. We were making somewhere between $30,000 and $35,000 per year on bingo. We paid people to run it for us. It was a Thursday morning bingo. We were surviving on that alone. We didn't do anything else. We had our banquet and a golf outing, but we were not making any money of these things. As soon as gambling took over in Canada, bingo has gone out the door as a huge money maker.

Our wild game dinner has turned into a large money maker. We just had it last weekend. It cost $50 per ticket. We had 400 people, and we made $30,000 at the end of the afternoon. You would not believe the door prizes. We collect things for a whole year. We would have enough door prizes to have another dinner next week if we really wanted to. I started it because I am in the autograph business. We started by getting sports memorabilia autographed and putting it out on a table.

We started selling raffle tickets on these items, and it began to expand. One gift we raffled off was interesting. The last ticket drawn got the "Couch Potato Special." This is one raffle ticket that cost $25, and we give away a Lazy-Boy that is donated to us. We give away a microwave oven, a small refrigerator, a 32-inch TV, and a CD system with surround sound for $25 a ticket. Most of this stuff is donated to us. People go wild over this.

We also had a "52 Pick Up" where we sold 52 cards for $20 per card. We gave away three prizes including two tickets to a Red Wing's game, a Sergi Fedorov autographed jersey, and a Steve Yzerman autographed jersey. You get a choice of the three if you are the first winner.

We provide a great meal with the best food that you can buy at the raffle. When we sell these tickets, kids go nuts over them.

The last thing Don wanted me to talk about was how do you keep your booster club from interfering with your football program? We have done it very simply. The head coach is on the Board. That helps to settle some of that stuff. Other coaches are also on the Board. All of these guys are former Bear players. So, they know not to interfere. They pledge their support to enhance the club but not to stick their nose in the football program. They have been very ethical and moral guys. I have never had a question about "Why do you play this kid?"

One of the other things that has turned into a real money maker for us occurs around the 4th of July. We are on the Detroit River, and we have two boats that hold about 300 people each that go out on the river. We sell tickets and provide hors d'oeuvres, drinks, and the opportunity to see the fireworks on the Detroit River. We cruise up and down the Detroit River, and one of the local merchants provides things for us. We beg and borrow about anything we can get. It has worked well for us. We have a little time before fall starts, and we probably will raffle off a jersey or beanie-babies. Thank you.

DR. JOHN FLOREK
Riverview High School Football Club

Good afternoon. As I was walking down the street to the lecture hall, I saw this blind man with his leader dog crossing the street. I kept my eye on him as he started to cross the street. A car almost nailed him. So as he was continuing to cross the street, a damn truck almost hit him. He got over to the other side of the street, and he pulled a cookie out of his pocket and gave it to his dog. I ran across the street and told him that a car and a truck almost hit him, and "you are giving your dog a cookie?" The blind man said, "I had to find his head before I could kick his ass."

The Riverview High School Football Booster Club has been very successful for many years in supporting the football program. This success comes from the dedication and involvement of our parents, coaching staff, athletes, and community. The Riverview Football Club is a group of responsible, organized, goal-setting, committed individuals whose priorities are primarily placed with the vision to support youth football. This is a group of parents who are focused, enthusiastic, positive thinking, competent, energized, self-starting team of individuals who are determined to develop and use all of their leadership qualities to make the Riverview football program the best it can be.

At this time, I am going to present some ideas about fundraisers we have used to enhance our football program. Here is some information on how I became the President of the Riverview Booster Club. It is important for you as coaches to recruit your coaches and your players. I think one instrumental thing that Don Lessner did is that he knew when players were coming up, he would take the parents off to the side and tell them, "You need to get involved in the Booster Club, and you need to make it happen"

When I became President of our group, we had about $80, and we needed to generate some money big time. So what I did was to recruit people that had kids playing on the team for the next few years. I wanted to find people I could count on, who were enthusiastic, and who would do the job without giving me any flack. I invited people over to my home in June for an informal meeting. We got to know each other, and we met to discuss and organize the different functions of our club

We had poster sales. A local doctor came up with the funds for printing the poster that had the schedules of all the home and away games plus the starting times for the games. All the freshmen, junior varsity, and varsity players took 20 posters and sold them for $3 a piece. So off the top, we generated about $3500.

Next, we tried to come out with a top-drawer game program that we sell before every home game. We have about a 60-page program. We started out soliciting businesses asking them to support our Football Club with a $25 business card-sized ad. The next slot was a quarter page for $50, the back page was $75, a full page cost $100, and we went all the way to $250 for the front inside cover. We generated a lot of money off the sales on game programs at our home games.

The next thing we did was to organize the concession stand. We sold pop, pizza, and popcorn, and we usually generated about $500 at each home game. Because our concession stand is quite small at Riverview High School, at half-time we had people lined up 50 to 60 deep. We are going to expand our concession stand with some of the additional funds we have. Then we can double the sales and maybe make up to $1000 per game. You may want to put a concession stand on the visitor's side if you have the ability.

We also had a souvenir booth with T-shirts, sweat shirts, and afghans. I was at a booster club meeting, and someone suggested we sell boxer shorts. Everyone thought we were half crazy. We purchased about 500 shorts at $7 each and we sold them for $14. We ran out of them in one home game. We ended up selling about $3500 worth of the boxer shorts. It was a little different twist, but both girls and boys were buying them. It was a big money maker for us.

We have a social after ever home game in the high school cafeteria. Our women put on a meal after the game. We invite all the parents, fans, and players. We charge $3 per ticket, and you can have a good meal with fine fellowship. Everybody gets to know everybody, and it has made a considerable amount of money for us.

One thing we do is to have a 50/50 drawing at half-time of home games. Most typical 50/50 drawings you sell a ticket for a $1. I came up with an idea where you could buy tickets from your nose-to-your-toes for $5. You cannot believe how many people came through and paid $5 for these tickets. At our home games, we usually generate $1000 on this raffle, and at Homecoming, we generated $2000. We kept $1000, and we gave two winners $500 each. That is a big return off a 50/50 raffle.

I want to share with you some special fund raisers. We taped our local JC's asking them if there was anything we could do to work with them to generate money for our football program. They told us we could get involved with their Haunted House, and they needed workers. Our Football Club worked the Haunted House for three hours a night for one week. It was a lot of fun, and they cut us a check for $2400. In one week we made $2400

We got involved with a group called Fun Services out of Georgia that had a big picnic for the Chrysler Corporation. We had about 80 people work that picnic, and we received a check for $2500.

Another big fund raiser we have is our golf outing. We use the local golf course, and we charge $75 per person. We have 18 holes of golf. We had sponsors for each hole for $100 per hole. We had prizes provided by the local businesses. We made about $3500 profit after all expenses. This has been an annual function for our Football Club.

We had a parent who worked at Chrysler to get a Jeep donated for our raffle. We sold tickets for $20 a piece, and we made $14,000 profit. It takes a lot of work, but if you get enthusiastic, you can really make things happen.

The next project we had was at the Pontiac Silverdome. We worked 14 events, including 10 football games and four other events with one being a motor-cycle crossover and a truck-pulling contest. It took about 20 people to work the concession stands in one designated area of the Silverdome. We made about $2,000 to $2500 per event. In one year, we made $23,000 working at the Silverdome. This year, we are going to contact Co-America Park and work concession stands at 10 home games there as well. We hope to make $20,000 on this project.

Our next money maker is the Pirate Memory Walkway. At the entrance of our stadium, we contracted an outfit that lays bricks. We had a landscaper come in and landscape the area at the entrance, and we sold these bricks for $100 or $200 for a family brick. We have sold about $10,000 worth of bricks, an amount that will more than take care of the expenses for the project. We stand to make a $5,000 profit so far, and this will be an on-going thing.

Someone told me nothing is achieved without enthusiasm. If there is anything I try to do as Booster Club President, it is to bring enthusiasm to the people I work with in the Booster Club. I don't mind sharing this with you. We are like a family. We became close, and some of the friendships were incredible. We had a group of people that went all out for these kids and the football program. Some of the things we were able to do is purchase over $20,000 worth of weight equipment for our football program. We charter busses to take the team to far away games like Frankenmuth, and the playoffs at the Silverdome. It was a great experience.

As I close I would like to read a letter to you. It is for football coaches. This was a letter written by our Booster Club to our coaches.

"Dear high school coaches. Some of the parents do not take even a few minutes to thank you for coaching their sons this season. We wanted to thank you at the banquet, but you know there is not much time for little more than a pat on the back. We thought writing a letter to you would be more meaningful.

There were times this season when we envied you when our sons came over to the sidelines after a big run or a crunching tackle, you got to congratulate them, and we had to wait until after the game. There were times when we questioned your decisions, but that is normal. Almost all parents up in the stands have their own ideas how they would run things if they were in charge. You take a lot of heat. That goes with the territory. You learn to accept criticism and let it roll off your back. Deep down inside it hurts, doesn't it?

Sometimes, we parents forget that you coach for about a $1 per hour, and you would not be out there if you did not love it. Sometimes, we forget how hard it must be when you prepare all week and then lose a game you should have won. Sometimes, we forget you and your family suffer when you are trying to teach our children a little about football and a little about life. We never realized football and life had so many parallels—the ups and downs.

Thanks for the never-give-up spirit you taught them as they learned how to deal with adversity. Sometimes, we wondered if you really understand how important you are coach in this age when broken homes are common and kids are looking for direction. They are tempted by drugs, drinking, vandalism, and even suicide. As you know, some of them come from sad home situations. Some of their parents have not seen them for days. Some don't care what time their son comes home or even if he comes home. Amidst all of these problems, you stand like a beacon.

Thanks for caring about all of them coach. They are richer for having known you. Our sons learned discipline, they learned what it is like to be yelled at, and they learned what it is like to be hugged. They learned that football players have to be tough, but they can be tender too. Did you know they told us they loved us when they lined up for Parents' Night. Even if you told them to say it, we are thankful to you. We are a lot closer to our sons now. Football has brought us together, and it has helped our sons take another step to manhood.

There are so many ruts and wrong-way streets on those journeys. We worry about our sons and are thankful that you care. You are more of a father to some of these boys than their own fathers. The next time when things go bad and you wonder why you keep putting the whistle around your neck, and you can hear the fans taking pot-shots at you from the bleaches, just remember deep down inside we are thankful for you caring for our kids."

BOB McQUISTON
Center Line High School Booster Club

I really appreciate being here, and I appreciate your attention. I do have some handouts. First, I need to ask you a question. All of the coaches here who are thoroughly happy with the level of support you get from the community, both financially and spiritually, raise your hands. All of you who feel you have an okay situation as far as finances and spirit, raise your hand. Any coaches who are dealing with a booster club that needs a major transfusion in some way to come up with some extra bucks, raise your hand. If you raised your hand, you need to hear this. This is Booster Club #101 time.

I would like to share some fund-raising ideas with you. You need to understand up front that we are a small Class B school in a working-class town. We do not have a lot of money, but our people do well. We have a relatively generous school board and a high tax rate with an extra milleage. We take care of our schools, and we are proud of our schools. The athletic department has relatively a good budget. The Mom and Dad's Club does the extras. The Athletic Director tells us what they cannot afford. The coach writes a letter and the Athletic Director and Principal signs it. We have only said "no" twice, and we asked the coach to rewrite the letter. We have never said "no" to any request.

Each case we look at the effort required and the return on the investment that we experience. You can get an idea what you can do in your town. I have about 48 adults that I can contact and get something done. So depending on what kind of enthusiasm you have at your high school, you can plug that into your activities.

We have spaghetti dinners. Sunday is our 28th annual spaghetti dinner. The way this works is we get the VFW Hall free. We order the food through the food services at the school. They give us an invoice, and we pay them back, and we get the food at a good rate. The cost of the dinner is cheap: $5 for an adult, $3 for a senior citizen, and free for children under 6 years old. We go to the local senior co-op, and they pay $3. You do not make any money on the seniors, but it is important to reach out to them.

We will have a 50/50 raffle at the dinner at $1 per chance. The dinner is a ton of work, and we walk away with $2600. We also call all the parents of athletes and ask them to make something for the bake sale. We get about a 20-percent response. We don't get angry or call them names if they do not participate. We thank them for their time. If someone brings a tremendous desert, we put it in the raffle. We get two or three attractive female athletes to go around and sell raffle tickets. It is like a carnival atmosphere.

We need horse power to do a golf outing. That is work. I have done it myself. What we do if have a bowling outing, beer, pizza, and door prizes might be a lower-end deal. We are about to have ours in a month, and we have 144 slots just for bowling. We are expecting another 100 for just the beer and pizza. We have a much bigger bowling alley this time, and it looks like we are going to do it twice a year. We can probably clear up to $2,000 this year. So if you feel a golf outing is too large an event, you might want to try the bowling outing. It is much more manageable and a lot easier to pull off. It is also a parents' night out and a way to get donated funds.

We do a low-end sports game program. We do not charge for our programs, and we basically make one for the entire year. We stuff the roster in the middle of the program, and it has things about sportsmanship and nice pictures of all teams. We sell ads in the program, and we make about $2300 per year.

The nice thing about the sport program is that you put it together in the summer. It is hard to get parents involved during the school year when the kids are playing. It is a very convenient fund raiser because you do it in the summer. We ask parents to donate their time. Time management is very important. It is really hard to get people to commit to a whole weekend during the school year.

Another thing we provide is event support. We support the school system at the football games. They take tickets, and they get the gate. We take care of the security, parking, change gang, announcing, and concession stand. We run the whole show for the school district. We get all the revenues except the gate. This includes the concession stand, 50/50 raffle, and any merchandise that is sold.

When you buy items for the sales, remember to buy in limited quantities and do not have your money tied up in merchandise. We do not make as much money as larger schools, but we want to make as much money as possible so it can go to the program. We do $900 at the football concession stand and $2500 at Homecoming. The 50/50 is usually $500 per game. If you grill the hot dogs and hamburgers in front of the people, you will double your money just from the aroma of the food.

Always consider effort vs. return. Nothing beats a 50/50 raffle. You need a $15 roll of tickets with someone to hold down a cigar box. There is nothing easier you can do to make $60 per hour with your volunteers.

In our situation, we are the Mom and Dad's Club for the whole high school. When I first took office, the first feedback I got was a letter to the editor in the school paper. It was from a member of the girls basketball team. She said football gets everything, and women's basketball gets nothing. This is the political arena I walked into. From my experience, football is a very organized sport. The football coaches have a more complex request form than the golf coaches since football is much more involved. You are going to have jealousy from other parents and kids.

We go around and look at all sports. If we think the cheerleaders need something, we have the coach write us a letter. If we feel the volleyball team needs new bags, we have the coach write us a letter. Then if the football team gets what they need, there are no questions asked. We reach out and take care of everybody. That is how we try to deal with political jealousy. We try to have community fellowship in everything we do.

We have had a pot-luck dinner for decades for our football team. We now have a fall sports banquet, a winter sports banquet, and a spring sports banquet. We have a dinner for every athlete and their family that plays a sport at Center Line High School to show our appreciation for their time and dedication.

When you want to build your support, share your strategy with your parents. You want them to identify with your teams. If they are there because of their son, they will be gone when their son is gone.

They are more likely to stay if they identify with a team. We have some parents who have been with us for 20 years. They love the kids in Center Line, and they want to stay attached to them.

Poll all your members and find out their assets. We have a concession stand, and we need a health license to operate the concession stand. One of our members works for the Krogers Stores who is in charge of our concession stand. We now have a license for the year. Everyone has talents and things they can do.

When I was Vice President, I had a rock concert and lost $700. I made $2000, and it cost $2700 to put the show on. They still voted for me as President, but I am not going to try to do that again. You don't do a first event and hang yourself out to dry. If you are going to try something new, find the cheapest way to do it, and then make it better next year.

Have football parents work the non-football games. We want the parents to watch their kids play.

Always be aware that perception is everything. Always do things for the benefit of the athlete. Your common bond is not to make money, but love the kids and allowing the kids to have the richest experience possible. Thank you very much.

VIEWS ON COACHING FOOTBALL

Florida State University

Men it is good to see all of you again. When we played the University of Oklahoma in the Orange Bowl, I knew we were in trouble when we were warming up. If you noticed, Oklahoma has red and white uniforms. On their helmets they have that big O decal. I know it means a lot to them. As their players were warming up, one of them came over to pick up a punt at the fifty-yard line. I was standing there when he came to pick up the football. I looked at him and said. "young man, what does that big O on your helmet stand for?" He did not bat an eye. He replied "honor". I knew we were in trouble when he said that. I had some players that could not spell either.

I have a lot of notes here that I have used over the years. I have been coaching 46 years. I think this is the third time I have been to this clinic. It is amazing. It is still one of the largest clinics I ever attend. You people here have done a great job of organizing this clinic. We have clinics down in Miami and Orlando, and in other areas of our state, but we do not get as many people at our clinics.

The things I can help you with the most are things I have learned in my 46 years of coaching. These things have meant a lot to me over the years. When I get through, I will give you a chance to ask questions.

Some expressions that have meant a lot to me over the years include these. First, "You do not Win games, you lose them." I really think this is a true statement. It is true. You do not win games. You lose them. Take a look at the games you did not win last fall. Why did you not win those games? You find a way to lose games.

Missed assignments are reasons to lose games. I bet you if I could have five missed assignments back at Florida State, just five missed assignments in the last five years, we would have three National Championships. Just missed assignments have cost us a lot of games. Don't beat yourself with missed assignments. Turnovers get you beat. Blocked punts get you beat. Punt returns for touchdowns get you beat. So, I think the statement is true about not winning games. You do not win games, you lose them.

I remember when Woody Hayes was coaching at Ohio State. I was coaching at West Virginia at the time. I was at West Virginia for 10 years. I was the head coach for six of those years. I would go to Columbus to watch practice. Woody Hayes was the MAN back in those days. Bud Wilkinson and Ara Parseghian were big back then. But Woody Hayes was as big as anyone. We would go up to watch them practice. I always remember the story Woody would tell us. He always said the first thing you must do is to "make sure you don't get yourself beat."

But this is the story I liked best from Woody. One day a mother gave her son a dollar bill and told him to take care of it. The next day the little boy took the dollar bill down to the grocery store and asked the clerk to give his change for the dollar bill. He got two quarters, four dimes, a nickel, and five pennies. He took the change and went back to the bank. He asked the bank clerk to give him a one dollar bill for the change. The clerk gave him the one dollar bill. The young boy took the dollar bill back to the grocery store and asked for change. He got the change for the one dollar bill. He went back to the bank and asked for a one dollar bill. He did this for three days in a row. Finally, the bank clerk asked the young boy what was he doing. The young boy replied, "One day someone is going to make a mistake, and I can assure you it is not going to be me."

That is the way Woody Hayes coached. That was his theory of football. It is true today. If you coach the little things that get you beat, you will be a winner. If you take care of the little things, you can win.

This is my 26th year at Florida State University. When I went to Florida State, I put a big sign over the entrance to our practice fields. On the sign was the word "ENTHUSIASM." That sign has been up there for 25 years. We repaint the sign every few years.

After I had been at Florida State University a few years, I said I have another word I think is important to winning. That word is PERSISTENCE. We think that is the key to our program at Florida State with regard to work. We have enthusiasm and persistence written all over the place. Where we work out for our indoor program, we have those words written in big letters down the wall. Our players really get exposed to those words.

Out on our big tower that sits out in the middle of the practice field, we have the word "PERSISTENCE" in big letters. If you do not know what persistence means, then you need to look it up. You need to teach your players what the word means. If your players are persistent, they are not going to lose. If you are persistent, you can out fight your opponent. However, if your opponent is more persistent than you are, they will outfight you. That word is very important. We try to instill in our players to never quit. So, we put the big signs up with the words "ENTHUSIASM" and "PERSISTENCE" on them so our kids see them all of the time.

Last spring I put another sign up. I put the sign up all across my tower in the center of the three practice fields. The sign was "I AM THE BOSS!"

The sign was about three feet high. I wanted my players to see it everyday. Well, about the third day, my wife came and took the sign down and put it back in our kitchen.

You can watch two teams come out on the field to warm up. If they are equal in all things, I will take the team that is enthusiastic. I talk to our players about enthusiasm. I talk to them about being enthusiastic. A lot of the players do not know what it means. Enthusiasm is spirit. If you have spirit in you, then you will exhaust yourself physically to win.

If you want to know where that spirit comes from, in my opinion, it comes from God. I remember something Woody Hayes said about 30 years ago. He talked about the word ENTHUSIASM. He put it up on the board for everyone. Enthusiasm comes from the Greek word "EN THEOS." This means "full of spirit" in Greek. We all have kids with big builds that can run. I want those players full of spirit and full of enthusiasm. It is the spirit that makes you go. We all are looking for that button to press that will turn the kids loose. That is the key. The other part of the Greek word "En Theos" was GOD. God in you. Full of God. If you want to give a simple talk to your kids, this isn't a bad line of thought. If we have persistence and enthusiasm, we will be good.

Next, I want to talk about six commandments we use at Florida State. There are six things I go over with our players on Friday night before a game on Saturday. We take all of the players away to a hotel on Friday night. We get them all together in a room, and I make my last talk before we are to play the next day. I go over six reminders with them every Friday night. I have not missed doing this one time in the last 26 years the night before the game. I tell them there are six things we must do to keep from losing. We do not want to beat ourselves. Here is what I tell them.

SIX COMMANDMENTS

WE MUST HAVE NO BREAKDOWNS IN THE KICKING GAME. We do not have a kicking coach as such at Florida State. Some schools have a kicking coach. In college, you only get nine assistants, and I want all of my assistants to have a kicking-game responsibility. We break it down so everyone on the staff has an area of the kicking game.

In that meeting with the team the night before a game, I may mention some points in the game the week before to emphasize the importance of the kicking game. We may have lost the last game because of a blocked punt, a blocked field goal, or a missed field goal. We are really good at missing field goals at Florida State. We do not fool with the "wide left" stuff. We are always "wide right."

WE MUST HAVE NO MISSED ASSIGNMENTS. I just talked about keeping from losing before you can win. You must keep from losing before you can win, and these are things that keep you from losing. The biggest reason we lose games at Florida State is because of missed assignments. It is not the inability to block or tackle. It is missed assignments. We talk about that on Friday night. NO MISSED ASSIGNMENTS.

WE MUST PLAY GREAT GOAL LINE OFFENSE AND DEFENSE. We practice on the goal line everyday in the spring. We do not do it as much in the fall because we do not want to get people hurt. But this is what we do in the scrimmages.

We scrimmage 3rd-and-3 yards to go on the 3-yard line. Then we scrimmage 4th-and-1 yard to go on the 1-yard line. This is a low-injury drill because you are so close to each other. This is a compact drill. During the season, we may run this drill once a week, or we may not. It all depends on how we are doing with injuries.

If we run the drill on 3rd-and-3 from the 3-yard line, the offense can either run the ball or throw the pass. If it is 4th-and-1, they can only run the ball. It is a physical thing. We want the defense to bring all eleven players. We want the offense to take their eleven and run at them. We have to work on the goal line offense and defense.

Let me show you one thing I have learned about running your favorite play. Let me draw up a play for you. Let's say this is your favorite play, and you run it over and over from the middle of the field in practice everyday. Here is the play.

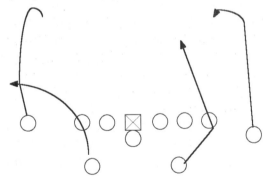

You run this play from the middle of the field, and it is your favorite play. You work on it from the 20-yard line to the 20-yard line.

Now you get down inside the 10-yard line. You want to run that same favorite play down on the goal line. The wide receivers run the same patterns and end up curling up in the stands of the end zone, and the tight end goes out of bounds on his route. What I am saying is this. Be sure you practice your passing game during the week on the goal line and on all other areas of the field. We practice it from the 3-, 5-, 7-, and from the 9-yard lines. One day we will work from one of those spots. We go to that area and every down it

will be 3rd-and-9. The next day we work on 3rd-and-7 yards to go from the 7-yard line.

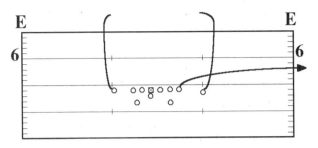

When I first started coaching, I was not aware of this. I learned it is different when you get down on the goal line. You need to have an open-field attack and a goal-line attack.

WE MUST HAVE NO FOOLISH PENALTIES. As soon as I tell the team this, I know we are fixing to get one. I know where it is going to come from. It is going to be on the punt return—blocking in the back. We specialize on that block. We tell our players if they can't get their head in front of the numbers of the defenders, not to block them. Our players have a hard time holding off on those blocks. It should not be that much fun to hit someone in the back. They can't hit you back. Anyway, stop the foolish penalties.

Let me cover the worst penalties you can have. It is 4th-and-4 and the offensive team is getting ready to punt. Then, the defensive man jumps off sides. Now they have a 1st down. Even worse than that is when it is 4th-and-4, and you line up off sides. I hate that penalty. Those are foolish penalties. That is a point that you must talk to your team about constantly.

WE MUST NOT GIVE UP LONG TOUCHDOWNS. Let me give you some ideas why this is important. Let's say we are on our 40-yard line. That means we have 60 yards to go for the touchdown. I know you do not have the best material in the country, right. I do not have the greatest material in the country. None of us do. But, we can still stop the long touchdown, right. You may not be able to stop 4th-and-1, or 3rd-and-2 because the offense just beats you to the punch. But, you can stop the 3rd-and-30 yards to go, can't you? You can back the deep secondary up when it is that far to go for the 1st down. Back them up, and they can stop the long play. You say they can't. Then back the linebackers up. Put the all backs deep. Give them all of that short stuff.

Now we say not to let them make a long touchdown. The offense takes the ball and picks up 3, 4 yards, then 3 yards, then 4 yards, and before you know it they are down on the 5-yard line. Now, what was one of our other goals? Great goal line defense. When we get backed up to the goal line, we tell our players it is to our advantage. When they get down on our 3-yard line we have 11 players against their nine players. The quarterback is going to hand the ball off to someone so we have the advantage. Last year we had three stops on 3rd-and-1 on the 1-yard line. That is because we scrimmage this situation. Our kids feel good down there. If the opponent can't score down there, they will have to kick the field goal. They get three points for the kick. No long touchdowns.

WE MUST KEEP FUMBLES AND INTERCEPTIONS TO A MINIMUM. The first thing we teach the players is how to hold the football. I know that sounds odd. We want our hands over the ends of the ball. We want the ball tucked into our arms which is against the body. We do not want any daylight between the cavities. When you look at the ball, that is all you see. We do not want to leave the elbow up or the hand out. We want to protect the football.

Once we learn to secure the ball, the second thing we learn to do is how to secure a fumble. We work on this the first day of practice. We want to teach the players how to lay on a fumble. When the ball is on the ground, they are going after it. If a player does not know how to recover a fumble, he may not go after it. We want them to fold their legs so they can bring in the ball. We do not want them diving on the ball where they get hurt. We teach ball security first, and then we teach how to recover a fumble. That is on offense and defense. We teach this the first day of practice.

We work on ball-exchange drills. When we are running the inside drill against dummies, we take walk-ons and line them up back in the area of the secondary. When the back gets through the dummies, the walk-ons try to knock the ball out of his hands. They reach in from the side and try to strip the ball.

Those are the six areas we work on with the players. I go over these points the night before each game. We work on these points all year.

Our offense has a motto. "DO IT RIGHT – DO IT HARD OR DO IT AGAIN." We have this up on our wall in the indoor room. When we are doing drills, I hear our coaches telling the players to go back and do it again. They must hustle or go back and do it again.

A couple of slogans that have meant a lot to me over the years are worth mentioning. When I get back to Florida State, I guarantee you that on Monday I am going to tell the players something that was told to me a long time ago. Vince Lombardi made the statement that has stayed with me for 40-plus years. He said, "Football is two things: BLOCKING and TACKLING." It has not changed over the years.

How many times have you seen a coach lose a game because his defense had a bad day, and then he goes in on Monday and puts in a whole new defense? He forgets to teach them how to tackle.

The other extreme is the coach who runs the offense but he can't make a first down. He gets shut out for a game. He comes in on Monday and changes the whole offense. It is the blocking that is the problem. He must teach them to block. If you get beat, go back and make sure your kids are blocking and tackling.

The way you improve your team is by blocking and tackling. If we could go out 15 days in the spring and get better blocking and tackling, we would be a lot better. We would not have to put in any plays. Don't neglect blocking and tackling. I try not to neglect them.

I heard this slogan back in the 1950's from Ara Parseghian: "It is not potential, it is performance." This is one of the biggest traps coaches get into. It is not the potential of a player, it is the performance of the player. We go out and sign a great high school player. When you get him, you think he is better than the player you have on the team who may not be able to jump as high, or run as fast. You decide his potential is better than the player you have now.

You arrange for them to compete, but you see to it that the new player gets ahead of the older player. You put the new player in and he drops about seven passes. You sit there waiting for his potential to come through. While we are waiting for the potential, we all get fired. If you have a proven performer, you need to make the player who has potential earn the right to play. That is my advice to you, but you must be careful, because that can be a trap.

Now, I am going to give you a chance to ask questions. I will repeat the questions and give you my comments.

WHAT DO YOU THINK IS THE TOUGHEST PART OF COACHING?

The toughest part of coaching for us right now is handling the players. Players are so different today than what they were when I first started coaching. The first year I coached was in 1953. World War II was over, but the Korean War was going on. The kids were much more disciplined. Anytime there is a War, everyone gets discipline all of a sudden. I expect it is the military carryover. When I started coaching, the players would do whatever you asked them to do and never ask WHY. If they did ask why, you told them to get gone. "We don't need you."

Today, you better must tell the players WHY. This is my thinking. When I tell the players to do something, I tell them why it is best for them. "Men, if do it this way, you will be better." Players think about themselves today.

The tough job is when you get a players, and he is not behaving like you think he should, or he does not act like you think he should act. When that happens, that player becomes a disruption to your team. You try to save him because you know he can make you a good coach. That is the biggest problem that college coaches have. We get to go out and choose our players. Most high school coaches have to take kids from the community. It is hard to bring in those players from different communities and make them a team.

Another of my favorite expressions is: " I do not want the eleven best players. I WANT THE BEST ELEVEN." Now, you may have to look at this again. Write it down. Now, you know what that is saying? It is not the team with the eleven best players that win. It is the best TEAM that wins. Football is a team sport. Your eleven best players may not fit together. Your eleven best players may have bad chemistry. One player may not like another player. This player may not block for another player. I want the best 11 players, and not the 11 best players.

WHAT WAYS HAVE I USED TO MOTIVATE PLAYERS?

I assume you mean other than cars. They love automobiles. I will try to give you some thought on that question. I am dealing with about 100 players. How are you going to keep 100 of them motivated? Each year I start out with this approach.

Men, our goal is to win the National Championship. That is our goal. All of you can not play. But everyone of you has a role to play. If it is on the first team, great. If it is on the second team, your job is to make the first team better, or get their job. For the third team, your job is to get that second team job, or make them better. First team, your job is to hold on to what you have. You better be good, or we will move you.

Now, we get on down to the fourth team, and lower, and we know they are not going to play. I try to sell them the need for them to give us a good look on the scout teams. They have to work hard to make us better. If they do not make us work hard to get better, we are not going to a bowl. "We will not win you a ring for the bowl game. If we win the bowl game, everyone of you will get a ring." I tell them with that ring, they will be an All-American twenty years from now. You may not play in a game, but twenty years from now your grandchild will be asking questions about that ring. You can tell him how good you were. No one can dispute their story because all of the other players will be dead. I can kid around with you on this, but you know what I am talking about.

I try to sell them on the fact everyone has a role to play. If I can get the last team group to really hustle and try, we have a chance. I have been very fortunate at Florida State. We have walk-on players that play halfback that only weigh 167 pounds. They get hit by our defense everyday. But their spirit is good. I pat them on the back and tell them what a good job they are doing. We try to sell everyone that they have a role to play in our success of our team. Our kids have bought into this. Some kids will not buy into this.

You must sell unselfishness. If you have selfish players where one player wants the ball every down, and this receiver wants the ball on every pass, or they want it more than the other players, then you have problems. It is a team game. We can't put the individual above the team.

Kids today just were not raised like we were. Today it is me —me—me. At Florida State, we feel that when we bring in a new player, we have to de-recruit them. "Son, you can not call me Bobby anymore. My name is Coach Bowden. You address my wife as Mrs. Bowden, and not Ann." You have to change them.

WHAT DO YOU THINK ABOUT HELMET DECALS?

Are you asking about those tomahawks on our helmets? I think most schools do this. What we do is to give small tomahawks to our kids when they do something great and beyond the call of duty. We have a spear on the side of our helmets. How can the players get those tomahawks? By blocking a punt—that will get them a tomahawk. Intercept a pass—that will get them a tomahawk. Recover a fumble, cause a fumble, to return a punt for a touchdown will get you a tomahawk. If a player gets straight A's in class, he will get you a tomahawk. After the coaches grade the film, they give out the awards. If they grade out 80 percent, they get a tomahawk.

The poor old offensive linemen have a hard time getting awards. If they knock someone flat on their back, they get a tomahawk. The kids take the awards and put them on their helmets the way they want to. Some players have a lot of them, and some do not have as many. We use the awards to motivate them. Men, that is what we are all looking for, and that is a way to motivate them.

HOW DO YOU REFLECT ON A LOSS?

This is one of the things I do not think has changed in my 46 years of coaching. That is the worst feeling in the world. I guess as I get older, I can get over them quicker. The ecstasy of winning is not half as bad as the agony of losing. That is the way I find it. I enjoy it that night, and I enjoy reading it in the paper the next day. Then it is over. It is over. I start worrying about the next game. Now, a loss stays with me a long time. I wake up at nights thinking about what I could have done to change that loss.

Some of you are young, and some of you are older. But the thing that is going to make or break you is how you handle a loss. Some coaches cannot handle it, and they get out of the profession. I have been as low as any of you here have been. I have been hung in effigy. I have been up the tree. I go walking down the street with my kids, and they tell me to look up in the tree. "Daddy, they have your name up there."

There have been about four days in my career that I contemplated getting out of the game. I asked myself, "Is this worth it? Is it worth taking all of the grief? I do not need all of this criticism." I do not want my wife discussing my career at the grocery. I do not want my kids getting heckled at school.

Every time something like this came up, I would ask myself this question. "What else are you going to do? What else would you rather do?" My answer was, "I would rather be coaching." You just have to be tough. You talk about being mentally tough. If you guys are not mentally tough, you will not be here five years from now when I come back to speak again. I may be stretching that, but I do plan to come back.

If you are not mentally tough, you will not make it in this profession. It is more difficult now than it has ever been, with all the talk shows and the media like they are, plus the TV programs. When one of our players gets in trouble, his picture is all over the world. It goes everywhere. You have the same problem in your community. We have to be tough, or we will not make it.

WOULD I TALK ABOUT THE OKLAHOMA GAME?

Offense or defense? After that game, I was thinking to myself that we were lousy. "What happened to us?" That was what I was thinking. "Why were we so bad?" Yet, I forget that our defense held them to 13 points. We usually beat teams when they only get 13 points against us. We had led the nation in offense and had averaged 42 points per game, and we could not score a touchdown. That is what I was thinking. But that was not fair to our defense.

Now, having said that I will tell you that Coach Bob Stoops and his staff did a great job. Nebraska may have underestimated them in their game. Kansas State may have underestimated them. Florida State may have underestimated them. They were a lot better than we though they were. Oklahoma is an example of what I have been talking about. They had perfect chemistry. We may have had better players than they had. It was their chemistry, and it was perfect. It was the team concept.

I know some of you may not like to hear me preach, because I do preach. I think the Good Lord is important in football, just like anything else. Every morning when our staff meets we have prayer. We have a little devotion, and we read scripture. Why do we do that? Do we do so God will make us win? God is not going to make us win. God does not care who wins the game. But what we are looking for is guidance. We ask for guidance to help us understand what we need to do. We have the FCA, but all of our kids do not participate. We have about 30 kids out of 100 that take part in the FCA. But those 30 kids work on the other players. What I am telling you is this. We are going to be successful if we can bond our team together. That is the key. Get those 100 players to act as one. That is why Oklahoma was so great last year. It was obvious when we played them.

I do not know anything that will bond your kids any better than the Good Lord. You can take this for what it is worth. I know what has happened to us. We started having prayer 15 years ago. You can do the numbers over those last 15 years.

HOW DO WE MOTIVATE THE COACHING STAFF?

The first thing I do with my coaches is to make sure everyone knows where they stand. I have an assistant head coach, an offensive coordinator, a defensive coordinator, and a strength coach, a trainer, and the rest of them are the assistant football coaches.

Here is what I do with my offensive staff. Number one, is my offensive coordinator. He gets the final say so. I tell them I do not want a dictator as offensive coordinator. But I do want him to make the final decision. When they meet as a staff, I hope they have some arguments but come to one conclusion. If they can't come to a conclusion, the coordinator must make the decision.

I tell the other coaches if the coordinator wants to do something and everyone agrees, then that is what we are going to do. If the other four coaches think the coordinator is wrong, they can come to my office and talk with me. They have that right. If that happens, I will call them all in and we will hear each other out, and then I will decide what we are going to do. I do that with both the offensive and defensive staff. The coaches seldom come to my office. But I want them to know exactly where they stand. They need to know who the boss is.

It is like I tell my nine assistant coaches. Each one of them gets a vote. Every time we have a staff meeting it is a DEMOCRACY. We have a vote on any issue we can't agree on. All of the assistants have one vote each. We have nine coaches. They get a vote, and I get 10 votes. I do, I have 10 votes. But, I do try to get their input a lot of the time.

DO YOU TAKE YOUR STAFF TO A HIDEAWAY BEFORE THE SEASON STARTS?

The hideaway is something we have been doing for about 15 years now. We go about two weeks before the season starts. We put this on our yearly calendar and call it HIDEAWAY. We take all coaches, equipment managers, team doctors, trainers, and any other group that is directly related to the football program. At one time, we went out in the country where we did not have a telephone or anything else to disturb us. We get all of our notes together and go over everyone's responsibility for that year. It is all written up. One day we have the team doctors come in and go over everything we need to know. We ask them questions and discuss all possible situations. Then we meet with the equipment man. He goes over everything related to our equipment. We take a week for this meeting. It is all football.

At the hideaway, our offense gives lectures to our defense, and then the defense gives lectures to our offense. They let each other know what they plan to do for the year. That takes about two days. When we come out of that session, we know exactly what our plans are for the year.

DO YOU MISS WEST VIRGINIA?

I was at West Virginia for 10 years and met a lot of wonderful people there. I left a lot of fine people up there. Football-wise, there just are not that many people there. Florida is about the third largest state now.

WHAT ARE THE TYPES OF QUESTIONS I WOULD ASK MY STAFF BEFORE A GAME?

I meet with the offense the night before the game. I do not meet with the defense. I have stayed involved with the offense. I hire a good defensive coordinator, and it is all his. Friday night before the game, we go over every situation that we think could occur in the game. We play a game of football on paper. We rehearse the plays and situations. We try to go over every possible situation. An example would be what we are going to do on the "two-point" plays. We have a check-off sheet that I have the coaching staff fill out with me. "It is 1st-and-10, what defense do you anticipate?" That is the type outline we follow.

HOW DO YOU HANDLE TEAM PRAYER?

Let me tell you what we do. We just signed 26 players last week. We feel we got some real good players. This summer I will write all of those recruits parents and tell them what I want to do with their sons. I want to take them to church two times. When they come to us in August, they are going to go to church two times. They are going one time to a predominately white church. This involves all of our players. The next Sunday, we go to a predominately black church. We take all of our kids to church those two Sundays. I want my players to see that they are welcome. I do not care what their race is; I just want them to see they are welcome. They can worship where they want to. This is what I tell the parents I want to do with their son.

I tell the parents we are going to have prayer, devotions, and other related activities. I tell the parents if they do not want me to do this with your son just let me know. If they do not want this for their son, I will not do it. In 25 years I have been doing this, we have had thousands of players, and we have only had two parents that said no on the church deal. I did not make those two players go to church. I made the others go. I never take the players to my church. I do not want them to think I am trying to get them to go to my church. We do have FCA activities, but they are not compulsory.

When I first started coaching it was a "hate" thing with football. Today, it is different. To be winning coaches, we must find something to keep the team together. I have not found anything any better to bond players together than love. The older I get, the more I see it is the love that makes you better. If I love my teammates, we are going to fight for each other. It is like brothers. They may fight with each other, but you better not hurt one of them. If you hurt one of them, you have to fight the other brother. I think it is the love that binds kids together and produces the chemistry that we want as coaches to make us a winner. That is what has happened to us.

IN 46 YEARS OF COACHING WHAT HAS BEEN THE MOST REWARDING THING?

I can't hide the fact that it is WINNING. That is why we are in the game. It is not any fun to lose. The thing that may rival winning is when I hear from players 20, 30, and 40 years later telling me how their lives turned out, it makes me feel proud. That is rewarding. All coaches go through this with their players. If you are young, you have not been through this. I am now coaching grandchildren. Today, I am coaching the kids of players I coached earlier in my career.

WHO IS THE BEST PLAYER YOU EVERY COACHED?

It would probably be Deion Sanders. He was the best athlete. He could do anything. He played football and played in a bowl game in his first year. He went on to play in three bowl games. He played baseball and played in the College World Series. He ran track in the conference meet. He just blew everyone away. This was against world-class sprinters. The track people wanted him to try out for the Olympics, but he would not do it because it would interfere with football. He could have been a very good basketball player. He was the best athlete. Charlie Ward had a lot of talent. He plays for the Knicks now. He won the Heisman, so we know he had a lot of talent.

HOW DO YOU HANDLE A CHARACTER LIKE DEION SANDERS?

Let me tell you about Deion. The first three years at Florida State, he was just like all the rest of our athletes. He never showed off or caused any trouble. He did not brag, or talk out of turn for the first three years.

When he got into his senior year, I guess an agent told him he could make a lot of money if he would do things differently. Then all of a sudden, he started being a showboat. His last year at Florida State, he was not on scholarship. He had signed a contract with the New York Yankees for a lot of money to play baseball for about a month. So, I tell everyone he is the best walk-on I have every had. He put us in the National Championship game. As a result, we put up with him a little that year.

The point I am making is this. All of his showboating came after he left us. I talked about faith and religion earlier. Do you know he has changed? He is a Godly man now. And I can tell you it is not fake. He is for real.

HOW DO YOU HANDLE TEAM LEADERS AND CAPTAINS?

I pick captains each year. I get with the coaches and make the picks. They have to be a senior. I select one each on offense, defense, and the kicking game. We talk about the seniors and come up with five or even eight names. Then, I will decide on the captains. I tell them it is week to week. If they do not do a good job of leading, I can change the captains. At the end of the season, I let the players vote on the three captains.

WHAT DO YOU THINK ABOUT PLAYERS LEAVING COLLEGE EARLY TO GO TO PROS.

I am not in favor of them leaving. I do not want them to leave early. I want them to finish their degree if they can. I cannot say that I have had a player that did not improve his position or standing by staying a fourth year. The players that have stayed another year have moved up in the draft the next year. For those that can't afford to stay, I can see why they come out early.

Men, I hope I have not rambled too much. It is good to see so many of you here. We are very proud of what you guys do. If college coaches are successful, it is because of the high school coaches. We are fortunate in Florida to have a lot of good football players. But they are no better than what you have. When people tell me we did not have good players when I coached in West Virginia, I tell them this. "Yes we did. We just did not have as many of them." There are good players everywhere. Some states are more populated than others. There are more athletes in those areas.

It is a shame we all can't win. Some one has to lose. I hope all of you here have a great year. Thank you.

LEADERSHIP AND MOTIVATION

University of Texas

I know anyone sitting in here on Friday night is serious about football. I was supposed to speak here three years ago when I was at North Carolina, but that December I took the job at the University of Texas. The clinic people here let me out of the lecture because my schedule was over loaded. I took the job at Texas, and I had never been to Austin. I got the call on Monday afternoon and met with them on Wednesday morning. By Thursday, I was speaking to a different football team.

I want to talk to you about some things we do with our team and our coaches. I am included in this as well. At the end if we have time, I'll show you a double screen that has been good to us. Also, I have a sprint throw back I can show you, if we have the time.

Coaching to me is really special. I was raised in a coaching family. Tommy Bowden is fortunate to have a dad that has won more games than anyone in the world. My dad coached one year as a high school coach. He went 0-10. They fired him and made him a principal. I'm sure you guys have a principal like that. After they have coached one year, they have all the answers. My dad was a lot better coach after he was principal.

My grandfather had the record for wins in middle Tennessee football. He had a record of 114-23. I was riding the team school bus with my granddad when I was five and my brother Watson was six. We were raised around high school football. That was all I knew, and that was all I did. My mother made all-state in basketball and volleyball. From a very young age, all I ever wanted to be was a coach.

After I got out of high school, I coached a short time in high school. From there, I became a graduate assistant at Florida State in the early 70's. I stayed at Florida State for three years as a graduate assistant, making $1,500 a year. I worked on my masters

degree so I could keep coaching. I wrote 106 Division 1 head coaches to see if I could be a full time coach for them. Out of the 106 letters I wrote, I got four responses. I was proud of that because they acknowledged them.

One day I was sitting in a staff meeting at Florida State, and I got a phone call from Bobby Collins. He offered me the receivers job at Southern Mississippi. He wanted to know when I could start. I asked him how far it was. He asked me if I wanted to see Hattiesburg. I said I didn't. I packed my stuff, got a map, and drove to Hattiesburg, Mississippi that night. I coached there three years.

From there, I went to Memphis State and got a huge raise to seventeen thousand five hundred dollars. I went to Memphis because the head coach, Richard Williamson, had played for Bear Bryant and coached for him. He had also coached with Frank Broyles. I thought for a young guy being able to sit in meeting with a guy who had worked for two of the most respected coaches in the country would be good for me.

From there, I went to Iowa State. If you have never been to Ames, Iowa, don't worry about it. That is the coldest I've ever been in my life. If you are not from there, you don't understand it. The only people that live there are from there.

From there, I went to LSU. That is a different deal if you've never been to Baton Rouge. They love football. Next, I went to Appalachian State. Then, I went to Oklahoma. Barry Switzer, who was the head coach at Oklahoma, called me and offered me the offensive coordinator's job. We had a great year at O.U. and played for the national championship.

I left that next year to go to Tulane as the head coach. When I took the job at Tulane, we had fifty-seven guys on scholarship. You could have had ninety-five scholarships. Of the fifty-seven guys on scholarship, forty-one of them were on academic probation. I hung in there at Tulane, and we won for two or three years and along came the North Carolina job. I took that because everything was going to be better there.

The first year we were 1-10. The second year we went 1-10. I made a critical mistake after the first year. I told everyone we would win twice as many game the second year. I was trying to be cute. Everyone laughed, but I knew we were going to win five or six games. We won one the second year, and they called me a liar.

One morning I was driving to work with my two little daughters. They were six and nine years old. All of a sudden a guy comes on the radio telling Mack Brown-North Carolina football jokes.

One of the jokes was "What do Mack Brown, Dick Crum, and Dean Smith have in common at North Carolina? None of them ever won any football games." I mean the jokes were good.

I was at North Carolina for eight years, and we finally got the program turned around and had some pretty good football teams. That is why I got the call from Texas. After I got the call, I talked to Coach Darrell Royal about what it takes to be successful at the University of Texas. I told him I had a whole lot at stake to move from North Carolina.

This was the answer Coach Royal gave me: "You have to like the state of Texas or make the alumni think you like it. You need to smile. If you are not smiling and happy, you are not going to make it. The most important thing is you need to win ALL the games."

I asked him if that were the case why should I leave North Carolina and go to Texas? Here is what he told me: "The best thing about the Texas job is this. Twenty million people really care about what happens in that job every day." I think that is true. I asked him what the worst thing about the Texas job? He said, "The worst thing about the Texas job is this. Twenty million people care about what happens in that job every day."

There are twelve hundred high schools that play football in the state of Texas. Everybody that has ever graduated from the University of Texas has a coaching degree. Everyone knows everything about coaching. You never need any more help than you have there.

Coach Royal told this story to a coach last year that was real interesting to me. Coach Royal is the neatest guy. He is seventy-six years old, has won three national championships, and has a stadium named after him. I told him one day that I wanted his job. He plays golf every day. Everybody loves him and tells him how smart he is every very day. That is the job I want. He said if you win three national championships you can have it.

This coach came up to him and asked him to tell him how to become a successful coach. Coach Royal has an amazing way of taking complex things and making them simple. He told the coach, "If you've got IT, you will be successful. If you don't have IT, you won't be successful. And if you don't know what IT is, you have no chance to be successful." The coach turned and looked at me, and I shrugged my shoulders. He turned and walked off. Coach Royal looked at me and said, "He ain't got It."

There is something to being happy and feeling good about yourself. There is something about if you lose, you can't wait to get back and get started again. If you win, you better get back to work sooner than if you lose. Because when we win, that is the time everyone is after us, and we lay down and get lazy.

I was concerned about everyone complaining about our recruiting and being negative. Coach Royal said that will just keep you in shape. The more people that complain, get on you, and question you, the less likely you are to get lazy. Coaches don't get in trouble when they work or when they are honest. They get in trouble if they lie, cut corners, get lazy, or believe when they won a game it was because of them. That is when they get in trouble.

Let's talk about things that matter. These are things I live by. A coach is in a situation that is responsibility without control. Why do coaches worry all the time? We are putting our checks in the mouths of young kids. We are letting them run up and down the field in front of a bunch of people. If they drop it, we get fired. If you think about it, we have responsibility without control.

If the player fails in the classroom or sells drugs, it is the coach's fault. If he doesn't play, it is your fault. There has never been a mom who didn't love her son.

My high school coach quit about six years ago, and I asked him if kids were different today? He said they weren't different, the parents were. The parent wants us to be the disciplinarian, because they have no discipline themselves. They want you do it, but don't be too hard on their kids. If you don't play them, they get depressed, and you've hurt their self image. If you play the bad ones, you are going to get fired.

What you have to do is be a strong leader and play the ones that give you the best chance to win. If the administration will not give you a chance to run your own program, then you have a bad job and need to find another one. You can't be a part-time coach. It is either your job, or it's not. That is very simple. Dwight D Eisenhower said "*Leadership is the ability to get a person to do what you want him to do, when you want it done, in the way you want it done, because he wants to do it.*" If you can get your team to make decision that you want and get them to do it because they think they wanted to do it, you are going to be successful.

Leadership is poise under pressure. Leadership doesn't matter when you are winning and things are going good. Everyone is patting you on the back and telling you how smart you are. You have to be a great leader, when Oklahoma beats you 63-14, and you are heading back to Austin. You have to figure out where you are going because everyone is watching to see how you respond. I actually get sick after we lose. I can't sleep for three nights. That is one reason I won't be able to coach as long as Joe Peterno or Bobby Bowden. I can't handle the losing.

I don't enjoy the wins as much as I hate the losses. Don't take it wrong if you can't take losing, because that is not a bad thing. But you have to have some balance in there. I haven't found that balance yet, and that is really tough for me.

I asked Coach Royal if he still got nervous after winning three national championships? He told me it was a year and half after he retired before he realized everyone didn't gag after they bushed their teeth before a game.

If you look at Vince Lombardi, he said, "*It is not so much in leading, as it is having people accept you. You have to win the hearts of people with your own personality and style.*" If you try to be someone else all the time, it won't work. You have to be yourself. The worst thing you can do is come in here and take everything everybody says, and try to put it in your program. I tried to take pieces for everyone I worked for. I've really been lucky. I worked for some great people. I've never had an original thought in my whole life. But I've found a lot of good people to help me along.

The first thing that you need to do is <u>observe people you admire</u>. Find somebody that is doing it like you want to do it. Then go find out why they are winning. There are a whole bunch of guys that are winning. There is a fine line between winning and losing. It is not what everyone thinks. You want to emulate the good and eliminate the bad.

There are some guys here that have talked to their teams about not drinking. Those guys are going to go out tonight and get drunk as a skunk. It is hard to be drunk all week end and tell your kids not to drink. It is hard to be a role model for kids all of a sudden.

On the field, we don't cuss. We don't grab them, we don't scream at them, we coach them. If a guy is not going to hustle, getting all over him is not going to help. Figure out who are the ones that want to play. Then don't cuss them or grab them.

You can't tell a woman she's pretty any more. It used to be a compliment, now it is sexual harassment. You have to go to work every day and give duties out. We have a bunch of young women that work in our offices called the Texas Angles. They help us with recruiting. I don't know their names. You have to be really careful about what you say and do now.

The second thing I think is important is <u>communication</u>. That means if I say something to you, you understand what I meant. That is a hard thing these days. What I am trying to do is listen more. I have each member of our football team come into my office, and we talk. I ask them by name, what they think of this staff member? What they think of the doctor, trainer, academic staff, and me? What do you think of our offense? That may not be very flattering because they will tell you. But you are better off knowing what they are thinking. After they get it off their chest, they go back to work. Of course, I tell them what I think of them.

There are two or three ways you can get feedback from your team. Listen to them, but make sure they are listening to you. Make sure they don't leave your office not knowing what you said. Make them tell you what they heard. You may have said, "I think you are great, you're hustling all the time, and you are doing a good job, but I wish you were better in the classroom." Don't let them leave thinking all that happened and that you talked to them just about the classroom, because they are going straight to their mom and tell her what you said.

If I have a kid get in trouble, I have him come to my office, and we call his mom. He tells her in front of me what he has done. Then I get on the phone, and we try to work something out. That is important.

This factor also has some relevance to your assistant coaches. They are going to talk and have opinions. I want to know their opinions. After I get their opinions, I tell them, I'll make all the decisions. One head coach was asked what the difference is in being a head coach and an assistant coach. He said it is simple. Assistant coaches make suggestions, and head coaches make decisions. No one every remembers suggestions, but everyone remembers those decisions. If you go for it on fourth down and don't make it, they remember that. It is easy to throw out a suggestion, but hard to make decisions.

Don't speak as an authority until you have researched it. So many times as a young head coach, when someone asked me a question, I would give them an answer? I wanted everybody to know what I knew. The best thing for you to do when asked a question and you don't know the answer is to ask for time to research it. That is the reason we go to work at seven in the morning and home right after practice. At the University of Texas, we go home and eat dinner with our family. We don't spend all night at the office. There has never been a good decision made after ten o'clock.

I hate to meet just to meet. Get your work done and get out of the office. If you want to stay because you don't like your wife, that's fine. But don't act like you're working. I've been there and done that. You need to get home, so you can be fresh for your coaching responsibilities on the field. You need to have some energy at the end of the year. At Texas, we are going to a bowl game every year. Our coaches work from the first of August through January. In January, they are going to go recruiting for another month. At the end of February, we start spring practice. If our guys don't get some sleep and conserve their energy, they burn out.

It is important to listen to your players. I learned this from my little daughter. She would tell me that a little boy at school was bothering her. I told her it didn't matter, because she wouldn't even know his name when she grew up. My wife chewed me out about that piece of advice. She told me if it was a problem for my little girl, it should have been a problem for me. At her age, she didn't want to hear that she would grow out of it. It was a problem right then. Your football players are the same way.

They have some issues that aren't issues. But, they need to talk to somebody. Coach Royal said, "Those that are going to talk are going to talk to someone. You better get them saying the right things." Show genuine concern to your players. Show them you really care about them.

It is amazing to me when you go out to recruit a kid, and you ask his coach what his family is like. Some of them don't know their family. You need to drive to the kid's house and find the parents. Because they are talking to him about football, you need to get around the parents and find out what the kid is all about. That will help you in the fourth quarter.

In 1992, Bo Schembechler was doing the color on a Georgia Tech game. I asked him how he made decisions in recruiting when it got down to the end? He told me it was real simple. When it got down to the end, if I didn't like him, I didn't take him. Because in the fourth quarter, if he didn't like me, and I didn't like him, he wouldn't play for me.

If you have a player you don't like, you better be careful, because he will screw you. You better be playing the ones you trust. Pat Dye told me Coach Bryant had a rule. If a kid had potential, don't play him. That meant he wasn't using what he had, and he wouldn't help you.

Be positive in what you do. Don't talk about the negatives. You can eat your life up being negative. The old statement about the glass being half full or half empty has merit as far as I am concerned. I think there is something to that. If you want to sit around and be miserable in your job, you can. All of us have bad jobs. You guys don't get paid what you are worth. But, you are never going to get what you are worth. Some days, I get paid way too much, and other days I don't get nearly enough.

If you are talking about someone on your staff or your head coach, you should quit your job. Your team is going to be only as happy as your most unhappy staff member.

If you have problems on your staff, you'll have problems on your team. I believe that today. It has been about five years since I've gotten really direct with our coaches. I want them to know what I like and what I don't like every day. I'm paying them to smile and be happy. I don't want a coach who pouts all the time.

Coach Switzer told me one day that he had enough problems without me bring him some more. He told me he hired me to run the offense and fix all the problems. He had Gary Gibbs to fix all the defensive problems. He told me not to bring him any problems until they were fixed. If they are fixed, they won't be in the paper, and I don't want to hear about them.

If you are the head coach, you are supposed to be working for the administration. If you can't do that, quit. I did that once.

I ask each of our coaches to figure out why the kids in their recruiting area signed with another school. I want to know if we liked him why we didn't get him. If we didn't like him, what didn't we like about him? If they look at the glass being half empty, they'll think I am jumping on them about the kids in their area they didn't sign. I'm looking at the glass as half full. I want to know what we did wrong so we can do something about it next year.

We won nine games at Texas this year. We were twelfth in the country. We were three games away from playing for the national championship. Two years ago in our last game, we were leading Texas A & M

16-6 at the half. We were going to play Nebraska the following week for the Big 12 conference championship. If we had won both those games, we would have played for the national championship. We lost them both. As a head coach, you are not happy, but you look at it and evaluate it to see why we didn't get to that point.

You must have some goals, but you can't be looking for another job all the time. I've never looked for a job in my life. I have never been asked a football question in my life in an interview. That is unusual. After I was at Tulane, I never went for an interview before they offered me the job.

I've got a good job. My first coaching job at Southern Mississippi, I said yes without even seeing the school. You are not going to get the best job the first time out. If you do, you're probably not going to be able to handle it. If I had taken the Texas job the year I took the Tulane job, I would have been fired before I got started. I was lucky that the Texas job didn't come up until I had been beaten up some.

I don't have all the answers, but I know if Coach Royal calls me I leave a meeting and call him right back. If the other twenty million call me, I don't answer.

I asked Coach Royal what he did with demeaning letters. He said he never saw them. The secretary read them and threw them away. I told my secretary to keep them in a file, because I am going to write a book when I quit. I am going to put all those idiot letters in the book. When you get one of those letters, you call the guy who wrote it and tell him that someone just sent you a really dumb letter and signed his name to it. You just thought he would like to know about it.

When you look at your goals, you have to understand what you are going to do. If you don't enjoy coaching, quit and do something else. Coaching is hard. I think you have to be a little obsessed. You have to love those kids. You have to get excited watching them play. You have to set personal and professional goal. You need to set short- and long-term goals to get a direction.

There are guys on your team that don't like football. Every one of us has some of those types, and we are depending on them. The team has to put their goals together. If they are not going to live up to those goals, they are not worth having.

Constantly work on ideas to evaluate and approve. Every year, you should add or take away something that didn't work. Coach Royal won a national championship in 1963. He said people bragged on him so much, the next three years that he almost got fired. He spent more time speaking for those people bragging on him than he spent working on football.

You must exercise great time management. We waste more time in coaching than any other business. If business men wasted time like we do, they would be fired. Most of the wasted time is at night. Go home and come to work early. You have sixteen-year olds that will never learn what you know. Go home and get some rest.

The last thing we have to do is to manage stress. I have tried to learn more about stress. If you exercise enough, you will sleep better at night. I don't exercise like I should. To manage stress, you need to get on an exercise program. I am going to try to make myself walk for twenty minutes three days a week.

Another thing I really believe in is honesty. If you cheat and nobody ever catches you, you will still know that you cheated to win. You have an inner soul that knows. It is a whole lot easier to tell the truth. If you are going to cheat, you are not really winning. What message are you sending the kids, if we are sincerely trying to help them? If you evaluate why you are in this business, you'll remember it is for the kids. My high school football coach, my dad, and my grandfather have been the three most influential people in my life.

Two years ago 82 percent of the teams that had three or more turnovers in a game lost the game. The number one reason people win or lose games is turnovers. If you are not protecting the ball, or not taking it away, you are going to get beat.

The second reason people win and lose football game is explosive plays. That means runs over twelve yards and passes over sixteen yards. If you make big plays, you've got a chance to win.

We have studied this for over 15 years, and when we have explosive plays and win the turnover ratio,

we have won the game. We have not lost a game where we have done those things.

Let me give you a play. This screen has been good to us for a long time. We can run it from a variety of formations. You always run the quick screen to the right. The quarterback takes five quick steps and dumps the ball to the back to the right. It is the tailback if he is coming from the I formation or the right halfback coming out of split backs.

If the defensive end charges hard, the tight end blocks the inside linebacker. The right tackle pulls hard and blocks the man covering the right flat. The guard pass sets and turns up inside and blocks. Basically, we have the tight end blocking down, the guard pulling in the alley, and the tackle kicking out. As a result, the play becomes a sweep.

If the play is not there, the quarterback steps up three steps and looks for the split end coming inside for a similar screen. The split end comes back three to four yards, and catches the football three yards outside the left tackle. The fullback is running hard to kick out the flat cover man. The left tackle cuts the rusher playing on him. The left guard is the lead blocker for the split end. The center leads down on the safety.

QUICK SCREEN

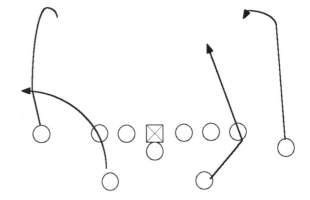

You can run this play from trips, four wide receivers, or just about any set you choose. This play will slow down a pass rush in a hurry.

The last thing I am going to show you is something you can use out of a tight formation. We get into a twin set left. The tight end is right. If you have a good tight end, this is a great play. We run this play from a sprint-draw fake. If it is zone coverage, the tight end hooks up. If it is man coverage, he works outside. If he can get deep, he can get the corner on his back and take him deep up the seam. We run a waggle with the running back.

SPRINT DRAW PASS

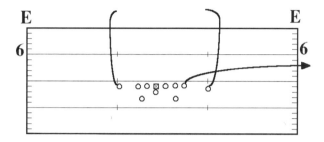

We do very few things, but we try to look complicated when we do them. We look like we are doing a lot, but it is the same things over and over.

I appreciate you inviting me here. If you get to Austin, Texas, come see us.

SECONDARY TECHNIQUES AND DRILLS

University of Louisville

It is a pleasure to be here representing the University of Louisville. I am going to talk about the secondary today. I will start out with the corners and go to the safeties. I'll talk about their fundamentals and then get into some of the drills we use.

Our secondary did fairly well this year. We led the nation in interceptions. At the end of each season, we look back to see how we did during the season and how it compared to past years. In eleven games this year, we gave up 211 pass completions. That was primarily the same number we gave up in the 1998 and 1999 season. We gave up seventeen touchdown receptions this year. In our first year at Louisville in 1998, we gave up twenty-six touchdowns. In our second year, we gave up seventeen.

In our first year here we intercepted only ten passes. The next year, we intercepted thirteen. This year, we were fortunate to have a great safety who had ten interceptions by himself. We have one corner that had six more interceptions. We had a total of twenty-seven for the year.

What do you look for in defensive backs? Your corners need to be your best overall athletes. They have to have speed. We are looking for the 6'-1" to 6'-2" corners. They are out there, but they are hard to find. What we generally end up with is a 5'-9" converted running back or option quarterback. In our safeties, we need someone who is a good enough athlete to be your corner, but is bigger and a good tackler. We ended up playing a 5'-11" and a 5'-7" player at the corners. That is not what you look for, but they did the job for us.

When we start the season, we start by setting goals. This year our number one goal was to *stop the big play*. You can't give up a lot of touchdowns, and you certainly can't give up big plays in the secondary. If they do catch the ball, we want to *make the big play*.

We want to strip the ball and create a fumble. We want to *out-physical our opponents*. We want to secure tackles and prevent touchdowns. We have to *swarm the ball*. We have to be in position and pursuit the football. The last thing we told them this past season was to *suck it up*. Those are some of the things we talked about a lot.

We have expectations for each player in our secondary. We wanted them to understand *THE TEAM COMES FIRST*. Individuals have no place in our program. Everything they do has to be totally focused on the team. We want them to *compete, compete, and compete*. They can never give up. If they do not compete they will not play. We want them to *play smart*. We don't want what we call, "no D.A.P." That stands for "No Dumb Ass Penalties." We do not tolerate dumb plays. They must *respect everyone in the program*. Most of all, we want them to *have fun*. When a player is having fun in the game, he plays better. We also want them to be on time to all meetings and team functions.

There are some points of emphasis we have to preach to our secondary as far as coverages. We want them to *align correctly*. They have to know their *responsibility and assignment*. They have to know where their help is, or is not. They have to *communicate*. The formation, checks, and automatics have to be relayed throughout the secondary. They have to make their *pre-snap reads*. They have to know who the WR-X, Z, Y, TB, or wing is and where they are lined up. They need to know the split, speed, and tendencies of the wide receivers they will face. The last thing is they must *compete* and rely on their techniques.

They must have complete focus on the details that go with the skills they have to learn. The more confidence we can instill in our players, the better and more relaxed they will play. The bottom line is, if a player cannot play with confidence, he cannot play.

The way we break this down is to start with our every-day drills. We start with our stance. We have two different stances, one is normal and one is square. The normal stance is usually used by the corner, while the square stance is used by the safeties or defensive backs in man coverage.

In our normal stance for our corners, we want a balanced stance. We want our outside foot forward. The foot stagger is a heel-to-toe or a heel-to-instep relationship. The arms hang loosely with the hands positioned in front of the knees. We bend at the knees and waist with the hips positioned underneath our shoulders. We want a flat back with a slight arch in the upper and lower regions. The eyes are focused on the quarterback. The head is set in a stationary, level position. The center of gravity is on the inside part of the ball of the front foot. They know their first step is going to be a six-inch step, usually with the inside foot. We want the stance relaxed and comfortable.

The safeties are in a square stance. Their feet are parallel and positioned slightly less than shoulder-width apart. Their arms are cocked with their hands up in a ready position. The other properties in the stance are the same as the normal stance. Their first step is generally a lateral step.

We also use the square stance for a bump-and-run technique on receivers when we are playing close to the line of scrimmage. A comfortable stance is essential in secondary play.

The most important skill for a defensive back is the backpedal. To start, we push off the front foot. We transfer the weight to the back foot by taking a short four-to-six inch lead step. We keep the hips positioned underneath the shoulders during the first step. We try to maintain our center of gravity while moving backwards. We use our arms to generate initial momentum. The speed at which we backpedal is determined by the coverage called. We want to come out slow into what we call a read step. We like to refer to it as *push and sit*. The linebackers, safeties, and corners all use a read step.

The corners are eight-yards deep and one-to-two yards inside. They are keying the quarterback. They are looking at the quarterback but seeing the number-two receiver to the number-one receiver on which they are aligned. They are keying the quarterback for a three- or five-step drop. If they recognize the three-step drop, they have to throttle down and lock on. If the drop goes past three steps, we consider that a five- or seven-step drop. From there, we start to weave or stem into whatever the coverage calls for.

In the backpedal, we are not running backwards. We are taking short strides. We want the feet gliding across the grass as light as possible. We want the feet touching the grass. If they are not touching the grass, we are too high. We want the arms locked and the hands loose.

We have drills we do daily to teach our backpedal techniques. The first drill is a simple fundamental drill. We have two lines. We use the sideline as a starting point. The defender assumes his proper stance and start. He pushes off the front foot, sinks, and pumps his arms gaining ground and speed. The objective is to develop a proper backpedal technique and body control while maintaining form. You want to make sure he pushes off the front foot with short steps. This will prevent false steps. His balance is maintained by keeping his hips underneath the body and getting his pecks in line with his knees. Do not let them over-stride. We do this drill two times. We go down and come back.

BACKPEDAL DRILL

CB: ~~~———————

SLOW

C

CB: ~~~———————

The next thing we do is a stem drill. We do a quick stem and a second-level stem. What we are trying to develop is the ability to backpedal in different directions while staying square and maintaining cushion and proper leverage on a receiver. On the quick stem, the receiver breaks into his pattern off the line. We angle pedal two to three yards off the line while staying square to the line of scrimmage. After securing the inside leverage, we straighten and continue our backpedal.

In the second-level stem, the receiver will stem after he gets downfield. We want to stay in our backpedal as long as we can. We backpedal five to seven yards, and angle pedal for two to three yards, staying square and securing leverage. We want to make sure they steer with the hips while staying square. We want to shuffle the feet at an angle without crossing over with our feet. In our stem drill, we also use a change of direction as part of the drill, depending on the game or technique we want to work on.

STEM DRILL

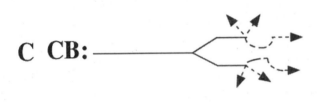

After the stem, we turn and run or break on an angle given by the coach. If a team uses a lot of stem and curl routes, we break back. If they use a stem and fade, we turn and go under the pattern.

The next drill is a change-of-direction drill. We focus on what we call a *W-angle cut*. The only thing we do differently in this drill is to machine our feet. The reason we do that is to keep our feet underneath our hips when it is time to plant and drive on the ball. Machining the feet involves taking short choppy steps before the plant. That keeps the defender from reaching with his stride and slipping. The defender backpedals straight or on an angle. He cycles his feet while keeping his hips underneath his feet. He plants his outside foot and drives by pumping his arms and leading with his inside foot. His shoulders should be slightly over his knees when he is planting and driving. His arms must be hammering as the defender breaks and bursts. The defender must accelerate three hard steps after he plants and drives. We use a straight drop and an angle drop. The angle drop is *angle-W*.

CHANGE OF DIRECTION DRILL

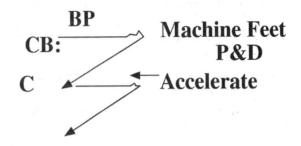

The next drill is a *bail drill*. In the diagram above, the two dots illustrate the defender's feet. In this drill, we have two different techniques. We have an inside bail, which is inside leverage, and an outside bail, which is outside leverage. These techniques give the impression of man coverage, when in fact, it is zone. The two techniques are called *5 o'clock* and *7 o'clock*. We start in a square stance in a press position disguising man coverage. On the snap of the ball, the defender opens the inside foot at 5 or 7 o'clock, depending on the coverage called, while pivoting the off foot. Then, he open steps vertical and uses a crossover step running to gain depth. His shoulders and head are turned to the key threats. We are checking to make sure he doesn't false step with his pivot foot and is accelerating at the proper angle.

BAIL TECHNIQUE DRILL

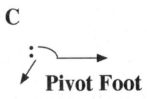

Those drills are footwork drills. We also use reaction drills. The next drills are called *open-open* and *open-whip*. We use the open-open drill to develop the ability to redirect our movement from a change of direction. The defender backpedals 3-5 yards and opens in a 135-degree angle, which is a post angle. He redirects by planting with his upfield foot, flipping his hips and shoulders in the direction intended, and accelerating through the move. He has to hammer his arms and keep his feet moving at all times.

On the open-whip drill, the defender completes the 135-degree turn and makes a center-field turn called a whip-turn. The defender has to rip his head and elbow around to turn his body and then accelerate. We want to make sure his shoulder level stays down. If they don't hit balances up, he will be thrown off. He cannot stop his feet.

OPEN-OPEN DRILL

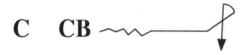

All these drills happen in the first five minutes of individual drills. We do two reps of everything. However, we don't do our bail drill every day.

Next, let's go to some of our tackling drills. This first one is a simple angle-tackling drill. We set the tackler and ball carrier in a normal wide receiver-defensive back alignment. You can call this angle, open-field, or sideline tackling. We develop the ability to breakdown, come under control, and make a sure tackle. We want the head across the body. The defender keys the quarterback. The quarterback takes a three-step drop and throws a hitch to the wide receiver. The defender breaks back and then up to make the tackle. The receiver has to run the ball through two cones. The defender accelerates to the wide receiver on the release of the ball. He squeezes the gap from the receiver with leverage and executes an angle tackle.

TACKLING DRILL

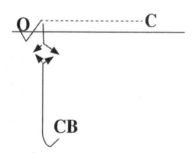

That for the most part would be the end of our warm-up period. We work our safeties and corners separately during warm up. They have different footwork drills and tackling drills which go with their position.

We usually have a tackling circuit. We have three drills set up and work different techniques in each drill. The first one is called *tackle fight*. The players line up one yard apart. The defender cannot move until the ball carrier touches him. The object is to teach the defender to grab cloth and take down the ball carrier. The ball carrier will lunge his near shoulder into the defender and scramble to get away. The defender must attempt to grab cloth and take down the ball carrier by any means necessary. The focus in on grabbing cloth and not on perfect tackle work.

The next drill in the circuit is *stalk tackling*. We set up four cones, positioned in an area five yards wide and ten yards long. The defender aligns in his normal off-man position, keying the quarterback. Once he recognizes run, he gets his eyes on the wide receiver. He initiates contact with the receiver's block. He sheds the block with leverage and makes the tackle. We make sure the defender takes his read steps. He has to fight pressure and not run around the block of the receiver.

STALK DRILL

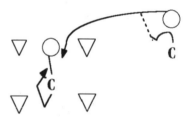

The next drill is a *cut block tackle*. We set up three cones two-yards by two-yards apart. We put blockers behind the first and second cones. A ball carrier is behind the third cone. The defender moves up field at an angle, with his pads level and his eyes on the blockers. The defender strikes the blocker by punching his near hand to the shoulder and his far hand to the helmet of the blocker. He has his inside foot up and his outside foot back, so he can escape the blocker and accelerate through the tackle.

CUT TACKLING

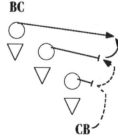

Let's get to some fundamentals of man coverage. When we play man coverage, we align in a press position with inside leverage. The defensive back is responsible for executing proper bump-and-run man coverage on designated wide receivers. He will cover the receiver all over the field. The first route the defensive back must expect is the fade route.

The defensive back will assume a square stance and align with his outside eye to the inside eye of the receiver. When aligning, the defender must squeeze the line of scrimmage as much as possible without being off sides. He must recognize the alignment and split of the wide receiver. The defender must know if he is aligning on a split end or on a flanker. Pre-snap recognition is a must. The defender must also recognize the size, stance and overall ability of the receiver over whom he is aligned.

The defensive back's focal point is on the outside belt loop of the receiver. If the opponent is in a bent stance, and the focal point to the belt loop is obstructed, the defender should focus on the bottom of the receiver's outside jersey number. The defensive back will mirror the receiver's outside loop on all moves.

Patience and quick feet are a must when executing this technique. The defensive back will encounter different types of releases by a receiver. He must be able to stop either an inside or an outside release. The defensive back must take short, quick mirror steps versus any lateral moves made by the receiver. He must not overplay these moves, but work to maintain inside leverage on the opponent. He should stay in the middle of the man. He must demonstrate great patience versus any vertical moves.

The goal of the bump technique is to disrupt the receiver's release which will buy pass-rush time and disrupt the timing of the route. We must establish this technique early in a game.

There are five fundamentals of man coverage. You must compete, have a good stance, be able to keep your feet under control, use your hands, and finish. To play man to man, you must make the play. That is the attitude of the defense. Your stance has to be balanced with your weight on the ball of your toes. It must be comfortable. Your feet have to be under control and balanced open with the wide receiver. You have to use your hands to neutralize the speed of the wide receiver. The finish is the most important part of all. You have to compete for the ball, intercept it, knock it down, or strip it out.

We use two different types of man coverage. We play bump man and press coverage. Our first concern is with the feet of the defender. We teach foot fundamentals first. The main feet fundamentals of the bump technique are good lateral step, mirror, open step, and maintaining the top shoulder. In the press technique, we use inch, mirror, open step, and maintaining the top shoulder. We teach these techniques and make the defensive back put his hands behind his back. We want them to move the feet. The coaching point for all foot fundamental drills is to never cross over with your foot placement. If you do, it allows the receiver to cross your hips.

In teaching the hand fundamentals in man coverage, we use drills that require the defensive back to kneel. The first drill is called *punch and replace*. While the defender is on his knees, it teaches the defender to use his hands. This drill helps neutralize the upper body of the receiver. The receiver and defender kneel facing each other at arms-distance apart. We focus on punching the aiming point. The aiming point is the shoulder/arm pit region. The defender punches and retreats his hands as quickly as possible. The receiver tries to block the punch using receiver techniques like the swim, rip, and other moves. We want to make sure the defender does not lose control of his upper body and lunge forward. We stress punching with the arms, not the entire body. We do ten to fifteen reps of this drill.

We do the same drill with the receiver holding a bag. This is done on the knees also. The receiver will move the bag as if he were releasing off the line. The defender will assume the same position as the punch and replace drill. On the receiver's movement, the defensive back gives a two-hand jam to the bag. We want the defenders thumbs up when he jams. If it is an inside release, we emphasize a two-handed jam, an open step with his off-hand, and a lean-back move. On an outside release, the defensive back executes a one-hand jam and open step. Depending on his leverage, he double punches or single punches away from leverage. We don't want him to lunge. Make sure you over emphasize the open step.

After we work the feet and hands separately, we put both fundamentals together and work with hands and feet. We get in a good square stance. In bump coverage, we are five yards off the receiver. Our key is the quarterback. We teach the defender to react accordingly to the different routes that he sees out of the quarterback's drop. We are keying him for the first three steps. If it is a three step pass, the defensive back throttles down and locks his eyes on the receiver he is covering. If the receivers hips are offset, he pins the up-field hip/ top shoulder and plays the ball. If the receiver pushes up field, the defensive back open steps to meet the receiver at five o'clock and accelerates with his eyes on the hip of the receiver.

FEET AND HANDS DRILL

If the quarterback's drop exceeds three steps, the defensive back accelerates his backpedal and reads the receiver's hips. He maintains leverage as he drops. His eyes must lock on to the receiver after reading the three- or five-step drop. We do not want to lose ground or gain ground during this time. That is when we use the techniques of stemming and weaving in reaction to the receiver's moves. We work over the receiver in film study to try and pick up any clue to the way he makes his moves. If he has any type of tendency to the way he runs his patterns, we can pick that up. That gives us an advantage in the drive on the ball.

We run drills to produce turnovers. In these drills we teach how to properly recover a fumble. When the ball is on the ground, coil your body around the ball to secure the fumble. If the ball is bouncing around and takes a high hop, scoop the ball and score. Only attempt to scoop and score when there is a high hop or no one else is around.

We have a drill to teach the club/punch on the ball. We want to develop the ability to strip the ball carrier from the ball. We align five yards apart, with the ball carrier two yards ahead. We squeeze the gap, secure the tackle with the far arm, and attempt an aggressive club by coming downward with the near arm on the ball. We use the punch when we see a gap between the ball carrier's rib cage and the ball. We punch through the inside of the elbow.

CLUB/PUNCH

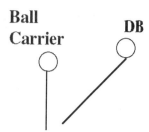

We teach interceptions in a four-phase drill. The first part is catching the ball like a wide receiver catching a fade. The second phase is to have control of a wide receiver with good downfield positioning. We want to ride the receiver away from his aiming point by making him widen out. The third phase is when the defensive back has no control on the receiver running the fade. The defensive back chases the receiver from behind and attacks through the near shoulder to the up field arm and strips the ball. The fourth phase is having no control on the receiver, but catching up and applying the techniques in phase two. We use all phases of this technique in a drill.

We try to read the releases of the receivers. In general, you can get a clue to the receiver's route based on his release at the line of scrimmage. Usually the tighter a receiver releases, the shorter the route. If he is going deep, he wants to clear quickly and avoids contact. That means he tries to get wider.

WR RELEASE VS BUMP

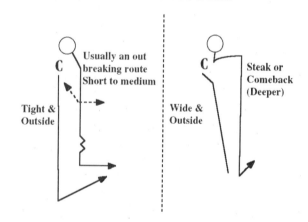

If the release is tight and outside, it is usually an outbreaking route, either short or medium in depth. A wide and outside release is generally a streak or deep comeback route. If the release is tight and inside, the pattern is an inside-breaking route either short or medium in depth. If the release is inside and wide, that is the toughest read. We know the pattern is going to be a deeper route. But it could be a corner, dig, or post from this stem.

WR RELEASE VS BUMP

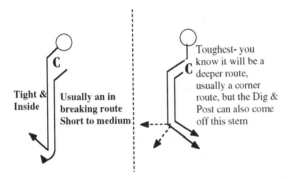

Tight & Inside

Usually an in breaking route Short to medium

Toughest- you know it will be a deeper route, usually a corner route, but the Dig & Post can also come off this stem

When we align our coverage with our defensive scheme, we make calls in the secondary to match the secondary strength to the receivers strength. The tight end may go to the right, but if there are two receivers in a left formation, our secondary strength will be left toward the passing strength.

We play quarter coverage as our zone coverage. The corners have the number one receiver to their side. They will carry him deep if he goes vertical. He knows he has help from the safety to his side on a post cut by his receiver. But he must help the safety on a corner route run by the number one receiver. The safety has the number two receiver to his side. If the number two receiver comes vertical, the safety has to get over top of the number two receiver going deep. If the number two receiver does not threaten deep, the safety picks up the number one receiver on any deep move. The corner is reading the number one receiver to the number two receiver. If the number one receiver runs a curl route, and the number two receiver runs a corner route, the corner has to help the safety with the deep-corner route of the number two receiver. If the ball is thrown short, he reacts back up to make the tackle. Everyone is running this coverage these days. It helps to defend those teams that are trying to get four vertical routes run on a one- or two-safety defense.

This defense gives the secondary an opportunity to make plays. This year we played ten teams that threw the ball twenty or more times. Eight of those teams threw it thirty or more times. We had one team throw the ball seventy-two times. We were very fortunate to get a lot of reps in the passing game. We are also fortunate to have a great defensive line. They kept pressure on the quarterback all year long. We had twenty-seven interceptions this year, but we dropped some balls that could have been interceptions. When you have success, you generally have good kids who are motivated. Our kids were hungry.

I would like to thank you for coming out. I hope I gave you something you can take back to your program. If I can be of any help to you, feel free to come visit.

THE USC PASSING GAME

University of Southern California

I am a little overwhelmed here. Everyone goes through life and has heroes. Perhaps my biggest hero is sitting right here in the front row. Let me acknowledge Coach Charlie Ane. When I went to Punahou High School in the 9th grade, it was rough. This coach was relentless. He was on my rear end everyday. I may have been the worst football player, ever. I had never put on pads before. I will never forget Coach Ane. To go to USC and hear people talk about him gives me goose pimples. I will always acknowledge him.

I have seen a lot of people in the audience that I have played against and coached against. I will acknowledge Coach Don Botelho who taught me a lot about the game. It is an honor for me to be here. It really is an honor to come home to speak. I started coaching down the street here at Waialua High School. We did not win many games, but it was an enjoyable experience.

I can remember sitting in clinics like you are doing today. I was always trying to learn something. I would tell myself if I could just learn one thing or get one thought that would help our team get better, it would be worth my time. If one idea would trigger a thought in my mind, it would help me become a better coach it would be worthwhile. I hope I can do the same for you today. I will not try to change your mind about the way we do things, but I will tell you what we do.

I told Coach Don Botelho to come up here and speak because he knows the passing game a lot better than I do. He has forgotten more football than I will every remember. So much for the introduction.

I want to talk about offensive football. As far as teaching the quarterback, I have some very simple rules. I copied this from someone a long time ago. The quarterback must always give a command that is understood, and must never give a command that will be misunderstood. This is just good common sense,

right. You can fool a lot of people, but you had better not fool the quarterback. He needs to know what is going on all of the time. That is the number one rule that I ask of our young players. "Never give a command that will be misunderstood, and always give a command that will be understood."

The second rule for the quarterback is this. You always ask him what he saw on a play. "What did you see?" It is not "I thought!" It is not what he thought; it is what did he see. What he saw may be accurate or inaccurate, it does not matter. We can adjust to that. If he saw one thing, he should have done this. If he saw something else, he should have done this. We want to know what the quarterback saw on the play.

The third rule for the quarterback is that he is never wrong. The quarterback is never wrong. I learned this from Doug Scovill. I was very lucky in my career to work with some excellent quarterback coaches. The quarterback would screw up, and he would never get on them. This used to bother me. He would put his arm around the quarterback and talk to him in a low tone of voice. On the other hand, I was coaching receivers for him. We would throw a pass downfield that was near impossible to catch. He would yell at the receiver, "catch the damn ball." It finally hit me what he was doing. He was showing the football team the quarterback was the key to the team. He was treated differently, and he was handled differently. He did not get extra shoes or anything like that, but he was special.

You think about this. Until the quarterback says "GO," nothing will happen. There can be 100,000 people in the stands but nothing will happen until this player decides the play will begin. We always make him feel like a million dollars, because he is the man. If he makes mistakes, we talk about them in the film room. But as far as the rest of the team is concerned, he is never, ever, wrong.

The fourth rule is this. Always throw the football to the receiver. Throw the ball straight ahead. Think about how easy that is. If the receiver is over there, throw the ball to him. If he is over there, throw him the ball. Basically, what we are saying is for the quarterback to move his feet. Get the body in position so you are throwing the ball to the receiver. Always throw the ball straight ahead. Step and throw the ball to the receiver.

With that idea in mind, we work with our feet, our hips, and our eyes. Notice, I did not say one word about the arm. When you get most quarterbacks, they have been throwing the ball for several years, and you are not going to change them. You are not going to change their delivery. But what you can work on are the feet, hips, and eyes. That is what we try to emphasize with our quarterbacks.

Bill Walsh wrote an article about developing the quarterback. He said the work is done in the off-season in the gym. That is when you work on the feet, hips, and eyes. However, when the quarterback gets on the football field and takes the snap, you do not want him to be thinking about his feet, hips, and eyes. You want him to be thinking about this. "I take the snap. If the receiver goes over here, I am going to throw the ball to him." That is the difference in a teaching and coaching situation. You do not want him thinking about all of the mechanics when he gets to the field. He wants to be thinking, if the safety goes here, I am going to throw the ball over here. That is the way you want him to think.

That is our philosophy on coaching the quarterback. We can talk about stance and delivery and all of the other mechanical aspects, if you want. We are all different on taking the football from the center. Some coaches want the quarterback to take the ball with the feet straight; some want the feet staggered. There are a lot of right ways to do things.

As far as putting the passing game together, we have a couple of rules. First is the pass protection. We are going to protect the quarterback. That is the reason we spend hours and hours in the meeting room talking about schemes. You may beat us because your players are better than ours. But as far as the scheme goes, we are going to protect the quarterback. Before we ever start discussing pass routes, we talk about pass protection.

We make it easy for the quarterback. We tell him to look up. If he sees two safeties back in coverage, we do not worry about protection. We have seven blockers and we can handle them. We do not teach our quarterbacks to understand the fronts. He is concerned about throwing the football. He has enough to worry about. All he has to do is to look for the two safeties. If they have two safeties back, you assume they have two corners, and that means they have seven rushers. We have seven protectors.

If we are in the one-back set, the numbers change. Now, that seventh protector becomes his responsibility. Here is how we do it. We all point at the seventh man that we cannot block. That is the man on whom the quarterback must key. If that seventh man comes on the rush, the quarterback must get rid of the ball. If he drops off, the quarterback keeps the ball. We call this the movement key. He watches the coverage. He sees the seven rushers, and he reads his progression, 1, 2, and 3.

If we have our six-man protection, the line points to the one rusher we can not block. That is the man the quarterback must key. We do not care if everyone knows that the quarterback is keying that seventh man. Now, the read becomes the blitz. He checks the blitz and goes through his progression, 1, 2, and 3. That is how simple we try to keep it.

The second rule as far as putting the passing game together is this. We are going to try to control the football with the forward pass. This is a contradiction.

Statistics are whatever you want to make of them, or however you want to use them. But one statistic is the time of possession. We feel we need to win the possession battle. The other statistic we want to win is the turnover battle. We do not want to turn the ball over. Those two points are very important to us. If you can accomplish those two things you will control the football. But, we are going to try to control the football with the forward pass. What does this mean in our terms? Check downs. The quarterback looks for the number one receiver, then the number two receiver, and if they are not open, he looks for the three-yard pass. Bam! If the first two receivers are not open, he takes the three- or four-yard pass. He throws it to the receiver for a three-yard gain, and then we hope he can run for four more yards.

When I was coaching with Doug Scovill, I would see the quarterback look at the post receiver and then throw the ball to the back coming out of the backfield. Doug would go over to the quarterback and tell him that was a nice job. I was thinking what the hell is going on. It looked to me as if the wide receiver on the post route was open for a touchdown, and the quarterback drops the ball off to the swing man. Finally, I realized what he was doing. That is the hardest thing the quarterback has to do. He has to be able to throw the check down.

The third aspect related to the passing game is this. We are going to KISS it. We all know what that means. KEEP IT SIMPLE, STUPID. I think the biggest mistake coaches make is that we are too smart. You come to a clinic like this, and we get an idea from Coach Herb Meyer. Then you try to incorporate it into what you are doing. You need to develop a philosophy. When you develop that philosophy, you need to stay with it. There are lots of ways to move the football. You need to develop your own philosophy on moving the football, and you need to keep it simple. I can not overstate that point.

Because of the nature of our business, we get to sit in an office and spend time drawing up plays on the chalk board. A lot of plays may look good in a playbook, but is it going to help our team. With that in mind at USC on the drop-back passing game, we will have nine passes. We call it our 60 Series. We have a pass for each of the 60 numbers. We may call the play 65. This means the linemen know it is basic 60 cup protection. The 5 is the pass pattern. Everyone has to remember the pass routes. We have nine basic pass patterns. We teach four one day and five the next day. That is all we have. We feel very strongly about this. We are going to keep it as simple as we can, so our kids will go out on the field confident that we are going to make the play, and we are going to know what we are doing.

The mistake coaches make is to make it too complicated. It is a football game. It is not a physics class. If we were that smart, we would not be sitting here not making a lot of money. That is our basic philosophy.

In the scope of setting up the passing game, we feel there are a couple of things we need to consider. We need to include the 3-step drop, the 5-step drop, and play-action passing game. We want to be able to establish the run to some extent. Also, we need the ability to sprint out at times. The reason you need the ability to sprint out is this. If you can't handle them on the inside, you can take the ball outside. If we get beat on the outside, we can step up in the pocket. If they come up the middle, then we have to move the quarterback outside.

The last thing in setting up our passing game is that we try to control the blitz. There are so many things happening with the fire zones, and zone blitzes, and there is so much suffocation with the coverages, and disguises, that we feel the best way to control the blitz is with the screen pass. We run a lot of screens. We run a lot of receiver screens and a lot of pop out screens where we just throw the ball outside to the receiver. When those screens get blown up or knocked down, I do not think you should be that upset about it. It is no big deal. It tells the defensive line they cannot be in a hurry to get upfield because we may throw the screen pass. It is all done with our blitz control package.

Then we look at our running game. It is very simple. We run a trap-draw. All we are trying to do is to trap the outside rush man. That is the man that gets his butt up the field. I was fortunate to coach against Florida State for a couple of games. They have defensive ends that are 6'4" and 250 pounds. All they do is to get their butts up in the air and look for the snap of the ball. When that ball is snapped, they come across the line very hard. They do not know where the quarterback is. They are great upfield rushers.

We do not run the 7-step drop game because we cannot protect the passer. We run the football. We throw the ball on time, we run screens and draws, and we are going to run some gimmicks just to slow the game down a little. That is our game plan every week. When you formulate your offense and decide you are going to throw the ball, these are the things you should consider. Let me show you how we go about doing that.

When we decided to implement the passing attack, which is not new to what is going on today, there were a couple of things we had to do. In designing the passing attack, the concepts remain the same. We have curls, flats, man routes, option routes, crossing routes versus man coverage, and the four vertical routes. The last thing we have is what we call building triangles. That is what the passing game amounts to. I do not think those concepts will ever change. This is true if you run the run and shoot, or a drop-back attack.

I am going to talk about building triangles. I could go through the entire passing attack for USC because it is that simple. But I will talk about building triangles in our passing game. This is what we do against the teams that play zone coverage against us. We call these passes oblique passes. Everyone knows the horizontal- and vertical-stretch passing game. We say we use the oblique stretch passing game.

We try to create oblique stretches to force the defense to cover the entire football field. We call it movement keys and receiver progression. Movement keys simply means the coverage. You know the defense can be confusing when they put seven or eight men in the box. I can't tell what the defense is when that happens. It is hard to figure out what the coverages are when that happens. They move around so fast you can't tell what they are doing. When we get to that point, we are going to attack with triangles.

We have a strongside vertical, and we have a middle vertical, and a weakside vertical. We have a couple of horizontal stretches, and we have a couple of man routes. We have a few one-man routes. We have a route to attack cover two, and we have the four verticals game. That is our passing game. I have told you everything we do, and I did it in two minutes. We have one strongside vertical route, one middle vertical, and one weakside vertical. We have two horizontal stretch routes, a man route, four verticals, and a cover two beater. That is all we do. We attack everyone we play with these plays. Our kids know these plays the second day of practice.

BUILDING TRIANGLES

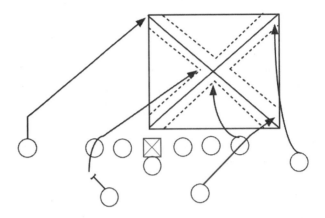

I am assuming everyone knows how to break down the passing zones. We figure there are eight defensive zones on the football field. If the defense rushes three men, they can defend with eight men. It is simple, if you rush three you can cover eight zones. If the defense covers all eight zones, we are going to run the football. If the defense rushes four men and covers seven zones, it is our responsibility to find out the zone that is not covered, and that is the zone we are going to attack. If you only cover seven zones, it is our job to find out the open zone. We are going to throw the ball to that area.

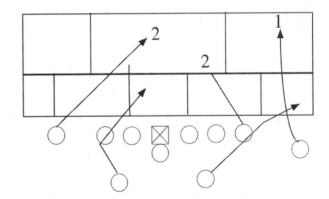

With a strongside vertical, we send the Z back on the go, or whatever you want to call it. We tell the split end to go to the middle deep area. The tight end goes to the area where the deep and underneath areas meet. The back checks the rush and runs an arrow. The backside back runs a little check down. That is how we try to design our passing game. That is a strongside vertical route for us. If the defense is playing a 3-deep with four men underneath, we feel we have a chance. That is our 65 pass.

The deep man is number one. We always look for that long ball first. We have learned the quarterback can throw the deep pass if he can throw it on five steps. If he hits five, he can throw the deep pass. If he hits on that fifth step and has to hitch to make the throw, we tell him not to throw it. Why? Those cornerbacks are good enough today if you have them beat, and the quarterback hesitates in throwing the ball, they are so fast they can recover and make the play. You can not hesitate. If the quarterback can throw the ball on his fifth step, that is fine. But anything after that, we do not want him to throw the long ball.

The two man is the tight end down in the area between the deep and the underneath zone. We want him to sit down and look for the quarterback. We call this our sail route. We find the dead spot in the zone, and we sit there. The end has an easy release. He comes out and sits inside. Most teams run this play with an out route for the tight end. They want to get a 1, 2, 3 vertical look. We do not want to do that. We want a 1 and a 2 and a 3 look, so it looks like our triangle we talked about. It makes it tougher to cover.

If the quarterback has an open window on the outside, he will throw the ball. If he has an open window inside with the tight end, he will throw it. The tight end wants to get into position where he can shield the defender from getting the ball if it comes to him. It is just like playing basketball. If the ball is over his head, he can still make the adjustment and make the catch.

In our playbook, the split end is also number two. We draw it up with both receivers being number two. If the quarterback drops five steps and does not see the wide receiver open on the called side, he looks to the inside to the tight end. Then, he sees a flash of light coming over to cover the tight end. It is the free safety. The quarterback now looks up to the split end who is running the deep route down the middle. When the free safety comes over to cover the tight end, it leaves the split end open. Now, the quarterback can throw the deep ball down the middle.

If we can not get the ball to the first three receivers, we look to the backs. It is a four- or five-yard throw. We tell the right halfback to run a five- to six-yard arrow route. Once we get the ball out side to him, he can run the ball up field. Now, if the defense takes

the arrow route away from us, we still have a chance to go to the backside on the dump to the back. We look at the three deeper routes first, and then go from there. That is a strongside vertical pattern.

We can add a tag to the pattern to make it a little more sophisticated. If the defense has taken the deep patterns away, we come back with 65 F-Angle. As the onside halfback sees the stud linebacker leave to cover the tight end on the curl, he cuts back inside on the angle route. Now, we have an open spot in the defense. This all comes from this one basic route.

65 F- Angle

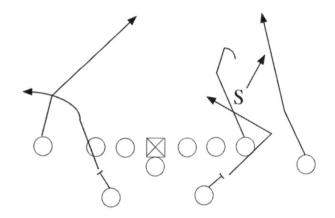

If we face some type of man coverage, and our tight end sees the strong safety come up to stop the inside route, we want the tight end to make a move at the top of the route and push outside. It is man coverage, and he can get to the outside and get open. Now, it is 1, 2, 3 progression. This is how we design our pass offense. It is very, very simple.

65 VS. MAN

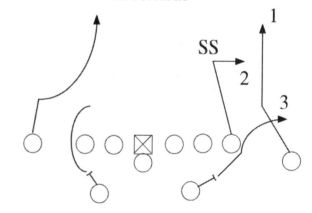

The other way is the same idea. We are going to run the play to the weakside. The weakside vertical is the same idea. We send the split end on the up or go route.

We take the tight end 5- to 7-yards deep and then across the middle at 15- to 17-yards deep. We bring the wide receiver down the middle on the split. The onside halfback runs the flat. The other back runs the check down. We have the same play as before. We have the triangles as we had before. This is the weakside vertical.

WEAKSIDE VERTICAL

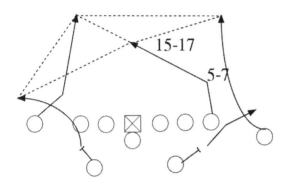

We can do different things with the backside halfback. We can bring him down inside. This is what it looks like with the split end, tight end and onside halfback in the triangle.

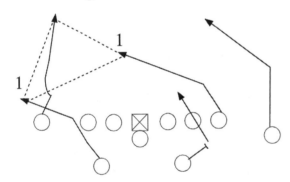

Protection-wise, we are going to block big on big. We block backs on the linebackers. If the defense is better than we are, we will have the backs check the rush. If the defender gets by the line, we will have the back block him if the linebackers are not coming. That is the weakside vertical.

Now, we tag this route as well. It probably is our favorite play. We call it 69 weak. We tag it with a get-a-way route for the halfback. It is an option route. It is a free release for the halfback. He is not going to block the Will linebacker. It is our 69 H option play.

As I said, we block big on big. Our backs block linebackers. The halfback has the Will linebacker, and the fullback has the Stud linebacker. The front five have the four down linemen and the Mike linebacker.

If we split the H-back out, or if we are not going to block the Will linebacker, and we still want to throw the drop-back pass, we call the play 69 Will. We cannot block Will. Will could be in a different area, and we can not block him. If the Will comes on the blitz, the halfback is hot. As Will comes across the line of scrimmage, the H-back must turn and look for the ball. We dump the ball to the H-back.

If we want to free the fullback on the other side we call it 69 Sam. The Sam tells us we cannot block the Sam linebacker. Everyone knows who is assigned to block Sam. If Sam comes on the blitz, we throw the ball to the fullback on the hot.

We call the play 69 H option – Will. We played the University of Michigan for the National Championship several years ago. We ran this play 17 times in that game. For some reason, they were trying to defend the H-back with the Mike linebacker. We try to free release the H-back. If Will comes, we throw it hot.

If the defense is playing some type of zone defense, the H-back will come up to the line and sit in the hole. It is just like you do on the playground. He sits at the hole on the line, and we throw the ball to him. As the quarterback comes back on the H-option, he eyes the back. When he gets open, the quarterback throws the ball to him.

69 H – OPTION – WILL

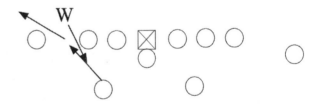

If the defense is in man coverage, the rule is this. If the Will linebacker has the H-back reinforces the defender's position. If the defender is outside, we push him outside and then cut back to the inside. If Will is on the inside on some type of knockdown coverage, we bring the H-back down inside toward the Will, and then we break outside. Now, I have the chalk, and I should win this battle. We tell our receivers the defender cannot be right. If he is on the outside, we run inside. If he is on the inside, we run outside. If he splits the difference with another defender, then we want to run in the middle of the two defenders.

If the defense takes the Mike linebacker and squeezes the play and does not allow you to throw the ball to the H-back, we look for the tight end. If Mike goes over to help Will, it leaves a lane open for the tight end. That is where we would throw the ball.

When we ran our normal 69, the look is long, and then short. It is the triangle we talked about. When we tag on H option, the look is short to long. It is down, and then back up to the top.

We have covered the strongside vertical and the weakside vertical. Now, we add the middle vertical. It is the same idea. Now, we want to stretch it down the middle of the field. We send the tight end 10 yards deep and drag him straight across. The Z-back runs a post cross route at 18 yards. We run the X-end on a split route. We take the fullback and check him down to the flat. The H-back checks down at three yards inside. Now, we are stretching the defense down the middle.

MIDDLE VERTICAL

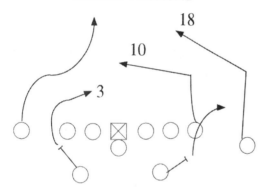

If the safety stays high, we come off the X-end. If we move the coverage underneath, we have a shot at the Z-back. If we do not get movement underneath, we look for the tight end at 10 yards deep across the middle. If that is covered, we look for the H-back on the check down inside. We throw the ball at three yards, and hope he gets four more yards out of the play.

You had better cover the deep routes of the two outside receivers. The defense must cover everyone for us to get to the check down. If they cover everyone, we get the ball underneath and get up the field, and see what we can do.

With this in mind, all of this gives us a chance to run what we like to run. When I coached against Coach Ane and the University of Hawaii, he always

told me the post-corner route was something they were always nervous about. So, we run the post-corner route with the wide receiver. Everything else stays the same. We teach the wide receiver one route. We call this our 63 Route.

If we want to run 63 and put the Z-back on the post-corner route, we call it 63 Z corner. If we want to put X on the route, we call it 63 X corner. We can put the Y-end on the corner. The play stays 63. It looks like we are running about six different patterns. It is the same route run over and over.

63 POST CORNER

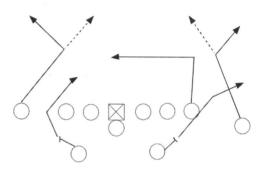

This system allows us to run a lot of different looks with the same pattern. It is one basic pattern. That is basically the way we put our offense together. We have one strongside, middle, and weakside vertical stretch play. We have a couple of horizontal stretch plays to go along with this. This is as basic as we can get with our passing game.

One of our favorite routes is the horizontal stretch route. I have showed you the three vertical routes. Now, I am talking about the horizontal stretch. We run 14-yard curl routes with the wide receivers. The fullback runs a 4- to 6-yard arrow route. The tight end runs 8- to 10-yards deep in the middle. We start with movement keys. Let me show you what we do against the basic cover 3 which is a basic 4-3 defense. On the first step, the quarterback takes, he is reading the Mike linebacker. Mike will give the quarterback direction. If Mike goes to the weakside, it means the Will linebacker has taken the flat away. If the Mike has taken the curl away, the read now becomes inside out to the strongside. We have three underneath receivers, and the defense has two defenders on that side. If the strong safety hangs on the curl and runs to the flat, we throw the ball to the curl inside. If the Sam linebacker takes away the curl by the tight end, and the strong safety takes the curl by the Z-back, we throw to the flat. If Sam goes to the middle, and the strong safety goes to the flat, we throw to the curl with the Z-back.

When we call 6 Y bench, we have recognized that something is going on. The defense is giving us something that allows us to stay strong. Now, we are not reading Mike. We are staying on the strongside. Now, we go with the Y-end toward the bench. We read the routes, 1, 2, 3.

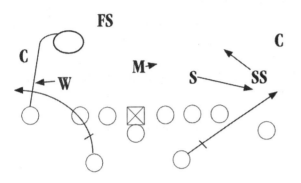

66 Y BENCH

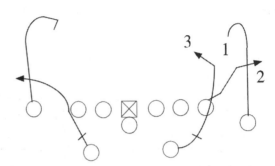

You have four defenders underneath. We have five receivers underneath. We have to find the open receiver. We do not run this play against cover 2 where the defense has two deep and five underneath men.

If the Mike goes strong or goes straight back, we respond accordingly. If Mike goes straight back, he takes away the curl to the tight end. If they take away the strongside, they only have Will underneath on the short side. If Will hangs to cover the curl, we throw to the flat. If Will goes to the flat, we throw to the curl. This is how we attack the defense. Again, the defense has four underneath and we have five horizontal. The area the defense vacates we are going to hit.

If the defense is in cover 2, and we do not check out of it, we do not have a very good play. We tell the receivers if they see the pressure on the five-under two-deep coverage to attack the defense on a high-low route. If we can get the ball to the open man, we will. If we can't, we go back and call another play. We have to be smart. If the defense covers with five underneath, it means they only have two deep men to cover. That is why we go high-low. That is the way we attack cover 2.

The next play is our 66 play. We can call 66 Y bench. Some people call this play Hank. It is 66 to us. It is the same route over and over. All we are doing is tagging one man, and everyone else is adjusting to that tag. We hope it looks to you like we are running a lot of different plays.

This gives us a chance to take advantage of what the defense is giving us. This is a good route for us against the blitz. We call it 66 Y bench – Fred. It is a delay route for us with the fullback.

We have one crossing pattern against man coverage. We tell our quarterback this. When we put a game plan together, we list all of the different situations. On the bottom of the game plan, we put the audible checks in. Against man coverage, we only allow two calls. Against cover 3, it is two calls. Against cover 2, it is two calls. The quarterback knows he only has two calls against any defense. If he comes to the line and sees the defense is in something that will give us a problem with the play called in the huddle, he has two plays he can check off to. We do not have a complicated list.

This is the route we use against man coverage. It is our crossing route. We tell the tight end that he is responsible for the <u>depth</u> of the route. We tell the X-receiver that he is responsible for the <u>mesh</u> of the route. The X-receiver comes underneath the Y-end. If Y goes six yards deep, then X has to go five yards deep. They are going full speed. It is not a pick route. It is simple a crossing route. The quarterback watches the mesh occur with the crossing routes. The quarterback turns his shoulders to the receiver that comes open and throws the ball to him.

CROSSING ROUTE

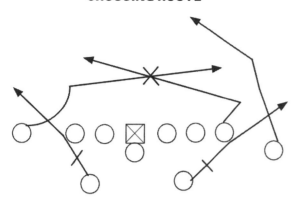

If we make a mistake, and the defense is not running man coverage, and they are playing zone, and we are running crossing patterns, this is what we tell the quarterback to do. He looks at the back on the two-receiver side, which is the tight end side, and he turns his shoulders and throws the ball to the back in the flat. We want to throw the ball three yards and get three more on the run. Now, we have a 2nd-and-4 situation. We have to be able to look for the crossing receivers, and if they are covered, we go to the backs.

I heard Y. A. Tittle say this about playing quarterback in the NFL. "If you are going to be an NFL quarterback, you have to know where the number 3 receiver is going to be." I think it is our job as coaches to make sure our quarterback understands where number 3 is going to be. It is not that hard if you work at it.

Teams used to man blitz against us in the red zone. When teams played the man blitz, we had a variety of things we could do. We run our 62 Z pac. We call this route a pac Route. It stands for post or corner route. The Z-back runs the corner or post.

62 Z PAC

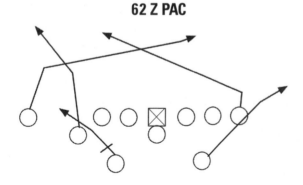

You could line up in a split look with two backs split wide with the X-end. You could line up in a stack look with two backs stacked behind the split end. You can do anything that is different. But basically, it is the same route over and over. We have X and Y cross; Z runs a post or corner, and the backs run out.

I do not mean to minimize this, but it is a basketball game. We tell our receivers they have to get five yards deep. We tell them there is a hole on their side, and they need to find the hole. If they understand the concepts of the routes we have taught them, they should know where to run. We tell them we are not teaching robots. We are teaching young men, period. We teach them to play football, and that is all.

You can be as complicated as you want with the passing game, but if your players do not understand what you are doing, it will not matter. We feel our players can understand what we are doing, and they are comfortable with what we are doing.

As we get older, we do not remember who our chemistry teacher was. We do remember who our coaches were. But, I can remember Coach Ane like it was yesterday. I was in the 9th grade on the third-string JV team. The season was over, and he was taking some of the JV players up to the Varsity. He called the names out, and he called my name out. I will never forget that.

The point I am trying to make is this, and I want you to remember this. We are in the best profession in the world. We can go to work in shorts and tennis shoes. Don't forget to teach kids techniques. Teach kids values and character. If we can do that, we will all be successful. I say this from the bottom of my heart. I appreciate you listening to my lecture. Thank you.

QUARTERBACK TECHNIQUES AND DRILLS

New Orleans Saints

It is good to be here. Most of my life I lived just outside of Pittsburgh. I lived in Morgantown, West Virginia, and Indiana, Pennsylvania. The New Orleans Saints have a very strong Pittsburgh connection. A lot of our staff has connections to this area. Each day, we are on the Internet looking for the high-school scores for this area.

I am going to talk about training the quarterback and drills for the quarterback. Then, I have a few pass plays I want show you.

The material I am going to discuss is not material I have made up. As you know, my coaching background goes down through the generations. I have my father to thank for his input. He was one of my mentors. Also, our offensive coordinator, Mike McCarthy, who has been with us for ten years, has helped me. The ideas I will present are a mixture of a lot of different people. This is the New Orleans Saints' quarterback material. In March, we have a quarterback school in New Orleans. It is the material we presented to them in the classroom. This will not be as detail, but it is what we use.

In anything you do, it must be well planned. This is especially true in working with the quarterback. The quarterback is the key to success. You must have goals and objectives. We sit down with our quarterbacks in March and talk about our goals and objectives. We are constantly talking about goals and objectives. We talk about goals for the spring, summer and the season.

Next, we talk about building blocks. Everyone has heard the statement "Rome was not built in one day." Every coaching session you have must build on the last session held. There must be a sequence to the meetings. The head coach, the quarterback coach, and the offensive coordinator must work together. It may be that all three of those jobs may be one person, two people, or three people. The people involved in these three jobs must plan and work together. Everything that involves the quarterback must be planned. You must work together with all three people involved. It is imperative that you speak the same language. When a play is called, it is important that all three people understand what is going to take place. All of this starts in the classroom.

We cover three areas of concentration in working with the quarterback. This is the nuts and bolts of training a quarterback. The first area involves from the neck up. This is knowledge. Knowledge is power. It is not what we know, it is what the quarterback knows. That is the most important thing. This comes mainly from classroom sessions. We go three days a week in the quarterback school. It is a time to relearn the entire system and all of the drills.

The second area of concentration involves from the waist up. This relates to the mechanics of playing quarterback. The third area of concentration addresses from the waist down (i.e., the footwork). Those are the three areas of concentration for training the quarterback.

We start with the first area which is from the neck up. This is the same format we use at New Orleans. It is the same format I used when I coached at Kansas City and at IUP. Coaching is coaching. The game of football is still the same. It is true in high school, college, and in the pros. It is teaching.

The big thing in the classroom is communication and information. The information and communication must be spoken in the same language. Let me give you an example. I am the quarterback coach of the New Orleans Saints. Mike McCarthy is the offensive coordinator. Mike calls the plays. It is his offense. The quarterback coach and the quarterback are an extension of the offensive coordinator. When you go back to the first idea we discussed, it is the head coach, offensive coordinator, and quarterback coach who must work together. If you do this, it all makes sense. The group must communicate together, and they must speak the same language. Again, it all starts in the classroom.

The first information we teach is the offensive system. When we start out, we assume the quarterbacks do not know anything. We teach the system, the training drills, and the defenses to the quarterbacks. We teach the whole phase of football. That is the great thing about being a quarterback coach.

There are several items we can utilize in teaching the quarterback. The first is the playbook. We utilize videos. We constantly look at cut-ups on film from the season before. We have training tapes that we view. We use the overhead projector to illustrate different points. One area we stress is that it is not what we know, but what the quarterback knows. In our situation during the season, after we have taught the quarterback the game plan, we have him stand up in front of the group and present the game plan to the team. The coaches knew the game plan. We ask our quarterback to go over the plan. Get the quarterback on the chalk board, and you sit back and observe. You can make the corrections when necessary.

Make sure that the quarterback understands the goals and objectives of each session. It has to be well planned, and there has to be a sequence to the sessions. Every time that the quarterback steps on the field or gets up in front of a group in a meeting, make sure he understands what the goals and objectives are. That is the great thing about the classroom. That is the first phase in training the quarterback. It occurs in the classroom.

The second phase is from the waist up. This relates to the quarterback's mechanics. I do not believe there is only one way to teach football. You have to believe in the best way for you to coach. This is the way we do it at New Orleans. We start this phase by talking about the quarterback's shoulders and eyes. We want his shoulders perpendicular and slightly open. If I am a right-handed quarterback, I do not want to close my left shoulder. We talk about a get-away drill. It is getting away from the center, or the drop from the line of scrimmage. We want his shoulders perpendicular and slightly open.

His eyes must be focused on the read area. However, in the first step, his eyes must be focused downfield. Then, his eyes must come around to the read area. Now, we say on the first step away from the center, his eyes are downfield. Some coaches tell the quarterback to keep his stripes on his helmet pointing downfield. But, it is imperative for the eyes of the quarterback to be on the hot linebacker. If the hot linebacker is on a blitz, the quarterback must be ready to throw the ball. If the linebacker does not come, then the eyes of the quarterback must go to the read area.

Next, we talk about ball carriage. We want the quarterback to keep the ball high on his retreat. We coach that the tip of the ball should be held at the top of the numbers on his jersey. We want him to keep the ball in the framework of his body. We say keep the ball in from nipple to nipple. We want the quarterback to be as functional as possible. We want him to keep his elbows close to his body, and we want him to keep his arms relaxed. You can look at these areas, and you can film them and study them.

The draw of the ball is the immediate action of the ball being taken away from the carriage. When we breakdown the quarterbacks from the combines, these are the things we go to. We can correct problems with the shoulders, the eyes, and ball carriage. The draw of the ball is difficult for us to correct. Different players have different draws. What we look for is the player with the better draw. The right-handed quarterback can use his left hand to help in throwing the ball as the ball is released. They use their left hand to push the ball up to their right hand. It makes it a lot easier to throw the ball.

We do not try to change a quarterback's throwing motion. We may do some things with the mechanics, but we do not change the throwing motion.

The pull is the left-arm action after the draw. We are drawing the ball up with the left hand. The pull is the left arm coming through the left side. When we evaluate the quarterbacks, we do not coach the pull. But, we do look to see what the pull is like.

We want the elbow out in front. We want the quarterback to point his elbow to the target. Once again, this is an evaluation thing. We want to see his elbow out in front and pointing at the target.

The last point is the arm release. Where does the follow-through end up? Where would we like it? We would like it down toward the left hip. We do not want it across the chest. We want the wrist snap to be down, not across.

We do not talk about all of these points with our quarterbacks. These points are evaluative factors in the players we are going to draft or take a look at as prospects. We do talk about the shoulders, the eyes, and the drop. The other things are things we look at in selecting a quarterback.

The third phase is from the waist down. This phase involves the quarterback's footwork. I think proper footwork is imperative. When I first started coaching, I used to spend a lot of time on footwork. I would bring in quarterbacks before practice and spend the whole session on nothing but footwork. If the head coach gives you five minutes of individual time to work, you must understand that you need to work on footwork with the quarterback. In pro ball, it is imperative for the quarterbacks to get on the field early and spend a lot of time on footwork. There are a lot of different phases to footwork. There is the 5-step drop, 7-step drop, and counter steps, play-action passes, movements, sprint outs, and a lot of other different steps.

The first footwork aspect to be considered is the get away. This is the most important phase of the drop. The second phase is the control. This starts the conversion of the quarterback's weight distribution and body control. The next aspect is the get back. This involves getting into position to make the throw. It is getting the body turned toward the target.

When we talk about footwork, we talk about get away, control, and get back. Simply, the quarterback needs to drive away from the center smoothly, come into balance, and be in position to throw the ball. That is what we talk about. They have to drive away from the center, come back and get balanced, and get into position to throw the ball. Those are the three basic steps of footwork.

Let me talk about the get away. As we said, the get away is the most important factor in this process. The quarterback must get away from the center in one fluid motion and get set. We could spend the next three hours discussing the method of getting away

on that first step. In New Orleans, we teach the punch step. This is the initial footwork in getting away from the center. There are three ways to do this. Again, we teach the punch step. It is a six-inch step. We want the butt down, the hands up, and the quarterback to pull out in one fluid motion. It is like cranking a lawn mower to start it. It is one fluid motion.

There are criticisms of this method. It all goes back to what you believe in working with the quarterback. The most common way to get back is the pivot. His toes are pigeon toed, with the weight on the balls of his feet. We push off with the opposite foot. If I am a right-handed quarterback, I would push off with my left foot. The third method is the staggered get away. During the pre game warm-up, I watch the other quarterbacks to see how they get away from center. A lot of teams have gone to the stagger on the get away. In this method, the quarterback comes up under the center with his left foot out from under the center. I think all three of the methods are good. It all depends on what you believe in and what you are trying to accomplish. You have to sell it to the quarterbacks. It is the most important phase of the drop.

The first step of any drop is the reach. The first step is across the midline with depth. You want to stretch it and run with the toes pointed upfield. As the quarterback comes back from the center, he wants his toes pointed upfield and his left shoulder perpendicular to slightly open to the other shoulder. His eyes are on the read area. Don't forget this is where ball carriage begins. We have talked about this in the classroom, and we have covered the ball carriage mechanics. The most important thing is that the quarterback must get away from the center smoothly, and he must get depth. He has to stretch that first step.

The second step is the crossover. He wants to maintain his depth and maintain body mechanics. This completes the first phase of get away.

The second part of the drop is the control. Now, we are into the third step. We start teaching our drops from a 5-step drop standpoint. If we can teach the 5-step drop, we can adjust to the 3-step and 7-step drops. The control starts with the conversion of the weight distribution and body control. On the third step, you either have one of two different methods to apply. You either have a control-and-gather step, or a no-hitch throw. If you are throwing the 5-step pass, there is no hitch. On the third step, you are getting ready to throw the ball. If you are going to hitch to throw the football, you have to crunch that third step. If you are going to throw the ball without a hitch, you must make a control step on the third step. If you are going to hitch to throw the football, you have to stretch on the third step so you can reach and cross step. The first three steps should be a smooth transition. In fact, the whole drop should be a smooth transition.

On the fourth step, you are going to dig it into the ground in a comfortable manor. You have to dig it into the ground to break the momentum. Digging it with a possible kick or roll, this is what I mean. If we are going to throw the out or hitch route to the right, the quarterback is going to roll toward the route on the last two steps. If he is throwing to his left, he wants to kick to open his hips toward the receiver.

The first two phases are the get away and control. The quarterback must know if he is throwing the ball with a hitch or without a hitch based on the third step. The last phase is the get back.

The get back is getting in a position to make the throw (i.e., getting the body toward the target). We have talked about the first four steps: reach, cross, control, and stretch or dig. On the fifth step, he has to plant his foot in the ground.

On a possible hitch step, this is what we do. All the hitch step amounts to is a gather step and then getting ready to throw the football. You have a re-set step, which is half a hitch step to find an outlet. The passes I will cover later are all related to the footwork done properly. We throw a 5-and-hitch, and a 5-and-a-re-set step. Just remember the hitch is a gather step and then throwing the football. The reset is half a hitch to find the outlet. It could be your third receiver.

We have just covered reach, crossover, control step, stretch, dig and crossover, plant, hitch, and reset. A relevant example of all of this that was taught to me was this. The quarterback's footwork is like a rubber band. It is big and smooth in the beginning.

Those first couple of steps must be big and smooth. You have to get away from the center big and smooth. After that you have to make the rubber band small and under control. You have to get ready to let the football go.

In our game plan, we may have 140 passes. But, we have spent time in the classroom with the quarterback. We group passes into concepts. I will show you four pass plays, but to the quarterback, it is only one pass. We may have 140 passes, but to the quarterback, it will only be 30 or 40 concepts or categories.

I am going to show you what we do in teaching the quarterback these concepts. The triangle read drill is how we teach the quarterback the progression of the passing game. It is a 5-step drop type pass. It is a triangle read drill because the receivers form a triangle. We want the quarterback to read the receivers in progression 1, 2, 3. The #1 man is the primary receiver. The #2 man is the second receiver, and the #3 man is the third receiver the quarterback reads.

In our offense, this is a pure progression route —1, 2, 3. We have three types of passes in our offense. We have pure progression. When we say Z hook, the quarterback knows the Z man is number 1, the back is number 2, and the number 3 man is either the tight end or the fullback, based on the variations. That is it for the quarterback. It is pure progression. When that play is called, we are looking for a completion. It is a triangle read. The other two reads we have are the read with an option, and then a pure PSL which is a pre-snap look. I am going to be talking about the pure progression read for the quarterback.

PROGRESSION TRIANGLE PASS DRILL

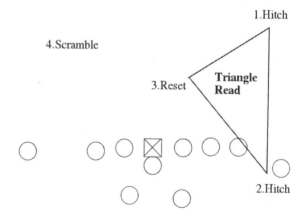

This is a great drill. I need one person to stand 12 yards deep where the number 1 man is located at the end of the route. I need another person to stand outside where the back ends up as number 2. I need a third person to stand inside for number 3, which represents the tight end or fullback. We need a fourth person on the backside to represent a receiver on the scramble.

As the coach, I stand behind the drill where I can watch the quarterback on his footwork. Before the quarterback gets away from the center, I am going to point at one of the receivers. Now, the way I start out on this drill the first day is to point to number 1. Everyone stands in the receiver's position. As the quarterback takes his drop, the receiver that I pointed to will raise his hands. That is where we want the ball to go.

If I pointed at number 1, it is a 5-step drop and a hitch and throw for the quarterback. Next, I will point to the back who is number 2. Now, here is the catch. When the quarterback throws to the number 1 receiver, it involves five steps and a hitch, and he throws the ball. When he throws to the back outside, he must take the hitch step. However, he must turn his toes to point toward the back on the wide route. When I point to the number 3 receiver, he takes his five steps and the hitch, but he has to reset his feet to throw to the number 3 receiver.

Also in the drill we teach hot routes. We use the tight end or fullback as the hot receivers. In our progression scheme, our fullback is the hot receiver on this route. The first part is to teach the progression and then to teach the hot phase of the drill. The first day in the classroom, I would only teach the progression 1, 2, 3. The second day in the classroom, I would add the hot concept.

If the number 4 defender comes off the edge, the fullback knows he is the hot receiver. If the Sam linebacker comes, the tight end is the hot receiver. If the pressure is coming from the inside, the quarterback wants to get the ball off on the third step. If the step is coming from the outside, the quarterback should get it off by his fifth step.

The next phase is the scramble. This phase of the drill does not happen a lot of the time. You have to cover the drill in the classroom and on the field as well. The quarterback goes back and takes his five steps and his hitch step. He sees that the hitch is not open, the wide hitch is not open, the reset to number 3 is not open. As such, the quarterback must now get into the scramble mode to the backside away from the triangle. We put the backside man or number 4 on a post curl route. If the ball is passed to the triangle, number 4 just runs the post route. If it becomes a scramble, the number 4 man must hook it up and make eye contact with the quarterback. He will work back and to the sideline. I will show you the scramble drill on a tape later.

After you feel confident the quarterback can work the triangle drill, 1 through 3, then the next stage is to teach the hot and the scramble. The hot depends on the type of pressure. There are only two types of pressure. For the quarterback, it is either from the inside or the outside. A team can run all the blitzes they want, but to him, it is either from the inside or the outside. Once the quarterback understands all of this, he should have a good idea of what is going on.

On most pass plays, if you can connect the dots, you get a triangle. On all of our pure progression passes, I should be able to connect the dots to form a triangle. You can move the triangle wherever you want. The footwork does not change. The hot and the scramble do not change. After you have covered all of this with the quarterback in the classroom, you need to go to the field and actually run the drill.

HOT THROW

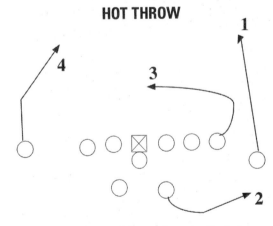

On this route, the tight end must find the eyes of the quarterback. Again, you can see the triangle

I will show you different ways to run the hook route. We call this route the Z hook – Y post. We use speed moves on the hook route. When the defense is in man to man, the receiver has to make a move away from the man. You can run this play from most formations.

Z HOOK – Y POST

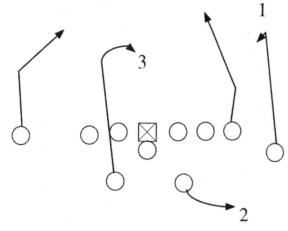

We want to run the safety out of the play against teams that play cover 2, or they are playing quarter-quarter, half cover. We then call Z hook – Y post. To us all hook routes are triangles. We send the Y-receiver on the post so we have to put someone else in the triangle. We put the fullback in the route as the third receiver.

The next route is the X hook. We still release the tight end against number 4 strong. If number the number 4 strong man is coming on the rush, our tight end has to block him. So, we lose the triangle if he comes. We are a protection-first football team. If number 4 defender does not come on the blitz, our tight end is going to run the hook. It is the same as the Z hook. The weakside running back has the free release. The fullback has the hot. It is the same play. The quarterback takes five steps and a hitch to the X-end, five steps and a hitch to the back, and five steps and a reset to the tight end. The scramble phase is to the Z-back.

X HOOK

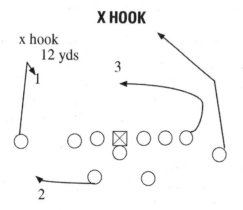

Now, we have covered three plays, but it is really only one play. It is the hook route, and it involves the triangle concept.

Now, we need a slot or twins set pass. We call X hook – Z post. Now, you can see it is the same pass as we looked at before. It is pure progression. The called man is the number 1 read, the back is number 2, and the tight end is number 3. The Z-back is running the post route.

X HOOK – Z POST

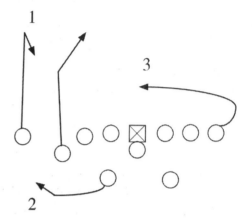

Now, we have a concept. While it is four plays, it is really just one concept. You can do this with most of the passing game.

I want to talk about some of our basic fundamental drills we use with quarterbacks. The first thing we do is to show the players the drills they were going to be using.

The first drill is jumping rope. Everything the quarterback does starts with his two feet. We stress being on the balls of the feet. We do speed jumping, left foot, right foot, and all of the rope-jumping drills. We make everything competitive, and we chart every drill.

On every drill we do, we talk about the big toe of the quarterback's foot. When they get away from the center, they have to push off on that big toe. When the hips are out front, they are on their big toe. All of these drills have to do with the footwork of the quarterback. The quarterbacks do all of the bag drills. We do the drills at 10-second intervals.

On the football drills, we have the quarterback handle the football on every snap. Just as we grew up playing basketball, and we did all of the individual ball handling drills with the basketball, we do the same drills with the football. We have a warm-up with the football. We take it around our waist, between our legs, and all of the other moves used in basketball handling drills. We do the left leg, right leg, and figure-eight drill.

Next, we have them take five steps and their hitch step, and then run through the bags. We want them to get speed and depth, while keeping their feet and shoulders square. They are scrambling, and then they throw the ball to the target. We start them with one foot in the hole. Then they go to the left, two feet from the hole. We constantly coach mechanics.

Next, we do our redirect drill. This is where we work our feet in the pocket. Now, we want to slide in the pocket. We want to push and pull our feet. We have to slide opposite the pressure.

We teach the scramble drill. We teach two throws on this drill. We teach the quick throw when the quarterback has to throw the ball inside, and we teach the throw when the quarterback is outside the numbers on the scramble. We have found that either you have to throw the ball in a hurry, (i.e., you have to get rid of the ball fast), or you will have time to scramble and throw the ball to a receiver working back to you.

We teach the quarterbacks how to slide. It is the baseball slide. They run the scramble drill, but now they have to keep the ball. They have to protect both themselves and the football.

We work on the fade drill. We try to take all of the different things that happen in a game and apply them to the drills.

The next drill is what we call our net drill. If you do not have a net to run this drill, I would purchase one. Put the net under the bottom part of the goal post. In quarterback school, we do the net drills every day. During the season, we run one of these drills per day. We work with the quarterbacks on their mechanics during this drill. You get a lot of work done by using the net.

A couple of other drills that I will not have time to show you are very good. If you have a quarterback that does not have a high release, and you want to work on him getting his elbow up, use this drill. Take him behind the goal post and have him throw the ball over the goal post. This will help him get that nice high release.

We get the quarterbacks during the special team's period and have them go through the pass patterns they are going to run for that day. We get them on a line and have them all go through the footwork on one cadence. We just call out the play, for example, "22 Hook, number 2 man." They know they are going to throw the triangle pass to the 2 man. We have them go through the footwork on the drill. We do all of the plays we are going to be running that day. It helps us to get ready for the day.

Now, I want to get to the films.

THE BEAR 46 DEFENSE

Bloomfield High School, Cincinnati

I want to get to my topic, which is our 46 Bear Defense. We base out of the 50 package, but this has been a compliment to our defense. I would like to recommend a book by Fritz Shurmur. It may be the greatest source of defense I have seen. It is called, *The Eagle Five Linebacker Defense*. If I had to select one book, I would pick this one. Also, If you have a chance to visit with Donnie Brown at Northeastern University, you could learn a lot about the Bear defense. He is the Huskies' defensive coordinator, and they run a Bear defense.

I am going to move fast and go through all eleven positions on the defense. I have video tapes to show our practice drills and how we install each technique by position. I have some tapes that show the techniques in game situations. First, I want to cover our defensive philosophy and defensive personnel. If you are going to run this defense, you need to decide how you are going to chose your personnel and how you are going to decide who to put into each position. Also, I will show you how we adjust to different sets. We have seen every set known to man.

We make a decision as a coaching staff on Sunday night if we are going to play this defense against our next opponent or not. This is how we make our decisions for that week. If we are playing an option team, we want to know if they are a real option team or a great option team. We want to know if they just run the option as a part of their package, or if they are a true triple-option team. A lot of teams are not sold on the option and run it as a small part of their offense. If this is the case, we will stick with our Bear defense. We will determine this from the film and scouting report.

If we are playing a real one-back team or a shotgun team that runs the drop-back passing game, we will make the same decision. If the one-back is just a small part of their package, we run the Bear defense. In the last seven years, we have run the Bear look about 75 to 80 percent of the snaps.

Our philosophy on defense is to disrupt and destroy the opponents. Our first goal is to hold the opponents to ZERO rushing yards. We have been able to accomplish this in almost 80 or our games in the last eight years. We are trying to force the high school quarterback to throw the football.

Our second goal is to win the critical downs. We practice 25 to 30 minutes a day on 3rd-down situations. Our third goal is to create turnovers. All turnovers come from our attack defense. We want to get our people in the backfield to the mesh point and strip the ball. This year we were plus 26 in our turnover ratio. Our last goal is to take away what the offense does best with our Bear defense. We want to make the offense play left-handed. We take away their best running plays for each set.

Next, I want to cover how we pick our defensive personnel. People will think I am crazy but we start picking our personnel after the State Championship. We have to decide who is going to play each position on the Bear look. We do it in five different ways.

We do a Sunday morning basketball clinic. It is an open event, and all of our football players are invited to take part in it. We just play basketball in this activity. It does two things for us. One, we can get them into shape. Also, it builds camaraderie. But, the most important part of this activity is that it gives me a chance to evaluate talent. I am watching to see who can move east and west, who can change directions, who can jump, and who can play man-to-man defense. We can evaluate all the players coming back and all of the new guys that want to come out for the team.

We use our winter weight training and our spring weight training and conditioning periods to evaluate our players to see where they would fit in on our defense. I often watch gym classes. I visit them during my free period and frequently find a freshman that did not come out for our team, and I invite him out for the team. We have spring football practice for 10 days. We evaluate talent during this time. We do a simple game. We have two competitors go for the ball. One man gets the ball, and he has to run to the goal line. The other man has to tackle him. You can find out who your running backs are in this drill.

We are going to select the 11 best athletes on the team. We never sacrifice speed for size. We do make one exception to this rule with the nose guard. We want playmakers and competitors. We want hit men.

CHOOSING DEFENSIVE PERSONNEL

DEFENSIVE ENDS (2)

- Best athletes on the team.
- Quickest on the team.
- Toughness a must.
- Ability to change direction.
- Hit men.

The first two players we select are our two defensive ends. We pick the two best athletes on our team for these positions. We are looking for speed and aggressive players, but more importantly is the fact that we are looking for athletes. In the last four years, we have had seven All State defensive ends. We feel we have our best athletes three or four feet from the offensive tackle. We feel this is a defensive mismatch. This is the whole key to this defense.

SAM LINEBACKER (1)

- Great football sense.
- Great work ethic.
- Ability to think analytically under fire (cerebral).
- Toughness a must (no injury rule!).
- Great leader.

Our Sam linebacker must have an incredible work ethic. He has to be the type of kid that is going to take video home and study it, or he is going to stay two hours after practice with the coach. He will make all on-field calls, blitz calls, and adjustments. We tell them every spring that they are not allowed to get hurt. We do not feel the back-up Sam can make the calls as well as the first team Sam can. We do not get in a huddle on defense. We do not make any calls from the sideline. All of our calls are made on the field by the Sam linebacker. He does not have to be strong or fast. He must be articulate, and he must be an analytical person.

STRONG SAFETY (1)

- Ability to play man coverage on wide receivers.
- Strong enough to jam a tight end on the line of scrimmage.

Our strong safety is usually the hardest person to find for this defense. He is a hybrid. We call him the freak. He has to be able to go out in space and play a slot man. He has to be able to line up on a tight end and not lose ground. He must be strong enough to stay in the C gap and not get knocked into a linebacker. He must be a great cover man who also has some physical strength.

COVER CORNER (1)

- Best man coverage player on the team.
- Confidence and a short memory.

This is always a basketball player. Bloomfield is still a basketball town. I am like a vulture looking at the basketball team. This is where I get all of my corners. I look for those players who have been cut from the basketball team. If they can play basketball, they can play cover corner. I tell them they will not have to tackle anyone. They can be like Deion Sanders. I tell them to come and cover #11 for forty-eight minutes, and then they can go home. They are going to play man-to-man the entire game.

STRONG CORNER (1)

- Second best man coverage player on the team.

- Great football sense.

- Great tackler.

This man is also a basketball player. He has to play some tight-end defense. He must play the tight end is a two-tight end set. He must be tougher than the cover corner. He must have some tackling ability.

FREE SAFETY (1)

- Best tackler of team.
- Great football sense.
- Ability to think analytically under fire.
- Speed is vital.

Our free safety is the best tackler on our team. If the ball breaks loose, he is the man who must make the play. He must make all of the coverage calls and all of the motion adjustments in the secondary.

WILL LINEBACKER (1)

- Third best man coverage player on team.
- Speed, Speed, speed.
- Great tackler.

Our Will linebacker is the third best cover man. We do hide players at Will linebacker. Size does not matter here because we want speed. The drill we look for the Will linebacker is the shuttle drill. He must run this drill in "great" time.

NOSEGUARD (1)

- Take size for speed.

- Strength most important (18-inch rule).

Our nose man is the only exception when we take size over speed. We want someone that is strong enough to blow the center back 18-inches off the football. We try to make this player flexible.

DEFENSIVE TACKLES (2)

- Fastest linemen on the team.
- Speed, Speed, speed.

We can play anyone at defensive tackle. All I do is to take all or our linemen and pick the two fastest players. Size does not matter. We may end up with a 165-pound player in this position. We want them to be a 1-gap player. A lot of times, they get down in a sprinter's stance.

I want to go over the alignment for each position and talk about the techniques we use. Then, I want to show some a tape of each position in a game.

We start with the defensive ends. We use the term line technique with them. It is a simple theory in practice. It takes a lot of time to master this technique. Our ends spend 45 minutes a day working on this technique. The ends line up in a tilted stance. Basically, their feet are three inches apart. They are in a track sprinter's stance. They are cocked tilted.

We have a three-foot rule. We want them three feet outside the end. They are watching the tip of the football. When the ball moves, they go off in a rage. If the offensive tackle does not move, the end's inside shoulder should hit the butt of the tackle.

We set our line on the near back. In the I formation, we draw a line from the nose of the end to the fullback's inside foot. We want to run a straight line to that position. We are going to stay on that line. We do not want to come off that line.

The first threat is the near lineman. If the lineman blocks out, the end is reading on the run. We call it a high read. All high means is that the back is coming high. It is from the C gap to the outside. If we get a high read, we use a quick swim and get right back on his line. We call this a swim-and-replace move on a high read.

If we get a low read, it is anything from the A gap, B gap, C gap, or flow away. When we get a block out on a pass set, we use a squeeze technique. We keep the shoulders square as we are coming. We make contact and push down the line to restrict the play down to the gap. We want them to be able to bounce outside if the ball goes outside. We call that technique squeeze.

DEFENSIVE ENDS LINE

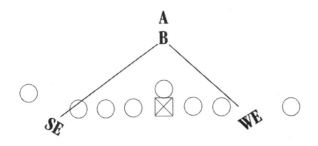

We do not get a lot of block outs. We get a lot of down-blocking schemes. They block the end or tackle down. That is what we want. We continue down the line.

The next person that is going to show on the line is the fullback or the frontside guard. Now, we use the butt technique. This is the best technique we have ever put in. We put it in four years ago. It is not a spill. We do not spill the fullback and bounce the play. We do not contain the play. He hits the fullback head-to-head and nose-to-nose and tries to knock him back on his butt. Then, we play the ball inside or outside. We are going full speed on that line, and we are not breaking down or stopping. We go as fast as we can and hit the fullback.

The next set for the ends is the open set or split back set. This defense was started in the NFL to stop the west coast split-back offense. Now we have a 1-by-1 rule. The ends will cock the tilt a little tighter. They go one yard inside the back, and one yard in front of the back. They draw an imaginary line. Now, the ends become quarterback players. They are going straight to the quarterback. They hit the quarterback on a veer option, and they hit the quarterback on the drop-back pass. They react late to the run.

DEFENSIVE ENDS LINE VS SPLIT BACKS

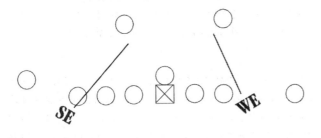

They have the same rules. If the tight end pass sets, they get a low read. They are going to squeeze and strip the hole. They want to keep their shoulders square and be able to play the bounce. If they get a high read, they are going to swim — replace and get back on the line.

When do we change our line? We may change our line through out the game. We call our "change" and tell them to aim at the tailback instead of the up back in the I formation. Now, we set our line to the foot of the deep back. Anytime on a passing situation, we change our line to the tailback for the ends. What we do is to make a "FIRE" call. Now, we are playing pass first. We are looking for a pass-set line.

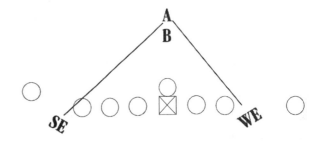

We do not come off our line until we see the ball in the stomach of the running back. It takes the ends a long time to accept this rule. If the ends believe in this concept and practice this, and can execute it in a game, you will get a sack on a play-action pass. They will not get fooled on play-action passes.

Will they make the tackle once the ball is handed to the running back? Yes, they will. When we get a fire call, we move out four feet from the tackle. We have more room against the tackle with our best athlete. We are thinking fast first.

Here are the rules: on, inside, and outside. One of the two backs is going to block the defensive end. If the tight end releases, one of the two backs will try to block the end.

If the fullback sets up on the same line as the quarterback is, it would usually be a 5-step drop. If he is on the line, we stay on our line, and it becomes a bull rush. It is the same as the butt technique. We hit them nose-on-nose and drive them into the quarterback. We do not get a lot of sacks when this happens. As soon as the quarterback comes back with the ball, we use the jump rule. We jump in the air to block the pass. That is the reason I like the tall defensive ends. That is on-the-line move.

If the back were to set up _inside_ the line of the end, we use our swim replace move. We swim and get back on the line to the quarterback.

The thing we see the most against this defense is the 3-step drop or the quick pass. They try to throw the ball on a fade or slant because you are in man coverage. We see the back set _outside_ the line. We love to see this. If we have a strong end, we want him to stay on the line and use a rip move. We want to run through half of his body. If we do not have a strong end, we use a quick head-and-shoulders fake like we use in swim replace and then we use the rip. If we see the back outside the line, we make our move and head for the quarterback. (Tape)

The defensive tackles use what we call the slingshot technique. The strong tackle is lined up on the side of the tight end in a wide 3 technique on the outside shoulder of the guard. The inside foot is lined up even with the outside foot. Why the 3 technique? We want to penetrate in the gap two yards into the backfield. That is our two-yard rule. If we get a base block, our rule is to under hook, and run upfield two yards. We are wide enough that we will never get reached.

If we get a cutoff block, we are not going to stay in our gap. We are going to run and use our speed. This year, we had two big men play these positions, and we used the cross-face technique. Two years ago, we had two fast and underweight tackles, and we used the dip, speed, and run technique. This is how they played it. If they got a reach block, they would dip, and spin down the line. We do not want to go behind the block.

DEFENSIVE TACKLES ALIGNMENT
A
B

ST   WT

Any time there is no fullback in the set, no one can threaten the A gaps. Our Sam linebacker makes a "Y" call. He calls out "Y – Y – Y." It may be a split set or a one-back Set. Now, we are going to get the tackles almost in a 4-eye alignment. The call is made on the line of scrimmage by Sam anytime the offense can

not hit the A gap on a midline play by the set of the offensive backs. This is built into the package.

"Y" SET

B   A

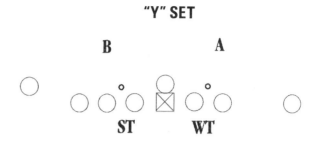

ST   WT

When the tackles get a pass set, they are allowed only one pass-rush move. They get to use the bull rush. This year I had two tackles who could not rush if you gave them 30 minutes to get to the quarterback. They both weighed 350 pounds. All they were allowed to do was bull rush. The only sack they could get was to take the offensive guard and throw him into the quarterback. We want big strong tackles inside. We do let them pass rush on a "fire" call. If we have quick tackles, we let them pass rush.

Using this technique, we feel we should never get blocked by a scoop block. We are sprinting to a two-yard spot across the line. We tell them to check the split of the guard and tackle every time they come to the line. If it is a tight split, they know they are going to get a tom block down or they are going to get a scoop block. They must read the split. If it is a tight split, it is going to be a tom or cutoff block. They want to race across the line and get into the backfield and disrupt the offense. They want to stop the guards from pulling.

This is how we play the double-team block. As soon as we get pressure, we are going to let go of the guard. We turn and focus on the tackle and attack him with all the power we have. We want to get two hands on the tackle and run his butt to the sideline right through the B gap. We let go of the guard. If they want to combo block and get the guard off, let them try it. Our linebackers are outside. We are not going to let the tackle come off the line.

The tom block is the biggest block they are going to get at tackle. The key is the offensive tackle. This is his split rule. If the split is less than two feet, he is going to use an across-the-face or a spin move, depending on the personnel. We want to dip and run. If the split is more than two feet, we want to penetrate and run until we get into the backfield. This is a pre-snap read. It is his call before the snap. If he screws it up, we will see it in the film.

The nose guard is the simplest man to coach. He has his 18-inch rule. He spends 30 minutes a day on a sled that we have. It was made for linemen. It was a two-man sled, but we made it into a one-man sled. We get one of those big GILMAN body pads that weighs about 200 pounds. We put that pad on the dummy, and he drives it five yards each time. We put a jersey from our opponent on it, and he pounds it four days. He has to get 18 inches on that first move. If you can get 18 inches against the center, they are not going to score on you. We tell him this is his house. No one runs in the A gap. We do not expect him to get sacks. He does make plays on the screens.

NOSE GUARD

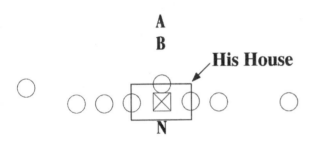

If the nose man gets the "Y" call, we want him to shed the center and run with the guard. He takes the first two steps the same, but runs to the guard. They do not have a threat to the A gap.

If we make a "nasty" call, it means the nose will slant left or right. We call it nasty left or nasty right. If we call Lee and Roy, it is a three-man slant with the tackles. All the nose has to learn is shed and nasty.

Our strong safety must find the tight end and line up on him before the ball is snapped. Some teams will try to screw us up by moving the tight end around. They will line him up at the shortside tackle. They move him around. A lot of teams will go on the first sound against us.

If it is a normal tight-end split, we want him to split two to three feet. His outside foot is on the inside foot of the end. We want his hands one inch from the grass. He plays very low to take away that drive block. He plays a mirror technique. He has no run responsibility. All he is going to do is to keep the tight end from blocking our linebacker. All he has to do on run is to hold the C gap.

STRONG SAFETY

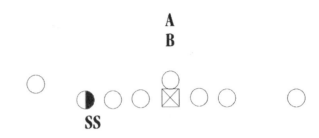

You can not play someone here who is not disciplined. The rule for the strong safety is straightforward. If he looks into the backfield and gets beat by the tight end on play action, he can not play the rest of the season. This is in practice or in a game. If he will do it in practice, he will do it in a game. He is out for the season if he gets beat on play action. You must be a disciplined person to play this position.

If we get a tight split of one foot, they more than likely will be running outside. Now, we want him to go from inside foot to head up with the tight end. It is always a mirror step for him. If the tight end goes out, he steps out. If he goes in, the strong safety goes in. If he goes straight out, we "bucket" step him. This is the base block, and we can get more power against him on the bucket step.

Teams are starting to flex the tight end by moving him outside. We have our call for that. Now we call "switch" and the strong end comes down and plays the same as a weak end. The strong safety goes to the inside alignment and plays it like it was a twin set. We must make the call to the Sam linebacker.

I told you that the strong safety has to be a special player. If we get three wide receivers, he has to go out and cover the inside man of the three. He is our fourth best man-to-man cover guy. We always give him help over the top. If we get three wide receivers, the free safety makes the "off" call.

Techniques for the linebackers are called a hot spot. We have hot spot A, C, and alley. They have their feet at five yards deep. They are no tighter than four yards. The Sam linebacker has three hot spots. He has the A gap 2, the C gap 2 that we call the bubble, and he has alley or 3 area. It is easy to teach.

The Will linebacker has two hot spots. He has A gap 2 and C gap 2. Both linebackers key the fullback in an I formation. If the fullback runs midline, both linebackers run through the A gap. That is their hot spot, and they go at top speed. If the fullback goes at a 45-degree angle, the Sam linebacker runs through the bubble at top speed in the C gap. If the fullback goes to the outside, the linebackers go to the alley which is the 3 area. All of this is on flow to.

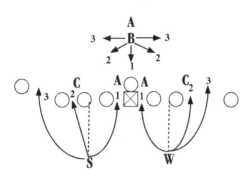

We have an away rule. We always have a third linebacker in the game in our free safety. He is reading number 1, first as a linebacker. He has no pass responsibility. This is where you can play with this rule. If we are playing a great I formation team, and they have a good tailback, we put the free safety on the tailback. He has the tailback everywhere he goes. If we face a team that likes to run a lot of counters to the backside, we will let the free safety be the alley player and let the Will be a slow player on flow away. The free safety is always the adjuster on all blitzes. If we blitz the Sam linebacker, the free safety takes the place of Sam.

If we get flow away from Sam, his rule is this. He never crosses the face of the center until he sees the ball beyond the line of scrimmage. The Will is reading slow until he sees the ball in the stomach of the running back. He is different. We let him go crazy when he sees the ball. If he sees the ball, he runs.

If we get wide flow away, we tell Will he has no counter responsibility. We tell him to run through the first seam he can find. On split flow, he goes right to the back. We are in man coverage. If the back is pass blocking, we grab his jersey to take away the screen.

When the two backs cross in the backfield, it makes it tough for us. We have to cross our linebackers on cross flow and hope we do not get picked. You have to work on this if you are going to run this defense.

We teach our corners four different man-to-man techniques. If the wide receiver is up on the line of scrimmage, we are in a bump technique. If the receiver is off the ball, we use what we call a cowboy technique. It is an inside leverage man-to-man technique.

COWBOY AND BUMP TECHNIQUES

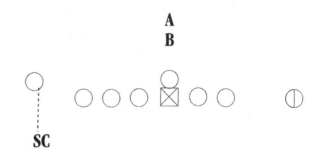

Anytime there are two wide receivers next to each other, we go to special coverage. The outside corner takes an extra inside alignment, and the second corner takes a deeper alignment to guard against the pick play.

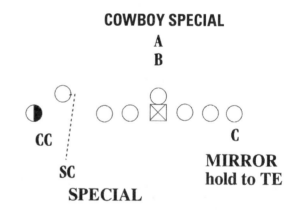

Anytime time we see two tight ends, one of the corners must become a strong safety. They must be strong enough to play the C gap.

Let me show the tape of the other positions. When we go over the drills for the linebacker, we have little orange dots or spacers to show them where the hot spots are. All they have to do is to read the fullback and run to their hot spots.

Thank you. Let me close with a Confucius quote that expresses my feelings about coaching:

"CHOSE A JOB YOU LOVE AND YOU WILL NEVER WORK A DAY IN YOUR LIFE."

BASIC PRINCIPLES AND DRILLS FOR RECEIVERS

University of Florida

It is a pleasure to be here. It was tough getting here, and I did not know if I would be able to make it or not, but fortunately I was able to make it. On behalf of Coach Steve Spurrier and Coach Buddy Teevens, I want to try to give you some ideas that may help you with the passing game. I want to cover the things we do with our receivers. One thing Coach Spurrier believes in is getting the ball to the open receiver and to the playmaker. I want to pay a tribute to the high school coaches that send us the athletes to get the job done.

Last year, we had a 10-3 season and were fortunate enough to win the SEC championship. We were a very young team. We had to play a lot of young players because of injuries. Once our guys catch on to what we are doing, it is easy for them to have success in our system. We have had several players that made it in the NFL. We had two players in the Super Bowl this year.

Inside our 20-yard line, we face a lot of different coverages. We have a few plays that are built in to cover the zone, the blitzes, and man coverages. We use our two wide receivers to run the defense off to give the quarterback time to throw the ball. We want the halfback and fullback to protect the backside. They can run motion, or they can run it from a regular set. We run the patterns and form our triangle for the quarterback to read. We try to hit the route at 10 yards and let them get as many yards as they can after the catch.

We run the draw play a lot. It is one of our best plays. We use that action to keep the linebackers in. We have a zone and man route built in for that particular play. The thing you must do is to have a route you can use against both the zone and man

coverage. We like to use two backs and the tight end inside the 20-yard line. We can run these routes from different formations.

We run option routes where the receivers have a "choice" route. Our quarterback and receivers work together a lot. We may take a 30-minute session with the quarterback and receivers. We want the receivers to know what the quarterback is doing on each play. Once they learn that we are confident, they can do a better job making proper adjustments on their routes. This helps us eliminate mistakes by the receivers.

Our quarterback is taught to throw to an area. It is our job to get the receivers to understand this and to make adjustments to be in a certain area when the ball is released.

I want to talk about some of the techniques that help receivers. These are basic principles for pass receivers.

The first principle is to keep your eyes on the ball at all times. Your first responsibility is to catch the ball. After you make the catch, think about additional yardage and scoring. The fun part of being a receiver is what you do after the catch.

A lot of receivers do not realize how important it is to see the ball. I will ask the receivers what they use to catch the ball. Most of them will reply their "hands." I indicated to them the hands are useless without the eyes. The eyes are the most important part of their body they can utilize in a game.

We chart every catch in practice and in our games. We utilize a manager to keep this chart. We list all of the passes that go to each receiver in game-type situations in practice and in a game. We keep track of the number of receptions and the yards after the catch. We can see each day which receiver has had a good day catching the football. This makes the receivers accountable in games and in practice. It makes them competitive.

We try to show the receivers how valuable the receivers are to the team and how important it is for them to do their job right. I keep a chart of several other teams around the country that throw the ball a lot and compare them with our receivers. In our offense, the receivers have a very important part of each score. Our receivers are involved in 75 percent of our scores. For us to be successful, they have to accountable for doing their job. We compare pass efficiency with those other teams and show our guys how they stand with those teams.

#2. When we are on offense, and the ball is thrown, it is not a "free" ball. It is ours — go get it! Never allow an interception. Anything goes. Most receivers are the type players whom you try to keep away from the action. You try to keep them out of the contact, and do not put them in drills that are too rough. Now, I do not want that type of receiver. I want a guy that has a mentality that he can run into a hole where the linebacker is and make the play. On offense, you are supposed to be attacking. We want to attack and go get it. They must do everything they can to go get the football. We are attacking the ball.

#3. Whenever possible, catch the ball in your hands and not against your chest. We want to "frame" the ball if it is coming straight at us. We have our thumbs together. If the ball is going to the sideline, we teach the receiver to put his inside elbow down. To stop the ball, we put both hands up with the thumbs out. If someone threw you a small baby, how would you catch the baby? You would turn your hands up with the thumbs out and your little fingers together. If the ball is behind, us we will turn our back and go to the ball.

#4. In practice, after you catch the ball, tuck it away securely and sprint at least 10 yards. Put in a fake, a spin, etc., to simulate what you would do in

a game. Demand a lot of yourself. Take pride in your work.

#5. When you warm up, don't just jog around. Run in spurts, change of pace, weaves, cuts, stutter steps, etc. Start from your stance. Use head fakes to release from imaginary linebackers. We find time at practice to catch a lot of different types of passes (high, low, behind us, etc.).

When we teach the stance, we want them in a two-point stance. We want the knees flexed and the weight evenly distributed. We teach the stance like a baseball player trying to steal second base. You have first base on the left and second base on the right. We want them where they can watch the pitcher so they can go either way. They can go to second base, or they can get back to first base. Their hands are dangling with their shoulders square.

#6. Always run your patterns at full, controlled speed. We can not get the correct timing at half speed. If you can stop on a dime, you can run at full speed. You have to be able to go get the ball when it is in the air. We cannot get a good pattern at half speed. We practice all of our routes at full speed.

#7. Pass receivers are made — not born. They are made by practicing day after day until all of your body moves and receiving techniques are second nature. Whenever possible, have a ball in your hands. Play "catch" with your partner. Never let the ball become a stranger to you. Protect the ball when in a crowd. Raymond Berry caught over 630 passes and fumbled only one time.

Before practice we do a lot of receiver drills. Coach Spurrier has the receivers catch the ball with their hands up next to a wall. They see the ball hit the hand.

Another thing we do is the "Jerry Rice" drill. Jerry Rice worked for his father who was a mason. They used to throw the bricks to him on top of a house all of the time, and he had to catch them with the strength of his forearm. In practice, we have the receivers catch 50 to 100 bricks tossed to them. If they drop a brick, they have to start over. It helps them concentrate on not dropping the brick. We will have them catch about 200 red bricks in that drill with each hand. We try to get better everyday before practice.

#8. Always be alert for the ball, even though you are not the primary receiver. You never know when the quarterback will throw to you. Do not loaf because you think the pass is going to someone else. Carry out your assignment at full speedy on every play. This is an easy way to tell the difference between the "good ones" and the "great ones."

#9. Concentrate at all times on what you are going to do and why and how you are going to do it. Keep in mind the object of the pass play and what your part of it is. Know the complete picture and not just your part of the play. We want our receivers to be thinking about the adjustment they are going to use when they break the huddle and come to the line of scrimmage. When they get to the line, they should know what the defense is going to do, so it should not be a shock to them when they get to the line.

#10. Always know field position and where the sideline is. Know the time remaining, the down and distance, the sun position, wind conditions, lights, condition of the field (high or low spots), pitcher's mound, infield dirt, ball position with regard to goal posts. Remember that goal posts are the receiver's friends.

When players leave the huddle, they must look at the clock to make sure they have time to run the play. Coaches must know these conditions as well. Some of you may play on fields that have a pitcher's mound on it.

#11. The sidelines and end zone lines are not enemies. Always know your relative position to them. Respect them, but do not let them bother you in catching the ball. Remember the catch comes first. The officials will never call you "in bounds" if you drop the ball.

#12. Always expect to get your jock knocked off after, or as you catch the ball, then the jolt won't surprise you. You have to "want it." We catch the ball and pay the price. You must have utter disregard for contact while catching the ball.

#13. When you are breaking past a defensive man and have him beat, be alert for holding or tackling. They are taught to take the penalty rather than give up the touchdown. You must clear the defender. You can get away with a push or straight arm in this situation.

#14. Get in the habit of going all out after the ball every time, regardless of how the ball is thrown. Soon, great catches become routine. We work on "bad passes" everyday. We throw the ball in every area to make the players aware of how to catch bad passes. They get used to catching all types of passes. We do not accept any excuses for dropping passes.

#15. Fake the man and not the area. Don't telegraph routes with your body. Maximize the reception area vs. zone coverage and misdirect the defender vs. man coverage. (Vertical – lateral momentum.)

#16. All of us want to catch a lot of passes on game day, but it doesn't always work out that way for whatever reason. The important thing is that we win the game. Have a little patience, and your opportunities will come. In our passing scheme, our receivers are going to have a lot of opportunities. All they have to do is to carry out their assignment and let the quarterback take his proper reads. If he is taking his proper reads, the ball will be distributed fairly evenly.

At this point, I am going to put on the tape and show you some drills of the things we just talked about. Hopefully this will help you to understand what we are doing with our receivers.

THE VIDEO SHOWN COVERS THE FOLLOWING DRILLS:

CARIOCA OUT DRILL

The wide receiver is in a football position 10 yards from the quarterback or the coach. On a "go" call, the receiver starts to carioca within 10 yards. The receiver must snap his head around to find the ball. His eyes should not go to the ground. This drill is designed to develop better vision on the ball. The receiver must not put his hands out until he sees the ball. We do not want the defender to knock the ball out of his hands when the receiver puts his arms out. After he catches the ball, he should turn up field.

TOE TAP DRILL

The wide receiver is aligned in a 2-point stance. On the signal "go," he runs to the sideline looking over his inside shoulder. He wants to keep his eyes on the ball. He toe taps at the sideline as he catches the ball. The quarterback throws the ball to a spot — not to the receiver.

OVER THE SHOULDER CATCH

The receiver stands 10 yards looking over his shoulder. He catches the ball at its highest point. His eyes do not go down until the ball is in his hands. We look at his arm action and head position on the catch.

CARIOCA CURL DRILL

The receiver is in a 2-point stance 10 yards away from the quarterback or the coach. The receiver plants at 10 yards and squares his shoulders. He shuffles to keep within his frame if possible. He catches the pass on the curl and tucks it away, and turns and runs up field.

SNAP DRILL

The wide receiver stands in a 5-yard-by-5-yard area, looking over his inside shoulder with his inside foot back. On a signal, the ball is thrown, and the receiver takes his step, plants his foot, and snaps his head around looking for the ball. His eyes do not go down until the ball is in his hands. He tucks the ball away and turns to run up field. We try to get everything we can after the catch.

EYE TO THE SKY DRILL

This drill is use to help players catch the deep pass. We want the receiver to keep his shoulders square downfield, and not turned toward the sideline. The wide receiver stands directly in front of the quarterback. On "go," he comes off the line at half speed. The ball is thrown on the call. As the ball nears the receiver, a "ball" call is made when the ball is directly over the head of the receiver. The wide receiver looks upward and finds the ball. He does not look at the quarterback. He must get in the habit of looking up, not back.

NEAR ARM SWIM – RIP RELEASE

The receiver gives a jab step or a drop step opposite the direction in which he is going. He must use head-and-shoulders action. He uses his inside arm, with his elbow down, to execute the swim or rip motion to release from the defender. He keeps his shoulders square and downfield.

SIDE STEP LINEBACKER DRILL

The receiver aims directly at the linebacker or the defensive back and tries to get within arms distance from the defender. As the receiver approaches the defender, he plants his foot in the ground and sidesteps the defender, either inside or outside. He does not want to cross over his feet. He must keep his shoulders and head upfield. The throw is made to the receiver, so he can catch it at its highest point.

I really appreciate the chance to visit with you. If you get down our way, you are welcome to come see us. Thanks a lot.

DEFENSIVE LINE TECHNIQUES AND DRILLS

Western Kentucky University

It is a pleasure to be here representing Western Kentucky University. We had an exciting year. We ended up fifth in the nation in Division I-AA. We led the nation in scorning defense and turnover margin. We led the Ohio Valley Conference and ranked in the top ten in the country in rushing defense. We recorded four shutouts and did not allow a touchdown in six games. We had three players post 100 or more tackles. Our defense recorded 33 sacks and 94 tackles for loss.

We forced 50 turnovers, which was the most since 1975. We had 29 interceptions, which was the second-highest total in the school's history. We allowed only one 100-yard rusher in thirteen games.

Our overall record was 11-2, which tied the second highest win total in school history. Our head coach is Jack Harbaugh, who was named American Football Coaches Association Region Three Coach of the Year.

He is the type of coach I like to work for. He lets you coach and supports you in every way. It was certainly the right fit for me. It was a good fit for my family. Whenever I go back to my home, I really brag on Kentucky. There are great people around here. I think they are wonderful. We have a young defensive staff. That is what I like about it.

In my presentation today, I'm going to take you through my day. I'll tell you what I actually do with my players.

This was my first year at Western Kentucky. We didn't have a lot of big kids. They all worked hard and were dedicated to the weight training. On the defensive line, I don't worry about size. When I look at a recruit on film, I want to know if he can use his hands. If you find a player who knows how to use his hands, he can play for anyone in America. Our players showed up and worked hard. They busted their butts to improve every day.

We are an attacking defense. We have a 4-3 package as our base defense, but we are going into a 3-4 look. Actually, we will have a 50-defensive look next year. Before I get into my practice routine, let me give you some general thoughts I have about coaching in general.

The first question I think you should answer is, "What is coaching?" Coaching is the best chance your team has to win. Coaching is the best way for your team to succeed. Coaching is the ability to transmit information to your players. Use teaching videos. They are the best form of information transference that you can use. Don't be the blackboard coach. Don't simply think that X's and O's can win for you.

I have a couple of thoughts on drill work. I think you should do drill as close to full speed as possible. Your drills should be as game-related as they can be.

When you select personnel, you should have some things in mind. Get to know each individual that plays for you. Get to know his abilities. You have to learn about his attitude. Never ask a player to do something he can't do.

We have "three nevers" we talk about. #1) Never get knocked down. I know players are going to get knocked down, but they never stay there. #2) Never run around a block. That is taking the easy way out. Always go the hard way. #3) Never get knocked off the ball. We want to play on our opponent's side of the line of scrimmage, not on the defensive side.

There are three things that lead to team success:

• Play great defense

• Have great special team play

• Have the ability to run the football.

There are three things the defense has to do to help win the game. First, they have to stop the run. If a defense cannot stop a team from running the football, they are not going to win the game. Second, the defense must win the third down. If you cannot win on third down, the offense will drive the ball all day. We want the three-and-out type of defense. Third, for a defense to win, they must create turnovers. The defense has to take the ball away from the offense.

Before the ball is snapped, a defense has to understand four things. They have to get into their <u>stance</u> before they can come off and play defense. Good fundamentals always start with a good stance. The defenders have to be sure they know their <u>alignment</u>. To have a chance to make a play, the defense has to align properly. They have to know their <u>keys</u> are their <u>responsibilities</u>.

There are some basic fundamentals we try to practice. We have to get into the gaps for which we are responsible. We want to come to the point. That gets them into a position to make a play. To get to the ball, we must fight pressure and locate the ball. After we have found the ball, we have to shed the blocker. The last and most important thing is to pursue and gang tackle. We have to have eleven guys running hard to the ball.

I have worked for some good people over the years. They all told me to develop a philosophy of coaching if I wanted to be successful. There are some things I teach and believe in. The first thing I believe in is the defense has to be physical if you want to win. The second thing is to give second effort every time you line up. The third point is when you are playing defense, you have to dominate your position. The last thing you have to do is to make a commitment to excellence. Those are factors I believe have to take place to win.

Practice is the most important thing you can do. That is where you do your teaching. When the players come to practice, they have to accept responsibility for some important thoughts. They have to come to practice ready to work. They must be intense while they are in practice. They must strive to improve every day. If they are not getting better, they are getting worse. You don't stand still.

When players come into practice, they have to develop an attitude. They need to be aggressive. To play defense, you have to be tough. You want to intimidate the offense. For any defense to be successful, they have to be dedicated. They have to play as a team and put team goals in front of individual goals.

We set some defensive goals in 2000. We wanted to stop the run. The tough yardage comes from a team's ability to run the ball. That is how you get the ball into the end zone or pick up the first down. If the defense can stop the run, their chances to win are very good. We want to have four sacks a game. We wanted to stop the run, force a team to throw, and sack the quarterback. We wanted to play smart. We wanted to play without mental mistakes. To us, lining up wrong is a mental mistake.

When you play the type of defense we play, it is important to play assignment football. If a player starts to play his own game, the defense breaks down. He has to do the best job he can of executing his technique. Our last goal was to win, win, and win.

We have twenty-minute periods in our practice schedule. I get my players out early because we won't have enough time in the individual drills if we spend too much time in a warm-up period. I call this pre-practice. We start with a front-leg kick. All we are doing is high kicking with our leg. We kick the leg as high as we can kick it forward like a punter would do. We work the right leg, and then the left. This really helps the defensive linemen. We are working the hips, groin muscles, and the leg. We want to kick as high as we can. That also works on the hip flexors.

The next thing we do is what I call a crusting kick. That is a round kick. The players stand forward and kick with a round-house movement to the side and back to the front. Again, we kick first with the right leg, and then with the left. It is hard to kick with the off leg. This improves the players' flexibility.

From there, we go to a side kick. This kick is performed by standing forward and kicking to the side like a karate kick. That develops balance and flexibility. We use a walking-high kick to end our kicking drills.

The next thing we do is to work on arm flexibility drills. We work in pairs on this drill. You've all seen this drill. One player stands behind his partner. He grasps the wrists of his partner and lifts his partner's arms up as far as his partner can reach. It's a super stretch of the shoulders and arm. These drills are used to loosen up our players and to help improve their agility, flexibility, and balance.

The next thing we do is to go on the sled. On the sled, we work our stance and get-off drill. The thing we emphasize is to run with the knees. We don't tell them to run with the feet. If you tell them to run with their feet, they take baby steps. If they run with their knees, they take longer steps. The sled helps a lineman with his footwork. We work on playing the veer block on the sled.

I am big on eyes, hands, and feet in teaching defensive line drills. As a coach, you shouldn't watch your drills from behind. Get in front of the drill so you can see your player's eyes. A defensive player has to use his eyes so he knows where to shoot his hands.

The first thing I built when I got to Western was the china post. It has been my trade mark every where I've been. I use it to teach attacking hands. I am into karate. I used to teach it. Karate teaches quick hand movement, and part of the training is punching the china board. They use a board used in karate class, I use a post. It is a square post wrapped with half inch rope. I use railroad ties buried in the ground. There are two feet of the ties above the ground. I wrap them around the top with half-inch rope. That becomes the target for the hand punch. I have five posts spaced to represent the A and B gaps.

CHINA POST

We start out in a six-point stance. That is the hands, knees, and toes, on the ground. We work an explosion drill like you would on a sled. The difference is we are punching with our hands into the railroad tie. It obviously doesn't move. We punch out with the hands with our knuckles up, not out.

We work from the six-point stance, then to the four-point stance, and finally to the three-point stance. In each stance, we are working on attacking with the hands. We want them to imagine they can rip the top of the railroad tie off. We want them to punch out with the knuckles up. Here is a coaching point on this drill. The defensive movement is always triggered with a ball. I have a ball on a stick, which I move to make them get off. Never use a cadence. We play defense on movement of the ball.

When we get in the three-point stance and explode, I am looking for a good power step. That is the short six-inch step they take as they break their stance. After the power step, I want the second step as quick as possible. I call it a drum beat. I should hear the feet like a drum beat. It should sound like bam-bam. If I don't hear that beat, they are not doing it right. It is not a hop. It is two distinctive steps.

The kid you will see in the film had a lot of trouble doing this drill. He is a great kid and has a lot of heart. If all my players had this kid's heart, we could beat the world. As a coach, you have to be patient with your players. If they have the right attitude and heart, they will help you. This kid was an offensive line cast-off. I took him, and he ended up starting for me. If my kids work hard, I reward them. I give them playing time. I rotate my players in and out of the games. If a kid works hard for me, he plays. Kids come to school to play. Reward them by playing them in the game when you can. If you don't work hard, you will be down so far on the bench, you'll never play.

On the china post, we work on shooting the hips. We come off, punch the hands, and shoot the hips to one side or the other. We come off, shoot the hands and flip the hips, which is a half turn so they end up between the posts with their shoulders perpendicular to the line.

HIP FLIP

The next thing we work on is shooting the hips and ripping through with the arm. We get off, flip the hips, and rip through with the inside arm. We always finish this drill with the rip. We want to bring our hand all the way up to our ear hole on our head gear.

The next drill we go to is the chute drill. I picked these drills up from the University of Tennessee. All coaches are big copy cats. The chute is four-feet high by three-feet wide. The chute is made out of pipe. This is the second piece of equipment I built at Western. I have two of them. They are light and you can move them around.

We put our defensive players under the chute and work on our get off. We get off the ball and get our hands out. We always want to have something to aim for. Make sure you have a landmark for your players to finish the drill. I set a cone five yards to the side to sprint to.

We are watching their stance, their eyes, how they get off ball (i.e., the shooting of the hands, ripping through, staying low), and the finish. We are an attacking team. We are not a reading team. That is why we have our hands out. We are in the attacking mode.

CHUTE DRILL

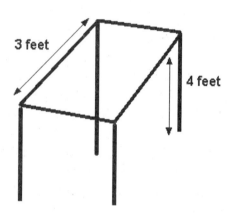

3 feet

4 feet

The next thing we do is our torque drill. We work on twisting stunts in this section. We align under the chute. When the ball moves, we step over from one section of the chute into the other section and up the field. We watch their footwork and body movement.

TWISTING

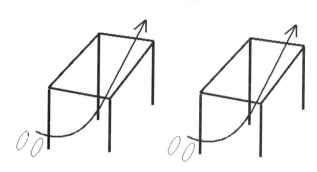

From there, we go to our partner drill. We repeat the same drills we did in the chute, except we are working with a partner. We line up a defensive player with his partner. The first drill is called push back. We shoot the hands into the target. We are making sure the knuckles are up and the thumbs are in. We push our partner back to a cone five yards behind him. We are looking at the shooting of the hands and the power steps to the running knees.

PUSH BACK

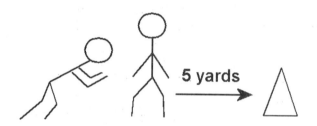

5 yards

The next thing we do is the push and pull drill. It is the same drill except we take it one more step. We shoot the hands, push back, and pull past the offensive man. When we pull by, we are using a rip or swim move. If the blocker is high, we want to rip. If he is low, we are going to swim.

The next drill I got from the Tennessee Titans. It is called red ball. You can use any color ball, but our colors are red and white. This drill is done with a big rubber ball about three feet in diameter. It is a weighted ball like a medicine ball, but larger. The coach has the ball five yards from the players. They must get in their stance. The coach rolls the ball either at them or to either side. The player gets out of his stance, attacks the ball, shoots his hands to the ball, and continues punching it back to the coach. They really hate this drill.

RED BALL

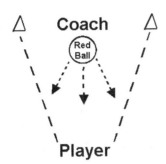

We work a partner drill where we are keying high hat or low hat. If we get a high hat, we are thinking pass rush. If we get the low hat, we are thinking run. We work against different types of block for run reaction. It is like the push back drill, except we are getting movement right and left depending on what the offensive player is doing.

When we are playing run blocking, we do not run around blocks. We play through blocks. We want to align our shoulders square to the line of scrimmage. When we key, we are looking at a small element on the helmet. We tell them to focus on two screws on the helmet. We want to win the line of scrimmage.

In this drill, we align with our partner in a locked-up, hands-on position. The defender's hands are either inside the offensive blocker's arms or they are outside his arms. If his hands are inside, I want him to turn the opponent's body and rip across with his opposite arm. If the defender's hands are outside the opponent's arms, he wants to slam his outside forearm across the arm of the blocker and pull across the top with a swim move. The offensive partner moves one way or the other. The defender shuffles down the line and executes an escape move. He rips or swims to the outside.

The next drill is called wrist-elbow-shoulder. I use this to practice the pass rush. The players face one another in a standing position. The players are off set, so one player's left shoulder matches up with the opponent's left shoulder. The offensive player ex-

tends his left arm toward the defender. The defender uses his left wrist to strike the offensive player in the wrist while turning his arm away from him. He takes his right hand and pushes the offensive player's elbow the same way. His left arm extends into the shoulder of the offensive man. It is a three-step move which is done rapidly. Use the left wrist to left wrist, the right hand to left elbow, and the left hand to left shoulder.

As soon as the defender's hand strikes the shoulder of the offensive man, the offensive man becomes the defender and does the same thing to the other player. This is done in rapid fire. One player executes the move followed by the other player doing the same thing. We off set to the right and do the same thing.

We have some everyday drills we use for pass rush. We always work on take-off. We use hoops to work on our lean. We play chase around the hoops. It teaches proper lean, so the rusher's speed can be maintained. Remember in the pass rush, speed kills.

Here are some general principals of the pass rush. There are a number of things you can do to improve pass rush. The first thing is to move up on the ball. Have a teaching progression breakdown for your skills. Have a slogan to get your players to focus. An example would be "Pass rush is an attitude." Use motivational charts and videos to improve your player's attitude about themselves.

There are goals in the pass-rush game. First and foremost, we want to sack the quarterback. If we can't get to the quarterback, we want to throw the quarterback off his rhythm. We want to hurry him and knock him down whenever we can. If you can't get to the quarterback, get in the throwing lanes and get your hands up. If you are supposed to contain in your pass rush, make sure you don't give it up because you think you have a chance to get to the quarterback.

There is a mental aspect to the pass rush. The defensive lineman has to know the drop and distance the quarterback is going to take. Once we know the drop, we can take the proper angle to get to the quarterback. The defensive lineman has to know his opponent. We want to know if he is a quick setter, a deep setter, or a weak pass protector. In the pass rush, the operative phrase is "The best man wins."

The most important element in the pass rush is the "get-off." The defensive lineman has to close the distance between himself and the blocker as quickly as possible. We do that by seeing the movement of the ball. We want to take as big of steps as possible. We clasp the offensive lineman's hands and get on his face as quick as we can. Never allow the offensive blocker to get his feet set.

In our pass rushing techniques, we want to gain ground on the first step. If we use the stab and grab, we stab with the inside arm across the arms of the offensive blocker. With the outside hand, we grab the offensive blocker's outside hand at its weakest point. Make sure to run with your knees for faster and more powerful movement. Turn the shoulders of the offensive blocker as the defender moves upfield. If you have to bull rush, go over the lineman.

We also use a grab and shuffle. You have to find the target area first. Close down quickly and take off deeper. Grab the back of the blocker with your outside arm. Turn your shoulders and hips parallel to the blocker. Shuffle your feet twice, keeping your arm lowered out. As the original move, use the rip-and-counter with the swim or torque.

In the rip-pick, start out with a slap with your outside arm. After the slap, set the rip with your inside arm. Lift with your rip arm. If you feel the blocker start to lean, continue to lift the blocker. Make sure to point your toe toward the quarterback. You pick with your outside arm. If the rip is set deep, grab the back of the blocker.

We use the arm bar for inside and outside rushers. On this move, we want the blocker to think we are going to speed rush up the field. We match our inside hand to the inside hand of the blocker. Grab the inside hand of the offensive blocker and swim move to the inside with your outside arm. We don't use this move for a containment rusher.

The dent rush is used by outside rushers only. We get into a wider alignment. It is essential in this rush move to get a good take-off. We sprint upfield using a big first step. Don't make contact with the offensive lineman if you can help it. This is where the hoop drill pays off. We have to lean in on the quarterback, so we don't run past the quarterback.

The rip and spin is a good inside-counter move. You set up the move by making it look the same as the rip. Never get your inside hip away from the blocker. Don't lean and go more upfield on the charge. Set your rip arm and spin back inside. Grab the lower back of the offensive lineman when spinning. Make sure you always gain distance on the spinning move. The most common mistakes made in this move are spinning in place, stutter stepping, and telegraphing the move.

Suit your escape moves to the ability of the offensive linemen. Use a stab-and-grab with smaller offensive linemen. Use the power swim against bigger, but shorter, offensive linemen. Use speed against slow linemen and strength against weak ones.

When you pass rush, have a plan of what you are going to do if the initial move is stopped by the offensive lineman. Make your counter moves quick and natural. Don't stutter step in your pass rush. Don't do any counter move that will stop the momentum of the defensive lineman.

When rushing the passer, the defensive lineman must have a target area. He has to know where he is going to end up. If his target area is seven-yards deep, he wants to get there as quickly as he can. He wants to attack the back shoulder of the quarterback. That means for the quarterback to escape, he must step up into the pocket.

In the defensive line, we want the ball. We want to create turnovers. We want to tackle, strip, and recover the ball. In our tackling progression, we want to eye the ball. Make sure you are close enough to step on the ball carrier's feet. Double upper cut with both forearms making sure to keep your elbows in. On contact, we want to roll the hips and grab cloth driving through the tackle.

We want to strip the ball if possible. If the ball carrier is carrying the ball on the same side as the tackler, we want to tomahawk the ball. That is a hard viscous club with the outside arm. The inside arm should be on the ball carrier to secure the tackle.

If the ball carrier has the ball to the side away from the tackler, we want to punch the ball from underneath. Make sure to secure the tackle with the inside arm and punch the ball with the outside hand.

If the ball comes loose and is rolling on the ground toward our opponent's goal line, we want to recover the fumble by cradling the ball. If the ball is rolling toward our goal line, scoop the ball.

Tackling is the most important skill a defensive man can have. We use all kinds of tackling drills. We use a drill we simply call sideline tackle. The ball carrier and tackler are three yards apart. It is a confined area with two cones at the end of the drill. The ball carrier is allowed one move on the defensive man. After that, he must run straight for one of those cones. The defender executes a sideline tackle.

We simulate the strip by using a one-on-one trail drill. We put the defender in a trail position behind the ball carrier. He can tomahawk or punch the ball depending which hand the ball is in.

We also use a two-on-one strip drill. The first man secures the tackle, while the second man goes for the strip. The strip man comes from the same side the as the ball carrier.

We run fumble drills with our strip drill. We have a two-on-one cradle drill and a three-on-one scoop drill. In the scoop drill, the tomahawk or the punch may be used. Remember we want to cradle the ball towards the opposite goal line and scoop toward our goal line.

The most important aspect of tackling is to make sure you don't have any injuries in practice. Use a port-a-pit or some kind of cushion to practice tackling. That helps to prevent injuries from ground impact.

To play in the defensive line, a player must learn to deliver a blow. In this regard, we have five essentials to remember: stance, elbows, base and leverages, toughness, and escape.

In our stance, we want to get as tight to the ball as possible. We want the hand down and the leg back to the side that covers the offensive lineman. Our alignment is usually some kind of shade technique, but it can vary with movement. We key the ball if we are close to the ball. If we can't see the ball, we key the opponent's helmet, watching a small focal point.

The defender's specific responsibility depends on the defense we are running. But, we are always in an attack mode. The thing you want to remember when you are striking the blow is we never want to roll our hips. If you do that, you have extended your power angles.

When we try to create separation, we never want to get on the corner of a block. There are two types of escape. To the playside, we want to keep our helmet outside and cross face if we can. We only rip if the play is run inside. It is hard to rip-and-run in a pursuit type of play. We cross face usually to a high cut-off block. We want to keep the blocker locked out to secure our responsibility. Again, we never want to get on the corner of a block because the offensive lineman can turn us. Drop set and swim across blocks, never rip across.

I've got more, but I'm out of time. If I can do anything to help you, don't hesitate to call us at Western Kentucky. Once again, thanks.

THE EIGHT-MAN FRONT DEFENSE

University of Kentucky

Men, it is my pleasure to be here. I appreciate you guys for hanging around. It has been a long day for everybody. I have heard a lot of great speakers today. I feel honored to just be on the same program.

My background has been mostly Oklahoma and Texas. All of my coaching career has been in Texas. I coached fifteen years in high school and nineteen years in college. I was a high school head coach for ten years. I learned more in high school than I ever did in college. The defense we are going to run at the University of Kentucky, I started running in high school in 1975.

We visited a lot of places back in the early 70's. We visited the University of Maryland, which is where we started with our concept of an eight-man front. Bobby Ross was the head coach then. In their playbook, the defensive tackles were listed as guards, defensive ends were tackles, and outside linebackers were ends. The two linebackers were the center and the fullback. The corners were halfbacks, and the safety was a quarterback. Those guys knew what they were doing, because they had been doing it for a long time.

We went to the University of Georgia and talked to Eric Russell. He had run the split-six in the South-eastern Conference for years and years. We took a lot of ideas from him.

From there, we went to the University of Texas. They were the first school to run a combination man-to-man coverage in the secondary. We took some of those principles and started to build the defense we wanted to run.

We visited with Buddy Ryan when he was with the Eagles and Cardinals, and got some ideas about pressure defense and stopping the run. We looked at his blitzing package. We were trying to make our minds up about what kind of defense we were going to run. We wanted something to hang our hat on.

You can turn your TV on and watch any football game. Teams like Nebraska run a man-free scheme with inverted safeties and do a heck of a job. Oklahoma ran mostly zone with a quarter scheme. They know exactly what they are doing. The national championship game was as good a game as you will see defensively. They didn't blitz, but maybe two times. Then you look at Joe Lee Dunn at Mississippi State. They blitz every snap. The point is that you can be successful a lot of different ways.

I read Bill Parcells' book all the time. I think it is the best football book that has ever been written. It is called "*Finding a Way To Win.*" You should get a copy. It is a damn good book. I go back and reinforce what I think by just reading that book.

He says that defensive philosophy is like any other philosophy. You have to have four points to judge what you are doing. The first point involves the fact that it has to be sound. What we are talking about being sound against everything you see. Your defense has to be based on sound principles. The second point is it better reflect the personality of your head coach. That is for all of your defensive coordinators. The first time you blitz about eight people on 3rd-and-long, and they don't get to the quarterback, and they complete a pass for a score, your head coach has to be on your side. He has to believe in what you are doing. You don't want him to think you are crazy. Your defense better be sound and reflect your head coach's feelings.

Your defense must be communicated and talked about with every member of your staff. They have to be in agreement with what you are trying to accomplish. We play a lot of man-to-man coverage. You better talk about that with your staff, because every once in a while the corner is going to get beat. If he gets beat and gives up a big play, we don't need a bunch of people pointing a finger at the corner. That is the kind of defense we are going to play. Sometimes you get beat. Everybody needs to know that.

The last point is the defense has to stay in place long enough to be successful. You can't cave in just because you have a bump in the road. All the good coaches have something in common. They all believe in themselves, and they all have a concept of how they think the game should be played. Joe Lee Dunn has a concept of how the game should be played. He challenges receivers and puts pressure on the quarterbacks. He understands that. They all have a concept of how the game should be played, and they don't cave in to pressure. They don't change the defense when they hit the first bump in the road.

You have to find out what you have to defend in your conference. I have already broken down Kentucky's games from last year. I wanted to know what we were going to have to defend against the people we will be playing this year. We are still seeing a two-back set about fifty percent of the time. We see the I formation, king set, queen set, and split backs. A king set is the fullback set in the strong halfback position. The queen set is the fullback set in the weak halfback position. We see three wide outs and one tight end about twenty-five percent of the time. We see the spread formation with no tight end about twenty percent of the time.

The ace set, which is a one-back set with two tight ends and two wide outs, we see about five percent of the time. That is about what we saw in the Big Twelve. We saw more ace sets in the Big Twelve than we do here. But, the rest of it is about the same. That is the trend. That is the way everything is going.

I take every two-back formation, and find out how many times that team was in the I formation. I don't want to guess at it. I want to know exactly how many time it was in the I formation. I need to know what plays they run from each set they get into. I want to know what the offensive coordinator is looking at. I want to know why he thinks he can run that play against us. If you don't find that out, I don't know where to tell you to start. That tells you what the offense is seeing when you line up. That is the first thing we try to do.

When people line up in an I formation, they run the isolation play into B-gap weak and A-gap strong. They run the off tackle power play toward the tight end. They run the toss sweep to the tight end and the isolation pass weak. That is what they run from this set ninety percent of the time. When a team comes out in an I formation, those are the plays we are going to defend. We are going to spend time defending those plays. We are not going to be screwing around doing other things. I want the players to know that. I can't play. I'm up in the press box, so it doesn't matter what I know.

I FORMATION PLAYS

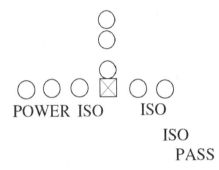

If the offense moves the fullback out of the I and into the halfback position to the tight end's side, their play selection changes. We call that set a king set. They can't run the isolation play weak. They can run a little bit of counter weak. Maybe three or four snaps are all I'm talking about. I keep a notebook each year on teams. I have done that for ten years. From this set, we get the stretch play, the outside zone, and the toss sweep. I know that about eighty percent of the time, the ball is going over the guard.

KING SET PLAYS

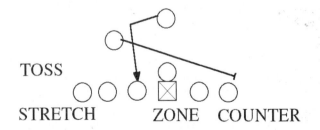

If they go the other way with the fullback, we call that a queen set. What can they do? They can't run the toss sweep to the tight end, because there is no one to block. They can't run the isolation play to the strongside. They could run it weak, but it is not a good play. They are going to run a ton of the inside zone play. You could get a counter play to the tight end.

QUEEN SET PLAYS

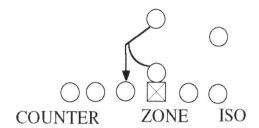

COUNTER   ZONE   ISO

I was listening to Gary Nord of UTEP talking about the offense getting a pre-snap read. The defense gets a better pre-snap read than the offense does. Every time they line up, they tell the defense something.

When the offense splits the backs, other than a draw every once and a while, they are going to throw the ball. Whatever we have called, if a team comes out in split backs and a shotgun, we are going to get in something to defend the pass. All we are trying to do is line up in the best way possible for every way the offense comes out and lines up. All you have to do is look at the formation and backfield sets. Talk to your kids about what can be run from each set, and you can pretty well get it done. It is easy and simple.

If the offense goes to a one-back set, and I'm talking about the run, all I want to know is where the other back is. If he is set in the wide slot to the split end, it is no different than the queen set. If I ask the linebacker what plays the offense runs out of the queen set, he will tell me inside zone and counter.

If the other back is set the other way in a flanked position outside the tight end, it is nothing more than a king set. We defend strong and weak one-back sets. It does matter if they have a spread, two tight ends, three wide receivers, or four wide outs. We try to be as simple as we can and defend what the offense can do from each formation.

At the end of the year, we are going to take every formation, and chart it. That tells us what people think they can do against us.

Let's talk about our defense. We'll talk about the run from the two-back set and go from there. All the coaches that are working on the defensive staff at

Kentucky believe in what we are doing. That is ninety percent of it. I believe in self confidence. I believe you can sell confidence to your coaches and kids. If your kids don't think they are going to be successful, they won't be. If you have one coach that doesn't think the defense will work, it won't. You have to believe in what you are doing and don't cave in to the pressure.

In this day and time, there are radio talk shows with experts who have all the answers. They can tell you what you need to do at Kentucky. You have a grocery store guy calling in and telling you how to get things done. You can't listen to any of that stuff. It is easy for me, because I don't read the paper, and I don't listen to the radio. But, I know it's out there, and you can't cave in to it.

We are an even-man front. We normally play a 3-technique and a 2-technique with our two tackles. We play both of the them head up sometimes. We want the biggest, fastest tackles we can get. We have got some pretty good ones at Kentucky. Those two freshmen that played last year are going to be excellent players. We are going to attack the line of scrimmage with those guys. But, we are not going to be out on the edge completely out of control. We are going to attack the line of scrimmage and try to read what is going on, rather than blindly charge up field.

Our number one goal is to stop the run. I know there are a lot of people throwing the football, but I promise you this. If you can't stop the run, you're not going to beat anyone. You can give up a few passes, but if they run up and down the field, you are in trouble. There is no worse feeling than to sit in the press box and know there is nothing you can do to stop the run.

I'll give you two examples. When Ricky Williams was a junior, Texas came out to Lubbock, and we couldn't stop him or the other running back. They beat us to death. They just ran up and down the field. They had a good quarterback and two good receivers. We tried to play them in an in-between defense, where we played pass and run. It was no good. The next year we went back to what we had always done. We were going to stop the run, and if they threw for two thousand yards, so be it. Ricky Williams was a senior. He rushed for sixty-nine yards on 35 carries and we beat them 24-7. They threw for 390 yards, and the game wasn't even close. They moved the ball all over the field, but they couldn't run it when they had to. If you can stop the run, you have a chance to win.

The defensive ends will be in 7-techniques. To the split-end side, we will play a ghost 7-technique, where we align in a 7-technique as if there were a tight end to that side. Toward the tight end, we will be in an inside-shoulder alignment on the tight end. We have pretty good ends at Kentucky. The guys I've seen can play. At Tech, we had little bitty ends. But they could run. I would like to have great big fast guys. But if I can't get those big fast guys, I'll take a little fast guy. I don't want a bunch of big slow guys.

We hope the guy on the tight end can control him and cause some problems in the running game. We hope we can get that done at Kentucky. We like Dennis Johnson and some of the other kids. They have got some size and athletic ability.

We play three safeties. All of them are defensive back-type guys. They have to be able to run and tackle. They don't have to be huge, but they have to be able to cover and run. They play like a double monster and free safety. I hear on TV that if your safety is your leading tackler, you are not very good. That is not the case with us. Our safeties will be in on a ton of plays, because that is where we are going to push the ball. The weakside guy has to be a better cover guy. He is almost like a third corner. We had a guy in 1994-95 named Marcus Coleman, who played this position for us. He is now the starting corner for the New York Jets. He is 6-3 and 210 pounds. He could run, cover, and tackle.

We play two linebackers. We would like them to be big and fast. We have some size at Kentucky. But, we are going to play the best guys we have. Speed is the number one thing we consider in a linebacker. We are hunting for linebackers that have intelligence. They must understand football. The Mike linebacker must understand the game.

We play two corners. Our corner guys are cover guys. They are guys that can run. They have to jump and have a good vertical leap. They have to be competitive as heck. We don't play them on the outside all the time man-to-man by themselves. We try to give them some help, but they have to know where their help is. We are very little zero coverage, which

is straight lock-up man. It is generally outside leverage with inside help. They always have some help, but they have to know where it is.

BASE DEFENSE

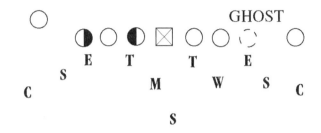

Let me get into what we do against the run. If the offense comes out in an I formation, our defense knows what they can run. Our linebackers' depth is about five yards. They are playing downhill from there. Our linebackers do not shuffle, they are attacking the line of scrimmage going downhill. The corners have a number of ways they align. They will press the receivers, play off them, play catch with them, and cushion them. We don't want them to line up the same way twice. If we are on the line pressing the receiver, we will bail out, open our hips, and get help from the inside. We play our base defense about forty percent of the time. We are going to pass rush with five guys about thirty-five to forty percent of the time. We rush six guys about ten percent of the time. We align in our nickel package the rest of the time. We don't do very much, because we want to make sure that what we do, we understand.

When the offense breaks the huddle and lines up in an I formation, all the quarterback is looking for is the number of defenders on each side of the ball. When he looks to his split end's side, he sees a defensive tackle and end, a Will linebacker, and a safety about six yards deep. They have a guard, tackle, and fullback. It doesn't take a rocket scientist to figure out we have one more defensive player than they have blockers. The isolation weak is a play that they are not going to run because they are outnumbered. The first year at Texas Tech when we did this, the offense ran the ball eighty-one times toward the tight end and none toward the split end. Now, the defense knows where the ball is going. That means you are in a half line drill. The thing we have to do is stop the isolation, power, and toss, to the tight-end side.

BASE DEFENSE VS I FORMATION

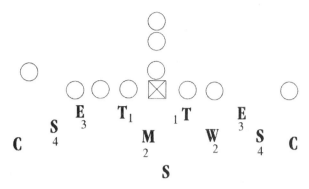

I learned more from Zack Thomas, when he played for us, than he learned from me. He is playing for Miami now. He understood formation football. He told me when the offense came out in an I formation, he thought he should move over toward the tight end. He knew if they were going to run to the tight-end side, that is where he should be. He moved over the offensive tackle to the tight-end side. He had outside leverage on the fullback. The other linebacker moved over also to avoid the center's block. We had our tackles in the 3-and-1 techniques. The ends were in 7-techniques. Our Mike linebacker was in an outside stack on the 3-technique tackle and the Will linebacker was head up the center.

BASE DEFENSE/LINEBACKER MOVED

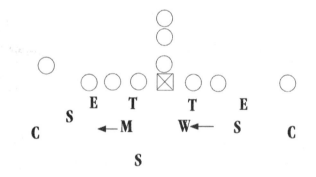

When we moved our linebackers over, the offense started to go back to the split-end side with the isolation play. They thought they could double team the 1-technique and chip up on the Will linebacker. They would split their tackle wide and cut the center-guard split down. When we saw that, we moved our tackle to a head-up position on the guard. That allowed us to get inside leverage on the fullback by the Will linebacker and bounce the ball to the safety who is unblocked. The Mike linebacker runs right through the center. The center is combo blocking with his left

guard, and the Mike linebacker is filling unblocked for the cut-back run. That worked good for us. We could over shift our linebacker and still cover to the split-end side. If we were to ever get hurt on the backside, we would tell the linebacker to move back.

BASE DEFENSE/G-ADJUSTMENT WEAK

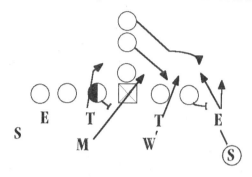

If the offense gets into the king formation and runs the toss sweep, they will block down and pull the guard. The pulling guard would go after our strong safety. We used to run hard at the pulling guard and take him out. The guard would kick out the safety, and the back would dip in and get right back out to the outside. We didn't like the way the play worked. Instead of attacking the kick-out blocker, we simply stay on the line of scrimmage and contain the football. We squeeze the play, but never get upfield where we can be kicked out. We want the 7-technique end to whip the tight end. He holds his C-gap until the ball crosses his face. When the ball crosses his face, he either slips inside or fights across the face of the tight end's block, depending on how good a player he is.

The Mike linebacker is coming downhill through the C-gap. He is taking on anybody that is blocking. He is taking on the pulling lineman or the fullback on an inside-out path. The Will linebacker is running like crazy right through the pulling guard's hole. We don't give up many yards on these types of plays.

BASE DEFENSE/POWER OR TOSS SWEEP

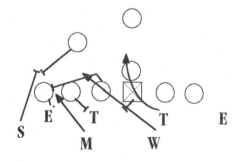

We have seen teams run a counter from this set to the two-man side. I heard the guy from Ohio State talk awhile ago, and he said they keyed the back and picked up secondary linemen pulls. We do the same thing we just call it differently.

We got this adjustment from Zack Thomas too. He was a smart kid. He could see stuff faster than anyone I've ever seen. Everybody would be running right, and he would be running left. But, he was right. The ball was going left. I asked him one day what he saw to get on a play so quickly. He told me the isolation, toss, and counter looked different. I asked him to explain that to me.

He said an isolation looks like an isolation, a toss looks like a toss, and a counter looks like a counter. When a team runs a counter, I play the counter. How can the offense make the isolation, toss, and counter look the same? They can't. That is like a fat girl and a skinny girl. How can you make them look alike? You can't.

We drill this in a read drill. I set up the cones at four different spots. The cones represent strong B and C-gaps and weak A and B-gaps. I put one back in the drill and tell the linebackers the formation. They know where the imaginary back is supposed to be. The Mike linebacker is always on the strongside. We drill all the plays using one back, and letting the linebacker run their patterns to the line of scrimmage. If they run the power to the Mike linebacker, he is leveraging blockers. The Will linebacker is inside the guard. If they double your 3-technique tackle and don't protect against the Will linebacker running through the B-gap, he goes through. If they do protect the run through, he works over top of the double team. If the back takes his counter steps, the linebacker reads it right away, and pursues toward the counter play.

KEY DRILL

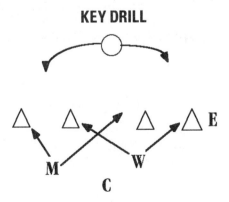

In addition to keying the back, they are getting reinforcement of plays that can be run from certain sets. If I change the set, their set of plays change. If I say "queen." They know they are going to play inside zone, counter, and stretch. We do this drill over and over and over. I want them to play fast. The faster we are, the better off we will be.

We tell our defensive linemen, we are not going to allow the offensive to stay on a double team. That linebacker is coming right now. The offense on the stretch play will send the tackle and tight end on a combo block for the 7-technique end. We tell our Mike linebacker if there is no movement by the end, he gets downhill into the gap right now. He can't let that tight end come off the block on the 7-technique and block him. He attacks the C-gap and makes the tight end come off before the tackle can get into his block on the 7-technique. The 7-technique end can whip the block of the tackle on his own. The quicker we can see those plays, the better off we are. When people ask us what we key, I say we play plays.

I really believe in recognition, execution, and repetition. If you want to execute well, get a lot of repetitions. Find out what the offense is going to do. Find out what you have to stop. Then, line up and run those plays over and over against your defense. We try to track how many plays we see during the week. If we are playing Tennessee, which runs the counter, I want to see that play fifty or sixty times in practice. Because when we see that play on Saturday, we better be getting after it. If you rep plays over and over and over, you will be able to defend that play.

I believe in great effort. Let me tell you how to get your players to play hard. Be simple, and they will play hard. If you confuse them, they will not play hard. Spike Dykes was the head coach at Texas Tech when I got there. He was a piece of work. When I first got to Texas Tech, we would have coaches meetings where everbody was taking notes. I thought they were really into what he was saying. They weren't taking note, they were writing down Spikeisms. He would say things like, "We've got to get better at whatever it is we are going to work on." We would have a recruiting meeting, and one of the coaches would say, "We've got this linebacker who is 6'-4", 220 pounds, and runs a 4.5 forty yard dash." Spike would say, "What's the matter with him? Is he a homosexual?"

Spike was the real deal. He was funny, he liked to kid around, and he liked to do a lot on defense. We had our rules, and also had Coach Dykes' rules. Whenever we started to get too many things in the defense, we would get Zack to go to Coach Dykes and ask him to put us back in base defense. That is all he liked to play. Most of the time, he would do it.

Effort is tied to simplicity. I really believe that. You can take the best player in the world and confuse him, and he won't play hard. He can't play hard because he is worried about making a mistake. That doesn't mean we don't do a bunch of stuff. But, we package it simple. If the players think the defense is complicated, and they have to think too much on the field, you are going down the wrong path.

Let me talk about two or three other things, and then we can open it up for questions. I'm going back to Bill Parcells' book. He said there are three ways to fail philosophy-wise. The first thing was to put a sorry product on the field. If your defense isn't any good, it will get your butt fired. The second thing is public perception. If the public perception is that you are sorry, you are going to get fired even though you may be doing a heck of a good job and winning. That is what happened to us at Baylor. You must have a decent relationship with the media. You will never win a war with the media.

The last way to fail is from division from within. That means your team is split on the direction you want to go. That is what I like about Coach Guy Morriss. The first day he got the job, we started talking about the off-season. That is where you build everything connected with your football team. That is where you build teamwork.

We have a Monday-night meeting during the season. We get together with our defensive football team, kickers, and snappers. On Sunday, when the coaches grade the film, we have a production sheet, where players are awarded points for accomplished tasks. The biggest statistic to stopping the run is a take-away.

We use our production chart in our Monday meeting. We get little candy treats for this meeting. What we are doing is recognizing guys who did some good things on Saturday. That is whether we win or lose.

We go through the entire roster off those productions sheets. If a guy had a sack, we gave him a little sack of candy. If a guy had a big hit, we gave him a Crunch bar. If someone recovered a fumble, we gave him a Payday. Don't think this doesn't mean something to your kids. It is important for them to be recognized.

People play the game because it is fun and because they want to be recognized. The reason I bring the kicker and snapper into this meeting is to let the defense know how important they are to the defense.

We use to meet Friday nights when I was at Baylor. During that meeting, we had a highlight film of the previous Saturday's game. That video stuff is great. You can put all your big hits and the great plays on one reel. We showed them the film, and they would go crazy. They loved them. It was a time to enjoy the game. We have a big hit of the week. We would get the shot from every angle we could film and play it over and over. We would select three guys and have a competition for the biggest hit. I would stand behind them, and the guys would cheer when I held my hand over his head. Whoever got the loudest cheer got a T-shirt. It had a picture of a dead cockroach on his back with his feet stuck up into the air. I am here to tell you they would kill for that T-shirt. Anything you can do for teamwork should be done.

Another thing we stress is accountability. If we play poor defensively next year, it will be one guy's fault, and that will be mine. Accountability starts at the top. If a kid messes up, it is because we didn't coach him enough. Spike was great about doing that. He would never point a finger at anyone. I believe I coach them, and they play like I coach them. If we don't play hard, it is my fault. I promise if you approach accountability like that, your kids will take that approach also. As soon as I talk to them that way, I have ten kids come up afterwards and tell me it wasn't my fault. If it starts at the top, it will work its way down through your team.

Coaching is hard. We are trying to get kids to play hard in our off-season. When I am in my drill, I'm trying to get my kids to bust their butts every time they go through that drill. If they don't, I'm on them. Then, I go talk to them. There is not a lot of difference between ninety and a hundred percent. We are trying to teach them to play full speed all the time. If you don't coach the same way on the fifth day as you did on the first day, they will quit working for you. It is hard for a coach to keep going with that intensity every day. On the 20th day of practice, when they jog through your drill, are you going to allow that or are you going to coach them like you did the first day?

The good coaches I've been around coach everyday and on every play. I recruit all over the country. I see a lot of players and a lot of programs. I see a lot of guys, that after a week, coaching becomes old. They don't demand what they did the first day. The first day your players will be fresh and ready to go. On the fifth day, it won't be like the first day, unless you make it that way. You get what you accept. I believe that more than anything.

One more thing, then I'm done. I believe in coaching. I don't think the best players always win. You heard Bobby Bowden this morning tell you he believed Florida State had better players than Oklahoma. The best players don't always win. The best teams win.

I think we have something to do with the way our kids play. That goes for effort and discipline. I believe that, and I believe in coaching. If you coach hard, you give your kids a chance. I've been around some guys that are never going to be satisfied. I believe you take the players you have, or you recruit and do something with them. In the NFL why is it that the same coaches win all the time? Why is it that Bill Parcells wins everywhere he goes? I don't believe that the water makes a team better. It is the coaching that does the trick. You take what you've got, coach them, and get better.

Men, I know I've rambled around, but I appreciate being asked to speak here. It has been an honor for me. You are always welcome at our place. I promise you, everything we are doing is open to you. We have no secrets. What we do on defense is very simple. It will work in high school, and it will work in college. If I was coaching in the pro league, it would work up there too. I believe in what we are doing.

If you can, come see us. I appreciate it. Thank you.

BUILDING CHAMPIONS FOR LIFE

Lutheran High School, California

It is a real pleasure to be in Hawaii. It is interesting, the last clinic I spoke at was in Southern California, only an hour's drive from our campus. None of our staff accompanied me. But, when they found out I was going 3000 miles to Hawaii to speak, they were so concerned about me, four of them volunteered to come along to support me. That's the type of staff unity we have.

Seriously, it isn't just a pleasure to be here, it's an honor. On the West Coast, we are familiar with how outstanding Hawaii football is because we see so many great players from the islands peppering so many Division I rosters, particularly in the PAC 10.

Eight years ago, when our staff took over at Orange Lutheran High School, we had 45 kids in our entire program and averaged maybe 150 fans per game, that is, when all the distant relatives showed up. Today, we have about 130 boys participating, and our average home attendance is around 3500. Half of our games are against schools of similar size (around 750) and the other half are two to four times our size. I just want to share with you some of the things that helped us grow and affect lives in a positive way.

Every successful organization has a significant mission and purpose. For us, "our mission is to build champions for life – to forge the foundation that will yield a lifetime of success for our young men." In order to fulfill our mission, we first have to a have clear understanding of what success is. Society says scoreboards determine successful coaches and players, or that it can be found in the accumulation worldly possessions and/or the attainment of fame and power. We think there are some flaws with these commonly held perceptions.

First, we can never win enough or acquire enough to satisfy ourselves or our fans. Second, we are left with a gnawing emptiness when our pursuits are lim-ited to short-term, self-centered pursuits. Third, we know scoreboards don't always tell the whole story. Abraham Lincoln's election record was 2-8, hardly Hall of Fame numbers, and he also suffered two business failures and a nervous breakdown. Yet, he is revered as our country's greatest president. Or as Coach Tom Osborne put it in athletic terms, "Even though you might have finished 3-8 last year, if your players grew significantly under your leadership then you were successful." We believe in an alternative view of success, defining success as "giving and developing our best everyday." We teach our kids to never measure success in comparison to someone else, but rather in John Wooden terms: "Success is peace of mind, which is the direct result of knowing you did your very best to become the best you are capable of becoming." The number one cause of kids having low self-esteem or a poor self-image is comparing themselves to others. We do our best to get them off that destructive path of thinking and shift them toward an understanding of coming to know their particular purpose in life or on a team, growing to reach their potential while developing an unselfish outlook which sows seeds to benefit others.

We instruct our players to focus on the things they have control over, especially in the realm of attitude and effort, and we assure them that they will only be held accountable for those areas. We rarely throughout the course of any season discuss winning per say, instead we concentrate on daily maximum improvement.

We take a process-oriented approach in contrast to thinking that failure or success is an event or person. Winning becomes a by-product of traveling the success road, but it is not one of our core objectives. We believe that seasonal awards and recognition mean little if we do not establish a foundation for our players that enables them to become men who are great contributors to their families and society. Each season our staff views the collection of young men in our care as men who will one day build the "city set on the hill."

We have found however, that it is not enough to teach the players what our mission is and what success really is. We need to educate groups critically linked to our program and players. The first of these groups is our school's teachers, staff, and administrators. We make sure they know the Mission and Objectives of our program go far beyond winning football games. We support our teachers 100 percent, and never ask them for favors with regard to players. Our teachers, in general, enjoy having football kids in class because they know unacceptable player behavior or effort will be dealt with swiftly and firmly. Our permanent football theme, "champions for life," has become the school's theme as well and is printed on our school's application materials.

The second and more difficult group to educate is, of course, the parents. We generally have three parent meetings a year, and a good portion of each is set aside to explain our program and how they can effectively support and partner with us to help their son achieve maximum growth and success. We are blunt with them about making playing-time issues an off-limits area of discussion. We explain to them that we don't have the luxury of making decisions solely based on an individual, that every choice we make is made with regard to the entire team's welfare.

Once parents understand that their son's success is not based on playing time or statistics and that success, then, is not a "zero sum game" that can only be experienced by a select few, they can begin to let go of their own ego's interference with their son's success journey. Ego, by the way, we tell them is an acronym for edging god out. When parents begin to evaluate their son's contributions on factors he has control over, namely attitude and effort, the parents are also liberated from a destructive form of thinking.

We also talk to our parents about how to deal with their kids' complaints regarding playing time or how demanding or unfair the coaches are. We tell them to ask their son if he really is making the best, most unselfish effort he can. Of course, 99.9 percent of the time, an honest answer is "no," and the parent is able to steer their son back to a healthier outlook and approach by encouraging him to do everything he can to improve his attitude or effort. If the player remains mired in a funk, we tell our parents to encourage their son to talk to us about ways he can improve or increase his playing time opportunities.

Also, we candidly admonish our parents that the minute they engage at all with their son in bashing a coach or other players, they are setting their own son up for failure. Because his effort level will inevitably decrease due to his perception of "unfairness," a downward spiral for him will inevitably ensue.

The third group that it is critical to educate and share with is the coaches within your own staff, particularly new additions. We want coaches who are teachers at heart and who have a passion for helping people. Head coaches need to do everything they can to equip assistant coaches by helping them to grow, develop and find success. A Stanford study on success found that 92 percent of the reason a person experienced success was attitude, compared to only eight percent who achieved success on innate ability. Creating staff unity with that common sense of shared purpose makes it possible to achieve great dreams.

To fulfill our mission statement, we are going to relentlessly pursue three core objectives. The first is to strengthen their faith. Active, living faith is believing in and trusting in something greater than ourselves that gives us hope, purpose, and a reason for living. Faith is the assurance of things hoped for, the belief in things not yet seen. As coaches, we have a choice in dealing with the issue of faith. As Tom Osborne says, "we as coaches either approve of spiritual growth or disapprove of it. We believe either you are here to serve and honor God, or you are here to serve and honor yourself." Grant Teaff's advice for coaches includes believing in God and teaching players that next to love, believing is the most powerful force in the world. Woody Hayes' ten virtues of a good leader includes never underestimating the spiritual power of people. At the 1997 AFCA Convention, Zig Ziglar shared a nationwide study that noted the following if people attend church regularly: suicide, crime, drug and alcohol abuse rates are reduced; people are happier and healthier; and that it helps poor and inner-city youth escape poverty.

There is a great true story of the transformation of a young boy named Ben Hooper who grew up in a rural area of Tennessee back in a time when there was a stigma attached to children born out of wedlock. Ben grew up with his mom being shunned and ostracized by the community because he was fatherless. One day, Ben heard about a new young minister in town who was preaching a powerful, positive message. Feeling lonely and hopeless, Ben began attending services sitting in the back quietly. He was careful to always leave just before the sermon was over so that no one would notice him and condemn him. One Sunday, Ben was so enraptured by the sermon that he forgot to make his early exit and was instead caught up in with the people leaving. He began to feel the uneasy stares of many people who surely thought he wasn't worthy to be in church. His anxiety reached a climax when he heard the minister's voice boom out, "boy!" He stopped dead in his tracks as the church came to a quiet standstill as the young preacher walked up to him. "Whose boy are you?" the preacher asked. Ben stood motionless as a big smile came over the minister's face who continued: "I know whose boy you are. The resemblance is remarkable. You, son are a child of God. Since you are the son of the King, go out in this world and claim your inheritance." That was the day, Ben Hooper recalled, that he was elected and re-elected Governor of Tennessee.

For coaches who find themselves in settings where there are restrictions on sharing faith, we can remember the words of St. Francis of Assisi, "preach the gospel at all times, if necessary use words." The way we live our lives and model for our players is always the most powerful statement we can ever make.

Our second core objective is to develop *leadership through character*. We believe athletics and football do not teach character and leadership, coaches do. We must have a plan for inculcating character-based leadership. We see leadership as a strategic process of moving a group of people in a direction that is in their best self-interest. It's being able to influence others to their maximum performance. It's a powerful, positive presence that creates improvement in people's lives. And it is the ability to take people where they can't take themselves. When Dennis

Franchione was introduced as Alabama's new coach he said: "Our job as coaches is to take young people where they cannot take themselves academically, athletically, socially, and maybe even spiritually for that matter."

But more important than any definition of leadership is what lies at the heart of effective leadership. Bill McCartney said it best and most succinctly: "The foundation of leadership is concern for others." The old saying is true, people do really want to know how much you care before they care about how much you know. John Maxwell, an outstanding authority on leadership, says effective leaders encourage and lead by doing three things: 1) valuing people, 2) praising effort, and 3) rewarding performance. Great leaders are "people-first" leaders. Eddie Robinson put it this way: "I love the game of football, but I love the people who play the game more than I love football."

After defining leadership and understanding what lies at its center, our next step is to instill an uncompromising work ethic in our program. In his book, *Success Is A Choice*, Rick Pitino discusses and explains how the right to success is captured through a relentless work ethic that creates the mindset of deserving victory. In other words, hard work is the basic building block of every kind of achievement. When the investment is great, the will to succeed is palpable.

Vince Lombardi said: "We are going to work so hard that we will never surrender." Another quote we believe in is attributed to Bud Wilkinson, "The will to prepare is more important than the will to win." Every coach I've ever met or heard always talks about how badly they want to win. To us that is virtually meaningless. Every coach of course wants to win. What separates coaches and teams is that willingness and desire to prepare, to have the thorough attention to detail which produces excellence.

Next, we identify the key characteristics of character-based leadership. We always talk about the first and most important trait being to lead by example. The English philosopher John Locke said: "I have always thought the actions of men the best interpreters of their thoughts." The next characteristic we talk about is integrity. Integrity is honesty plus doing what is right when no one is watching. I heard a

Texas high school coach, Dennis Parker, give a great illustration of this when he walked into his weight room one day and gathered around him three or four kids who had a reputation for dogging it whenever a coach wasn't around. He handed each of them a wallet size picture of himself and told them to carry it with them wherever they went. When the players looked at him puzzled, he told them that since the only times they seemed to work their best was when a coach was watching, he wanted them to act knowing he was always watching. Finally, Bo Schembechler states that honesty is the most important attribute of a coach.

We also emphasize humility, teaching players the word itself is derived from a word which means "to harness power". Another key characteristic is the appetite for learning and improvement. Bill Snyder of Kansas State said their staff's number one goal is to improve. We strongly embrace this concept as well. The Japanese call it "kaizen", the process of continuous improvement. We also see it as the third most important attribute of a quality staff; the first being a passionate shared commitment to and belief in the program's mission and objectives, and the second being loyalty. Lou Holtz says, "the biggest room in the world is room for improvement....Morale improves when players and coaches improve." Having a passion to "learn as though you are going to live forever" is vital according to leadership expert Kent Schlichtemeier.

Teaching players to make and keep commitments is fundamental to their long-term welfare. British Prime Minister Benjamin Disraeli believed that the secret of success is constancy of purpose. Commitments preclude giving ourselves an 'out'. Commitment demands that we "burn our ships," as the Spanish conquistador Cortez did so that his men would be completely focused and highly motivated. Pat Riley put it bluntly in his book *The Winner Within*: "There are only two options with regard to commitment to the team and what it stands for; you are either in or out. There's no such thing as life in between." Lastly, we believe teaching our players to be faithfully consistent to their commitments is fundamental to them becoming the men that God intends for them to be.

Discipline and unselfishness are also core values we want players to embrace. As Joe Paterno says, discipline creates pride and pride creates morale. We instruct our parents and our kids that discipline (which comes from the word disciple) is carried out to help kids, not hurt them. To achieve long-term gains for a player, sometimes short-term pain will be administered. We want them to understand being disciplined and unselfish creates power; in other words, when people work for a common cause, their unity multiplies their strength.

Zig Ziglar tells us that you can get everything in life you want if you help enough others get what they want. This is a way of life like the Golden Rule, not a self-centered tactic. We believe then in the concept of servant-leadership based on the best role model history has ever produced, Jesus Himself. Throughout the ages, kings sent people out to die for them. Jesus was the King who went out and died for His people. One of the best cures for kids with low self-esteem is to learn to go out and do things for others. Their sense of self-worth rises as they discover they are needed and appreciated.

The behavior of geese also gives us insight into the power of unselfish teamwork. Research shows that when geese fly in a "V" formation as each bird flaps its wings, it creates an uplift for others, which adds at least 70 percent to their flying range in contrast to if they were to fly alone. Whenever a goose falls out of formation, it suddenly feels the drag and resistance of trying to go it alone. It quickly gets back into formation to take advantage of the bird in front of it.

We also emphasize the power of persistence and perseverance, and the importance of responding to setbacks or failures in a positive way. According to John Maxwell, the difference between average people and achievers is their perception of, and response to, failure. That is also where persistence comes in, understanding that most people who fail are not actually defeated, they simply give in. Perseverance and proper response to failure demand that we be responsible and accountable as coaches and players.

Sam Rutigliano said it this way, "A man can make mistakes but he isn't a failure until he starts blaming someone else. There is one statistic we are proud of related to our won-loss record in eight years at Orange

Lutheran. It is not that we have won about 80 percent of our games, because a lot of teams have sound winning percentages. It is that we have never lost two games in a row. We believe that is due to two factors. First, we haven't succumbed to the natural human tendency to lash out at other coaches or players. Second, we've pulled together with great resolution the following week to see how much we can improve. As coaches, we believe since we are responsible for the design and implementation of our program and practices, and since we determine the game strategy and play calling, it is just plain wrong for us to hang a loss on the players. On the other hand, we absolutely expect and demand they give the maximum effort with the best possible attitude, and we will accept nothing less."

With regard to skills and strategies of effective leaders, it is critical to create and communicate your vision. When Gary Barnett took over at Northwestern, he stated "We're going to take the Purple to Pasadena." Setting high expectations is positive because they are contagious and people tend to perform to the expectation level they have for themselves. While we believe in high expectations, we don't believe in a multiplicity of rules. As Mike Krzyzewski says, too many rules get in the way of leadership. In other words, leaders who have a lot of rules often do so to avoid having to make difficult judgments and decisions. Norman Schwarzkopf puts it this way, everyone already knows the right thing to do, the hard part is doing it.

We have only one expectation for the players in our program: be a champion every day. We teach them that this applies to the five major areas of their lives. Consequently being a champion every day means: growing spiritually; enriching their families by being kind, considerate, helpful, and communicating well; and enjoying their social lives (this factor entails two things which we have taken directly from Kansas State).

First, choose good friends to spend time with. We have the players make two lists, with one column listing people who care about them and want to make their lives better, and the other for those who don't. We then encourage them obviously to spend their social time with those from the first column. The second thing we emulate from Bill Snyder is to give them

a decision-making process for when they encounter various situations or temptation. We teach them to take thirty seconds and step back and ask themselves two simple questions: First, if I do this, will it help me with my faith and family. Second, will this make me a better person, student, or athlete? If the answer is yes, go do it. If the answer is no, we teach them to have the courage of their convictions and walk away.

The fourth component of being a champion every day is to be an academic achiever. Here, we emphasize two things: 100 percent concentration in class and to complete all assignments and homework "and then some" (i.e. to go the extra mile whenever possible). We expect them to get the best grades they are capable of earning and hold them strictly accountable on this.

The fifth area is athletic improvement. Here, they are expected to model excellence in attitude and effort, and to be unselfish contributors who resonate a contagious enthusiasm. This type of attitude and effort will yield daily improvement. These are the expectations we have of our players, which we will not compromise. We firmly believe that this daily championship mindset will pay dividends for our players in the long run and will help them achieve the team goals they normally set for themselves which revolve around winning championships, and earning and commanding respect.

In addition to setting high expectations, it is also critical to teach players effective communication skills, including the importance of eye contact and a firm handshake, to say "yes sir/no sir", and to not use foul language. Tom Osborne says, "swearing is unprofessional, unethical, and uneducated." You know, I've never had a player call me after he has graduated to thank me for teaching him how to run a slant route. But, I have gotten calls that relate to them landing a job or earning a scholarship and them believing that the communication and life skills they learned in football had a great deal to do with it.

Linked to impacting communication skills is a leader's ability to motivate. Morale is more important than the skills a team possesses. It's a big part of why underdogs pull off an upset. We think the best way to motivate kids is through relationships, us with them, and them with each other. We try to create a family atmosphere based on love and unity, understanding that kids spell love, T-I-M-E. Or as Bill Curry says, "you can't motivate someone unless you spend time with them, care about them, and are honest with them". In short, while using fear and incentives at times can be effective and appropriate, the best and most enduring form of motivation comes from cultivating relationships.

The final component of developing leadership through character for us is to install a goal-setting program. Here, we differentiate between staff or program goals and team or individual goals. All of our staff's goals are intrinsically geared, having to do with the objectives, expectations, and values I've already discussed. We devote a week of our summer program to lead them through a goal-setting process, which we monitor throughout the coming school year. Over 95 percent of Americans play the game of life without goals. Goals need to be specific and reflect a player's passion sufficiently so that he will be persistent and patient in the march toward achieving his goals.

Our third and final core objective is educational excellence. Part of the goal-setting program I just alluded to deals with helping them set their grade goals. We monitor their grades the entire school year. It is not difficult to track them in-season, but out-of-season has always been a bigger challenge for us. So what we do in the off-season is to assign 10-15 players to a particular coach whose responsibility it is to conduct grade and behavioral checks. The coaches meet with the players at least once every two weeks to monitor their success and improve their relationship with those players.

We also help them with the college admissions process, regardless of whether or not they have the ability for, and interest in, college football. In February of their junior year, they fill out a college-interest form with their parents, that is designed to help them to begin to deal with the realities of the college-admission process. At our spring parent meeting in March, we give the parents of our junior players SAT materials and remind them that any juniors who want to play football their senior year must take the SAT for the first time no later than May of their junior year. General Douglas MacArthur once said failure in war almost always came down to two small words – "too late". We tell our parents their kids are never going to miss out on going to their dream college because they took the SAT's too late their senior year or scored poorly on an early- fall, Saturday morning test after a tough Friday night game because they were fatigued or unprepared.

Our players are required to turn in a sheet signed by their parents stating how in March and April they plan to prepare for the May SAT. While this has not been a foolproof plan, it has resulted in over 85 percent of our kids going immediately to a four-year college versus about 70 percent for our general student body. For our players who desire to play at the next level, we are candid with them in our assessment of what level we believe they could compete at. Our staff then puts together organized highlight (and game) tapes where we note for the college coaches where our player can be found on each highlight segment play. We always want to send the university evaluating our kids the message that he comes from a highly organized, disciplined program. All of the aforementioned has tended to yield strong parental support for us because they know we care deeply about our boys' welfare. It also facilitates an overall positive response from our players as we make large demands on them throughout the year.

To summarize; we have a mission statement and purpose which reflects a deep concern for our kids long-term welfare ("Champions for life") and three core objectives we are going to pursue to fulfill that mission: strengthen their faith, develop leadership through character; and educational excellence. We have a clear path we want to travel. However, we believe it is important to identify the chief obstacles that stand in our way.

The first one is societal in nature. Today, kids are growing up in a "what's in it for me society" as opposed to a "what can I contribute" culture. Some of this relates to a paradigm shift in the values and influences that impact most teenagers today. For example, in the year 1900, a teenager had a daily average of seven hours of quality family time. In the year 2000, that figure had eroded to seven minutes. Today, the top two influences on teenagers are peers and television. Children have turned to peers for status and approval in the wake of the void left largely by absentee or ineffective parents. There is a direct correlation between an excessive viewing of television and the dependence on peers with today's lack of values.

We also see as a major obstacle to kids' success in the fact that they live in an instant gratification, credit-card society. Many times, they are not taught that the truly worthwhile things in life come at a price, a price worth paying that is. The media celebrating talent over character is another issue we address with them. And of course, drugs and alcohol are an ever-present issue and stumbling block. We try to combat these enemies by providing something better for them that can make a radically positive difference in their lives.

We, as coaches, can build their self-esteem and equip them to face a world often off course with outstanding high school and college programs throughout the country. While the challenges to helping young people are greater today than they ever have been, so are the possibilities and rewards. Edmund Burke once wrote "the only thing necessary for the triumph of evil is that good men do nothing." It is a special privilege to be a part of a profession that has the capability of making such a significant impact on young people.

Like many of you, I'm sure, one of the two most influential men in my life was my high school coach, Paul Briggs. Thank you for your kind attention and a special thanks to Earl Browning and Nike for allowing our staff to visit your great island and to share some thoughts with you.

DEVELOPING TEAMWORK AND TRADITION

Columbine High School, Colorado

To start the program, I am going to plug in a video. It is our highlight video we do each year. Our technology guru started editing our highlight video tapes and put them together a couple of years ago. I want to show the film just to get some football spirit flowing here today. This tape includes all the years I have been at Columbine High School. I went there in 1994. This video covers the years from that time to the present at Columbine High School. (FILM)

We do not have, nor do we pretend to have all the answers for success, but these points have factored into some of our success. We bring our kids in a couple of hours before game time and show them this video. They start getting taped, and after they are taped they can come in the film room and watch highlight videos from year to year. One thing that has become a tradition with this is that we take all of the seniors and film a few minutes with each one of them. We film them talking about their high-school career. They reflect about their football experiences at Columbine High School. This tradition has been passed down from one team to the next each year.

Our coaching staff has been together for several years. We have some great people on our staff. We all believe in each other, and we work together very well. We are not brain surgeons by any means. We believe in each other and believe in what we are trying to sell our kids. They have bought into our program. Our kids make us look good. We have had some good athletes in the last four years. We had some talent, and our kids have a great work ethic.

We have had great discipline in our program. Our program is very simple. I know a lot of coaches could get up here and talk about discipline in the school and on the field. We all know discipline does not stop on the football field. Life does not work that way.

We have been lucky over the years. Our players have remained healthy. We have had some good bounces. We have had a lot of fumbles go our way. You must have luck in this game. Our kids have shown a lot of emotions in our games when breaks go our way.

The second thing I want to cover relates to what we have learned from clinics. We have taken bits and pieces from other people. Besides the beer and jokes at a clinic, we do get a lot of good information at clinics, such as this.

A few years ago, we went up to Pomona to a clinic. One of the lectures was on teamwork and motivation. I thought it was a very useful session. You can go to a lot of clinics and get X's and O's. But, we got a lot of ideas about selling our program to our coaches, team, parents, and community.

I want to go over some ideas used to build togetherness and teamwork. In 1994, we started to develop the idea of bringing the team and community together. We talked about selling rebel ball and pushing the school fight song. We came up with the idea to develop a slogan for the year. Our first theme was "PREPARE TO SUCCEED." We put the slogan on the back of T-shirts. We wanted to develop a work ethic. We wanted our players to get ready to work their rear end off.

In 1995, we were talking about kids not willing to step up and challenge themselves. They were afraid to sell out. They were afraid of pain. That year, we decide our slogan would be "CHALLENGE YOURSELF." We wanted them to step up and not be afraid. That year, we went to the state playoffs. We lost to Mullen High School in the first round of the playoffs.

In 1996, we selected the word "T-E-A-M" as our slogan. Then we added the other letters to the word TEAM = Together Everyone Achieves More. We wanted the seniors and juniors to develop respect for each other. We had a large number of juniors, and they were a good group. We only had 12 seniors in our program. The two groups did not get along very well in the spring of the year before. So, we decided to do something to bring our team together. That year, we came together and did better as a team.

In 1997, our slogan was, "FIND A WAY - MAKE THE PLAY." Our kids really took to this slogan. During practice and in the games, they would repeat the slogan, "Find A Way – Make The Play." We ended up losing to Bear Creek High School in overtime in the playoffs. But, our kids got a taste of what it was like to play against good teams.

The next year, we had some good players coming back. They were good athletes. Our quarterback was a good athlete, but he always found something wrong with the officials if we lost. This kid thought we were supposed to get all over the officials if things were not going our way. He had been taught that way. We wanted to come up with a slogan that would help our emotional players who tended to lose their self-control. Our slogan that year was "PRIDE – POISE – PERFECTION." We stressed to our quarterback to show poise, get our team back in the huddle, and get ready for the next play. They wore those three words on the back of their T-shirts. That year we won 9 games and lost 1.

The next year we were ready to have a big year. In April, the shootings happened at Columbine High School. You all know about that situation.

When you have a tragedy such as this, you try to be strong and help those that you can. There were a lot of blessings after the shooting. We had a lot of great people send us cards and letters, and call us. I can never tell you how important our profession is as far as support, the camaraderie, and respect and friendship. I have not had an opportunity to thank you for your support, but all the support we received was just incredible.

The day after the shooting, we called all of our kids and had them meet at one of our player's house. We met for about three hours, and we prayed together. We hugged the kids and tried to assure them we would survive this tragedy. I never will forget the love and emotion involved during that period. I think it made us closer at school as a football team. The game of football is filled with a lot of emotion. Our football ex-

perience took over for us. There were a lot of rough times for us. This is where our natural instincts took over.

About two weeks after the tragedy, the people stopped filling sorry for Columbine. They decided someone had to be blamed for this tragedy. It was not the kids that pulled the triggers that were at fault. It was someone else that was at fault. People started pointing fingers and trying to figure out which group had caused this terrible tragedy. Some people felt some of our athletes were bullies. They thought this was a problem at Columbine. After a few weeks, we were isolated as a group. We were the "jocks." The word "jocks" was not a popular word at school.

We decided we needed to pull everyone together as a team. So we selected the slogan "TOGETHER WE CAN – TOGETHER WE WILL." That is what we put on the back of our T-shirts. When we were doing conditioning and we were lined up, the man behind a player saw this slogan, "TOGETHER WE CAN – TOGETHER WE WILL." Before practice, we would get together for our chalk talk. As we broke the meeting, the players repeated the slogan. We did it everywhere we went.

After the tragedy, we had to take all of our football-related equipment down to a middle school until they could get the high school repaired for the fall. But the first day we had football practice in the fall, we went back to Columbine High School and took back the hill that had been taken from us as a result of the tragedy. It was an emotional scene. "TOGETHER WE CAN – TOGETHER WE WILL." Our kids did not really have to buy into this slogan. That was where our program was, and that was where we were with our lives.

We went on to win the state championship. It was probably the greatest thing I have every experienced. It was one of those things that was very, very emotional. It was one of those Cinderella stories. To see our kids come together under those conditions was very rewarding. I know God was with us through all of this.

After you win a state championship, where do you go from there? How could we match that year? We started doing things we felt we should be doing. We said we were going to "TAKE CARE OF BUSINESS."

That became our slogan for 2000. We decided to take one week at a time and just "take care of business." The kids responded and did a great job with this.

The playoffs are sudden death, because you are out when you lose if you are a senior. When you lose in the playoffs, it is tough. We lost in the playoffs in 1998, and it was tough for everyone. Our seniors were crying and very upset. Some of our sophomores came up to me after that game and told me they would not let that happen again. We lost that game, and they decided they did not want to go through that feeling again. They kept their word. We won the state championship in 1999 and 2000. They were proud of what they had accomplished. Our seniors were 41-9 in their high-school career.

The next part of my lecture, I want to go over some of the things we did to sell our slogans in-season and off-season. I will tell you that selling is hard. Some players do not buy into the selling aspects of this. Some players think it is cheerleading. I am not a cheerleader. But, if you want the players to buy into something, you better give a real effort. The assistant coaches are the ones that really sell our program. The players buy what they sell because they believe in them.

We have given out T-shirts in the off-season with slogans on them including the following: "COUNT ON ME", "PAY THE PRICE", "ACCEPT THE CHALLENGE", "NEED FOR SPEED." It all depends on where your kids are. If they work hard, you do not need to give them a boost. If they are pumping iron and working hard, you do not need to give out T-shirts.

I learned one thing from a friend that won a state championship. He said after they won the championship the next year, the coaches did not expect as much from the kids. They let a lot of little things go here and there. This stayed with me.

I have found the conditioning period provides us with an opportunity to sell. The head coach is always the "bad guy." The head coach has to take care of all of the discipline. So, when we do our conditioning, we have another coach lead us. It is a new energy with Coach Ivory Moore leading them. This helps me, because I do not have to be the bad guy with conditioning. He really gets the team worked up. Just when they think they are through with an exercise, he will ask them "can you do one more?" The kids respond with "yes sir!" They are a great with Coach Moore.

We talk to our kids about conditioning. We tell them they have to be in shape, and that we are not punishing them. We try to build mental toughness. We try to sell the importance of conditioning to the team. Conditioning will prevent injuries. "We cannot get tired and lose a game because of fatigue." We use the terms "together we can" and "together we will" during the conditioning drills. We call out the word "TOGETHER" and the kids will respond "WE CAN." Then we call out "TOGETHER," and the kids respond with "WE WILL."

We break the groups down and try to sell them on our program. For the Team, we sell "rebel ball." Rebel ball is something we believe in, and we get our kids to believe in it. For our linemen, we use the term "hog pride" to describe them. For our defensive backs, we use the term "get it up." For our backs we use "brothers."

During practice and whenever it is fitting, we sell the message, "Find a way - make the play. Take care of business. Go 100 MPH."

For teamwork, we used the theme of the Wolf Pack. There is a poem by Rudyard Kipling about the Wolf Pack.

TEAMWORK

Now this is the law of the jungle,
As old and as true as the sky,
And the Wolf that keeps it may prosper,
But the Wolf that shall break it must die.
As the creeper that girdles the tree trunk,
The law runneth forward and back –
And the strength of the Pack is the Wolf,
And the strength of the Wolf is the Pack.

By Rudyard Kipling

The bottom two lines mean the most to our group. We have used T-shirts, decals, pre-game and post-game speeches about the Wolf Pack. We had some of the seniors from the year before come back and talk about their championship ring and what it meant to them. I have never been big on decals. We give the decals of a wolf to put on our helmet. We try to find videos on wolves to show players the idea of the pack.

One of our players did a lot of research on the wolf and wrote a story about the wolf. He came up with the way the wolf pack lived and how they had to work and how they persevered. It was neat to see how the kids bought into this wolf-pack concept.

The next point I want to cover may be something many of you have seen. It is a poem about the LINK. The first time I saw this was in 1985, when I was a senior in college at Western State College. I have the link on my key change today. When I see my old buddies from college, they pull out their link. The idea is that you can keep up with the link. It is amazing how many kids still have their link. I can't keep track of anything, but I know where this link is at all time.

THE LINK

I carry a link in my pocket
A simple reminder to me
Of the fact that I am a team member
No matter where I may be.
This little link is not magic
Nor is it a good luck charm
It isn't meant to protect me
From every physical harm.
It's simply an understanding
Between my teammates and me.
When I put my hand in my pocket
To bring out a coin or key
The link is there to reminder me
Of what a team member should be.
It links me to the team
It links me to the school
It is a constant reminder
That there is no place for a fool.
So I carry this link in my pocket
To remind me many a time
That a man without conviction
Isn't worth a simple dime.
By Norm Parker

The next thing we have done to promote togetherness is the rope concept. It is called hold the rope. The idea came from Pomona, Dakota Fairview High School. We would scout Fairview, and they would bring out pieces of rope during their stretching session. The cheerleaders would have small pieces of a rope. What Pomona did was to cut little pieces of yarn, and the kids tied it to their belt loops. The theme was carried out through out the season. It is hard to do all of these ideas the same season. Some schools have used this as a special week when they try to bring the kids together. The idea of holding the rope is a good one.

HOLD THE ROPE

Every year, a professional football team wins the Super Bowl. Every year, a college basketball team wins a National Championship. Every year, the best high school team in their class will win a state crown. And every year, only one team for each sport will be able to hang a banner up in their school for them to remember their season for the rest of their lives. All these teams have one thing in common. No matter how tough it becomes throughout their season, they did one thing – "THEY HELD THE ROPE."

What is holding the rope? Imagine you are hanging from the edge of a cliff with a drop of five-thousand feet. The thing between you and a fall to your death is a rope, with the person of your choice at the other end. Who do you know that has the guts and courage to pull you to safety? Who will hold the rope for you? Who do you know that is going to let that rope burn their hands, withstand that burning pain, and maybe even shed a little blood from their hands for you?

If you can name two, three, even four people who would do this for you, that is great, but it is not enough. Those people may not be around when you need them to pull you up. You need a group of people who you would do anything for, and they would do the same for you.

The next time your team is together, look around and ask yourself, who could I trust with my rope? Are they going to let their hands bleed for me? And most importantly, can these people around me hand me their rope? Will I do anything and everything in my power to pull them up?

When a person can look every member of their team in the eye, and say to themselves that they will hold the rope, that is the team that is destined to win a lot of games. Skill individuals and luck can only take a team so far. You see, the team that holds the rope when the going gets tough is the winner with heart, and ten times out of ten, all bets are on that will be the team that walks away the winner.

If you are down by a point or two, yell at your team-mates to grab a hold of the rope, let it burn, but don't let it go. Every year, there are winners and losers in all sports. Every year the winners hold the rope. You don't have to be the best team on the field to hold the rope and to win big games. If you play with poise, and do everything that is asked from the coaches and the captains, and most of all put your hands and heart onto that rope — YOU WILL BE SUCCESSFUL.

No matter what sport you play, in order to win you have to have a commitment to your team. It is the team with the highest commitment and love for one another that will walk away with the championship title.

Don't let your team down. You've got to hold the rope. You must do everything possible both on the field and off the field, to make sure your teammates know they can count on you to "hold the rope."

I am sure most of you know who Vince Lombardi was. The problem is the kids do not know who he was. They know he was some old coach. But, he made some great quotes related to teamwork. Our parents decorated our lockerroom during the playoffs. They put up some of the Lombardi quotes in our lockerroom. I enjoyed the quotes, and I feel they were very helpful to us.

"PRICE FOR SUCCESS"

The dictionary is the only place success comes before work. Hard work is the price we must all pay for success. I think we can accomplish almost anything if we are willing to pay the price. The price of success is hard work, dedication to the job at hand, and the determination that whether we win or lose, we have applied the best of ourselves to the task at hand.

By Vince Lombardi

Another Lombardi quote we that have used is called "Heart Power."

HEART POWER

A man can be as great as he wants to be. If you believe in yourself and have the courage, the determination, the dedication, the competitive drive and if you are willing to sacrifice the little things in life and pay the price for the things that are worthwhile, it can be done. Once a man has made a commitment to a way of life, he puts the greatest strength in the world behind him. It is something we call "HEART POWER." Once a man has made his commitment, nothing will stop him short of success.

By Vince Lombardi

I do not know where I got this idea, but it was at a clinic or from another coach. After a loss, we were beat up and down mentally. The next week, we were on the practice field running a skeleton pass drill. I looked up and a saw a flock of geese flying over our field. It was really cool. These geese were in a V-formation. They took turns leading the group in that V-formation. I remembered reading a story before about the geese. I looked it up and decided to share it with our kids. The kids bought the idea, and it had a big impact in our turnaround. It goes with the team concept.

GEESE

As each bird flaps its wings, it creates an "uplift" for the bird following. By flying in a "V"-formation, the whole flock adds 71 percent flying range than if they flew alone.

LESSON: People who share a common direction and sense of community can get where they are going quicker and easier because they are traveling on the thrust of one another.

Whenever a goose falls out of formation, it suddenly feels the drag and resistance of trying to fly alone, and quickly gets back into formation to take advantage of the "lifting power" of the bird immediately in front.

LESSON: If we have as much sense as a goose, we will stay in formation with those headed where we want to go, and be willing to accept their help as well as give ours to others.

When the lead goose gets tired, it rotates back into the formation, and another goose flies at the point.

LESSON: It pays to take turns doing the hard tasks, and sharing leadership. With people, as with geese, we are interdependent upon one another.

The geese in formation honk from behind to encourage those up front to keep up their speed.

LESSON: We need to make sure our honking from behind is encouraging, and not something else.

When a goose gets sick or wounded or shot down, two geese drop out of formation and follow it down to help protect it. They stay with it until it is able to fly again, or it dies. Then they launch out on their own, with another formation, or catch up with the flock.

LESSON: If we have as much sense as geese, we too, will stand by each other in difficult times, as well as when we are strong.

We have used a lot of motivational pre-game gimmicks. We used the "jars-of-beans" gimmick. We took a ping pong ball and placed it in the bottom of the jar with the beans. The ping pong ball represents the team. As we face adversity, as indicated by shaking the jar, we see the ping pong ball rises to the top. This represents the team as they stick together through the adversity.

We did the deal of "burning the house down." That one did not go over very well. We made the house out of popsicle sticks. We tried to light it, but it would not burn. We sprayed it with lighter fluid. When we did get it going, we almost burned the place down. We put it in the showers to put it out.

We have used "keep the worm moist" trick. I got the worm ready, but it never got in my mouth. We sold them on the idea we must do whatever it takes to win. We have given out Superman T-shirts. We have showed videos from college and NFL teams. We have shown movies of Rocky, The Edge, Brave Heart and Meatballs. Now, I am not sure how much of this works. However, I do not believe it has hurt us over the years.

I have tried to give you a few ideas we have used over the years to build team spirit and to develop teamwork. If I have anything that you would like to see, feel free to contact me at Columbine High School. Thank you.

THE WING-T JET PACKAGE

Morgantown High School, West Virginia

As the head football coach at Morgantown High School, I am representing the football staff and our athletic department. We are located in Morgantown, West Virginia. We installed the wing-T seven years ago, and we have been in the State Playoffs the last six years. In 1998, we were the State Runner-Up, and in 2000, we won the State Championship.

In 1997, we installed the JET SERIES (split-end attacking series) because teams were loading up their defense to the tight end side to stop the buck sweep. Once we were successful in attacking the perimeter to the weakside, we forced teams to defend both the tight-end and the split-end side. Since our installation of the jet sweep series, our regular season record is 38 wins and 2 losses and our overall record is 46 wins and 5 loses.

The Jet Sweep is an outstanding compliment to the already hard to defend wing-T. Today, I want to cover our wing-T Jet package. I will go fast so I can cover the entire package. That way, you can get a better idea of what we are trying to accomplish.

We can run our Jet package from eight different formations. We have ten running plays and six pass plays with this package. I will show the plays from a couple of formations and against a few different defenses that will give you a better feel for what we are doing. I will go fast, so stay with me.

Our base formation is with a wing-T to the tight end, a slot to the split-end side, and one running back. We call this set our ace formation. The fullback heels are set at four yards. The wingback is one-yard wide and one-yard deep from the tight end. The tailback is two yards-by-two yards on the tackle.

We want the wingback and tailback in a two-point stance, slightly angled inside. They are going to be blocking down inside most of the time, or they are going to run the Jet route.

ACE RIGHT

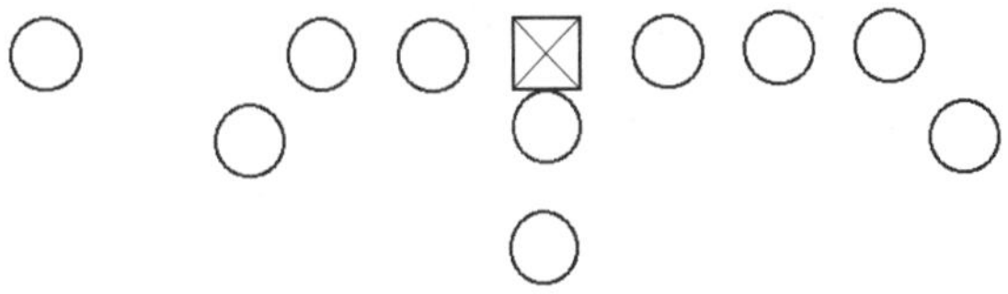

DEUCE RIGHT

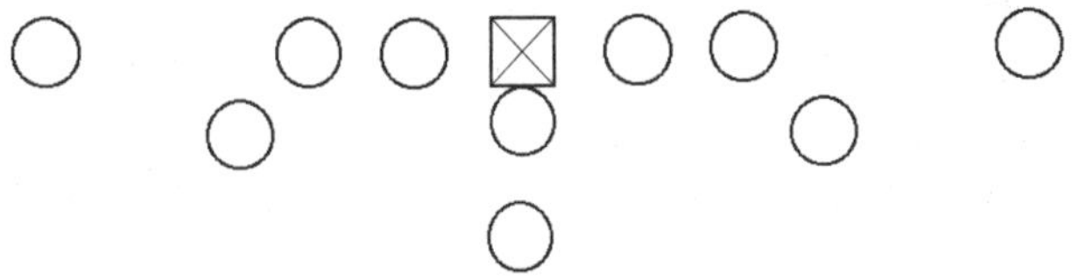

DEUCE QUEEN

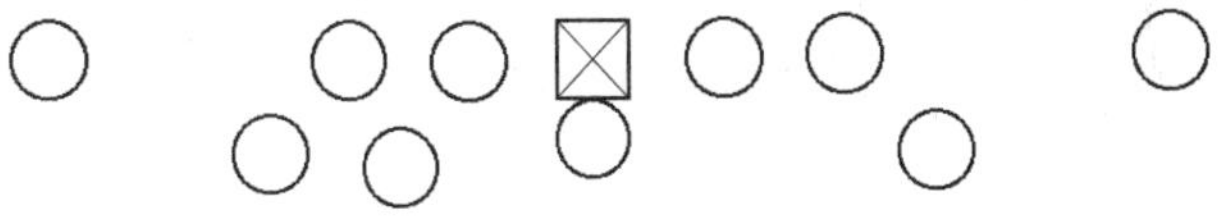

SLOT

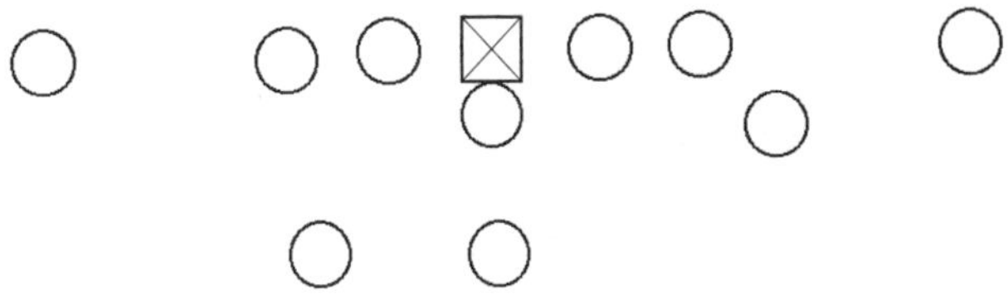

DEUCE OVER

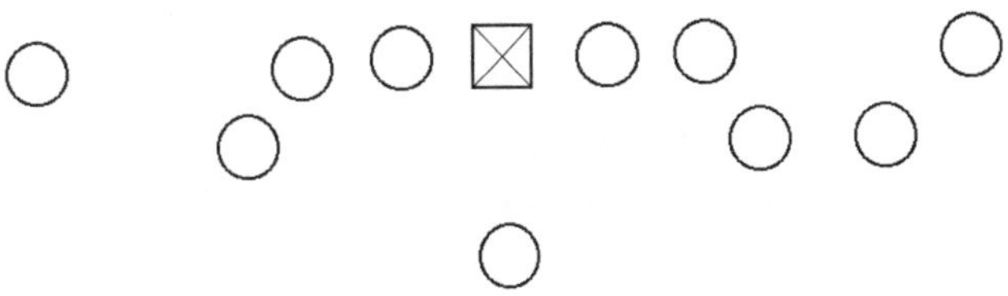

EMPTY GUN

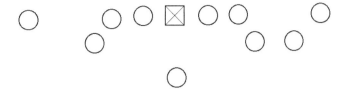

RIGHT TRIPS GUN

RIGHT TRIPS GUN

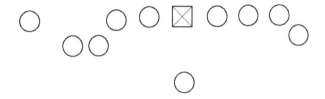

Next, I want to list the plays we run from these formations. Again, we run ten running plays and six pass plays.

The first play is our Jet sweep. I will show you the play from three formations. Here is what it looks like from the ace set.

JET SWEEP

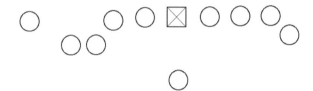

We can run the Jet from our deuce set against the 4-4 defense.

DEUCE FORMATION

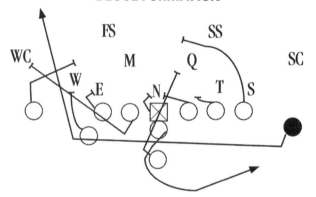

We can run the Jet against the 4-3 defense from the empty set.

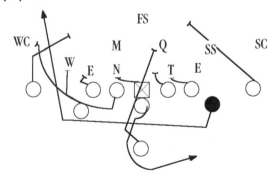

Rules for the Jet Sweep.

SE—Read crack block from FS to LB

S—Fire, on

SG—Pull and kick out contain

C—Fire, zone, backer

TG—Fire, zone, backer

TT—Fire, zone, backer

TE—Deep 1/3

TB—Fire, on, backer

FB—Jab step, run trap path

WB—Zip motion – receive ball and read block of SE and SG

QB—Open to TE side, hand ball to the WB, fake boot or waggle

JET TRAP

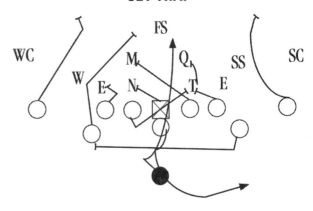

JET TRAP

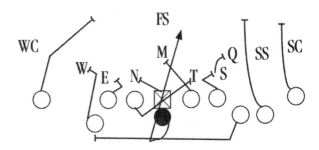

We see a lot of 3- and 6-techniques to the tight-end side. On the split-end side, we see the 2- and 5-techniques. If the defense is playing sky coverage with the FS coming to the flats on the motion of the wingback, our SE will crack on him. If they are playing cloud coverage, the SE will crack on the scraping LB, and the SG will kick out on the contain player. Our QB will waggle or boot according to our game plan.

Our next play is our Jet trap. We want the play to look as much like the Jet sweep as possible. I will draw the Jet trap against all three defenses using the same three formations as the Jet sweep.

JET TRAP

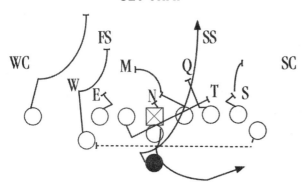

SE—Stalk deep 1/3

ST—Shut down, LB

SG—Pull and trap #2

C—On, gap

TG—Gap, down, backer

TT—LB

TE—Deep 1/3

TB—Cut off to 1/3

FB—Run trap path

WB—Zip motion, fake Jet sweep

QB—Reverse out, fake Jet sweep, hand off on trap, run boot or waggle

We can run the trap to either side with this particular motion. We always trap the short side with a defensive tackle in the 1-technique. Our guard will make a short call, and the trapping guard knows he is going to trap short instead of long. We like to keep the rules the same as much as possible.

The next play is the Jet sucker trap (SUBA) Against the 4-4 defense, we will not run the SUBA to the split-end side because we can not block the Mike LB. The SUBA to the TE side is a much better play because the Jet motion by the WB causes the Mike to scrape. We can run the play with either the TB or the WB motion depending on the formation.

On all traps, we can run them to either side with motion from either the TB or WB.

The next play is the Jet belly. We want the WB to fake the Jet sweep. The FB and TB run the belly path, and the FB cuts off the blocks of the TB and split guard.

JET BELLY

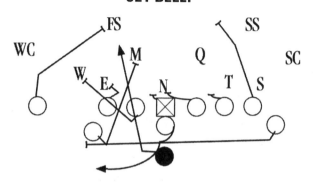

JET SUCKER TRAP

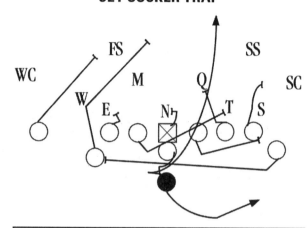

SE—Stalk 1/3

ST—On, gap, down

SG—Pull, kick out #3

C—Fire, on, backer

TG—Zone

TT—Zone

TE—Deep 1/3

TB—Drop step, backer

FB—Belly path

WB—Zip motion, fake Jet

QB—Reverse out, fake Jet sweep, hand off to fullback on belly and continue on option.

SE—Stack deep _

ST—Shut down

SG—Pull, trap #2

C—On, gap

TG—Pull, kickout #3

TT—Backer

TE—Stack deep 1/3

TB—Cut off

FB—Run Trap Path

WB—Zip motion, fake Jet

QB—Fake Jet, hand off on trap, run boot or waggle

How many of the wing-T Coaches here run the wing-T sally play? It may be the best play in wing-T football. Some teams pull and trap on the sally. We do not trap on the sally. The frontside of the line runs a Jet look, and the backside shows pass and blocks according to what the defense does. We want the tailback to fake a block on the DE, and then take three drop steps before he starts on his sally path. This gives him a better angle to hit the open seam. The wingback runs the Jet sweep and then blocks #3. The quarterback fakes the Jet sweep and hands the ball off inside to the TB and then continues on the waggle.

We needed another play to go back to the tight end-side other than the sally for our TB. We run the play to both sides. It is a counter trey off the Jet sweep look.

JET COUNTER

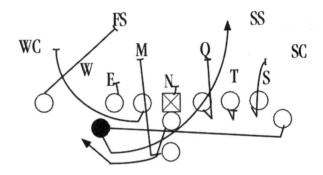

SE—Stalk deep 1/3

ST—On, gap, down

SG—Pull and block contain if uncovered. If covered, block on or gap

C—On, #2, #1

TG—Pass set, block #2 or #1

TT—Pass set, block #2 or #3 or #1

TE—Pass set, block #3 to #4

TB—Fake block on #3, drop three steps and receive ball on inside from the quarterback.

WB—Fake Jet sweep, block #3

FB—Lead on #1 to split-end side

QB— Fake Jet sweep, sprint to SE. Hand ball to tailback on the inside, then run the waggle

SE—Stalk/deep 1/3

ST—Pull and lead through on #4

SG—Pull and kick out on #3

C—On, gap, backer

TG—On, gap, backer

TT—On gap, down, backer

TE—Gap, down, backer

TB—Drop step three steps, receive ball on inside handoff, read block of SG and ST

FB—Fill for pulling guard

WB—Fake Jet and block 33

QB—Fake Jet, hand ball to TB on inside, continue running option path

We put this play in two years ago in the ninth game of the year. The first time we ran it, our tailback ran 75 yards for a touchdown. I thought it was a good play after that. We have been running it ever since. It is a better play against the 50 defense than against the 44.

The next play is the Jet reverse. We can run it from several different formations. Again, we start the Jet sweep action, and the #1 receiver will become the ball carrier after a handoff from the Jet sweep player.

JET REVERSE

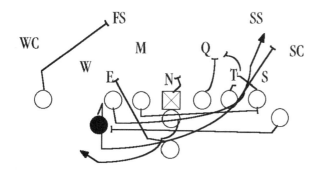

SE—Cut down split, run reverse, receive the ball on the outside

ST—On, gap, down

SG—Fire, on, backer, pull

C—Fire, on, backer

TG—Fire, on, backer

TT—Fire, on, backer

TE—On, gap, down

TB—On, gap, down, next level

FB—Lead through B gap on LB

WB—Receive ball on Jet, hand off to split end on outside

QB—Handoff ball on Jet, lead on reverse

The next play is the Jet power sweep. There is no difference between the Jet power and the Jet sweep except we put our FB in a queen alignment (between the tackle and guard). We now have two lead blockers — the fullback and the SG.

JET POWER SWEEP

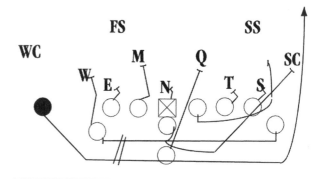

SE—Read crack block from FS to ILB

ST—Fire, on

SG—Pull and kick out contain

C—Zone

TG—Zone

TT—Zone

TE—Stalk deep 1/3

TB—Fire, on

FB—Queen alignment – lead block

WB—Zip motion, receive ball, read block on free safety by the SE, SG, and FB

QB—Handoff ball to WB , run waggle or boot

We lead with the FB, and everything else is the same as the Jet sweep. We can run the trap and sally from the queen formation, so we don't give away the fact that we are running the power sweep every time we align in the queen set.

The next play is the Jet option. We arc block on the #4 man with our tight end. We tell our quarterback to pitch the ball most of the time because we do not want him to run the football.

JET OPTION

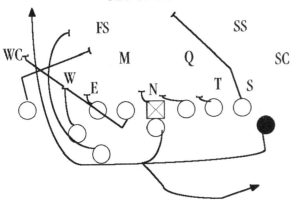

SE—Deep 1/3
ST—Zone, backer
SG—Zone, backer
C—Zone, backer
TG—Zone, backer
TT—Zone, backer
TE—Arc release on #4
TB—Deep 1/3
FB—Option path
WB—Fake Jet
QB—Fake Jet, run at #3, read for pitch

On the Jet cross buck, we can run it to both sides. We bring the wingback inside on the linebacker. He starts in motion, and the ball is snapped as he gets to the guard.

JET CROSS BUCK

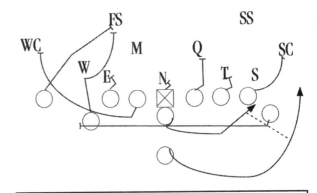

SE – Deep 1/3
ST – Fire, on
SG – Pull and kick out #2 or #3
C – Fire, on, chip
TG – On, gap, down, chip
TT – On, gap, down, chip
TE – Inside release, deep 1/3
TB – Drop step two steps, receive ball on outside handoff from quarterback, read block of pulling guard
FB – Fake veer dive, fill for pulling guard
WB – Zip motion, when wingback gets to the guard – turn inside on dive and block linebacker
QB – Fake dive to fullback, hand ball to tailback on outside and continue option path

I will show these plays so you can see how they look in a game. If you have questions, let me hear from you.

The Jet waggle is identical to the waggle. The difference is that we can motion either the wingback or the tailback.

I want to get to the Jet Boot real quick. It is the same play you run out of the Wing-T offense.

JET WAGGLE

JET BOOT

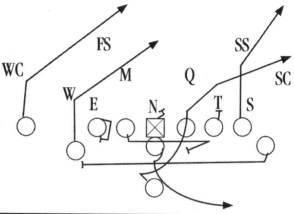

SE—Post corner

ST—On, gap, down

SG—Pull and log #3

C—Fire, on, backside

TG—Sickle pull, to backside

TT—Hinge block

TE—Drag at 12 yards, post route if split

TB—Fake Jet, block #3, release to flats at five yards

FB—Flats at five yards, control step and block #3 to TE side

QB—Fake Jet, fake to fullback, run waggle play

SE—Post, trail

ST—Hinge

SG—Sickle pull to backside

C—Fire, on, backside

TG—Pull and log #3

TT—On, gap, own

TE—Post corner

TB—Drag at 12 yards

FB—Fill for guard to five yards

WB—Fake Jet and block #3

QB—Fake Jet, fake to fullback, run boot

On the Jet pass, we make it a play-action pass. It is just like the run, except we throw the pass to the wide receiver.

JET PASS

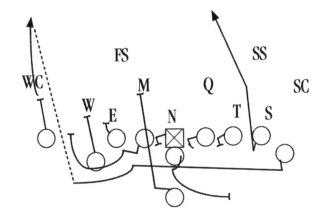

SE—Post / fake block on corner – release deep

ST—Hinge

SG—Hinge

C—Fire, on, backside

TG—Pull and log #3

TT—On, gap, down

TE—Split if ball is coming to you – drag at 12 yards if going away

TB—Fire, on / zip motion and throw the pass

FB—Fill for pulling guard

WB—Fire, on / zip motion and throw the pass

QB—Hand off ball on Jet and block backside

If the tailback is going to throw the pass, the wingback blocks onside. If the wingback is going to throw the pass, the tailback blocks onside.

Next, is our Jet throwback pass. This will keep the backside honest.

JET THROWBACK PASS

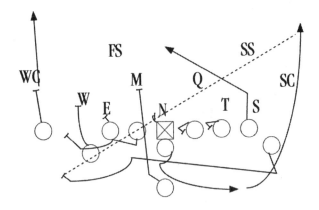

SE—Post pattern

ST—Hinge

SG—Hinge

C—Fire, on, hinge

TG—Pull and seal #4, to ballside

TT—Fire, on

TE—Drag at 12 yards if run to you, block #3 if Jet runs to your side

TB—Run Jet – pass ball to quarterback, fire, on

FB—Fill for pulling guard

WB—Run Jet, pass ball to quarterback, fire, on

QB—Hand ball on Jet run – run rail pass route

On our Jet reverse rail pass, we fake the Jet reverse. We like to throw the ball to the wingback down the sideline. The quarterback must make a good fake on the Jet and reverse.

JET REVERSE RAIL PASS

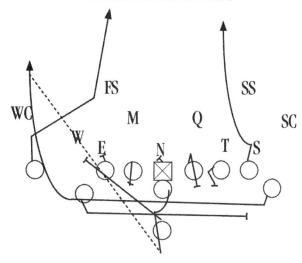

SE—Post pattern

ST—Fire, on

SG—Fire, on

C—Fire, on

TG—Fire, on

TT—Fire, on

TE—Skinny post

TB—Fake reverse and block #3

FB—Block #3 on TB side

WB—Fake Jet and run rail pattern

QB—Fake Jet, fake reverse, 3-step drop and read patterns

On our Jet screen pass, we can throw the ball to the split end or the Z-back. We can run it to both sides. We can motion the tailback or the wingback. We like to move the fullback up and run the man next to him in motion and screen to that side. We can run these plays from all of our formations. Let me show the Jet package on film. This is what we do with the Jet series.

JET X/Z SCREEN PASS

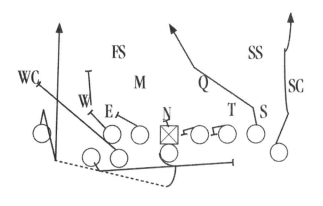

SE—Take 2 steps forward – drip step – come back and look for ball

ST—Pass block – release on WLB

SG—Fire, on gap, hinge

C—Fire, on, gap

TG—Fire, on, gap, hinge

TT—Fire, on, gap, hinge

TE—Skinny post / if split, 2 steps forward and drop step/ look for ball

TB—Fake Jet – drag at 12 yards

FB—Block corner on play side

WB—Fake Jet – skinny post

QB—Fake Jet – throw ball to X or Z (called side).

I hope you have gotten and idea or two that may help you. If you have any questions, feel free to contact me. I will list my address and email if you want to contact me or anyone on our staff.

COACH GLEN McNEW AND STAFF
MORGANTOWN HIGH SCHOOL
109 WILSON AVENUE
MORGANTOWN, WV 25601
SCHOOL PHONE – 1-304-291-9269
HOME PHONE - 1-304-296-0417
WEB: www.mohiganfootball.com
Email = coach@labs.net

Herb Meyer

MAKE THE SPECIAL TEAMS SPECIAL

El Camino High School, California

I will get started if I can get this wireless mike hooked up. This shows two things. I am old, and I am dumb. I have been around a long time. I started coaching in the 1950's. That covers six decades. I am not dumb, but I am not smart enough to know when to quit coaching. I was a graduate assistant for one year. I was a high school assistant for one year. The next year, I became a head coach. I have been a head coach for 44 years. It has worn on me a little.

You are here because you expect to learn something. You do not hear many clinic lectures on special teams. Not many people spend time on the special teams. That is why a lot of teams get beat in the special teams game. Special teams are special to us, and I will tell you some of the things we do that may be a little different approach to that phase of the game. I will not talk about schemes. I will talk about organization and our approach to special teams and what we think makes special teams special.

El Camino High School is in Oceanside, California. We are 35 miles north of San Diego and about 90 miles south of Los Angles. We have 2,600 students. We play in the largest division in our section.

I get a chance to travel around the country to lecture, and I tell everyone I live in God's Country. However, I have to admit Hawaii is a very close second. Hawaii has it own unique qualities. We go to work everyday in shorts. In January, you may have to wear a sweat shirt but you can take it off in the afternoon. It is great weather if you like outdoors.

I have been to a lot of clinics over the years. I have taken ideas from a lot of coaches. Coaches at all levels shared their ideas with me over the years. I think this is what makes coaching unique. In the business world, it is industrial espionage. You get thrown in jail or get fined for it if you steal an idea from another company. In coaching, we get together and share ideas. We try to make each other better. It helps us all in the long run.

I believe you must have everything you do written down. It must be concise. Everything is written down because I do not want anyone associated with our program not knowing what is going on. I never want a person associated with our program not knowing what is going on. I do not want anyone coming up to me and say, "I did not know." I let everyone know what is going on.

It all starts with a mission statement. You must have a philosophy for your overall program. We place our kicking game first, our defense second, and our offense third. Then, you have to have goals and objectives of what you are going to do. If you will take the time to write all of this down in a logical sequence, you will benefit from it.

Everyone can talk off the top of their head. The problem is you may not say it the same way the second time. When you put it in writing, it is there. Then, when you pass it out to others, they know what you want, and it does not get misinterpreted. I make this point a big deal with our staff. I have them put everything in writing for our summer retreat. We have a clinic with our coaches, and they have to teach the other members of our staff how they are going to coach their position.

This is our mission statement. The total effort is to develop consistency, and team unity, team pride, and a strong sense of moral value leading to continuing success in life. It does not say anything about football or winning or losing. Our goal, when we talk to parents, is to make every player in our program a champion as a human being. This starts with simple things such as saying, "please, thank you, yes sir, and no sir." These are things the parents do not teach anymore. We want to make the kids better than they were when they came into our program. That is our goal as coaches. To do that, we have to teach them a lot about moral values in today's society. It is important to us to teach kids to do things right. In order to do that, we must have a sound philosophy and something everyone can buy into.

Our overall philosophy for our total program is this. We want to be known for something. It may be for being physical on defense, having a high-scoring offense, and aggressive hitters. Our philosophy is defensive-oriented. If you play El Camino High School, you better screw your hat on and get ready to go war because we are going to knock the crap out of you.

Of the three phases of the game, we believe we are going to win with defense. We put our best players on defense first. The thing I have always felt was important about coaching is not what you do, but how you do it, and why you do it. If everything was equal, everyone would run the same offense or the same defense. You can be successful with anything. You must believe in it, and you must sell your kids on it. How you do it is the most important aspect of the game. How are you going to coach? How are you going to teach?

To be successful, you must have a plan. It does not matter if you believe what I am going to tell you about the kicking game. It does not make any difference. Make your own plan. You must have something you believe in. You must sell your coaches, and then everyone must sell the kids. Then, you have to teach the kids. It does not matter how much you know, or how enthused you are about something, if you can't get your kids to do it on the field, you will not be successful. You must believe in it, understand it thoroughly, and sell it, and you must practice it. It goes back to keeping it simple. If you have so many things going on that you can't practice it, you will not have great execution. You must select what you are going to do to fit the amount of time you are going to spend on it in practice.

In our overall philosophy, we have always felt that defense wins championships. We believe very strongly in the field-position, as opposed to the possession, approach to he game. Obviously, this means we put a great deal of emphasis on the kicking game. In the twenty-five year history of our school, we have been to the finals ten times and won eight C.I.F. Championships. The key to our success has been excellent coaches who are great teachers, and outstanding young men who have been willing to commit themselves to doing whatever it takes. One of the fundamentals of our program has been attention to detail, and that includes all phases of the kicking game.

In order to subscribe to our philosophy you must commit to two things. First, defense has a priority for the placement of personnel. Second, you must put a premium on the kicking game. Realizing that 25-30 percent of the plays in any game involve some aspect of the kicking game. We must give it: appropriate practice time; involvement by the total coaching staff; an approach where no players are exempt from being on special teams.

Since every game begins with a phase of the kicking game, this provides an excellent opportunity to set the tempo for the game. Also, the kicking game provides numerous opportunities for "big plays" that can change the momentum of a game. The head coach must set an example for the importance of the kicking game by his involvement and interest in everything related to the kicking game.

Everyone involved with the program must understand that all special teams have a high priority. We do not have separate coaches for the varsity and JV's. All of our coaches work with both groups. We have six offensive coaches and six defensive coaches. We play double headers, with our JV team playing first and then the varsity game. Our coaches work together with both teams. When the JV game starts, everyone except the defensive coordinator and the head coach are working with the JV's. The defensive coordinator and I go up in the press box and help with the phones. At half-time, we go in and address the varsity squad. When the JV game is over, one coach goes in with the JV's, and the rest stay out with the varsity for pre-game. Everyone works the varsity game.

In our program, we have an assistant as the "head coach" of each special team. Each of them chooses two to three other assistant coaches to work with them. They have complete freedom to select 15 to 16 players for their unit. They are responsible for establishing their own practice organization and meeting schedule, as well as determine the game-substitution patterns. Since our coaching staff works with all tenth, eleventh, and twelfth graders together in practice, we can work on punt or kickoff coverage with the varsity, while the junior varsity is working on punt or kickoff returns on the adjacent field. Each squad must scout itself. And it is the responsibility of the head coach of each unit to set up the scout teams for practice. Halfway through the team kicking period, the coaches will change fields and repeat what they did with the other squad (varsity/junior varsity).

When each coach has established his kicking group, our kicking coordinator will then make up a master list of all teams with all the personnel involved. If we find a single player who is on four or more of the six special teams, then the head coach will make a decision about removing players – especially starters who need to get off the field to rest.

Our overall philosophy is to provide opponents with as many "looks" as possible in all phases of our game – offense, defense, and special teams. This is to create as many preparation problems as possible for our opponents.

We are a double-slot punt team. We will motion to either side, line up in trips or bunch, and then have fakes off the different sets or looks to take advantage of defensive adjustments. We are a directional kicking team when we kick, trying to converge our coverage to a corner.

Since we are a pressure team on defense, we like to apply pressure on punt-return situations. We will almost always go for the punt block. We can block from either side, or we can go all out from both sides. However, there is always a built in return to one side of the block.

We are a directional kicking team on kickoffs. Usually, we kick from one of the hash marks. We want to box in the return by kicking to the corner inside the five-yard line. Most of the time we kick cross field. However, we use pop-up kicks to drop the ball in the deal spots.

We do not expect to spend a lot of time on kickoff returns. We ant to get the ball as close to the forty-yard line as possible. We are primarily a double-wedge return team, and we try to crack a seam. We do return kickoffs for TD's each year, but it is because of outstanding return men, and not by great schemes.

We vary our extra-point and field-goal alignments and have used the "swinging gate" pre-shift, both with and without a split end. Obviously, when people do not adjust properly, we have several fakes to run off this formation.

Our short-yardage and goal-line offense – RAMBO – is a special team for us. We utilize special team personnel philosophy.

Our entire squad comes on the field together – after meeting. Immediately following stretching, everyone goes to a special station. In this period our deep snappers, punters, place kickers, and return men work every day. During this period, we try to work on breakdown drills in the kicking game, much the same as we all do with our offensive and defensive practices. We work on breakdown and contain drills with the forcers; rushers work on blocking punts; and the outside blockers work on double bumps versus rushers. Immediately following this period, we have our team-kicking session that each day emphasizes a different phase of the game. On Thursday, as part of our pre-game practice, we go through a "kicking circuit" that involves all possible kicking situations as we move up and down the field. This drill is an adaptation of the "18-minute drill" that we got from Spike Dykes of Texas Tech.

More games are lost due to breakdowns in the kicking game than in any other phase of the game. We strive to have our special teams win at least two games for us per year. There are many great ideas that one can find to utilize in any phase of the game of football but we feel it is important to have a plan and not only have a what but a how in whatever we plan to do. We feel this approach to the kicking game has helped make it important to the players, and as such, it is a productive part of every game we play.

By using stats, we can show how various phases of the kicking game have helped us to achieve success over the years. We put as much time into the planning phase of our kicking as we do our offense and defense. This means viewing films and evaluating opponents personnel and schemes. We work just as hard perfecting our kicking game as we do with our offense and defense. We believe our players are going to perform well in those phases of the game in which we stress heavily. We strongly believe in stressing the kicking game. We try to "make our special teams SPECIAL.

PHILOSOPHY FOR THE KICKING GAME

Realize the kicking game makes up to 25 to 30 percent of every game. It is a great opportunity for "big plays." All coaches must be involved; no players are exempt. Be organized and allow adequate practice time.

KICKING GAME PRACTICE PLAN AND STAFF ORGANIZATION

- Early outs – specialists and groups. (Coach).

- Entire staff involved in teaching the kicking game.

- Training camp – practice time block.

- Regular season – specialty; two phases following stretching, two phases within practice, on Mondays, introduce kicking game. Thursday – Review, substitutions. (Kicking game coordinator).

- Game sideline organization.

SPECIAL TEAMS

- Kickoff coverage – alignment, assignment, drills, coaching points, cover 1, 2, 3, 4, safety.

- Punt coverage – alignment, assignment, drills, coaching points, fake punt.

- Punt return – alignment, assignment, and drills, coaching points.

- Punt block and return – alignment, assignment, drills, coaching points.

- Kickoff return – alignment, drills, coaching points: i.c. hands team.

- PAT – field goal – alignment, assignment, drills, coaching points: "fire," optional.

- PAT – field goal block – alignment, assignment, and drills, coaching points: situation drills and application of rules.

TEAM KICKING GOALS

- Do not field a punt inside our ten-yard line.

- We do not want a last second lunge to block on a punt return.

- We want to avoid the bad snap on the kicking game.

- We want to score or set up a score each game with our kicking game.

- We want to avoid the long run on the kicking game.

Because each game starts with the special teams, we must set the tempo of the game with great hitting and a big play on the kickoff or kickoff return, it is a question of how badly you want to get the job done. "We must have total commitment from all special team members." Each play of the kicking game is potentially a "gamebreaker" because one or more of the following events take place: ball possession changes; sizeable amount of yardage is involved (i.e. 40 yards or more); points may be scored.

SPECIAL TEAMS IDENTIFICATION

In order to make special teams important to our kids, we name our special teams. This makes it meaningful for them. The first name we identify is the team for the kicking game. The second name is the phase of the kicking game. The next name is the coach of that team. For example:

STORM

- Kickoff coverage

- Inside linebacker coach

VOLCANO

- Kickoff return
- Running back coach

PRIDE

- Punt protection and coverage
- Quarterback coach

MONEY

- PATs and field goals
- Offensive line coach

DEFENSE

- Punt block, PAT and FG defense
- Defensive coordinator

RAMBO

Our short-yardage and goal line team is made up of our double tight end and power I backs. It is a special team for us. It is not part of our offense as such. They are special to us. The head coach is in charge of the group.

HEAD COACH OF KICKING UNIT

- Select personnel (11 athletes).
- Pick two assistants to help.
- Set up practice routine.
- Establish game plan. (Film study).
- Responsible for substituting.

ESTABLISH PRIORITIES

#1 – Punt protection and coverage

#2 – Kickoff coverage

#3 – PAT's/fiel-goal protection

#4 – Punt block and return

#5 – Kickoff return

YEAR-ROUND DEVELOPMENT OF THE KICKING GAME

This is what we do in spring practice – identify kicking specialists: three each for varsity and junior varsity; deep snappers – punters - place kickers – holders - return men.

We do no team work in the spring. We work on specialty periods. Kicking coaches must identify the assistant with whom they want to work. We do not want 15 guys coming up to me in August and telling me they are punters. We find out who the punters are in the spring. We are going to send them to summer camps and they are going to work on punting all summer.

SUMMER PRACTICE

All specialists must follow the prescribed workout routine for their skill. They must be in shape and ready to go when practice begins in August. This includes kickers.

TWO-A-DAYS

All head coaches of a kicking unit evaluate personnel during conditioning circuit drills. They select 16 to 17 players for their phase of the kicking game. They give the names of the players selected to the head coach/kicking coordinator. They introduce the unit to team kicking situations. When they meet, only players on that kicking unit attend. We do not bother the rest of the team because they are the only players that need to know what we are doing in that phase of the game. We do a different team each day.

- Punt
- Extra point and field goal
- punt rush – block or return
- Kickoff coverage
- Kickoff return

The head coach of each unit will identify schemes to be used. In scrimmage situations, we work on the following: punt protection and coverage; PAT's; and field-goal protection.

IN-SEASON

Each coach will do their own film study to prepare for upcoming opponent. They establish meeting times for each unit. They develop the game plan for their unit. They set up the practice routine for the day their unit is to work. Also, they plan Thursday's circuit drill. They develop their own substitution plan.

GAME-WEEK PREPARATION

SATURDAY – Review previous night's game. Evaluate each aspect of special team play and evaluate personnel. Review and study of next opponent and give an overview of the opponent's style and personnel.

SUNDAY – Each special team "head coach" must do their own film study. They determine the approach for the week. They plan their phase of practice for the upcoming week.

MONDAY – Prior to practice, give overall scout report, meeting with entire squad. Our money team meets to review the weeks plan. The kicking period is for the money team and defensive team adjustment of opponent's PAT's and field goals.

TUESDAY – Pre-practice meeting time for Storm and Volcano teams. Team kicking period for Storm and Volcano.

WEDNESDAY – Pre-practice meeting time for The Pride team. Team kicking period for Pride team and defensive teams adjustments for punt block and punt return. Post-practice for "punt for points."

THURSDAY – Pre-game warm-up routine. Kicking circuit; review all situations.

FRIDAY – Prior to going on the field, any kicking team unit that needs review will meet. All special teams substitutions checked. I meet with them and have them kneel down. Then, I call out the kicking team and have them stand up as I call out their names. Kickers and kicking game personnel warm up early. Then, pre-game warm-up routine. expect to be "ready to execute."

I make the decisions on Friday night when we are going to punt and when we are going to fake the punt, and when we are going to go for a field goal, who is going to kick and who is on the team is up to the coach of that unit.

On Monday, Tuesday, and Wednesday, we have a 10-minute team special period. We do it at the beginning of practice. This is in addition to the individuals working on their specialty in individual sessions. On Thursday, our kicking circuit takes about 25 minutes.

THURSDAY PRE-GAME KICKING CIRCUIT

YARD LINE – SITUATION:

Yard Line	Situation
- 2	Take a safety
- 2	Tight punt; coverage
-30	Spread punt (two)
+40	Pooch punt
+40	Fake punt
+20	Field goal; kick and cover
+ 3	Extra point vs. block
+35	Pooch punt teturn/fair catch
-45	Regular punt return (two)
+30	Block: return or play safe
+ 3	Defense vs. PAT's
+ 3	Defense vs. PAT's regular/safe
- 2	JV tight punt – return (block or fair catch).
- 2	JV take a safety (defense: play for fumble)
-20	Kickoff after safety
+20	Kickoff return after safety
-40	Kickoff return

-40   Onside kickoff return

+40   Regular kickoff

+40   Onside kickoff

+40   Blooper onside kickoff

On Wednesday we do a drill called "punt for points." We punt the ball and cover the punt. We give points to the group, depending on where they down the punt. Early in the year at the start of the drill, it takes time to do the drill. After they learn the drill, it goes fast.

Let me show you this film of our kicking game . Also, I have a cut -up of the punt for points drill. (Film).

My time is up. Hopefully, I have said something that will help you.

Mahola!

THE TWO-MINUTE OFFENSE

University of Washington

It is nice to be here. The northwest has become the hot bed of college football. Oregon and Oregon State just had marvelous seasons. Congratulations to everyone, and let's keep it up. I've only been living up here for two years, but I am amazed at the quality of teaching these kids are getting from their high school coaches. Hopefully, we can have some fun tonight talking about something that all of us have to go through. It is my topic tonight, the two-minute offense.

It is without question the most screwed up portion of the game. Week in and week out, somebody makes a big mistake in the two minute offense.

If you watched the Cleveland-Pittsburgh game in the NFL, you saw an example of it. It was the first time they played against one another. It was late in the game, and Pittsburgh was down by three points. At that time, Cleveland hadn't won a game in the season. Pittsburgh ran a draw play to their big fullback, and he got all the way to the nine-yard line. There was 35 seconds left in the game, and they called their last time out.

They had a first-and-goal from the nine-yard line, with 35 seconds to go and no time outs. They called two plays in the huddle. The first play was another draw play for three yards. Their second-down play was an incomplete pass. It was third-and-goal from the six with 13 seconds left. On the next play, the quarterback got sacked. They watched the clock run out because they didn't have time to get their field-goal team on the field and had no time outs.

They lost the game to Cleveland needlessly. They might have lost the game in overtime, but it should have at least gone to overtime. That was a bad situation for the coaching staff of Pittsburgh.

As coaches, we have to tutor ourselves annually to get ready to play offense during this time of the game. During that last drive, you can't turn down the volume of the crowd. People get crazy in a close game in the last two minutes. The days after the game, we are continually second guessing ourselves, if we make a mistake during this time.

The way to avoid that is to practice this portion of the game. You need a plan of what you are going to do. We can practice a thousand situations and find out there are some things we missed.

My first year of college coaching, I was at UCLA, and we were playing against Washington State who was coached by Dennis Erickson. UCLA was ranked number one in the country, and Washington State had Tim Rosenthaul as their quarterback. They had a great team and came to Los Angeles for the game. We got ahead 27-6. Washington State played well and near the close of the game, the score was 34-30 Washington State.

Washington State punted the ball to us, and we decided to put in a personnel group which was different than our normal two-minute offensive team. We wanted to get four vertical patterns on the field. Our normal formation in the two minute offense was three wide receivers and two backs. We put in a tight end and took out one of the backs. We went into a two-by-two set, with two receivers to each side to get the four verticals pattern.

After the punt, we figured we could hit that play and go back to our normal two-minute offense. We had 35 seconds to go in the game. We had made all the choices of the plays we were going to do after the punt. We were going to run the four verticals and use a clock play to kill the clock. The punt-return man broke a tackle and returned the ball forty yards. Instead of having the ball our 25-yard line, we had the ball on their 45-yard line. We hit the pass just as we had planned and got the ball to the 7-yard line. The quarterback hurried up and used the clock play to kill the clock. Unfortunately for us in that situation at the 7-yard line, we could not get a first down. So, we only had three plays to get a touchdown. There were 22 seconds left in the game when he threw the ball into the ground.

We had three shots to get the touchdown, but we didn't score. I would have loved to have had the fourth down to try to get the ball into the end zone. Those are the types of things we are going to talk about. It is not going to be about plays. This is going to be a lecture on how to organize your two-minute drill.

The first question you need to ask yourself in the two-minute drill is, "who calls the plays?" A lot of teams have someone up in the press box calling plays. That is great, but at this time of the game, the more the communication has to travel to the field, the greater chance there is to get screwed up. How many different channels do you want in getting the play on the field.

The perfect solution is to have your quarterback call the plays. But, how many of you have a quarterback who is capable of doing that? I think the head coach should make the calls if someone on your sideline is going to call the plays. He is the one who has to be responsible for the outcome of the game.

The next thing is the signals you are going to use to get the play into the game. We all have different ways to signal the plays. Some use a messenger to get more kids involved in their program. Some people use hand signals given by one person or perhaps several people. Some people use a mixture of sending in the formation with signals and sending in the play with a messenger.

In the two-minute drill, you have to streamline your system of getting plays into the game. The next thing is the number of formations you want to use and the number of plays to use from each formation. Maybe you want to use two or three formations with a single play from each formation. These are the thoughts you need to have. What you don't want is a mistake. You don't want to lose a game that you had to win because some communication was lost because of bedlam on the sideline. You have to expect bedlam on the sideline during this period. That is the way it happens. You want to get the play into the game to give your guys a chance to run the play you think will work in that situation.

The next thing is your snap count. We all have different snap counts. We all have the ability to draw the defense offsides by using long counts. In the two-minute drill, your snap count has to be something different. At UCLA, our snap count was "DOWN, SET, HUT." If we wanted to draw someone offsides, we called freeze. We called the cadence, and used voice tones to draw the defense. If someone jumped, we snapped the ball, and the quarterback took a knee.

When we got to the two-minute drill, we couldn't use that cadence. If we did, we would lose three to four seconds on each down. That could be possibly the amount of time you need to win the game. We go to the first sound. But, the first sound also gives the defense the jump too. But, those are the types of questions you have to ask yourself in making your two-minute plan.

If you decide to go into a shotgun, the snap really becomes important. That is because of the noise. The shotgun also lets the defense get in on the snap, particularly if you use a nonverbal count.

You must have a plan, so you don't screw up before you get started. You have to answer all the questions before your get into the two-minute drill. You can't leave any stone unturned.

You must decide what personnel you want on the field in the two-minute drill. You have to get your best players on the field in the two-minute offense. Don't get so carried away with formations. If your best receiver is your tight-end, don't use a formation without a tight-end position. Don't get hung up on formations. Get your best guys on the field. They give you the best chance to win. Don't have a tight end who can make big plays for you standing next to you on the sideline.

The next thing you need to consider is formations. The three-wide out formation is a great formation, but it is limited. If you don't have that great tight end, it will be good for you. First, it gives you a protection scheme that can handle just about any situation you get from the defense. You can take on almost any blitz, except the eight-man blitz. You can also get your backs out on check-down patterns.

THREE WIDES/TWO BACKS

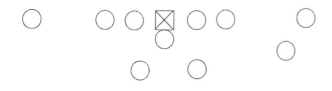

If you have a situation where you have a great tight end, and you want to use the four verticals pattern, you can use a formation we call DEUCE. It is a one-back set with a tight end and flanker to one side and a split end and a slot man to the other. It gives you a four-verticals pattern from any place on the field. You can work the two-man side and still have great protection by leaving your tight end in.

DEUCE

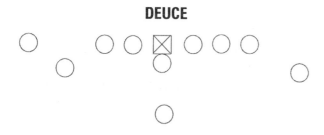

The TREY formation is a good formation without much adjustment. We simple move the slot back over to the flanker's side outside the tight end. It gives you the same personnel, but provides you the chance to get one-on-one with the split end. Also, in this formation, it is hard for the defense to disguise when they are blitzing. That gives you a chance to check to your max protection and get a one-on-one with your split end.

TREY

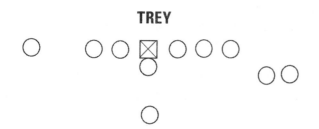

The other formation that fits into this thought is the TRIPS formation. That puts the tight end away from your three wide receivers. It gives you a chance to get what we call check throws. You can protect seven men, get things down the field, and still be able to run the ball to the tight end. Never lose sight of the ability to run the football in the two-minute situation.

TRIPS

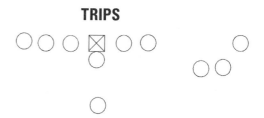

We run a speed option and zone play to the tight-end side. We also use motion by the fullback and to get to a no-backs set, and get five receivers in the pattern. As far as formations, you have to consider who your best players are and how to get them on the field in the two-minute situation.

However, the more formations you have, the greater the chance for a mess up when you are signaling. In college, the clock stops after a first down, when the pass is incomplete, or when the ball goes out of bounds. You are going to get a chance to get in the huddle when the clock is stopped for one of those situations. There aren't going to be too many times during the season when you are going to have to run two plays in a row without a huddle. Sometimes coaches put in too much in the two-minute package. But, you don't want to be caught with not enough. That is critical.

When I start talking about three and four wide receivers, the next important thing is the protection scheme you are going to use. Whatever offensive set you choose, you need the ability to protect against seven guys rushing. That keeps you from having to throw hot patterns and sight adjustments in a fourth-and-eight situation. When the defensive coordinator gets a little threatened, he is going to start blitzing. If your quarterback doesn't have the equipment to handle the blitz, you are not sound. I think you have to be able to block seven with your scheme. That doesn't mean you are going to keep seven in to block, it simply means you have the ability to block seven if you need to.

The next thing to consider is what we call special sitations. These are inventorying-type items that need to be part of any two-minute package. These are sideline passes or chunk throws, where we are going to throw the ball to the sideline to get it out of bounds. These patterns include comeback throws. We want the ability to get big chunks of yardage and get the ball out of bounds.

You do not want to forget your running game in the two-minute situation. This is a critical part of the drill. The draw play is an obvious play that you want to run. What we got good at this year at Washington was the option, especially into the boundary. That also was another way to get the ball out of bounds. We did it when we felt the blitz coming. Against Kansas State ,we were able to get a huge play from the option to help us win the game and get us into the Cotton Bowl. It ended up as a twenty-five yard run to the one-yard line. We later scored with about 45 seconds left in the game to win the game.

Along the same lines with the running game are screens. But remember when you put screens in the inventory, you are going to have to signal them into the game. The screen is a great weapon to have in your arsenal when the defense goes from a prevent defense to a pressure defense.

Make sure you change your drop point for the quarterback. Don't constantly drop the quarterback to the same spot. Use drop back, half roll, stop outs, or sprint outs to change where the quarterback is going to be in the pocket.

The goal of the two-minute offense is to get a score, either a field goal or touchdown. You need a red zone package in your signaling capabilities. That is where you go into a transition for the close area of the field where things get restricted.

You need to have a goal-line play. We practice our last play every Friday. You may never call this play, but you we have it in the package.

The quarterback needs to know how to execute the clock play. The easiest way to do it is to align in the same formation from the previous play. But, it has to be in a hurry so the quarterback can get the ball to the ground.

A perfect example of that was after I became a full time assistant at UCLA. We finally made it to the Rose Bowl. We played Wisconsin in 1993, the year before I left to go to Colorado. We didn't play very well and had a lot of turnovers. But at the end of the game we were only down 21 - 16 and had a chance to win it with a touchdown. There were about 40 seconds left, and we were going right down the field. We had it to the 40-yard line going in with a 3rd-down-and eight. We hit J. J. Stokes with a pass and he turned it in to a big gainer to the 18-yard line. There were 10 seconds left on the clock. We had a first down, but no time outs. We signaled the quarterback to throw it in the ground and run the clock play. He looked at us, took the snap, and got sacked. There was no way to get all our players back and snap the ball. Wisconsin knew we screwed up. That was the longest 10 seconds of my life. We could have gotten two chances at the end zone and probably could have won the game because of the momentum. Watching those 10 seconds come off the clock I made up my mind at that point, that any quarterback I coached would know how to handle that situation. You have to practice that situation with your quarterback and have a signal for the play.

Your quarterback needs to know how to POSITION the ball for a field-goal attempt. Using this play is assuming you have the time and downs to get the ball to the middle of the field. What you want to do is get the ball off the hash marks and into the middle of the field for the kicker.

I mentioned the last play earlier, but you have to have a last play depending where you are on the field. We have a last play from the 10-yard line to the 2-yard line. We have one from the 25- to the 10-yard line. We have a last play from outside the 25-yard line. You should know what your last play is in any situation.

When you are outside the 25-yard line, we start to think about the Hail Mary pass. I was fortunate to be at Colorado when one of the all-time great Hail Mary's was made up at Michigan. Everyone knows what happened. It was simply remarkable. The ball went 73 yards in the air.

After you get your inventory, you need to think about the situations you may encounter. The first situation is the obvious one: *you need a touchdown.* It is the easiest because all you do is hurry up. The next situation is difficult because it requires a lot of thinking. That is the situation when you *need a field goal.* The chief question you have to answer is from where your field goal kicker is most accurate. At what spot on the field do you feel comfortable that you have enough yards to give him a chance. You don't want to throw that last pass and have the ball intercepted when you were already in field-goal range.

The next situation is when a team *needs two touchdowns* at the end of the game. People make more mistakes here than anywhere else. I think people wait way too long to go to the hurry-up offense. In games where you are having trouble stopping the other team, you have to make the decision to go to that offense. Sometimes we go to the clock offense with 11 minutes to go in the game.

When I do that, I want to break the rhythm of the game. I don't want the game to go along at the pace it has been preceding. You may end up losing by a bigger score, but it only counts one loss. I think you need to consider how you are going to go about winning the game, instead of waiting around for the break that may never come.

The next thing is the transition. This is what you probably should spend most of your time on because it happens every game. That is the transition from clock offense to bleeding the clock that occurs just before the half in every game. That is the situation where you don't want to turn the ball over to the other team just before halftime. We want to go into the locker room with the score as it is. You want to nibble at scoring, but if things don't go well, you want to bleed the clock. It takes practice to do that.

The next thing is the most difficult. You have to manage the situation. The first thing we do is to go through our information gathering. That includes what kind of score we need and how many time outs we have to do it in.

A lot of people use their gut instincts on time outs. Time outs to me are used to add plays to your drive. When you get to the end of a half, we want to use our time outs solely for saving plays. We don't use them to save time on the clock. I have a sheet which I go over on Friday night for each situation and the way I use the time outs. We talk about it ahead of time and are ready to implement anything that happens into our game planning.

If I have three time outs left, and I need a touchdown, I like to use them like this. I will use the first time out at or around one minute thirty seconds. I'll use the second time out at or around one minute. I'll use the third one at or around 30 seconds. Rarely will we call the time outs on the 30-second marks. That is why I say at or around in the description of my time table.

I have some rules for time-out calls. I always use one after a sack, even if it is your last one. I have reasons for this thinking. First, your wide receivers have to run back from down field, and the quality of his next route is important. Plus, you are a little demoralized. Where the objective may have been 1st-and-10 is now a 2nd-and-long situation. You may not need to gain that many yards, but if you don't take a time out and calm the situation, it could get worse.

The coaching point here is to teach your quarterback where to unload the ball to avoid the sack. If the quarterback breaks containment, he doesn't have to throw the ball to anyone. All he has to do is run it out of bounds.

We never want to call time out after a first down. If we have two or three time outs left with twenty or so seconds left in the game, it is okay to call a time out after a first down. But, we don't want to waste a time out after a first down.

In the field-goal situation, we want to save a time out for our field goal. It gives us a better chance to go out there calmly to kick the field goal to win the game. Certainly, we practice the situation where we have to come in and align for the field with the clock moving, but it is better if you can take your time. That means we subtract 30 seconds from our time table. We are taking our first time out at or around one minute. The second one at or around thirty seconds, and the third one is before the field goal attempt. That gives you a chance to use your positioning play.

Next, I'll get into the *formula for the drive.* It is based on the principle of two pass plays. I call them chunk and control passes. A chunk is a pass that will gain 20 yards and has a completion rate of about 50 percent. The control pass is one that gains 5 to 10 yards and has an eighty-percent completion rate.

If I have to drive the ball 75 yards for a touchdown, I factor in ten seconds for every ten yards. It will take me 70 seconds to drive that ball 70 yards. If there is a minute and ten seconds left in the game, and I am on my own thirty-yard line, I don't have to throw a chunk pass. I can throw the eighty-percent passes and figure out a way to get down there.

If I have 50 seconds left, and I'm on my own 30-yard line, I'll need a chunk or two to get myself in position to use the control passes. I saw a NFL game on Monday night. The Buffalo Bills with Jim Kelly at quarterback had the ball with one minute and five seconds to go in the game. They had the ball on their sixteen-yard line and needed a touchdown. Jim Kelly threw the ball to Thurman Thomas six times in a row. The last play of the game he hit Andrea Risen for a touchdown.

He didn't panic and was patient. He took what the defense gave him. It goes to show you, if you are hitting passes, you are creating two things. You are picking up yards and are creating rhythm. The defensive coordinator is in an uncomfortable position, to where he thinks he has to do something. What he does is call the blitz, which puts you into some one-on-one situations where you can hit the big play. The offense wants to be in control of situations if at all possible.

If the clock doesn't allow for that, as against Stanford this year, you have to do something different. We had 47 seconds to move 80 yards and score a touchdown. We had to throw the ball downfield.

That is how we decide what type of drive we need. The next thing is red zone awareness. In this section of your planning, you have to have plays that will work in the red zone. Homer Smith was the coordinator when I was at UCLA. He always put three people into the end zone. His routes were varied, but he had three wide receivers. He used the post and wheel routes and the post-corner to get people open. He always had one receiver in each corner and one under the goal post. He wanted three chances to get into the end zone.

RED ZONE PASSES

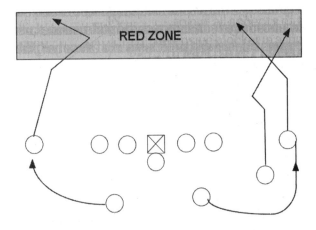

Red zone awareness also means the defense is in a pressure situation. You have to know if the defense is going to continue to give you something in the bend-but-don't-break mind-set or are they going to come after you. That has to do with your ideas on protection.

If you only need a field goal and you have a good kicker, the red zone starts when you cross midfield. Once you get to the 25-yard line, you can win the game. Once you cross midfield, you have to think the defensive coordinator is going to start to come after your quarterback.

I think the clock play is an overused deal. The clock play as far as I'm concerned does not come into play until there are about 20 seconds left in the game. However, you may want to use it to buy some time for your offense. I have a tendency to use it at the end of the first half rather than at the end of the game. The reason is you don't have to have a touchdown or field goal before halftime. You are just trying to get yourself in position for any type of points. At the end of the game when you know what you have to have, we use the clock play around 20 seconds. Each play is about five seconds long. In 20 seconds, I can run about four plays.

You have to practice these things on the field. You have to set a time aside each week when you are going to practice you clock offense. I generally do it on Thursday afternoon. We are not in full gear, but we will go up and down the field. I tell them the situations, and we have to react on the run. I play the referee. We go up and down the field with two drives. One field-goal drive and one touchdown drive is what we practice. Once a week is not really enough time. Because of that, in our fall practice we use the two-minute drill as a conditioning drill. It is a great conditioning drill, and you are killing two birds with one stone.

- EDITORS NOTE: Coach Neuheisel did a demonstration at the end of his lecture using four coaches from the audience. He let the coaches be his four quarterbacks. One of the coaches played his first quarterback, and Coach Neuheisel took the coaches through his teaching procedure that he uses with his quarterbacks on clock management.

- He has a board on the floor. The board is marked like a football field. He keeps track of the ball with a pin. He has the fourth quarterback make all kinds of noise. The first quarterback has to make the calls. The third quarterback is calling time out loud, as long as the quarterback is not speaking. If the quarterback is calling his play, he keeps the time to himself. Coach Neuheisel has control of the situation. He tells the quarterback the results of each play and when the clock is stopped for a first down.

- He gave a great demonstration about down-and-distance and clock management. Everyone really liked what they saw.

- The first quarterback called the plays; the second quarterback kept the clock; the third quarterback kept track of the time outs, and the fourth quarterback tried to cause confusion. Coach Neuheisel led them down the field and ended up in a last-play situation for the quarterback.

Thank you, gentlemen. It has been a pleasure. I appreciate your attention.

THE DROP-BACK PASSING GAME

University of Texas, El Paso

It is truly an honor to be with you and to be back home in Louisville, Kentucky. When I come back home and see people that have helped me get where I am today, it is a touching feeling for me. People do not appreciate what you have here until you get away from here. You have something real special here in Kentucky. Sometimes you have to get away from it to realize just how special it really is. The camaraderie you have here with each other is second to none. This will always be home for me and my family.

I will get right into football. I know you do not want to hear a lot of philosophy. When I was here at the University of Louisville with Coach Howard Schnellenberger, we were a football team that played with two backs all of the time. We had two backs, one tight end, and two wide receivers in our formation all of the time. We were real vanilla. We had a real strong weakside running game, and we had a real strongside pass game. We were able to keep the defense balanced. Back then, most teams were playing the 50 front with a 3-deep secondary. We were able to get away with this type of offense. Today, if you put two men in the backfield teams will play the eight man front and make it difficult to run the ball to the weakside. Then, they load up on you where you can't throw the ball on the strongside.

I thought it was a must for us to expand our package and to have the ability to take the backs out of the backfield, move our tight end around, and put our receivers where we wanted them. We are using a lot more personnel groupings. However, we are still based out of a two-back set. It is important for you to have a base to start from and then you build your offense from your base. If you have a lot of personnel groupings and a lot of different formations, it makes it difficult for the quarterback to learn. You have to keep it as simple for the quarterback as possible.

In our offense, we give the quarterback the ability to put any formation and any personnel grouping on the field and still have his same progression that he has to read. We lined up in a two-back set with a split end, a wide receiver, and a split end. We call that formation "East" because it is to the right side or east side of the map of the USA. If we wanted to line up in the I formation, we just call out east I formation. If we want to move the back to the tight-end side, we just call it near east. If we want to put him outside with the pro back, we call it out east. We keep all of our base formations the same. What we have started doing is to put in certain receivers against certain backs, and we use different personnel groupings.

BASE FORMATION

FORMATIONS ADJUSTMENTS

We can take four plays and run them from all formations. We can line up in about 15 different formations and run these plays. We will motion at times, but when you start moving people around you cause problems for your quarterback. If you can move the offensive people and feel sure you know what the defense will get into, you can use it to your advantage. I prefer to set the formation and let the quarterback see what he has to go against.

We are still based in the orginal set. All of our protections are based out of the two-back set. We have cut down on our protections to a minimum. At one time, we had about six different protections. We had a 3-step, 5-step, and a 7- step drop protection. We had problems when we moved backs out of the set, because they were involved in the protection when they were in the backfield. We were fully protected against the seven-man rush. If the eighth man got into a threatening position, and they were in man coverage, we would go to our blitz pick-up package.

When you take players out of the backfield, you are going to put more pressure on your quarterback. The quarterback has to understand protection. We have to spend a lot of time with the quarterback to let him know who the back was responsible for in the protection.

Our number one personnel grouping this year was our base set. We did it 38 percent of the time. Our number two personnel grouping was to put the H-back outside with the pro back. We moved them around. Just because we based out of a two-back set does not mean that we cannot move the formations around. You can adjust the formations to most any set.

If we want to go to a twins set, we put the back outside with the H-back. If we want to go to Trips, we can flex our tight end to the twins set. Our tight end was the number one tight-end receiver in the country this past year. He made first team All American. He is really just an average athlete.

To be successful, you must complete 60 percent of your passes. When I was with Coach Schnellenberger, we had to do a lot of different studies on ourselves. One study made a lot of sense to me related to pass completions in a ten-year study. When looked at the percentages of completions to our receivers over a ten-year period, this is what we found.

RECEIVER	COMPLETIONS
Z-back	= 43%
X-end	= 45%
Y-end	= 72%
H-back	= 74%

For us to get the 60-percent completion ratio that is essential to be successful, we have to throw the ball to the inside receivers a lot. We feel like a heavyweight boxer. We jab, jab, and jab, and then we are going to throw the knockout punch. We throw the ball to our tight end a lot.

It is important to stretch the field horizontally and vertically every time you line up. Formations are great, but they are not worth a darn if the quarterback does not understand what you are lined up in. We keep it as simple as we possible can for the quarterback. We progressive read everything. This takes the pressure off the quarterback. We have the 3-step, 5-step, and the 7-step drop passing games. A lot of people question the 7-step drop passing game because it takes too much time. But if you have a small quarterback, the deeper he can get on his drop, the more vision he will have on the passing game. He will be able to step up on the 7-step game.

The depth of our pass routes depends on the depth of the drop of our quarterback. This is what we want with our receivers.

QUARTERBACK DROP	DEPTH OF ROUTE
3-step drop	6 Yards
5-step drop	12 Yards
7-step drop	18 Yards

The depth this where we want the receivers to make their break on the route. We have to set up all of our progressions and packages. We have strongside combination routes, middle-of-the-field combination routes, and we have weakside combination routes. We have the ability to stretch the defense both horizontally and vertically.

I want to talk about progression reading. I will show you a base play everyone has, and then I will show you how we can get to so many different plays out of one formation. First of all, protection is critical. When I was a receiver coach and a running back coach, I always thought a pass play started out with the route structure. Once you become a head coach, and you understand the total picture, you realize you must protect the quarterback first.

Our number one protection is our 70 protection. If it is against an even front, we are going to count the defensive front. The way we count is by counting the men on the line. The center has 0 if there is a man on him. The guards have the #1 on the line of scrimmage on his side. The tackle is responsible for #2 on the line of scrimmage on his side. The tight end is incorporated into the route. The H-back is responsible for the linebacker to his side. The fullback is responsible for the linebacker to his side.

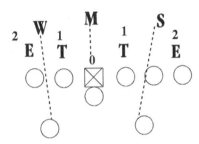

Our center and guards are responsible for the depth of the pocket. On a 3-step drop, the launch point or set up point for the quarterback is going to be at a depth of five yards. On a 5-step drop, our quarterback is going to set up at seven yards. On a 7-step drop, our quarterback is going to set up at nine yards. It is critical for the offensive line to understand where the quarterback is throwing the ball from.

Because the center and guards have that responsibility, they must vary their technique on each drop. If it is a 3-step drop, our offensive line is going to block aggressively. They are going to attack the defense on the line of scrimmage.

Our tackles are responsible for the width of the pocket. They have to be a little more athletic. They are going to get man-on-man a lot. They are responsible for the width of the pocket. They have to know when to put their head down and run the pass rushers on by the quarterback. They must know when they have to jump the defenders according on how wide they are. They have to know how deep our quarterback is setting up, so they can adjust their technique.

When our quarterback sets up at seven yards, we can be semi-aggressive. The quarterback is going to set up nine yards deep. If they are aggressive, we will "catch" them and drive them back. If they are aggres-

sive, the more we run the 7-step drop. It is easier to "catch" them and drive them outside. If the defensive line is knocking the line back into the area of the quarterback, he will not be able to see to throw the ball. The more talented the defensive linemen are, the more we ask our line to get back off the ball. That is when we try to get the ball to our tight end and backs.

If we have a question about which protection to use, we go to our 70 protection. Our backs have to learn to read on the way out of the backfield. If we face an odd front, we line the defense up and count them the same way. Our center has zero. The guards have #1 on the LOS and the tackles have #2 on the LOS. We will give the center help on the nose depending on which way the nose man is shading. We have the guard "tap" the back of the receiver to make sure we get help on the nose man. Then, we put the back out into the pattern. We have the ability to adjust the blocking if we want to here.

It is real important for our backs to be able to get out and into the route. Against the 3-deep look, we are going to run a flat and a slant route. We number the plays. That would be 72 for us. The 70 refers to the protection, and the 2 is a slant route. For us 2 and 3 are the slant routes. The 0 and 1 are the take-off routes. The 4 and 5 are out routes. You can number the routes anyway you want to. But once the quarterback knows the call, he knows the routes the receivers are going to run. When we call 72, the quarterback knows the two outside receivers are going to run a slant.

SLANT

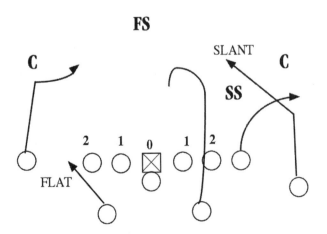

If we move the H-back outside to the wideside ,this is what it would look like. The outside men run the slant.

TRIPS – SLANT

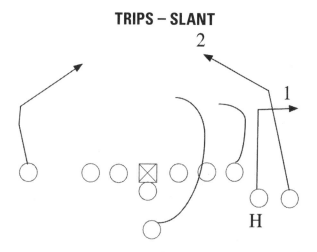

The progression time for our quarterback depends on the drop. Our quarterback is setting up at a depth of five yards. On a 3-step drop, we are telling the quarterback he has a maximum protection time of 2.0 seconds. On a 5-step drop, he has a maximum protection of 2.5 seconds. On a 7-step drop, he has a maximum protection of 3.0 seconds.

For us to get our passing operation done in that short period of time, it is almost impossible to have the quarterback drop back and then read the defense. If the quarterback is not coached well enough, we are going to get penalized for delay of game while he figures out what the defense is doing. The quarterback cannot react quickly enough, and we will get a penalty. So, we do not worry about the defense. We worry about our own people. If the quarterback comes back seven yards and looks for the safety man and then tries to find our receiver, it is too late. So we tell our quarterback he has two seconds on a 3-step drop to get the ball to our receivers.

His first progression is the tight end in the pro set. In the trips set the H-back is the first progression. If he is open, he throws the ball to him. If he is not open, then he knows the slant to the outside man who will be open. He is the second progression.

For the quarterback to get back and set up on 3-step drop to get five yards in depth, it takes 1.5 seconds. This is from the snap to the set up. It takes 1.5 seconds to do that. We give the quarterback 1.5 to 1.7 on his first progression. We give him 1.8 to 2.0 on his sec-

ond progression. If no one is open after 2.0 seconds he throws the ball away or tries to avoid the sack, or he tucks the ball and runs.

We do get our backs out into the pattern. However, on the 3-step drop, it does not give you time to get him the ball because you only have two seconds to get rid of the ball. We do get the back out for flare control, which I think is critical in the passing game. Make sure you get some flare control patterns in the offense. You can control linebackers with flare control. If you are going to throw the 3-step drop passing game, you must horizontally stretch the underneath coverage. Time will not allow you to get depth down-field to stretch the defense vertically. So on a 3-step drop passing game, you are going to horizontally stretch the underneath coverage. If you can get three receivers out, you are going to have bigger holes. You can keep the linebackers from sliding out on the slants and other routes you are going go to run off the 3-step drop.

It is critical for the back to read the protection responsibilities and then get to the spot to flare control the linebackers and keep them at home. We are worried about the corners when we throw the slants. We are concerned with the inside defenders, so we want to make sure they stay home. The only way they are going to stay home is to get your backs to check down. We tell our backs to check down over the inside leg of the onside tackle. He always goes there and he is there for flare control.

On our 3-step drop passing game, we can spread them out. We are throwing the take-off routes. You have to throw the take-off route in this part of the game. We spend a lot of time working on the take-off routes. The critical thing in making the play work is to make sure the quarterback throws the ball on timing. The other point is to make sure the quarterback gets set up properly.

I want to go over the way we teach the quarterback his footwork on the drop. Coach Howard Schnellenberger sent a lot of good quarterbacks to the NFL, and he used this procedure for the quarterback to set up. If you have a quarterback that understands techniques and keeps himself under control, he can be effective in this system. We did a study on the things that cause problems for the quarterback related to his mechanics that cause interceptions. First, is when he throws off balance. Second, is when he rushes his throw.

We do it a little differently than what some people do as far as technique is concerned in dropping back on the pass. I am not going to spend a lot of time talking about taking the ball from the center. There are a lot of different ways to do that but the key is to get the ball from the center cleanly. I have four quarterbacks now, and three of them take it differently from the center. As long as they take it cleanly from the center, I am not going to change them. We get a little bend in the knees. When we go back, we are getting our shoulders perpendicular to the line of scrimmage right now. We want the quarterback to bring the ball to his chest. We want him to go back breast plate-to-breast plate with the ball.

If it is a 5-step drop, the quarterback is going to stick his foot in the ground at five yards depth. We want him to stick the foot in the ground parallel to the line of scrimmage all of the time. I do not care if we are throwing left, right, or middle, we stick it in the ground parallel to the line of scrimmage. There are only a handful of people in the country that can stick their foot in the ground and throw the ball downfield. It takes a special person to do that. Not a lot of people are blessed with that ability. So, we help the quarterback out.

We make sure he stops his momentum from going back, and he gets all of his weight going back toward the target. We emphasize stopping the momentum with the plant foot. When we stick that foot in the ground at a depth of five yards, we have the weight distributed, we have the ball up, and we have a slight bend in the knees.

After this, we want the quarterback to gather and then throw. We do this the same way every time. We gather for direction. When we throw the ball, we throw with the lead foot. A lot of people will tell you if you are throwing the ball down the middle of the field, to point the "big" toe toward the target. I feel this prematurely causes you to open his hips. We want to keep the hips compact, and we want to get our lower body involved. The lower body is what gives you the accuracy on the pass. So we point our "little" toe toward the target. This keeps the hips compact and allows us to get the whip in the hips on the throw. It is like a baseball pitcher. He gets his lower body into the throw.

The target is where the ball and the receiver meet. It is not where the receiver is at the time. It is where he is going to be when the ball arrives. This allows the quarterback to keep all of his throwing motion toward the target. I do not want to spend a lot of time with the quarterback's throwing motion. Some people want the quarterback to get the ball up as high as his ear. If you have a quarterback that has a low release, you can put up a volleyball net and have him throw over the net to force the release to be higher.

But, I do not spend a lot of time on this. I prefer to work with the motion of each kid and try to help them get better rather than trying to break them down to start over. That may take a year just to get them back to where they were before.

I am going to get into what we do the most and that is our 7-step drop game. If you want to cut down the depth of the receivers to help you, I will cover the routes that we have been the most successful with. I want to cover a couple a couple of combination routes to the strongside, middle of the field, weakside combinations routes. Then I will cover our favorite screen pass off this particular protection.

You can run all of these routes from any formation and run them with any protection. I will draw these plays up out of the two back set, but it really does not matter if you use a one back set, trips, or whatever. We count from the outside to the inside. Our number one route is what we call "Y choice."

It is a route that we have made a living on for a long time. It is based on the tight end having the Choice to go wherever he wants to go in a 10 to 12 yard area to get himself open. But, a lot depends on what the tight end is going to do. It depends on how the defense lines up and how the defense plays him.

We call this play 78 Y choice. If it is a three-linebacker scheme, we have to find out who is covering the hook area. We describe the hook area from the inside legs of the two tackles. The strong slot area is from the inside leg of the tackle to five yards outside the tight end. The weak slot area is from the left of the weak side tackle to five yards outside. The flat area is from the slot areas to the sideline.

PASSING AREAS

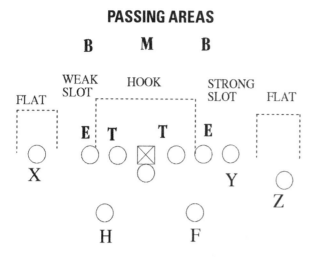

We try to horizontally stretch the hook, slot, or flat area on the strong side, or we are going to vertically stretch the flat, slot, or hook on the strongside.

We are going to find out who is responsible for covering the hook and we are going to work off that. On a 7-step drop, the tight end has his choice on the route. Our receivers are going to make their break at 18 yards. Our tight end is a little different. He has a man over him, and he is not as fast the wide receiver. So, we try to cut his route down to 12 to 15 yards. We will adjust the receivers' routes according to their talent. We do not adjust the quarterback. We want to keep the quarterback the same all of the time.

On 78 Y Choice, the tight end is going to come off the ball inside looking for the defender that is covering the hook. The way the defender plays the area will determine how the route is run. If the back goes deep with the tight end, he works to his depth and keeps the defender on his inside and then breaks away from him. If the defender overruns the play and gets wider than the tight end, we break back inside on him across the ball.

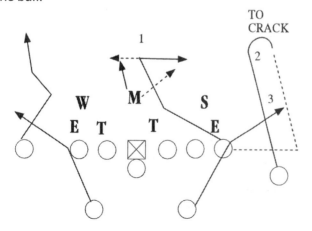

We get flare control with the two backs to take the linebackers outside. Our tight end is our number 1 progression.

On the 7-step drop we have maximum protection time of three seconds. We have three progressions built into the route. Our Z-back runs a comeback route. He drives off the ball to sell the take-off route. When he gets at the desired depth, he plants his foot in the ground and puts his chin on his chest and comes back to the "crack." We call it the crack to give him a landmark. The crack is where the sideline and line of scrimmage meet. If the receiver would keep coming back toward the bench, he would run into the crack where the sideline and line of scrimmage meet. The quarterback always knows the Z-back is going to come back on the crack.

It is important for the fullback to understand the type of protection you are using on a play. If he does not know the protection being used, he will get knocked off his track. We like to get him out wide and as clean as possible. He must be like an eel and keep his eyes open. He wants to get depth as he gets width.

On the backside, the X-end is running an arrow flag route. It is going to be dictated on the coverage. If it is a 3-deep coverage we are going to run it off a slant. He drives off the ball at a depth of six yards, he plants and takes three hard steps. If the corner hangs, he flattens out the route. If he jumps the route, we want him to go deep, and we lay the ball out to him. Our H-back must get depth as he gets width on his release. He is the flare control on the backside.

We are throwing the ball to the strongside. If the defense gives us a rotation and leaves us in a one-on-one situation on the backside, we will throw the ball to the backside. Our number 1 progression is going to be the tight end. Our number 2 progression is the Z-back. The number 3 progression is the back in the flat.

If we face a two-linebacker scheme with 3-deep coverage, we are going to attack it a little differently. We are going to use a horizontal stretch from the hook to the slot area. Now, the tight end works a one-on-one route against the Sam linebacker. Now, he will have a lot more room to work in. We run the corner out with the Z-back. If we face a two-linebacker scheme, we are licking our chops. We love to have our tight end working against a linebacker. The depth of the Sam linebacker determines the depth of the route for the tight end. If the linebacker is even with him, he breaks it outside. If he is deeper than the end, he hooks it up. If he is wider than the end, he continues to go across to the ball.

If it is against man coverage, he must recognize it. Now, all of the zone principles are off. Against a zone, you have spots to go to so you can stretch the defense. But, once you see it is man coverage the depth and width are off. Now it is the receiver against the defender. Now, we are looking for separation.

First, the end has to identify who is going to cover him. If the safety jumps down to cover him, he has to beat him. We are looking for separation on the route. We can cut the route down to eight yards or go up to 13 yards. He goes to a depth where he can get separation to beat the man that is covering him. He is still our number 1 progression. We are going to stay on him for 0.3 seconds. The quarterback gets set up and looks for the tight end. The end will try to get inside or outside leverage on the defender and break off to the open area. It is real important for the end not to get any more depth when he makes his break, inside or outside. He wants to make sure his hips and shoulders are pointed in the direction he is going, so he has enough speed to get away from the defender. He makes all the adjustments with his head. He wants to be under control. He catches the ball with the thumbs out. He wants to make sure he is going parallel to the line of scrimmage, or he may bring it back a slightly.

On the comeback route for our Z-back, the depth is no problem. He can cut it down a little, but he has to understand that he is the number 2 progression. He has to get enough depth down the field to let the quarterback work the number one progression before he comes to the Z-back. We give him a minimum of 15 yards and a maximum of 20 yards against man coverage. If he can make the defender think he is running a take-off route he can run the comeback. We want him to drive off to the man's inside numbers to condense him down. We sell the take off for two steps, and then drive the inside foot in the ground. Then, he comes straight back down to the crack.

The two backs flatten out their route against man coverage. They vertical push up the field and then flatten the route off to the flat. We do not care about depth, we want separation. Everyone is on their own, and they have to beat the man that is covering them.

We love to run the flag route against man coverage on the backside. We will work our progression to him if he can get inside leverage on his man. If the defender lines up inside-out on us, we want to drive at his outside numbers and keep outside leverage on him. We get a depth of 10 yards, and then we will separate. It really turns into a pressure-off out route. If the defender gets too tight on the receiver, we will go over the top with him.

If we throw this route 100 times, we will throw 75 of them to the tight end. Probably 10 of them would go to the wideouts. The rest of them will go to the backs.

Now, I want to cover the vertical stretch to the strongside. We can put a back out on the outside and run an H-back choice. We can put a twin set outside and make it a trips look and run the choice. We can make it a Z choice. We can TAG any receiver we want with the choice. We always designate the choice to the 3-receiver side for flare control purposes. You do not want to go to the choice on the 2-receiver side because you can get caught in two receivers going against three defenders. We always want to go 3-against-3 or 3-against-2. Our choice is always run to the 3-receiver side.

I told you earlier it was critical to be able to throw the take off. In the 3-step drop passing game, you have to keep the defense off you. If you do not have the ability to throw the ball deep, you will not be able to keep the defense off you. At all levels of coaching, you must spend time to make sure players know what you are trying to accomplish.

On the take off, you must break the cushion down before you can get separation. To break that cushion down completely, you must be patient. If you are moving back every yard you run with the ball in the air the percentage of completions comes down. The shorter the throw, the higher the completion percentage. We do want to give any yards away by running the width that makes it a longer throw.

We want the receiver to drive off the ball toward the inside numbers of the defender covering him. We want to get close enough to the defender where we could stick him on the inside of his breast plate with a pin if we had one. We want to overemphasize the inside head stick; we are going to avoid the collision; and we are going to get depth down the field. It is critical to avoid the collision.

We call this 78 Bat. We tell the receiver we want to throw the ball at a depth of 35 to 42 yards. We would like to throw the ball over his outside shoulder with trajectory and allow him to adjust.

78 BAT

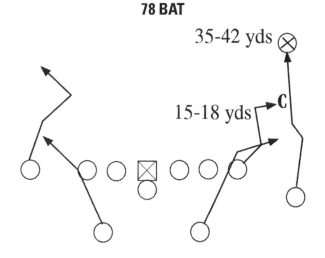

The number one cause for interceptions on the play is because the ball is under thrown. The second cause is leaving the ball inside. We want to make sure no one catches the ball but us. We make sure we leave the ball on the field.

The defender over the tight end dictates his release. We want him to get a clean release and get depth between the numbers and the hash mark at a depth of 15 to 18 yards.

Our back checks his protection responsibility and runs a flat route. We are vertically stretching the strongside. The number 1 progression is the deep ball. If you pass up the deep ball, you can never come back to it. We teach the quarterback to throw the deepest ball in the progression. If the deep man in not the number 1 receiver, the quarterback would have to re-

set to throw the deep ball if the shorter man was covered. Teach the quarterback to read the deep route, and then to look for the shorter route.

The Z-back is the number 1 progression, and the tight end is the number 2 progression. The back on the strongside is the number 3 progression. We are still running our flag on the back side. The H-back runs his flat route.

If it is against man coverage, things change. However, the take off stays the same. He will have inside alignment. We should have a lot of room to throw the ball over his head. We never want to take the take-off route outside of the area six yards from the bottom of the numbers on the field. The numbers are six yards from the sideline. We never want to take the take off outside the bottom of the numbers. This gives the quarterback the leeway to throw the ball so the receiver can adjust to it. He uses the same techniques against both zone and man.

If it is man coverage, the tight end runs an out route. It is the same technique as before. He identifies the man that is covering him. He pressures him off and gets separation. He will go parallel to the LOS, or he will slightly bring it back.

The back checks his protection responsibility. If his man does not come, he is going to get a vertical push and flatten it out.

Let me cover the middle-of-the-field operations. We are trying to vertically stretch the underneath coverage. We are trying to get all of our receivers involved. We do not want to give the play away. If you cut your splits down with the receivers, the defense will recognize the type of play you are going to run. To get what we want, we do what we call "run the lines." This will give the quarterback the vision to see the receivers. He can have a middle of the field read on a 3-progression read from short-to-deep, or deep-to-short each time. We keep our normal width, but we run the lines to shrink the zones. We drive off the ball at a depth of five yards, and three yards inside the original alignment. We vertical push the depth to 18 yards with a ninety-degree break to the middle of the field.

The tight end inside releases. We tell him to get across the ball as quickly as he can. I do not care what depth it is. After he gets across the ball, he is going to get a depth of six to eight yards as he crosses the ball. Our X-end runs the post route, using the same techniques as the Z-back. His landmark is the onside upright. The number 1 progression is the tight end. The Z-back is the number 2 progression.

Our fullback checks his protection and then runs a flare route. Our H-back checks his protection responsibility and runs a flair control route. He crosses the butt of the center on the route to clear the backside linebacker our of the way for the tight end. Out of 100 throws on this play, we are going to throw it to the tight end 60 times.

We can come back and run the play with the X-end and Z-back switching routes We run the square-in route with the X-end with the same patterns for the tight end and backs. The number 1 receiver is still the tight end, and the number 2 receiver is the deep man.

We do not want to throw the short pass over the head of the linebacker. We want to throw the ball between the linebackers. If the quarterback is undecided on to whom to throw the ball to, we want him to throw it to the underneath man. We have a better chance for a completion on the shorter route. You do not have to throw the ball 10 yards when it is 3rd-and-10 to get the first down. Throw the ball six yards and let the end run five yards with it, and you have your first down. We tell them, "don't get greedy, when we are needy." Dump the ball, and let them run with it.

Another middle-of-the-field play is also part of our two-minute drill. We get the backs involved on the play. The backs catch about 70 percent of the passes on this play. We run the lines again with the wide receivers. The tight end runs a flat-take off route. The backs check their protection responsibility and run their routes. We can do several things with them. We have them read the linebackers. We can move the backs to either side, or we can have them go in opposites directions.

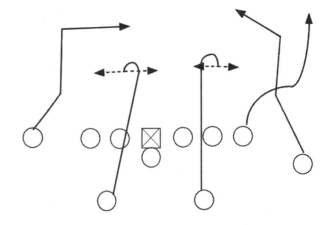

If the linebackers jump the backs, we have a hole inside with the deep receivers. This play is a high-percentage throw for us, and it is a good first down play. You can get the ball to your backs against linebackers. It has been good to us.

Next, is our weakside route to stretch the defense vertically on that side. Instead of calling the play BAT, we just flipped it over and called it TAB. We all this play 79 TAB. This tells the quarterback the direction we want him to work first. We go even numbers to the right, and the odd numbers to the left. After the numbers, we give a combination route for the play. TAB is a weakside combination route for us where we are stretching the weak flat to the intermediate area. It is the same play, but we are reversing the routes for the receivers.

79 TAB

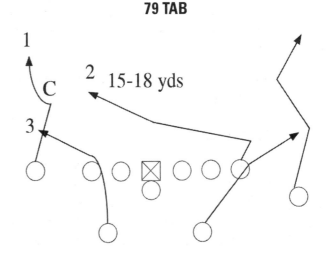

The tight end crosses the ball and climbs to a depth of 15 to 18 yards between the hash mark and the numbers. The H-back runs the flat. We are reading from deep-to-short. We read the progression from the X-end, Y-end, to the H-back.

We run a weakside combination route that is a lot like a choice route, but it is a lot shorter. It is a much higher-percentage throw. We call it Halfback Short Option. The X-end has an outside release and runs a comeback route at 15-to-18 yards deep. He wants to sit it down in the fade hole. He is the number 2 man.

The H-back crow hops for width. He wants to find out who is responsible for covering the slot area. He wants to sit down between the man that is covering the slot and the flat. Against the zone, we want him to split the difference at six to eight yards. If it is man coverage, he leans on the defender and then breaks it away. He is the number 1 receiver on the play.

HALFBACK SHORT OPTION

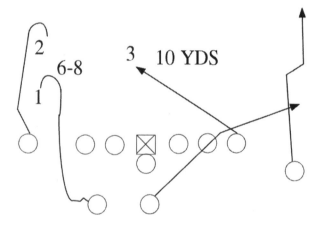

We want the tight end to sit down in the middle at a depth of 10 yards. He wants to get to that area as quickly as he can to make himself available over the ball. The tight end is the number 3 receiver.

A lot of teams make the mistake of changing their protection for the screen pass. Whatever you use for the most of the protection, you want to throw the screen off that protection. We use big-on-big so we throw the screen off that protection to sell the play. The screen is a great play. The key is to have a back that understands what you are trying to accomplish. The line must understand the timing on the play.

We call it 570 Screen. We use 500 to indicate our screen passes. All of our protection remains the same. The center is responsible for 0, the guards have

1 on LOS, the tackles have 2 LOS, and the backs are responsible for the linebackers. But, we do have a couple of exceptions. We never double team on a screen.

The tight end gets depth with an outside release to make it look like a pass. If it is man coverage, he runs opposite the direction we are going to run the screen. It is the same for the outside receiver. On zone coverage, we run them as deep as they will go, and then we stalk them. This clears the receivers.

570 SCREEN PASS

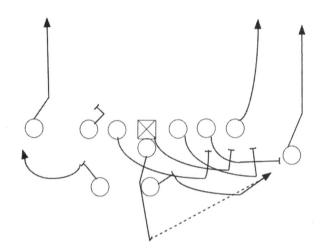

The key for the quarterback is to make sure he gets set up at a prescribed drop. We do not want him to keep drifting. We set him up at a depth of seven yards. He gets an aiming point and sets up. We run the play off a 2.5 count. Our center counts, 1001, 1002, 1003, and then he calls out "Go." The line stays in the entire time unless the quarterback overrules the center. If we do not get a blitz that we do not pick up, the quarterback can give a "Go" call, and the line drops their block and gets into their responsibility.

Our onside tackle runs what we call a 357-technique. He sets up at a depth of three yards. He fights the man for a depth of five yards, and he cuts the man at a depth of seven yards. It important for him to get back and to get depth. He must get his hands down when we throw the ball.

Our onside guard blocks his pass responsibility and gets into a position to release him, hopefully to the inside. If he can't, he will release him outside. He gets the first force on the "Go" call. He is responsible for blocking the first force, even if it is the strong safety.

The center is not going to get a double team. He sits inside and counts, 1001, 1002, 1003, Go. We give the center a landmark. He never turns upfield until he gets three yards outside an imaginary line outside the tight-end. He gets a depth of five yards and then gets upfield. We want to get the center and backside guard up the field inside out. We want them to get their shoulders parallel to the LOS. The backside guard gets on the inside hip of the center and looks inside out. Our backside tackle blocks full-time protection. He has nothing to do with the screen. We lock him on the down man, and he protects full time.

The back that is not in the screen runs a flare route. First, he checks his protection. If his man comes, he blocks him full time. If he does not come, he wants to get width.

The back we are screening to is going to get depth. He hides inside. If his protection responsibility comes, he nails him. He stops the momentum and stays with him until he hears the center give the "Go" call. He delays another one-half count. It is critical for the back not to beat the line outside. He must give them time to get outside. We tell him to set up five yards deep and three yards outside the tight-end position.

We tell the quarterback to throw the ball at the outside eye of the back five yards deep. He throws it firmly, but not hard, so he can catch the ball. If he sees man coverage, we like to get out of the screen. The quarterback is the key. If we get caught in it, we tell our guard to go block the defender that is responsible for the back that is getting the pass. That man can mess up everything. The quarterback is the key. He must get depth, and he must see everything.

On the goal line, we have had success with a few plays. It depends on the plays we are having success with in a game as to how we run them on the goal line. We call this short angle out. We stretch the squat coverage. If it is a three-linebacker scheme, we work off the Mike linebacker or off the man that is covering the hook. The tight end reverse pivots and works back outside. The back gets width and depth as quickly as he can. The Z-back runs a take off. He is our first progression on the pre-snap read. The coverage dictates our progression. On zone coverage, the tight end is the number 1 progression, and the back is the 2nd progression. If it is man coverage, we throw the ball to the back. The man covering the back will have a hard time getting outside to cover the back. It has been a good play in short yardage and on the goal line for us.

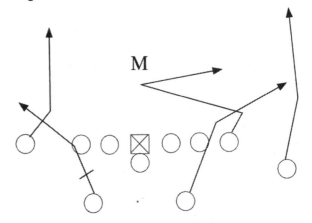

Once again I want to thank everyone for having me here. Thank you.

TIGHT END TECHNIQUES AND DRILLS

University of Lousiville

I want to thank the Nike Clinic staff for having me on the clinic. Offensively, we have been very fortunate at the University of Louisville in that we have had some very good players at the skilled positions. We have an excellent staff that enjoys going to work every morning. I think we have some good ideas on what you have to do to move the football. I coach tight ends so I am going to talk about things we do with them. I want to cover the way we work the tight ends to get them to fit into our scheme on offense.

Everyone has their own philosophy on how they are going to coach and teach their players. This is an area that Coach John L. Smith does not leave to chance. This is something he requires of all position coaches. We have a MUST list we have to turn into Coach Smith. We turn it in before spring practice, and before the two-a-day practices start. In the front page of the tight-ends playbook, we have these musts listed. We want them to know how important the must list is to us. Each position has a MUST list. These are the things we expect from our players. Here is the list the tight ends must do for us to be successful on offense

---

TIGHT END MUSTS

- Must be dependable and coachable.

- Must play physical and aggressive.

- Must play with good technique and be sound fundamentally.

- Must understand assignments and execute the game plan.

- Must be productive in the passing game.

- Must have ball security.

I stress point number five with them. In a lot of offenses, you can get a tackle and be successful at tight end in some offenses. But, we stress the point the tight end must be productive in the passing game. We probably could get some players that could block better than the tight ends we play with.

Our offense is very conducive for the tight end to be successful. Many of you may remember Ibn Green who played for us in 1999. He made All-American as a tight end. A lot of people told us we would be hurting for a tight end in 2000. But, we had two ends that redshirted. They stepped in and did a good job for us. They made All-Conference USA. Our offense allows the tight end to be successful.

The next thing the position coaches must do it to develop a fundamental drill book. It is a combination of all the fundamentals, techniques, and skills each position is going to be responsible for in order for us to be successful on offense. I am not going to go over all of the skills, but I want you to get an idea what we are doing with this drill book.

Our tight end is used in pass protection. If you want your tight end to be productive in the passing game, you must have a good deal of your passing game set up where he is not involved in the pass protection. If you want him to go out on the routes and catch passes, then don't have him involved in the protection as much. Have him release and get open. But, he does have to learn how to pass protect unless you want to throw a lot of hot routes and deal with all of the pressures the defense give you.

I will talk about the releases the ends have to use to be successful to get open. These are drills that I have thought about and have them down on paper. I know the drills we are going to use and the techniques we need to accomplish to develop certain fundamentals.

TIGHT END FUNDAMENTALS

Skill	Fundamentals	Drill
Stance	3-point: rt./lt. handed 2-point: rec. stance	On the line
Start	Snap count/communication	On clap, drill must continue to work st./start/1st step
First step	Zone reach footwork Drive - down Jab - pass sets Snap – Snap lateral Wide outside	Sleds – chutes – 1-on-1 – 2-on-2 Inside – skelly _ line – team
Run blocking	Reach – (power arm) Down/tex – fan Drive/base – sting Cutoff – bengal Draw block Pull - seal 2 Man blocks = ace – race – combo - scoop – coop – tight	Chutes Sled 1-on-1 – 2-on-2 Line Inside perimeter Team
Pass protection	Sets – stance Shuffle Vertical shuffle Punch Push and pull Man on Me/you – big	1-on-1 Punch sit Hit-hit mirror Set hold-eagles Bertha Blitz pick up
Releases	Arc – reach Jab - rip	1-on-1 Team
Pass catching	Head – eyes Hand placement	Jugs – nets Speed catch Route w/QB's Ball drills
Ball security	Pressure points Catch - tuck	Strip – gauntlet Angle tackle Agility
Routes	Arrow – out – option inside and outside Stick – read – corner – seam – drag – streak – over – swing - break	1-on-1 w/QB Skelly - team
Running with the ball		Open field – angle tackle 1-on-1 w/QB's – skelly Team - agility

As you can see on the chart, the tight end must work on pass-catching skills. They have to work on ball security, and they have to work on routes.

After we have looked at the list, we all know the things we have to do to be successful. After we have covered all of the things we have to do in our individual positions to be successful—fundamentally, and technique and skill-wise, then we have to start developing our long-range plan on how we are going to teach each one of these skills. We have to determine the amount of time we are going to spend on each phase of the drills and how we are going to teach them and the order in which they are to be taught. We have to determine how we are going to work with other positions on the field to be successful.

Here are some thoughts on why we have been successful the last three years. It is the organization, and time management, and the extra effort to work for a common goal. It is our schedule and plan for the offensive staff. We have thought about everything as far as when it is going to be coached and taught.

Now, you may have to adjust your schedule because you will not have a schedule like we have. Our schedule is really different for next year. We have Monday, Tuesday, and Saturday games. I am sure it will change for us, but I think you can get some ideas of what we do in our practice schedule.

On Sunday after a game on Saturday, we come in with the kids. First, the staff will grade the film and make any corrections we may need. Then, we start working on our charts for our scouting reports. Next, we start viewing our next opponent.

SUNDAY SCHEDULE

12:00 PM - Grade film

2:00 - 3:00 PM - Lift

3:00 - 4:00 PM - Lift

4:30 PM - Position meeting

6:00 PM - Special teams meeting

6:30 PM - Team meeting

7:00 PM - Practice

8:00 PM - Snack/finalize games for reports — cut-ups - QB tapes made.

One of the first things we do on Monday is to break up the offensive staff and take specific portions of our opponent to start getting an idea of what they do so we can focus on what we are going to do.

Next, we get together as a staff and watch a pressure tape of our opponent. If a team has a certain pressure package, there is no reason to develop a fancy offensive package if we cannot handle certain pressure. We have to make sure we know what we can do against pressure packages the opponents are going to use against us.

MONDAY SCHEDULE

7:00 AM - Offense meets/game video - formatmation cut-ups.

11:00 AM – Pressure tape

6:30 PM – Scouting reports/self scout.

8:00 PM – Posse/ace/plan

On Tuesday, we continue with our scouting report. We work on our personnel groupings. Next, we start putting together a plan of what we think the opponents will do against those packages. Tuesday is the first day we will practice after a game. We do our scripts, and we do our cards.

This is one thing we do that I think has made us a good team as far as preparing our players. Coach Scott Linehan, our offensive coordinator, will script the plays of what we think our base plans are going to be within a specific formation. All of the offensive staff stay in that offensive room because we have already put up on the wall and the boards how we think the defense will play us as far as the scouting report is concerned. After Coach Linehan puts up the game plan, we put up the defense we think we will see. We go over the play we are going to run and the defense we expect to see. Now, the different coaches will start drawing up the cards of how the scout defense needs to line up. We do this as a group. As we are drawing up the cards, we work with each other to make sure we have the defense in the techniques we saw in the film.

TUESDAY SCHEDULE

7:00 AM - Spread (bombers) thunder plan

10:30 AM - Plan practice/scripts cards

3:30 PM - Practice

6:30 PM - Practice video

8:00 PM - Critical zone, 2-point plays

On Wednesday, we start preparing a little more specific-type plays for the game plan. We script our first eight plays for the game. We want to attack a certain phase of the defense to see if they have the weakness we thought we saw in making the game plan. We want to see how they react to certain things we do on offense. Those first eight plays are not designed to win the game. They are designed to set the mentality of the game and to get ready to win the game in the fourth quarter. Obviously, we would like to score a touchdown on those first eight plays. This year, we scored five times on our first eight plays. We were very good on our first eight plays. We were looking at things we expected to see in the games.

WEDNESDAY SCHEDULE

7:00 AM - First eight plays

8:00 AM - Finalize two PP – do goal line plays

10:30 AM - Plan practice / scripts / cards

3:20 PM - Practice

6:30 PM - Practice video / 3rd-downs on board

On Thursday, the game planning and practice becomes something special that gives you the edge to get over the top. We have planned all of our third downs by down and distance. When the first 3rd-and-2 yards comes up in the course of the game, everyone knows what we are going to do, unless something drastic has happened. We know what we are going to do on 3rd-and-short, 3rd-and-medium, and 3rd-and-long. It is not just one call, it is a combination of our three or four best calls in the passing game and three or four of our best in the running game. Scott Linehan calls the plays. He does a great job of letting the other staff members feel they are part of the plan. We all give our ideas, so we can be successful.

THURSDAY SCHEDULE

7:00 AM - Third. downs, coming out, must calls, get it to's, 4-down territory, kill clock

10:30 AM - Plan practice / script / cards

2:45 PM - Offense meeting (road games)

3:15 PM - Goal line walk-through

3:30 PM - Practice

On Friday, we go out and view the offensive plan. We make corrections where we need to.

FRIDAY SCHEDULE

9:00 AM - Offense view practice – make corrections

9:30 AM - Round table

2:00 PM - Offense walk-through (home game)

2:30 PM - Offense meeting (home game)

4:00 PM - Practice / test

5:30 PM - Dinner

7:00 PM - Team meeting

If you are a head coach, make sure you develop a weekly plan on everything you are going to cover, coach, and prepare for each game. Any situation that may come up needs to be on that weekly plan.

In our pre-practice it is my job to make sure my guys are ready to do what they must to help us win the game. We cover the little things in our drill book to help our tight ends to be ready for the game that week. Each group has a different phase of what they need to work on.

The next area is the daily practice plan. On our practice schedule, we have each position on the chart. We break the sessions up into five-minute segments. Coach Smith will come into our meeting and tell us how much time he wants to spend on stretching and other phases of the game. The big thing is that you will know how much time you have to work on the things you need to work on. When I look at the Y-ends' schedule, I have to go back to the individual technique book to see what we must cover. I know the techniques we must work on to be successful for that practice and that game.

TIME	PD	RB'S	QB'S	WR'S	Y'S	OL	PLAN
3:30	1		<——STRETCHING————>				
3:35	2			Coop			

We know what each group is doing each period. Also, we have a copy of what the defense is working on. If we need to work with them, we have it on the practice schedule.

I have a film of our tight ends in the pre-practice. I had our video man go out and make a film of what we do in practice with our guys to let you see what we do.

I tell our players I want them on the field for the pre-practice. It does not matter if I am there or not. They are to be on the field. They may be working on making the catch and looking the ball in. I try to be creative and change the drills we use in this period. I do not want it to be boring. It is pre-practice. All I want them to do is to work on catching the football. (Film)

Now, we have to work on our plan on how we are going to block the defense. The first play we will put in our offense in the spring will be the zone play. It is our 34 and 35 Zone play. The even numbers go to the right, and the odd numbers go to the left. I am sure that is real shocking. Now, that is the play, but we have to come up with so ways to block on the play.

Each of our run plays has a position rule on it. Here is how we cover it. I tell them we are adding 34 and 35 Zone to our offense. Their rule against a strong tackle uncovered is to co-op; it is a pre-snap look for the lineman to the Sam linebacker. What does that mean? In my meeting with the tight ends, I will draw it up and be more specific. If there is not a man on he tight end, he looks for the Sam linebacker. The Sam linebacker is either inside or he is outside. That is all he needs to know at the time.

If the strongside tackle is covered by a down lineman, the tight end is going to reach block the man on. He must be alert to make a tight call. If the tackle is covered by a down lineman, he reaches the man outside. He has to come off the ball and block him one-on-one.

If the end thinks the down lineman on him is slanting inside, he tells the strong tackle he needs help. They work together on the block.

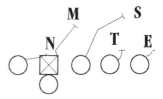

They must be disciplined with their footwork. In the drill book, they know they must be able to use the reach block. The reach block is drawn in the drill book. Everyone needs to know their objectives, techniques, first step, aiming point, and coaching points on the block.

When we run the 34 and 35 Zone play, the thing we want the tight end thinking about concerning his block is to knock his man off the ball as far as he can. On the first step, the wider the defender is the wider the first step has to be. We do not take a back step. We do not want to be going backward when the defense is coming at us. On the first step, we want to step to the outside toe of the defender. The second step is most critical. That step has to be in the center of the defender's body. The tight end's eyes are on the defender's outside breast. The hands are going to come thumbs up and clamp the arm pit with the elbows in tight. We want to push him back and knock him off the ball. We want as much push as we can get. If he needs help, he calls for the tackle inside. If he calls for help, he must be ready to work the two-man game.

What does this mean? It means to block the man on you if the tackle is covered. We go out and work on that aspect of the game.

I am going to go fast through the run-blocking techniques. I will start by defining our run blocks.

RUN BLOCKING

Single Blocks

- Reach — block used to block a contain defender from outside pursuit.
- Power arm — block used to throw the defender outside when you can't get reach him.

- Down (Tex)—block on the inside defender to keep him from the point of attack.
- Drive – block used to power block a man over.
- Cut off – block used to keep a defender from pursuit.
- Sting – cut block on the outside leg of man you cannot reach.
- Fan – big-on-big.

Two-Man Blocks

- Ace – double team with inside man coming off.
- Combo – double team with outside man coming off.
- Coop – zone block.
- Race – a read ace.
- Scoop – backside zone block for fast-flow linebackers.
- Tight – used when man on is a threat to come inside and our tackle is covered.

Drills

- Chute
- Sled
- 1-on-1
- 2-on-2
- Zone – cutoff
- Group — line/ inside
- Perimeter—team

Men, I want to give credit to Coach Art Valaro. He is the best I have been around. He will talk football with you as long as you want to talk. He is responsible for our blocking playbook.

RUN BLOCKS

Reach Block

Objective – The block is used to block a contain defender from the outside pursuit.

Technique – First step – 6-inch step with the playside foot.

Aiming point – Outside breast of defender.

Coaching points – Second step at crotch of defender. Make contact with palms of hands striking on the rise. Lock out with outside arm. Knock defender off the ball. Work hips around to outside.

Drills:

- Chute
- Sled
- 1-on-1
- Zone/cutoff— Line
- Perimeter – team

Power Arm Block

Objective – To throw defender outside when he can't be reached.

Technique - First step – reach footwork (6-inch playside foot).

Aiming point – Outside of pecs

Coaching points –

- Strike hands like reach block.
- Once he can't be reached, pull outside elbow to ribs and extend the inside arm.

Drills:

- Chute
- 1-on-1
- Zone/cutoff— Line
- Perimeter — team

Sting Block

Objective — To cut block the outside leg of defender who can't be reached.

Technique — Reach footwork

First step — Outside breast of defender.

Aiming point – When defender is out and running:

- Drive inside shoulder through the outside thigh.
- Drive inside arm through the crotch.
- Full extension on cut.

Drills – Bag cut.

RUN BLOCKS (TWO-MAN)

Coop Block

Objective – To be able to come off the ball and zone block the defenders.

Technique:

- *Inside man* – first step - zone step.
- *Outside man* – first step - zone step—8- or 9- technique with the outside foot, a 7-technique with the inside foot.

Aiming point:

- *Inside man* – center of down man.
- *Outside man* – technique of the defender.

Coaching points:

- *Inside man* – movement first; look to take over the block
- *Outside man* – second step to the crotch of the defenders; get movement first; be alert for an inside or outside call by the tackle.

Drills:

- 2-on-2—Line
- Inside—team

Cutoff Block

Objective – To keep a defender from penetrating or pursuing the ball.

Technique – *First step* – reach step with the inside foot.

Aiming Point –

- Drive outside shoulder and arm to the far knee.
- Get head past defender to inside thigh.
- Work hips around to square up.

Drills –

- Bag cutoff
- 1-on-1
- Zone cutoff
- Inside/perimeter—Team

Scoop Block

Objective: To block a down man and handle a fast flow linebacker.

Technique:

- Inside man – Reach step inside foot
- Outside man – Flat step

Aiming point:

- Inside man – inside arm
- Outside man – far hip of defender

Coaching Points:

- Inside man - push defender to linebacker. Clear down man square to offside linebacker. If down man stays on line, execute cutoff block.
- *Outside Man* – cut split down; get your head and shoulders past down man to playside. If down man runs across, the inside man goes up on the linebacker; do not allow penetration.

Drills –

- 1-on-1 bag drills
- 2-on-2
- Zone/scoop – same drill as zone cutoff with tackles in the drill— Line
- Inside/perimeter—team

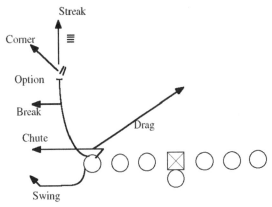

I want to cover the releases for the tight end. I want to get the ball to the tight end. I will define the routes, and then I will show you the route on the overhead and then show the routes on film.

After you figure out the routes you want the tight end to run then, you have to find a way to get him off the ball and to get open on the route. All ends are different. Some of them have a good releases, and some of them have poor releases. Knowing the ability of the tight end on his releases will determine a lot of your thinking in the passing game.

Arc – Flat step, crossover step, up field, avoid contact with speed. This is the key. Rip with contact. We use this release when we are going to run an out, read, or corner route.

Reach – Use over reach defender separate off any contact. If the defender is going to drop off this is how we release off the ball. We are going to run through the man.

Jab – Take a 6-inch drive step at a 45-degree angle opposite the direction your are going. Make a head-and-eye fake, rip the arm and shoulder through, drive the legs, and stay low. This is most effective when you face man coverage close to the line of scrimmage.

Rip – Take a 6-inch drive at a 45-degree angle, dip the shoulder closest to defender, drive leg through to clear the hips. We use this release mostly for our inside release.

Drills –

- Cones
- 1-on-1
- Skelly
- Team

Now that we have the releases, the routes come next. Here are the routes for the tight ends.

Option – We will use several option routes. Best release – speed upfield 10-12 yards, break away from leverage of linebackers, in-out, sit, over the top – vs. 0 coverage (get open):

- *Inside option* – restricted to side down to inside work.
- *Outside option* – restricted to sit down to outside work.
- Our *90 game* is at six-to-eight yards.

Corner – Outside release; push vertically to 12 yards; stick post break on an angle to 26 yards. Speed guys front corner of end zone, inside 25-yard line back corner of end zone.

Streak – Outside release; attack down the field with speed; get to two yards outside the hash mark. You could have an outside streak or a middle streak route.

Over – Best release – cross field to opposite hash mark; get over top of linebacker, don't cross the hash mark; get down field.

Stick – Best release – run off first linebacker from middle out 10 to 12 yards; plant, break out back to the ball.

Read – Outside release; get over the linebacker to the second level;. break into the open hole.

Seam – Outside release; flat crossover, stay outside Sam in man or cover 2. May slip release against a 9-technique.

Out – Outside release; push vertically 10-12 yards, roll or square out based on ability (97 – arc release – 6 – 8 yards).

Drag – Jab release; cross field six yards at opposite tackle 10 yards at the sideline; do not slow down on the drag route. If we have a drag route called, chances are we have something coming back inside, or we are going to use that area for a hot throw if the defense has two defenders coming, and we only have one man to block them.

Break – Outside release; push up five-to-eight yards; break out; make contact on linebacker. Against flat defender, sit down.

Swing – Protect gain to two-yards depth; arc to numbers.

Chute – Late slam release; block on the run, four steps, pivot out to the flat 3-yards deep.

Arrow – Outside release; break to point six yards on sideline; square up at the bottom of the numbers.

On the two-way option routes, we put a receiver in the backfield and release him outside in the flat. The tight end releases inside six-to-eight yards deep. He looks for the first linebacker. If the linebacker is inside, he breaks outside. If the linebacker is outside of the tight end, he breaks inside. He works a two-way option route.

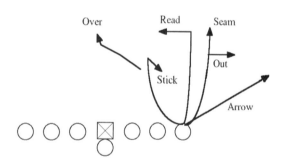

Now, we want to run an inside option route. He wants to push straight up the field as much as he can. At ten yards, he has his alignment to get open in his area. We use that route when a curl route is happening on the outside, and the tight end cannot go outside. He can go get open as long as it is inside his alignment.

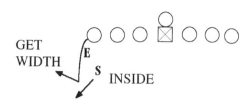

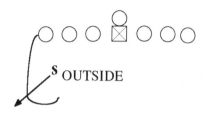

Let me cover the complete play. It is our Y outside option route. The play can be run from different formations.

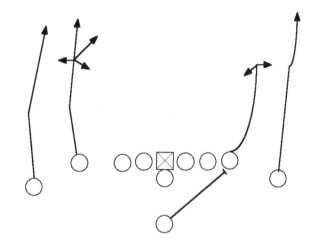

PLAY – Y – OUTSIDE OPTION
FB – 90 protection rule.
TB – 6 yard option route.
Y – 6 yard option route.
X – Protection release fade.
Z – Protection release fade.
QB – Progression:
• Pick best match-up for home run—either X or Y.
• Y
• T

You can run the play out of the trips set. It is the same play.

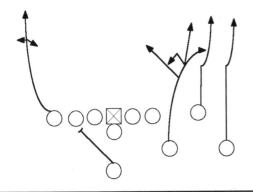

I hope this will give you some idea how we involve our tight end in our offense. I know I went fast, so if you want to talk with any of our staff, feel free to call us or come see us. If you want a copy of the drill book I use, leave your name and address, and I will be happy to send it to you. Thank you for your time. Come out and watch us practice anytime. We play a game on Tuesday, and two on Thursday, and the rest are on Saturday. Come see us play. Thank you.

Y – OUTSIDE OPTION PLAY OUT OF A TRIPSSET

FB – 90 protection rule.

TB – Protection release seam.

Y – 6-yard hitch or out route.

X – Protection release fade.

Z – Run 6-yard option route.

QB – Progression:

- Y/Z off MLB
- Pick best match-up for TB (TB/XE)

We can put our fullback in the route. We move him up and send him to the flat.

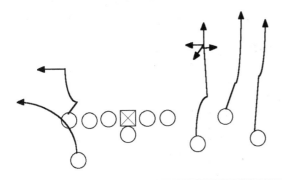

Y – OUTSIDE OPTION PLAY — FULLBACK IN THE FLAT

FB – Hot flat (two yards)

TB – Protection release seam.

Y – 5-yard stick.

X – 6-yard option.

QB – Progression:

- FB —flat
- Y — stick
- Z — option

OFF SEASON CONDITIONING PROGRAM AND DRILLS

Washington State University

Thank you. First, let me say how much I appreciate the job all of you do in helping physically to prepare your athletes. One thing I've noticed in the last 10 years or so is the marked physical improvement in high school players as you watch them on film, and visit with them during recruiting. I've borrowed a lot of great training ideas over the years from many people like yourself, and consider it a privilege to address this group today.

Secondly, I want to thank NIKE and Earl Browning, and Bill Jacobs of HAMMER STRENGTH, for giving me this great opportunity. They are two of the real "class" people I've met in this profession, and I have enormous respect for both of them.

I'm going to talk today on off-season conditioning. Conditioning should be the first priority in preparing your team for competition every year. Work capacity, or the ability to sustain effort, is critical both on the field, and even in the weight room. As an athlete, you don't need to be in great shape year-round. But you should *never* be completely out of shape. Again, it does not matter how strong or fast you are if you can't sustain effort play after play. There is no off-season program that gets a man totally ready to play football. The biggest part of preparing to play football is football. *However, athletes must have bodies that are ready to practice, and minds that are ready to practice!*

As we all know, football is a tough sport, and only for tough people. To me, it is the best sport there is for offering both a mental and physical challenge. We consequently strive to develop tough minds and bodies in structuring our program.

I have always believed the tougher our players are mentally, the tougher they will be physically. We strive to develop mental toughness by doing several things in our running program. First, we have what we call a mandatory *"stand tall"* philosophy when we are running. No matter what the circumstances, we do not allow any athlete to physically bend over, touch their knees, or lean up against anyone or anything for physical support when they are fatigued.

This includes even when you are in our weight room, unless you are performing an exercise. This is important for two reasons. Number one: if you bend over physically, you are bending over mentally. I always tell our players that this is a mental challenge that must be overcome. Number two, any appearance of fatigue is encouraging to our opponents. Also true, in the reverse, is the non-appearance of it is demoralizing. This is a mind set that must be cultivated into our players constantly.

Another toughness control is climate. Nothing builds mental toughness like hard work in extreme conditions. When I was at LSU I, purposely scheduled our running during what we researched to be the hottest part of the day. Rather than run from the "fire", we were going to run through it.

At the opposite extreme is what we did this winter in Pullman, which was to run our team outside all winter, rather than in a heated gym. As hot as it is in Louisiana in the summer, it is every bit as cold in eastern Washington in the winter. In both situations, I felt like the weather worked to our advantage.

At the very least, you should make every effort to schedule your pre-season running at the time of your afternoon practice. Scheduling makes it a temptation sometimes to just do all of your running in the early AM, and sometimes this is unavoidable. The concern here, especially in a hot climate, is not having your athletes acclimated to the heat and humidity of the afternoons when most people play and practice.

The bottom line to developing mental and physical toughness is this: you must create situations where your players are forced to think about quitting. The key word here is "think". I tell our players that it is no disgrace to think about quitting. We have all been in situations, at some point in our lives, where we have thought about quitting something. We want to create a mental proving ground for overcoming the urge to quit

Here are some other critical points of emphasis:

Group Accountability

Just as in a game, *all* of our players are held accountable when an individual makes a mistake. Knocking over cones, jumping off sides, missing a line, or failing to "stand tall" are all self-discipline issues. When this occurs, with any player, the whole group will do *five* "up downs" at the conclusion of the workout, for each violation. The players at fault lead the rest of the group. This creates peer pressure, develops leadership, and creates a sense of urgency that forces greater concentration.

Off the field, we believe strongly in this as well. If any player misses or is late to a lifting/running workout, or a training table meal, *his entire position group runs after our team workout.* Remember, it's the players' team, and they must take ownership of it.

Individual Accountability

We allow no excuses, or the old axiom "I'll try". The minute anyone says this they are giving themselves an out. Either do it, or don't do it. This starts with myself as a coach.

Great Effort

I'm stating the obvious here, but players must learn to *finish drills*. Full-speed effort must become second nature in your workouts. Finishing strongly must be demanded.

Competitiveness

You must develop competitiveness in your workouts. Our players are either competing against one another, or against a stop watch. We do as many agility drills as possible with players paired in two's with people at their own position. All sprint work is done by position group as well. Intrasquad "superstar" competitions, tug-o-war's, etc. also work well for this. You must identify the competitors on your team.

Specificity

We try to simulate the game of football as closely as possible, by doing the following (as you get closer to the season, prioritize football specific movements in all drills):

Winter (Off-Season)

* General agility – 30 min/workout

- 60-yd. shuttle/20-yd. shuttle/

- 3-corner drill, etc.

** Position agility – 10 min/workout

** Position drills

Summer (Pre-Season)

**General agility - 10 min/workout

Position agility - 30 min/workout. A typical program will last about 8-10 weeks. A normal schedule would be as follows:

Mon	Tue	Thur	Fri
110's	Agility/Metabolic/Agility		
	Ply./(40's/50's/60's)/ ply.		
	steps/hills/ X /form run		

(Ply. stands for plyometrics.)

An important reminder on all agility and speed drills is to allow full recovery between reps. A common mistake is to turn agility-type circuits into endurance workouts. Without full recovery, movements will slow down. Understand what you are trying to accomplish. Obviously, as your athletes get in better shape, it will require less down time to do this. Remember, agility is *controlled quickness.*

General Reminders

- *Be energy -system specific.* No aerobic running except for those individuals who need to lose body fat. Aerobic running will slow your players down, and potentially compromise explosive power output. The average football play in a game last between *4-7 seconds.*

- Use the *position stance* when at all possible when starting a drill.

- *Recovery:* The average time between plays on the field is approximately 45 seconds. In a "no huddle" offense, this will be as low as 25 seconds. Your athletes must be trained to recover accordingly.

Offense: Cadence/Defense: Ball Movement

On all running and agility work we start drills on the above commands. Depending on group size, we will normally divide in as many as four groups, for example:

Group 1	QB / RB / Receivers
Group 2	DB / LB
Group 3	OL / TE
Group 4	DL / K – P

In groups 1 and 3, a quarterback will be assigned to give a snap count. (This can obviously also be done by a coach.) In groups 2 and 4, a coach stations himself approximately 10 yards in front of the group and either moves his hand or a ball. We feel that if our players are conditioned to this stimulus in the off-season that it will potentially reduce offsides penalties in games and practice as well.

Note: Don't start drills with a whistle. This means "stop" during practice and games.

Depth of Your Team

Evaluate who is going to be playing, and how much. If you have little depth, you may have to place even greater emphasis on conditioning in your program. This is especially true on the *defensive* side of the ball, where unlike offense, you have all 11 players pursuing the football, regardless of position.

The following is an example of the agility drills we used this past winter: (eight stations)

- Start at two minutes per station, and gradually work up to 3:30.
- Allow one minute rest between stations.
- You'll notice that we don't use the same drills every day.
- Physically, this allows our players to develop quickness in a greater variety of movements.
- Mentally, it keeps the players' minds from getting stale by not doing the same thing every day.

Monday	Thursday
•Hoops	•Hoops
•Bags	•Ropes
•Triangle drill	•4-Square drill

Monday/plant and cut *(45-degrees)*

Thursday/plant and cut *(90-degrees)*

* 3-cone drill	* 60-yd. shuttle
* 20-yd. shuttle	*Mirror dodge
* Cross drill	*Cross drill
*Wave drill	*Wave drill

* NFL combine drills. Drills with an asterisk are covered at the end of the lecture.

In concluding this article, I'll address the most important attribute in any conditioning program: ATTITUDE.

There are two sure-fire ways that I guarantee will motivate young people to work, and be in regular attendance, provided <u>both</u> are in evidence.

- *Caring* – your players must know you care about them as people.

- *Results* – your players must see physical results from their program.

The most important attribute in any organization or group is high morale. If the aforementioned (i.e., caring and results) exists, you will have high morale. The drills we run are performed as follows:

FOUR-SQUARE DRILL

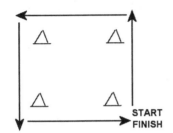

- Distance between cones is five or ten yards.
- Run: forward; carioca across; backpedal; shuffle.

TRIANGLE

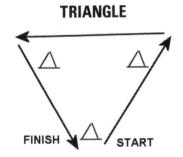

- Sprint entire perimeter of triangle.
- Reverse direction every other rep.
- Distance between cones is five or ten yards.

MIRROR DODGE DRILL

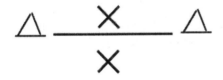

- Athletes are in 2-point stance , facing one another.
- Coach designates one athlete as a "rabbit"; the other players are "mirrors."
- Drill duration is approximately eight seconds; then they reverse roles.
- Players shuffle laterally.
- Distance between cones is five yards.

60-YARD SHUTTLE

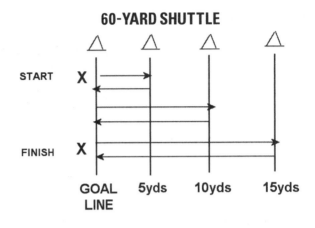

- Both athletes start on goal line, facing the 15-yard line.
- They must touch each line with either their foot or the hand.

CROSS DRILL

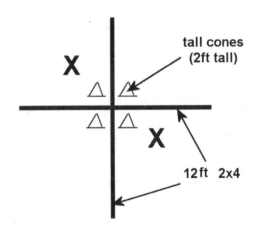

- Athletes start on all "4s" facing one another.
- On command, both athletes crab in a clockwise direction attempting to catch one another.
- On the whistle, players immediately change and both resume chasing in a counter-clockwise direction.
- Drill duration is approximately 15 seconds.
- Players must pick hands up over wood 2 X 4's. Cones are to prevent head butts, and to prevent cutting the pursuit angle short.

FIGURE 8 DRILL

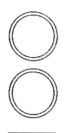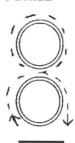

START   START/FINISH

- Athlete runs in a figure-eight pattern around the rings.
- They start to the outside and then to the inside.
- At the finish, the athlete will rope and finish through the next person in line.
- Rings are approximately 12 feet in diameter.

20-YARD SHUTTLE

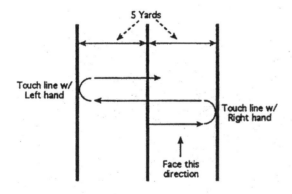

- Shuttle is set up with three lines that are five yards apart.
- To start, straddle the middle like, thus having one line five yards to your right and one line five yards to your left.
- Sprint to the right five yards and touch the line with right hand.
- Sprint back to the left line 10 yards and touch it with your right hand.
- To finish, sprint through the middle line five yards.
- Rest 30 seconds between each repetition.

PLANT AND CUT – 45 DEGREES

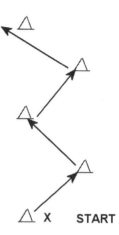

- Make sharp cuts, don't round turns.
- Distance between cones is five yards.
- Repeat drill from opposite side.
- Sprint THROUGH the LINE.

PLANT AND CUT – 90 DEGREES

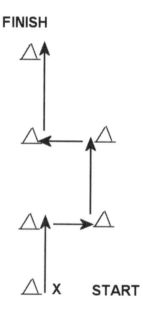

- Make sharp cuts, don't round turns.
- Distance between cones is five yards.
- Repeat drill from opposite side.
- Sprint THROUGH the LINE.

BUNNY HOP

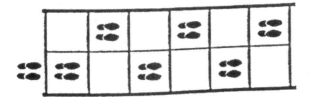

- Good high-knee action.
- Pumping arms.
- Square up hips and shoulders.
- Bend at knees, not at waist.
- Good football position.
- Eyes ahead and up.
- No false steps.
- Do not cross legs on lateral step.
- Keep the hands out in front.

LATERAL STEP

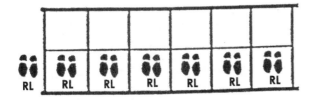

LATERAL STEP WITH DOUBLE CHOP

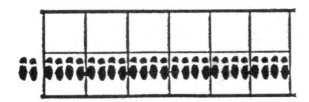

ROPE WEAVE

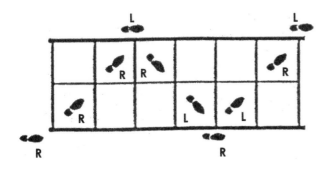

HIGH KNEES EVERY OTHER HOLE

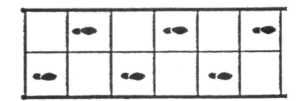

HIGH KNEES EVERY HOLE

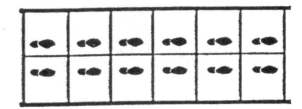

THREE-CONE DRILL

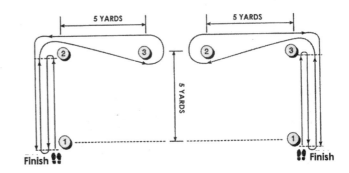

- Athlete begins in a right-hand, 3-point stance.
- On command, sprint to the second line, touching it with the right hand.
- Turn and sprint back to the starting line, touching it with the right hand.
- Turn and sprint around cone #2, (right-hand turn).
- Continue around cone #3 (left-hand turn.)
- Finish drill by making a left-hand turn around cone #32 and sprint past the starting line.

WAVE DRILL

10 yds

COACH
X

△   △

COACH   (coach between cones)

X → (arrow pointing up-right)

X   △   △ #1

START   FINISH

10 yds

- Cones are set up in a 10-yard square.
- Player sprints to the center of the square and chops his feet until the coach gives him a command.
- Player follows the commands until the coach releases him.
- When released, he sprints out of the box.

Commands are:
- Sprint forward
- Backpedal
- Shuffle
- "Up down"

TAP BAG DRILL

- Start parallel to the first bag.
- Using lateral steps, move across all four bags, tapping each with both hands as you cross the bag.
- The emphasis in on keeping your hips low as you move laterally.

WEAVE BAG DRILL

- Sprint around the bags in a zigzag fashion.
- Make sure to plant on the outside foot and make sharp cuts.

SHUTTLE BAG DRILL

- Shuffle facing backwards
- Shuffle in a weave pattern around each of the bags.

You can do sprint/backpedal drills with the bags.

- Start parallel to the first bag.
- Sprint forward and across the first bag.
- Then backpedal around the second bag.
- Sprint forward around the third bag.
- Backpedal around the fourth gag.

I have enjoyed this, and if I can help you in any way, let me know. Thank you and Mahola.

HURRICANES 4-3 DEFENSIVE PACKAGE

University of Miami

Thank you very much. It's good to be here. Last fall I was at the University of Miami. Recently, I moved up with Coach Butch Davis to the Cleveland Browns. We've got our work cut out for us. I was at the University of Miami for the past six seasons with Butch Davis. I am extremely happy for the opportunity I have been given and am looking forward to the new challenge.

This whole package I'm going to talk about started with Jimmy Johnson. In the late 1970's and early 1980's, Jimmy Johnson designed and came up with this package. He played two defensive tackles and ends, three linebackers, and four defensive backs. When I went to Miami in 1986, we were so good we didn't have to play eight in the box. We had so many good defensive linemen, we didn't have to use one of our safeties in run support like you see now. We were so good up front, we only played seven in the box and played a two deep secondary. If the offense came out in a twin set, we went to cover three, and that is all we ran.

But times have changed. It is very hard to find the defensive linemen to stop the run. Because of that, we have evolved to the eight man front. The number one thing we want to do is stop the run. We want the offense in 2nd-, and 3rd-and-long situations.

You see a lot of statistics today about yards per carry and so forth. We try to be simple with our people. We tell them to be successful on defense we have to stop the run, win third down, and create turnovers. When you force a punt that is just as good as a turnover. We have done an outstanding job on third down.

I want to talk about our base 4-3, our eight-man front, man-to-man coverage, principles of gap control, base-alignment run reads, some secondary play, and our eagle-reduction package.

We are no different in numbering our defensive techniques than anyone else. The head-up positions on the center, guard, tackle, and tight end are numbered 0-2-4-6. The shoulder alignments on the guard, tackle, and tight-end are numbered 1-3-5-7-9. The tight end has his inside and outside shoulders numbered. The 7-technique is the inside shoulder of the tight end, and the 9-technique is the outside shoulder. We also relate shade techniques as an inside shade on the guard and tackle are called 2-i and 4-i.

We letter the gaps of responsibility for our defense. The center-guard gap is referred to as the A-gap. The guard-tackle gap is the B-gap. The tackle-tight end gap is called the C-gap, and outside the tight end is the D-gap. The gaps and techniques are lettered and numbered the same going left or right.

If you count the gaps to defend on defense, there are seven gaps. We have a seven-man front which should be enough people to fill those gaps. As soon as the offense inserts the fullback into their game, they create an eighth gap. Defensively, until the fullback moves, we can't determine where that eighth gap will be.

We call our strong safety JOKER. The free safety is called JESTER. When you hear that in our defensive calls, that tells us who is going to be the eighth man in the box.

We align a 9-technique end over the tight end on his outside shoulder. How heavy or tight you play him depends on his ability or experience. The whole premise is he can't get reached. We try to align with the defensive player's nose on the middle of the offensive's player shoulder pad with his foot splitting the crotch of the offensive linemen. Our tackles are in a 3-technique to the tight end and a 1-technique to the split end. The defensive end to the split-end side is in a 5-technique.

If we are declaring the strong safety support in the box, we kick our linebackers to the weakside of the formation. The Sam is aligned in a 50-technique, which is a 5-technique at linebacker depth. The Mike would be aligned in a 10-technique. The Will would be in a 60-technique, which is an alignment over a ghost tight end to the weakside. He is basically splitting the outside foot of the defensive end.

BASE ALIGNMENT/JOKER

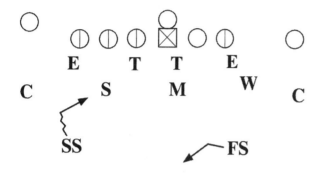

If we declared our free safety into the box, we kick our linebackers strong. The Sam aligns in a 70-technique, and the Mike and Will are in 30-techniques.

BASE ALIGNMENT/JESTER

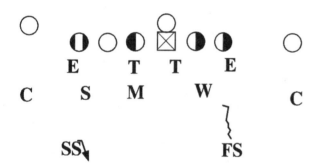

Next, are the keys we use. The tackle, nose, and ends key the man in front of them. We are an aggressive, attacking-style of defense. We are not reading. We want penetration and want to play in their backfield with disruption. The Sam, Mike, Will, and free safety are all keying the fullback. They key the fullback, because he is going to tell them where the eighth gap is going to be.

We teach our linebackers and safeties on run read through five different reads. The first read we teach is a *trap read*. That is a run action between the guard. The play could be a lead, slant, or trap play. In our terminology, a *lead* play is an isolation play to the strong-side. A *slant* play is an isolation play to the weakside. That helps you with your communication to your players.

The next read is a *belly read*. This is an open step by the back, keeping his shoulders square to the line of scrimmage. We read this as a zone-play step. We know the ball is going to be bent back.

The next read is a *stretch read*. That read to us is a run outside the tackles. We call it *stretch* to the tight-end side and *bounce* to the split-end side. The *toss* is to the tight-end side, and the *pitch* is the split-end side. We have a *counter read*, which is a misdirection run. It is *counter* weak and *power* strong. The last read is an *option read*, which I am glad we won't have any of those in the pros.

I want to go through these plays and show you how we defend them. The first one we are going to talk about is the *lead* play. That is an isolation play run at the Mike. We are playing single-gap defense. No one is covering two gaps. The Mike is responsible for the outside A-gap to the strongside. The defensive tackle has the B-gap. We are in a Jester support. Our defensive call on this type of defense is 90-Jester. The Mike is taking on the blocker and turning the ball carrier back to the Will linebacker.

The offensive left guard and center are going to power scoop the backside 1-technique with the center trying to get off on the Will. The Will is aligned in a 30-technique and has to get downhill in a hurry and beat the center's block. If the center comes off too quickly, the 1-technique should make the play. The Will takes the inside A-gap to the strongside. If the Will gets over the top, the ball carrier will break it back into the weakside B-gap. That is where the free safety is coming. Our free safety was more of a linebacker type than our strong safety. That is why we did this.

We didn't play Joker very much. We lined the safeties up eight-to-ten yards deep. While the quarterback was calling cadence, the safeties would be faking up and back disguising the coverage. When the ball was snapped, we wanted the free safety about a yard deeper than the linebackers. Ours line up with their toes at five yards. The reason we play them so deep is to get them downhill in a hurry.

We are working for a flat roll on defense. When you get beat in the run game, it is because you have guys at different levels. If the Mike can take the fullback's block on his side of the line of scrimmage, we will have more good plays than bad plays. We don't want the safety running at the line of scrimmage. We want him under control thinking play action.

LEAD PLAY

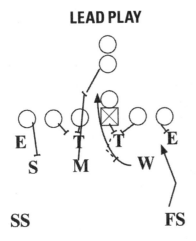

When we work our safeties in our seven-on-seven drill, they don't hit anyone. There are no receivers in the drill, and no one can block them. They learn their reads and reactions, but don't hit anyone. The Mike is attacking the outside of the A-gap and *boxing*, which is keeping his outside arm free. If we wanted him to attack keeping his inside arm free ,we call it *spill*. That is our terminology.

The next play we talked about is the *slant* or weakside isolation. The offensive blocking scheme is going to double the 1-technique tackle. The offensive tackle will try to influence the 5-technique end to rush upfield on a pass rush. The end has to read that move. If the tackle doesn't get depth and keep his shoulders square, the end should know it is an influence. An offensive tackle won't pass block like that. All he does is stay on the line of scrimmage and opens the gate outside. A tackle will not let an end have a free shot on his quarterback. The end has to recognize that and squeeze to the inside. He can't attack inside because he has his gap to protect. But he can't rush upfield and create a huge B-gap which puts the free safety on an island.

Sam, once he sees the fullback going to the weakside, knows he has to beat the block of the tight end.

He can't get cut off. The 3-technique stays in the B-gap. The Mike, when he sees the fullback go weak, runs through the A-gap. He made a ton of plays doing that last year. We don't need him to the weakside.

The Will takes the fullback on in the inside B-gap as deep in the backfield as he can. We want him to spill the ball. The free safety has the outside B-gap. The thing that can hurt is the end retracing his steps too soon and letting the ball bounce outside of him. He has to squeeze the B-gap, but make plays in the C-gap.

SLANT PLAY

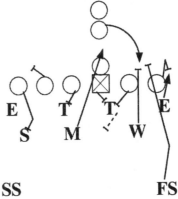

On the *trap,* we like to get the 3-technique underneath the trapper and spill the ball. The Mike has to beat the block of the tackle who is coming down on him. The 3-technique has to flatten and squeeze the guard as he tries to get backside for the Will. There are two schools of thought when you get a guard pulling and the center blocking back. We have done them both. Once the guard pulls, and the center blocks back, there is no backside B-gap. The 1-technique squeezes the center and keeps his outside arm free. There are only two gaps to the weakside when the guard pulls. The 1-technique is in A-gap, and the end is in the C-gap.

The Will reads the strong A-gap. If it has been flattened, and everything has been bubbled outside, he plays over the top. If there is some air in the A-gap, he bores into the gap. If the Will fills the A-gap, the free safety plays over the top of the bubbled area.

The Sam plays in the C-gap. If the offense ran a trap option, with the tight end arcing on the strong safety or Sam, we brought the end up for the pitch and played the Sam linebacker on the quarterback.

TRAP OR VEER TRAP

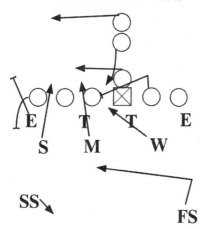

On the *belly* read, you really have to work. The combo block will come on the 3-technique tackle and the 1-technique tackle. The offensive line is reaching strong, and it looks like a full-flow play. The backside end has to squeeze down and close off the backside B-Gap. The free safety plays behind him if the play bounces back there. The Will can still run over the top and the Mike can fill the strongside A-gap.

BELLY PLAY

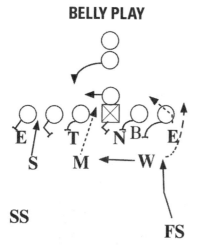

The next play is the *inside zone* play. They can block it by putting the tackle on the end and the fullback on the Will. But, the one we see the most is the offensive tackle blocking down on the Will and the fullback kicking out on the end. That is really tough on the Will because he has to beat the block of the tackle, but not get washed or pushed by the hole. He is in a 30-technique, so he shouldn't have a problem beating the block. As soon as he starts to feel the pressure, if he can beat the tackle with speed, he does it and maintains the B-gap. As soon as he feels the pressure, he has to get the same foot and same shoulder into the block and fight pressure. If he high or late getting there, he will get washed by the play.

If that happens, the end has to squeeze and get up under the block of the fullback and spill the play. The fullback is coming so tight to the butt of the offensive tackle, that the end may have to give some ground to get under the block. That happens if you are aggressive with your ends at getting them up the field. Teams are starting to bring the fullback and chopping the end. If the end can't get under the block, he takes the fullback on head up and tries to reduce the C-gap with the fullback's body. Ideally, we want the defensive end to take the inside portion of the fullback, and the free safety to take the outside portion. But a lot of times, the defensive end gets cut, and the free safety has to be a football player and make the play inside the end. This is tough on the Mike because he has to see the split flow. He stays and works to the weakside.

We drill the reads by using five trash cans or cones aligned as the gaps. The linebackers read the coach and react to what they see. We do it over and over again.

INSIDE ZONE

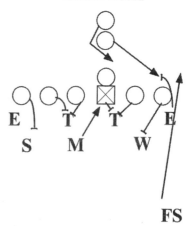

The next play is the *power 0* off-tackle. The offense will kick out with the fullback on the strong side defensive end. They combo block the 3-technique tackle up to the Will. The tight end comes down on the Sam if he is filling, but goes on to the Mike if he is scrapping. The backside guard pulls and turns up in the hole for the frontside linebacker.

We want our defensive end to squeeze down and spill the fullback's block. We are hoping for a two-for-one trade-off. We hope the pulling guard will be caught in the pile up. The Sam is scrapping outside. The Mike is on the tight end. He fills outside under the Sam, who is boxing the pulling guard.

The Will is filling the A-gap. If he hits and tries to get fancy and get over the top, a lot of times the ball will hit up in the A-gap. He has to bore his way into that gap. The free safety fills the B-gap weak and pursues over the top.

POWER 0

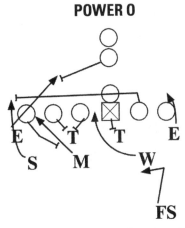

On the *counter,* we are getting the off-set fullback strong. The tailback is counter stepping to the weak-side and coming strong. It is the same blocking as the power 0 play, and the defense plays it the same way. The free safety has to be disciplined. He is mirror keying off the fullback.

COUNTER

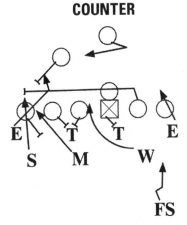

If you put together a read tape of all these plays and show it to your linebackers, by the end of the week, they will be able to recognize all the steps they see and to recognize the plays.

We give names to the fullback's position in alignment. If he off-set to the strongside in the halfback set, we called that JACK. If he set to the weakside in the halfback set, we called that QUEEN. If he sets in the wing position outside the tight end, we called that KING. If he sets in the weak slot position, we called that ACE. If he is behind the quarterback, we called that I.

This all comes back to communication. We need to have a meaningful conversation with your kids in the meeting room and on the sidelines on game day. That's why terminology is so important.

The next play we call *stutter*, which is counter weak. The left guard and tackle are down blocking on the 1-technique and Mike. The right guard is pulling to kick out the end. The center is blocking back on the 3-technique. The fullback is coming for the Will. We want the end to spill the guard, the Will to spill the fullback, and the free safety is outside making the tackle. The Mike to the strongside is under the tight end's block, to the weakside, he is under the tackle's block. The Sam is playing the cut back.

STUTTER

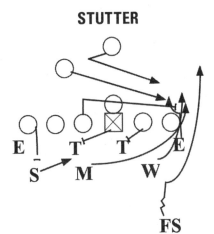

The *stretch* play is an outside read to the tight-end side. It is an outside zone for us because both backs' shoulders are turned. The offense is trying to reach everyone. We tell our end he can't be reached. The Sam has to beat the block of the offensive tackle. The Mike is attacking downhill. We tell him if he sees a window or run-through, run through it and make plays. Sometimes they make plays, and sometimes they don't, but we don't get on their butts if they don't.

STRETCH

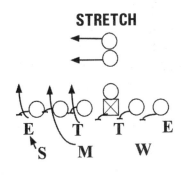

If they run the *toss* play, which is the sweep toward the tight end, they will pull with the onside guard. We are a penetrating defense with our down linemen. They are going to penetrate and come flat. More times than not, our 3-technique is going to try to get in the hip pocket of the pulling guard. You will see our 3-technique actually grab the guard and slip his hip and try to pull himself through. On the backside, we want our players to stay alive and not get cut off. The Mike and Will linebackers are running and ripping all blocks. The free safety is playing the severe cut back.

PITCH

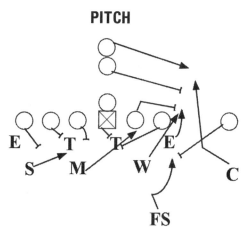

TOSS

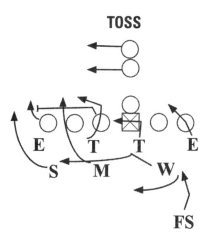

The pitch play is a toss play to the weakside. We don't see much of this. The offense will try to zone off the weakside. They may try to put the pulling guard on the free safety or crack him with the wide receiver. You must know what they are going to try to do to the free safety. It is very important that our free safety be down to six-and-half yards before the ball is snapped. If he is late, he is probably going to get cracked. If the crack comes, we want the safety to stay underneath the crack block, because the corner is reading and replacing the safety outside. If the fullback is outside, the Will is outside. The quicker the safety is coming up, the flatter the split end has to get to crack. That is an easier read for the corner. On the wide plays, kids have to know that the gaps move as the play goes wide.

Let me cover pass responsibilities. We call this coverage *10-FREE*. The corners have the number 1 receivers man-to-man. We play them with an inside alignment. We play our outside shoulder on his inside shoulder. They align seven yards deep. We line up inside on the man, not the line of scrimmage. The corner on the flanker side is tighter to the line of scrimmage than the other corner. This is because the flanker is off the line of scrimmage two yards.

On the snap of the ball, the strong safety wants to be ten yards deep over the top of the tight end. We start out two yards outside and ten yards deep. Both safeties go through their disguise movements. When the ball is snapped, the strong safety is zero-by-ten yards, and the free safety is six-and-half yards deep in the weak B-gap.

The corner's outside foot is up, and his inside foot is back. He keys the quarterback for three steps. The reason we do that is for the three-step drop by the quarterback. After the quarterback's third step, and he is not throwing, the corner focuses back on the number one receiver. He watches the split of the receiver he is covering. If the split tightens, it is to crack back on the safety or run an outside route. If the split is widens, we get inside and deeper.

The strong safety reads the quarterback to the number one receiver weak. If the one receiver is pushing inside, the strong safety works a little more inside to help the corner on the post. We call that a read middle 1/3 technique.

In this coverage, the Sam has the tight end man-to-man. The Mike and Will linebackers and the free safety have the backs. The flow of the backs determines who has a particular back. We play them three-on-two. The Mike has the first back strong, and the free safety has the first back weak. The Will has the second back strong.

10-FREE

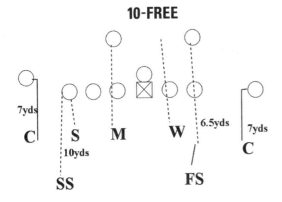

We talk to our kids about concepts. One concept we teach right from the beginning is what we call FIRE-PASS. That is a four-strong distribution. The rules are easy to learn, but the techniques are not so easy to play. Our corners have the number one receivers. The Sam has the tight end. The strong safety goes to the middle third. The Mike, Will, and the free safety work a combination on the two backs. Sometimes based on game planning, we tell the Mike and Will linebackers to lock on the I formation. That allows the free safety to play the low hole in a free position. The low hole is ten to twelve yards right over the ball reading the quarterback.

Everyone has tendencies. We see a lot of what we call the NCAA route. That is a crossing pattern, the dig, and the post. Where ever you like to throw the ball is where we are going to play the free safety.

FIRE PASS

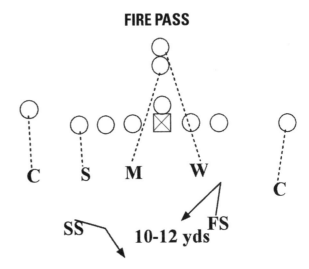

The FLOOD PASS comes off full flow weak. Everything is the same, except the free safety rolls up to take the fullback slipping out to the flat. The Will takes the tailback. The Mike clears the run and drops into the hole.

FLOOD PASS

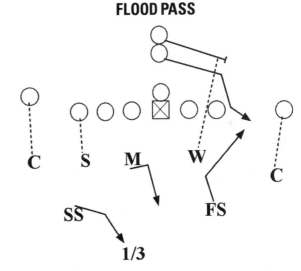

If the offense goes to a drop-back pass, and the backs split with the fullback going strong and the tailback going weak, the Mike takes the fullback and the free safety takes the tailback. The Will has no responsibility, so he drops into the hole and plays free. If the free safety is a better robber than the Will, you can go to a lock call. It allows the free safety to play the hole as a free under player.

DROP BACK PASS

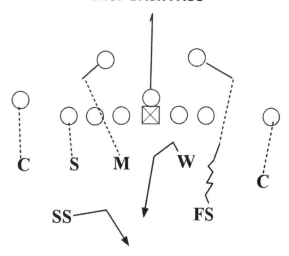

When the offense goes to a twin set, we bring both corners over and play man-to-man on the two wide receivers. The Sam has the tight-end, and the strong safety is still going to the deep middle third. The free safety is moving up, and nothing else changes for the linebackers.

TWIN SET

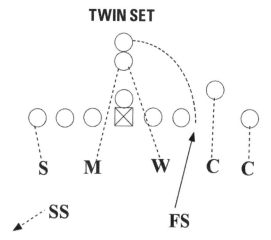

If we get a one-back set with a two-by-two look, the free safety adjusts up to take the number two receiver weak. We play the free safety in what we call an outside catch technique. He lines up five or six yards off the receiver in a head-up position. When the ball is snapped, he slides to an outside-catch technique. We want him to catch the receiver and absorb him as he comes off the line. We want him to dominate the outside shoulder of the receiver. Once we get a one-back alignment, the strong safety gets to thirteen yards and splits the set. The corners are inside at seven yards. The Sam has the tight end. Since there is only one back, the Mike and Will linebackers give a DUO TOUGH call. That means their gaps are de-

fined on the run, and they play the one back to their side, and the other linebacker goes to the hole. If the tailback steps right, the Mike takes him, and the Will goes to the hole. If he steps left, the Will takes him, and the Mike goes to the hole. We play the free safety in an outside technique because he has help to the inside, short and long.

ONE BACK - 2 BY 2

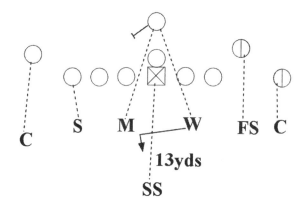

If the offense lines up in two backs and motions to the one-back set, the free safety does the adjusting. We want the best match up we can get. A match up between the free safety and the tailback is better for us.

If we don't want to play man coverage with the Jester, here is something we do. We call this BUZZ. Florida State has made a living at this. When you play man coverage with the Sam on the tight end, it is hard on him. It is hard for him to play the tight end man-to-man and make the plays we expect of him on the run. A lot of time, the tight end runs free in the field. We have to depend on the player in the hole to pick him up. It helps him by playing zone behind him.

The formation corner is still playing inside at seven yards. He is going to settle there and play a 1/5 underneath coverage. The strong safety is aligned at ten yards. He sinks and plays one half of the field. The weak corner is aligned at his normal inside seven yards. He cheats back and inside before the ball is snapped and plays one half. The Jester yo-yos up and down, but is at six and half yards as the ball is snapped. He is going to the weak flat. We are playing two-deep coverage and taking the pressure off the Sam in man coverage. It also gives your corners a break.

The only place this coverage is weak is to the weakside. The more you play this coverage, the more people are going to stand up and hit some hitches and quick routes to the split end.

The strongside corner reads the tight end. He plays with his outside foot up and inside foot back. On the snap, he opens his hips and shuffles outside. If he gets a run read, he tries to beat the block of the wide out and get back for the run. The strong safety plays over the top of him deep for the halfback pass or play action.

If pass shows, and the tight end goes vertical, he matches up with the wide receiver. The coverage turns into quarter coverage. We still have the eight-man front. The cheat corner knows he has the split end almost man-to-man. If pass shows, he knows he has help underneath from the free safety in the flat and the Will in the curl area. That is a good zone change-up to take the heat off your corners and the Sam linebacker.

BUZZ

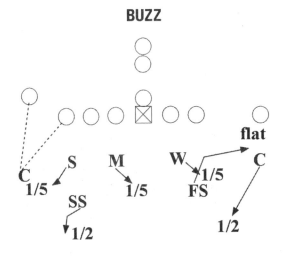

The next coverage goes with our under package. This is our eagle defense. We call it 70-Joker-3X. The X stands for exchange. The front reduces to the weakside. The Sam plays the 9-technique. Everyone else shifts weak. The ends are in 5-techniques and the tackles are in a 1-technique strongside and 3-technique weakside. The free safety rolls to the middle of the field. We cheat the linebackers weak, and the strong safety moves up into the run support strong.

70-JOKER-3X

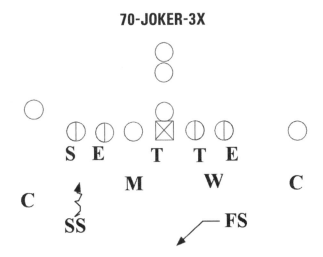

On the lead play instead of boxing to the Will, Mike will spill the play to the Joker. The Will plays the backside A-gap for the cut back. On the slant play, the Will boxes the fullback and forces the ball carrier back to the Mike, and the Joker has the cut back run. It is opposite of our base reads.

LEAD AND SLANT

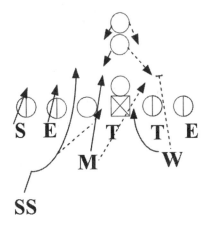

We can play 10-strong and put the strong safety on the tight end man-to-man and play three-way on the two backs with the three linebackers. Or we can play zone with a 3X, which means we are trading pass drops between the Sam and the strong safety. The Sam plays curl-to-flat, and the strong safety mirrors the tight end. If the tight end runs an arrow, the Joker looks for the curl. If the tight end runs vertical, the Joker jams him and carries him to a depth of ten to twelve yards. If he runs the flag, the Joker becomes a robber. If the tight end crosses, the Joker carries him all the way across the field. The Will plays curl to flat on the weakside. The Mike runs to the curl weakside.

ZONE 3X

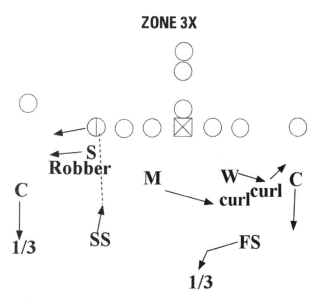

Y-MOTION

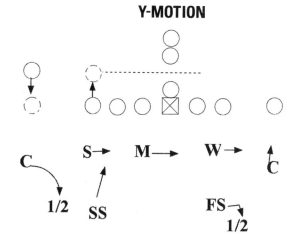

During training camp you need to take time to put in the adjustments to the base defense. Set aside time to go over adjustments to all situations. Take a single adjustment on one day and a different one the next day, and go though your adjustments to both the run and pass game.

Let me get to the film and show you what I have been talking about. I hope you got something out of this lecture. Thank you.

Before I close, I want to go over some simple adjustments. If the offense brings the tight end out on one side and trades him to the other side, we recall the front. The Sam and Will flip sides. The Joker and Jester exchange with the tight end. We call it Y-Walk.

Y-WALK

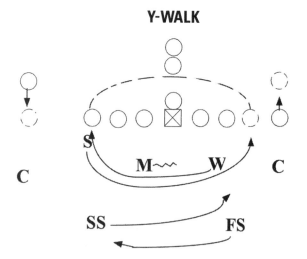

If the tight end comes out and aligns right and shifts back to the slot position, he can come in motion and align on the other side, continue in motion, or stop. Once he establishes himself as an off-the-line player, we can't trade our front. We bump the linebackers toward the motion and check the coverage to a sink coverage, which is a soft cover two. All the linebackers go to a tailback read.

If teams take advantage of our zone, we get out of the adjustment and assign a man to the tight end. We go to man coverage with the eight-man front concept and tough gap control.

THE WING-T SPEED SWEEP SERIES

Portland High School, Tennessee

It is a privilege for me to be here. Over the years, the Coach of the Year Clinic has been good to me. I see on the program it is the 41st year for this clinic. That speaks for itself as far as I am concerned.

I can recall Coach Jerry Claiborne speaking here when he was the head coach at the University of Kentucky. He made the statement several years ago that the high school coaches of the state of Kentucky needed to keep fighting for spring practice. I understand that spring practice is included in the football programs now in high schools in Kentucky. We all know the importance of having spring practice.

In 1999, Portland High School played in the state championship game. The game ended with our offense on the four-yard line when the clock ran out. We came up a little short. It was much like the Tennessee Titans of the NFL when they played the St. Louis Rams in the Super Bowl that year. The Titans ended up down near the goal line, but time ran out on them. Our story was very similar.

This past season, we were able to come back and win 15 games and the state championship. We have a lot to be thankful for at Portland High School. Before I get into my topic, I want you to know that our defense only gave up 1.87 points per game. In the state championship game, they blocked the first two punts and scored touchdowns on them. We were up 14-0 before we had to run a play. I call the offense, but I can tell you, I like that kind of start.

My topic today is the speed sweep series. We are a wing-T offense. One of the high school coaches from the state of Tennessee asked me how many different formations we run. I told him we run one basic offensive formation. It is the standard wing-T formation with a split end and a slot back to one side, and a wingback to the tight-end side. We have a fullback in the backfield. We are in that formation 90 percent of

the time. We have lined up with the split end over on the same side of the tight end. Also, we have lined the wing man deep in the I formation in short-yardage situations.

We have followed the Delaware wing-T philosophy over the years. As most wing-T coaches know, if you put in a wing-T play, you need to add another play that will complement the new play. We feel the speed sweep series is a great compliment to the wing-T offense. I believe you should give credit where credit is due. Coach Hershel Moore of Cumberland University in Tennessee is the person that gave us most of our ideas. If you want to learn about the wing-T, you need to get in touch with him. He is the master mind. We got the speed sweep series from him.

This is our base set. I will show it against the 50 defense and the 4-3 look. Also, I will go over the personnel for each position and cover our blocking rules.

SPEED SWEEP STRONG VS. 50 DEFENSE

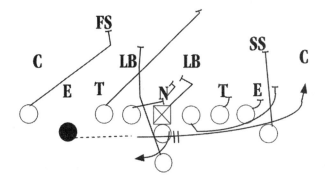

I am going to share something with you that helped us a great deal. This past year we played with three fullbacks. We played with two players that we call halfbacks. They are in the slot set. We played with two wingbacks. They rotated in the game. I let the position coach work out the number of rotations for each man.

Some of you may be thinking that we must have outstanding talent to play that many players. I do not think that was the case. I have been coaching at Portland since 1990, and we have not had a Division I player go to college in those 11 years. I feel it is important to play as many players as you can in this offense. In our third game in the playoffs, our junior fullback broke his ankle. We had a senior and a sophomore left at fullback. That sophomore stepped up, and we never missed a beat.

I want to cover the speed sweep strong play blocking rules:

TE – Reach man on. If defensive end is too wide to reach, make a switch call with the wingback and work up to the linebacker or pull to pin the linebacker.

PST – Reach man on. If uncovered, pull flat to pin the playside linebacker or free safety.

PSG – Pull flat and fast and read the wingbacks block. Read – wingback's butt to sideline or to the backfield; get outside and run to the numbers (think hook). Read – wingback's butt to you, cut up and look inside (same as backside guard on buck sweep.)

C / BSG / BST – Big scoop; scoop to next playside. If you come clean off, he LOS take a cutoff angle downfield. (C will look to cut off MLB or BSLB.)

WB – Reach first man outside TE's block. If he skates outside, turn him out and drive him to the sideline. If he is too wide to reach, seal the linebacker. Block the first man past the tight-end's block, attack chest, work feet outside or kick.

SE – Take a cutoff angle to the free safety. If the safety is gone, peel back on the corner.

QB – The quarterback is going to seed the ball, pivot playside foot, both heels in the A-gap, handoff over the outside knee, and then fake the bootleg to the opposite side. He pivots on the playside foot. He wants both heels in the A-gap. Then, he hands the ball off his outside knee. Then, he fakes the bootleg. This is something we struggled with for about a year and one half. I went back to see Coach Moore, and he helped me straighten it out.

FB – Step through backside A-gap, cut-off free safety, do not block on line of scrimmage.

HB – Full speed on snap count, open inside toe, cross over, sprint heel depth of quarterback, read frontside guard.

We do not block anyone in the A and B gaps on the speed sweep. Have we been tackled by defenders coming through those gaps? Yes, a few times. The most important thing I can stress on the speed sweep is TIMING. We started this series three years ago when we visited Coach Moore. We made a lot of mistakes when we first started. So, in those three years, I can tell you that timing is very important on the play.

I do not now the kind of snap count you have. We have a rhythmic count. "SET – RED – READY - GO". On the Red, the slot man is coming in motion. He is laying his ears back. He is coming across the formation full speed. When the ball is snapped we want the slot to be at the heel of the backside guard. When the quarterback makes the handoff it is over the front side leg. Hopefully, out onside guard will be out in front of the ball carrier.

This past year, our guards were only 160 and 165 pounds. They ran decently. One ran 40 yards in 4.8, and the other was 4.9. They got the job done for us. They had a lot of heart, and they wanted to play. They worked hard to get out in front of the ball carrier.

I get a lot of questions about the speed of the running back running the speed sweep. In all of my years of coaching, I have only had two players that ran 4.4. This past year we had one back that ran a 4.7, and the back up man ran a 4.6. They ran the play well. I have a tape at the end I will let you see them in action.

Here is the speed sweep strong against the 4-3 defense.

SPEED SWEEP STRONG VS. 4-3 DEFENSE

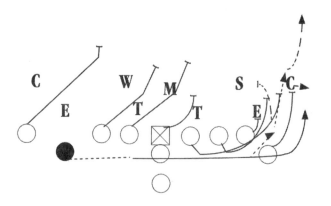

We like to run the play from the end over set. We bring the split end over on the strongside. The play is basically the same with the split end coming down on the strong safety.

Let's move on to the speed sweep weak against the 50 defense. We like the speed sweep weak play as much, if not more that the Speed Sweep Strong. It really depends on the game play. The following blocking rules apply to the speed sweep weak play blocking rules:

SE – The split end is going to stalk block or crack back. He will crack on a cheating safety or a wide outside linebacker that the halfback cannot reach.

PST – The playside tackle reaches the man on. If he is too wide to reach, he makes a call to the halfback and either pulls and pins the end, or bumps straight up to the linebacker.

PSG – The playside guard pulls flat and fast and is thinking hook. He reads the halfback's block to the split end's block, and then takes it as wide as possible.

C, BSG, BST, TE – The backside has the big scoop block. They scoop to the next gap, and then to the cutoff point downfield.

QB – The quarterback seeds the ball, pivots into the A-gap, hands off over the outside knee, and runs the bootleg play.

FB – Runs the backside A-gap, and then wants to cut off the free safety.

HB – The halfback blocks the first man past the outside tackle, depending on a tight or loose call. He attacks the chest and works his feet outside, or he kicks the defensive man outside.

WB – The wingback leaves on the snap count, opens the inside toe, takes a crossover step, and sprints heels depth on the QB, and reads the frontside guard.

SPEED SWEEP WEAK VS. 50 DEFENSE

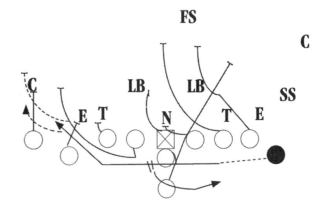

This is a great football play. We like to attack the weakside with the speed sweep weak.

Against the inverted secondary, we bring the split end down on the free safety if he is breaking on the motion. The motion by the wingback does a lot to the teams we play. Some teams will bring that free safety on the run to the slot when they see motion to the split-end side. We crack block with the split end and bring the guard outside on the corner.

SPEED SWEEP WEAK VS. INVERT

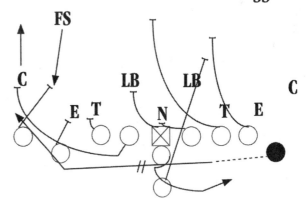

We can bring the fly man across the formation and hit him with the pass down the sideline if they continue to bring the free safety on the invert coverage.

Against the eagle shade defense, we bring the onside tackle on the defensive end and send the slot man on the linebacker on his side.

SPEED SWEEP WEAK VS. EAGLE SHADE

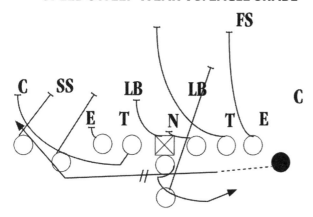

Against a hard corner that wants to come inside with the free safety coming outside to take the outside third, we have the pulling guard pick up the corner on the blitz.

SPEED SWEEP VS. HARD CORNER

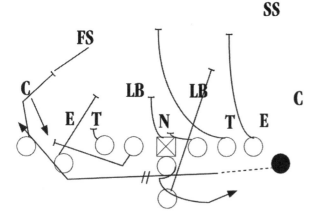

We tell our split end, if he knows the corner is in man coverage, to run him off deep. There is no need to block him. If the corner sits on us, we want to turn him outside.

Against the 4-3 look, we can crack down inside with the end or send him on the corner, depending on the game plan. A lot depends on the athletes we have in the game at split end and slot back, and it depends on the defensive players as well.

SPEED SWEEP WEAK VS. 4-3 DEFENSE

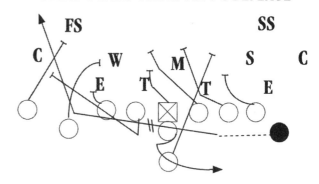

If the defense over shifts the front to the slot side, we can pull the tackle if he is uncovered. We pull both the guard and tackle.

SPEED SWEEP WEAK VS. OVER FRONT

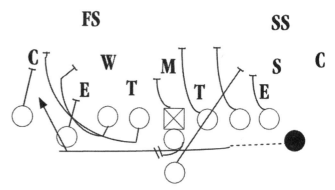

If the strong safety comes up in the slot and plays head up with the slot man, he has to be aware of that. He must take him on at the line of scrimmage and not let him penetrate.

SPEED SWEEP WEAK VS. 4-4 DEFENSE

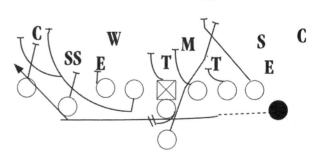

Our wingback is one-yard deep and one-yard outside. Our halfback is three-yards outside our tackle and one-yard deep. Our guards and tackles are two-feet apart. Our tight end is three feet from the tackle. We have not included a lot of splits like some of the Delaware wing-T teams have been doing recently. The base split for the split end is 12 yards.

In 1999, the belly play was very good for us off the speed sweep. We are talking about plays complementing each other. This is the play everyone asks us about when they see our films. I love this play. It is our speed-G vs. a 50 defense. If you are a wing-T coach, you already know the blocking scheme. It is basically wing-T blocking. Some people call it down blocking. We call it G blocking.

SPEED-G VS. 50 DEFENSE

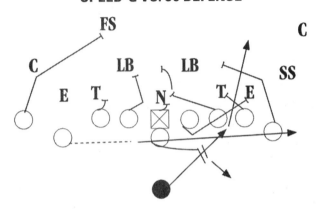

The thing about the speed sweep is that some people call it the jet sweep. It is the same play. The following blocking rules apply to the speed sweep play:

TE - Block down.

PST – Block down on LOS.

PSG – Pull and trap the first man outside the tight end's down block.

C – BSG – BST - Scoop block.

SE – Cut off safety man.

QB – Seed ball, pivot heels into A-gap, let Halfback pass (keep ball seeded). Take a crossover step down the line, hand to the fullback on the third step.

FB – Step playside foot to the outside cheek of the offensive tackle. Hit the C-gap behind the guard. Read the block of the wingback on the linebacker.

HB – Sprint and fake one-half yard deep to avoid the wingback.

WB – Influence step, avoid the kick-out block, (behind or in front), cut-off nearest linebacker.

Against the 4-3 defense, we have the wingback read the Sam linebacker. If he sits inside, the wingback seals him off. If he comes outside, the wingback turns him outside. This is a good play against this defense.

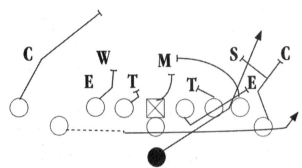

If you are going to run the speed-G play, you need to put this next play in your offense. It is our speed-G pass. We run the tight end on an out route, or we run him on the flag route. We can do several different things with the tight end. We want to do the same thing on the pass play as we did on the run. Because he steps down on the run, we want him to step down inside on the pass.

All of the linemen use a hinge block across the line of scrimmage. The split end runs his post route.

The quarterback pivots into the A-gap and lets the halfback clear. He sprints out of the A-gap off the tail of the fullback to four yards deep. He squares his shoulders to the line of scrimmage and reads the cornerback.

The fullback steps with his playside foot to the outside cheek of the offensive tackle. He blocks the first thing that shows in the C-gap.

The halfback runs the fake on the sweep one-half yard deep. He runs through the outside shoulder of the defensive end.

The wingback runs the route called. We can run different routes, including the out route, with him.

SPEED-G PASS VS. 50 DEFENSE

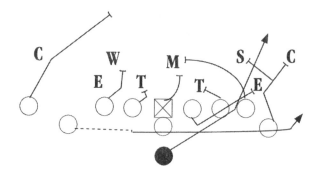

SPEED-G PASS VS. 4-3 DEFENSE

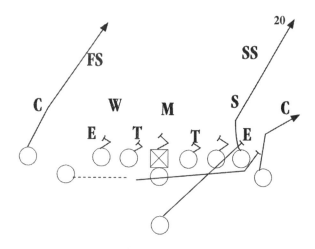

We very seldom throw back to the split end. If we see something in the scouting report, and we think our quarterback can throw the ball back to the split end, we will work on it.

I love the pass to the wingback down the sideline. If we run our end over, we are still going to throw the football. We have several combination routes we can run with that formation.

SPEED-G PASS END OVER

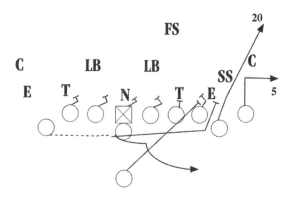

Against the 4-3 defense, the blocking is the same. We hinge block on the line. It is the same look with different patterns.

I want to show you the plays on film. I will say this before we get the film going. If you do not have an end-zone shot of your games, you should think about it. It is a great teaching tool. We feel it is important to have the end-zone shots.

I want to thank you for this opportunity to share with you what we do with our offense. Hopefully, you can pick up a point or two from what I have covered. The most important thing I have to say to you today is this. "JESUS CHRIST — DON'T LIVE WITHOUT HIM."

DEFENSIVE PHILOSOPHY AND GAME PLAN

Marshall University

I want to talk about a number of things today. We are real proud of what we have been able to do at Marshall. One of the reasons I wanted to come up here, is we have not had a lot of success recruiting in Ohio. It is not because we didn't want to. I was an assistant football coach at Marshall in 1979. From 1979-82, we were probably the most losing program in NCAA football. We played so many homecomings, that we began to take our own float. We are trying to make inroads into this area and get some of the players from this area. We feel we have a lot to offer the kids because we are close.

I was a high school coach for 14 years so I know what you guys have been through. Today, we are going to talk about game planning on defense and some of the fundamentals I believe in. We have had 17 straight winning seasons at Marshall. When I came to Marshall, we were on a plateau, but we have jumped to another level. I am going to talk about some of the things we have tried to do to get us to the level we are on today.

One of the things we look at is the perception of our program. This is true of the high school program, college program, or whatever program you are in. Your must raise the level of perception. At Marshall, we have tried to do it on two or three different fronts.

To build a successful program, the first thing you have to do it to have everyone who is involved with your program to be thinking in the same direction. The first year after we went from I-AA to Division I-A, we were going into the Mid-American Conference. We have won the MAC Championship four straight years now. That is the first time in the history of the conference that any team has won it four straight years. When I talk, I stress the fact we have been in position to play for the championship each of those years. We play for championships.

Marshall had been in the MAC once before but left and went to the Southern Conference. When we returned to the MAC the first year, we knew Marshall had once been the doormat for the Mid-American Conference. Although, we were 15-0 the previous year, we had not played anybody, even though we were the I-AA National Champions. We had not played any teams from the MAC or anyone who had played a MAC schedule. We didn't know how we would do in the MAC.

One of the goals we sat that year was to have a winning season. Marshall, prior to the 1997 season, had not had a Division I winning season since the 1964 team. I played on that team.

We set seven goals that year that we wanted to achieve. We set a goal to have a winning season. We set a goal to go to a bowl game. Marshall had only been to one bowl game in the history of the school and that was in 1949 – the Tangerine Bowl. Another goal was to win the MAC and to win the Motor City Bowl. Those were some lofty goals for our first year. The first year we were 10-3 and lost to Ole Miss 36-33 in the Motor City Bowl. We were able to achieve six out of our seven goals.

After that game in the post-game press conference, the reporters asked me if I was proud of the way our kids played against Mississippi. I told them I was proud of their effort, but we play for championships at Marshall. That was the only championship that we have played for in the last five years we have not won.

At one point this year, we were 2-4 in our won-loss record. In the four previous years, I was 50-4. We lost more games in the first six games this year than I had lost in four years. That was the first time these players had faced adversity. We were ahead of Michigan

State, North Carolina, and Western Michigan going into the fourth quarter, and lost them all. And then, Toledo just kicked the dog crap out of us. It was 35-0 at halftime. I talked to them at halftime, and that is where our season turned around. We ended up losing 42-0, but the points came on an offensive turn over.

We had a bunch of guys who had not faced adversity. If we had not laid a good foundation, we were going to crumble. If your fans, players, and coaches don't believe in what you are trying to do, you are in trouble. You have to set high goals and standards. That is the foundation. Set your goal, standards, and expectations high.

It didn't matter that we had lost eight offensive linemen by the time we played our first game this year. It didn't matter that we had lost three running backs for the year after the third game. It didn't make any difference that we were playing four true freshmen and ten sophomores. It didn't matter if we were playing Michigan State. Our fans expected us to win. Our players and coaches expected to win, and that was the reason we were able to turn our season around.

I want our kids to compete as hard in the classroom as they do on the football field. I want them to play as close to perfect as possible, realizing that no one is perfect. I want them to have fun. Those are the only things I talk to them about before a ball game. We talk a lot about faith, also. Faith is something you really have to talk about when you are building a program. That is true even if you have a good program. Adversity is going to strike in every football game you play, and in every day of our life. Your ability to overcome, manage, or deal with adversity is going to be critical in how things go for you the next day. In the lockerroom, I tell them adversity is going to strike sometime in this game, and they have to have faith we are going to pull this thing through. They must have faith in their teammates.

Faith is really something. We believe in God, but we never see him. We have faith that he is there. On the goal line, they have to have faith that everyone is going to do their job to get the ball into the end zone. You have to have faith in your coaches and teammates, because when things go bad, that is when your principles and beliefs desert you. You have to have strong faith in them.

You want to point fingers, blame people, and make excuses for why you are not successful. I saw that in the faces of our players after our first six games. Our faith was shaken. We were 2-3 and down 35-0 at half to Toledo, when I went in at halftime to talk to them. We were not doing things the way we knew how to do them. We were doing them fair, but not like we needed to do. Things were going bad for us. We started going the wrong way.

I know a guy named Hank Evans. You wouldn't know him. He is a sales guy who comes in and talks to our coaches about recruiting and selling. At one point, he told me in recruiting a player, if things aren't getting better, they're getting worse. When things are not getting better, you have to stop it right there. You have to make the sale, and if you can't, go on.

At halftime of the Toledo, I figured it out; it was not getting better. It was getting a hell of a lot worse. I told them at halftime they had to have faith in what we were doing and to have faith in me. I told them to go back out there and fight. We went back out and got better defensively. Our offense struggled, but we got through the game.

The first thing we had to fix was their mental approach to the game. Our players were going in different directions. We weren't doing things right. The best players don't make the best team, but the best team wins. We had good players. They were young, but they were good. We had to somehow become a team. I gave each one of them a rubber band. They wore that rubber band every day and every practice until the end of the bowl game. One rubber band by itself is not very strong. But if you put a bunch of rubber bands together, it is strong as hell. Our saying was: *"WE WERE GOING TO BAND TOGETHER AND GET BETTER."* We were going to have faith, and we were going to believe.

The next thing I did was to go out and buy a bunch of flashlights. I gave them to every starter on offense, defense, and special teams. I had the whole team get in a room like this one. We turned every light off. I had the offense stand up front. I had them turn those flashlights on one at a time. When we got all eleven of those lights on, it lit up that part of the room. I had one of the guards turn his flashlight off. I asked the player if they could see the hole it made when someone on offense did not do their job. I was trying to demonstrate to them that we were a team that had won 50 games in the previous four years. We had broken every record there was in winning games. I was the first coach since Alonzo Staggs to win 50 games in four years. We won more games in the 90's than any program in America. And now, we were floundering. We were bad.

I had the defense turn their flashlights on and then the special teams turned their flashlights on. When we turned all 33 of those flashlights on, we lit up the room. If a team pulls together, they can light up the room. By turning off some lights, they could see the holes and weaknesses of not playing together as a team.

We turned it around and beat a team in the championship game that had beaten us by 28 points in the regular season. At the end of the year, we were playing as good as any team that has every played at Marshall University. We did it with the same players that had gone 2-4 in the first six games. We are a young football team, and we are going to be pretty good the next couple of years. We have no fear of telling everyone we are going to be good because that is the standard and expectation we go by. If you are content with just being competitive, that is all you will ever be.

I think the MAC is a hell of a conference. People talk about us leaving the conference. The perception of our conference is going to get better, the more you see of it. When we compete against the Big Ten and Conference USA, they are perceived to be better than the MAC. We have beaten BYU, South Carolina, Clemson, Cincinnati, Louisville, and a bunch more. Toledo beat Penn State last season. We have a good conference. We have to raise the perception of the MAC. We want the perception that when the HURD comes to town, we are coming in there to kick your butt. We lost a little of that last season, but we gained it back. We will be competitive next year. Everyone in our league is up grading their schedules. They are trying to play better people.

Next year, we open up with the Florida Gators down there. I used to coach there. There is nothing good about going to play them in Florida. People want to know how we came about playing Florida. We know they are going to be good next year. But, I am the one who scheduled that game. If we are going to compete, let's get after it. Let's see what we have to do to get to where we need to be.

We were ranked 10th in the nation. That is the best the MAC has ever finished. We want to see if we can go on and get better. We are not going to be content with that.

People ask me why I'm not looking for a better job. The three coaches before me left Marshall and went to better jobs. They are all fired right now. I'm at least working and am satisfied with where I am. When I leave this job, I want to get a better job. I haven't seen one better yet. That is the way I perceive it. I won't do anything just for money. I almost did a year ago, but my driver would not take me down there.

When I set my goal in our football program, I try to look two years ahead. I have this year's team and what we are going to look like two years from now in my two-year plan. If I have a freshman or sophomore, I will start bring them along so they can be a starter two years from now. When we open up against the University of Florida, I don't want to start anyone in that game who has not been in a game.

I also have a 5-year goal. That covers finances, facilities, and things of that nature. For the actual football teams that play the game, I keep to a two-year goal. What I am looking for in recruiting is for two years from now. We never want to turn down anything better than what we have, but that is what I am looking for.

How the kids do in school certainly reflects how they play on the field. I think this has helped us. I don't think you can separate the two. We have been very fortunate at Marshall University. For the last four years, we have been in a bowl game. The Boston Globe did a survey. In the last four years we have been second, third, or fourth each year in the graduation rate of our minority athletes. The graduation rate for our team has been 85 percent for the last four years. That is pretty damn good. I know the worse we do academically, the worse we are on the field.

To build a good program, EXPLOIT YOUR STRENGTHS AND MANAGE YOUR WEAKNESSES. One of the problems we had this year was a young quarterback. He is an outstanding football player. I think he will be the best quarterback in the history of the MAC. I think this kid will be better than our last two quarterbacks who are playing in the NFL now. Going into last season I told our coaches he was not ready to win game for us. I told the coaches to just make sure he doesn't lose them.

The Michigan State game was the first football game he had played in since high school. Because of injuries, we got into some situations where we couldn't run the ball. That put more pressure on him to perform when he wasn't ready. We were trying to get him to win games, and he was not ready. We were inside Michigan State's 15-yard line six times and only got 10 points. If we had been smart and taken field goals instead of trying to force touchdowns, we may have won the game. Had he played at the beginning of the year like he played at the end, we would have won those close games. But, he wasn't ready to do that experience-wise.

We didn't do the fundamental thing going into the season of exploiting our strengths and managing our weaknesses. We tried to use our inexperienced quarterback as a strength instead of managing him. At the end of the year, he was that strength that we exploited. When we had Randy Moss, that was a strength. Anytime the defense single-covered him, we threw the ball to him. It didn't matter if it was third-and-an inch. We checked the play and threw it to him. If we had not thrown him the ball, I would have fired the coordinator. He was the best player in football. He had 55 touchdowns in two years. Exploit your strengths.

We have led the nation three out of the last four years in TD Passes. We want to take what the defense gives us. We want to exploit the strength, on offense or defense. Exploit the strengths and manage your weakness.

We want to be in great condition. We felt a great contributing factor in the bowl game against Cincinnati was our conditioning. We learned something playing in the Motor City Bowl indoors. It is dry and humid, and you get dehydrated. The first year, when we played Ole Miss, we were ahead at halftime 17-7. I looked at our players, and it looked like we had played three ball games. They were wet and dropping like flies. We got into the fourth quarter, and all our defensive backs started to cramp up. We couldn't play

man coverage. We knew what we needed to do, but we couldn't do it. Now, before we go up there, we do our conditioning in our field house with big space heaters on. It really paid dividends.

There are three things I talk to our players about related to fundamentals. It is very simple, but I believe this with all my heart and soul. These have to do with fundamentals. The first thing is *stance*. If you have to "move to move" out of your stance, you are in a poor stance. If I am a defensive back, and if I have to step forward to go backward or if I have to squat to move, I'm in a poor stance. I have to move to move to the direction I want to go. If they are high and have to move down or down low and have to move up to get started, there is something wrong with their stance. If I have to move one direction to go the other direction, I'm moving slower. If I have to stop the momentum of going one direction to shift it the other way, it slows me down.

You can't play the game of football straight-legged. I tell our guys not to be straight-legged, but to have their wrists down below their knees. That means they are going to have to bend their knees. From that position, you can do anything in the game of football when I get in this fundamental position. When the defensive back comes up to take on a block, we want his wrists below his knees. If he has changed levels too quickly to get from a straight-legged position to a position with his wrists below his knees, his weight settles. He has to transfer his weight before he can react to the block.

Another simple point is to *point your toes* in the direction you want to go. That is simple. If you want to go in a certain direction, you have to point your toes to get moving toward that direction.

There are two basic kinds of stances in football. There is a stance for *speed* and one for *power*. The *power* stance has the feet shoulder-width apart with the wrists below the knees. It is used to explode into someone. The *speed* stance has the feet in a narrow alignment. It is a running stance.

One other thing we do in our program is go one-on-one every day we have shoulder pads on. We do this with our offensive and defensive line for 10 minutes. This is the reason why. In today's football, so much of it is retreat pass blocking and passive blocking. The kids don't learn to hit, move their feet, and do all those basic principles that we just talked about. This year after we lost those eight offensive linemen before the season we stopped doing it. We went 2-4 in our first six games. We went back to doing it after that. I don't know if that was the reason we turned around, but we got better.

NEVER TRY QUITTING – NEVER QUIT TRYING. We talk to our players a lot about this.

Let's get into the *game plan*. Some of these next things I'm going to go through quickly. You must have a #1) *POSITIVE WAY OF COMMUNICATING WITH YOUR PLAYERS*. Instead of saying don't fumble the ball, we say squeeze the ball. I coach defensive backs. I tell them we have the best players, and that we have to be the best team. Coach the players positively, not negatively. No matter where I've been, if the defensive back's IQ dropped a point, they would be some kind of plant, and we would be watering them in a flower pot. I have to tell them exactly what I want. What they hear last is what they remember. Always find a way to talk positively to them.

The next thing is so fundamental but true. We call it simply #2) *ALIGNMENT, ASSIGNMENT, GOOD STANCE*. You have to align right, do your assignment, and get in a proper stance. When your team gets beaten, how many times did you line up wrong, didn't know what to do, or got the call in time. Those are three things a player should be able to do every time. If you can't get your players to that point, you need to stop and start over. You should be able to get him lined up, teach he what he has to do, and get him in a good stance. If so, you will win more than you lose.

#3) *POINT THE TOES IN THE DIRECTION YOU WANT TO GO – YOU CAN'T PLAY STRAIGHT-LEGGED*. We've already talked about that.

#4) *WALK THROUGH*. I am a firm believer in this. We do a lot of walk through. The reason I do walk throughs is because it is a good teaching technique. I go back to my high-school experiences. I really enjoy coaching. It doesn't make any difference to me whether I'm coaching a junior high, high school, or college kid. Now, economically, it does makes a big difference, but as far as the coaching goes, it doesn't matter. If a player can't walk through a play right, how

do you expect him to do it right at full speed? Go at a speed where the players can do it right. It may be walk through, or half speed, three-quarters speed, to full speed. Basically, that is the way our practice is organized. We do a lot of walk through.

I think this next point is really important: #5) *PICK OUT THE TEAMS YOU HAVE TO BEAT AND DO A STUDY ON THEM*. We have lost our offensive coordinator every year since I've been a head coach at Marshall. They have gone to better jobs. The coordinator at Minnesota was with us. They're running our offense. The coordinator at Southern Miss two years ago was with us. The coordinator at Texas was at Marshall. The coordinator at North Carolina State was on our staff. If I was in the MAC and had to play Marshall, I would go all over the country to find out everything I could about Marshall University, and find out what I had to do to beat them. That is what we do.

I was the defensive coordinator for Coach Spurrier at Florida. Florida had just won the Sugar Bowl that year for the first time ever in the history of the school. They beat West Virginia in the bowl game, but he fired his defensive coordinator, and hired me. I was at Tulane at the time. We had only won four games that year at Tulane. He hired me as defensive coordinator because he remembered me from Wake Forest. When he was at Duke, we beat him three straight years, and he remembered it. I had done a study on him while I was at Wake Forest. I understood what he was going to do. People are starting to do some things differently. If you are going to defend it, you better go study it. That's what happened when the wishbone came out. No one knew much about it. It took the defense time to catch up with the formation. They had to do studies to learn how to defend it.

People in the MAC are beginning to recruit like Marshall. They are starting to run our type of offense. They are starting to get the type of players we are getting. They are not big and slow any more. They can run to the ball just like we can. That's what making it a more competitive conference. If they want to get to a bowl game, they have to whip Marshall. When we come on the field, you have to understand what we are going to do or you won't stand much of a chance. But, understand this, Marshall is doing a study on you too.

When we played Clemson two years ago, their staff had just come from Tulane. I spent four days at Tulane. I found out everything I could. I talked with everybody and anybody I could that had worked on either side of the ball. If anybody had been fired, I went and talked to them. When we played Clemson I understood what they were doing.

My first year at Florida, we went to the University of Tennessee and shut them out 31-0. I did the same thing. I visited Penn State and everyone else that played Tennessee the year before. I understood Tennessee's offense. When Tennessee had a tight end or fullback in the game, the offense was the same. It did not matter where the fullback was lined up. If they have three wide outs and a tight end in the game, the offense was the same. The tight end is just a fullback, and the plays were the same. The formations were different, but the plays were the same. When they had one back in the offense, they were running the draw. We shut them out. That was when Peyton Manning was a freshman.

#6) *HAVE A SYSTEM FOR DEVELOPING A GAME PLAN WITH THE PLAYERS*; GIVE DRAFTS TO THEM EARLY AND A FOLDER TO KEEP ALL THE SCOUTING AND GAME-PLAN MATERIAL IN. We get the television copy of the game of anybody we play. We played the University of Cincinnati. We went back and got every game they played on television. On television, they give close ups of the quarterback. You can hear snap counts, checks, and signals. If you get enough tape, you can figure out a whole lot. Find out everything you can about your opponent. However, it doesn't make any difference how much you know. It is how much they know and can execute. When you do it, find a good system that works for you.

One thing that we do is this. We make an improvement list after every practice. Each coach makes a list of any player that is going to play in the next game and what he needs to improve on in the next practice. We do this from what went on in practice and from practice films. We list what they did wrong and what they need to improve on. We give those lists to each player. What it tells the coach is how well he is communicating his techniques. If they are making the same mistakes on Thursday that they made on Monday, there is something wrong with the teaching methods (i.e., it's too complicated, they don't understand, or they can't do it). If that happens we take

out whatever the technique or play was.

If they are making the same mistakes in fundamentals, the coach needs to spend more time on fundamentals and less time on schemes. If you want to be a consistent winner, you have to do those things.

Here are some #7) *PRINCIPLES OF GOOD DEFENSE*. You have to keep leverage on the ball, gap control, have an alley player, and take care of the cut back. It doesn't matter what scheme you run or stunts you use if you have the principles of good defense. If you teach something that doesn't have one of these principles in it, you better tell your players. If you run a stunt that leaves you with no-cut back player, you have to tell your defense so they can make the adjustments to play that type of play. Someone has to get off a block to cover that. If you don't tell them, they will lose faith and think you do not know what you are doing. If it goes against the principles, tell them so they know you understand.

#8) *KEEP IT SIMPLE SO THEY CAN LINE UP AND PLAY*. A confused football player is a slow player. He has to know what to do. Do lots of walk through with them.

#9) *KNOW AND UNDERSTAND YOUR OPPOSITION.* Do they count people? Do they count five in box, six in box, or seven in box (run or pass, what do they do?) Do they favor the 3-man side, 4-man side (what runs?) Do they have two high safeties, one high safety (find the Mike linebacker)? To the reduction side or to the Okie side?

#10) *KNOW AND UNDERSTAND THE BLITZ CONTROL AND PASS PROTECTION.* Do they ID to The Mike linebacker or to the 4-man side? Do they ID hot defense by pointing)? You should know how the offense is going to protect according to the look you give them. If you know their offense, you can dictate where they will run the ball by your defensive alignment. Hot receivers are tight ends or backs and sight adjustments are generally wide receivers. The sight-adjust receiver is usually 2 weak or 3 strong.

#11) *TAKE THE GREAT PLAYER OUT OF THE GAME.* Do not let them wreck the game? Make them go somewhere else to make plays. When we played Miami, they had a great running back. We put enough people in the box so he couldn't run the ball. We made them throw the ball.

#12) *MOVE, STEM, THE FRONT AND SECONDARY.* With 12-15 seconds on the 25-second clock, we distort the quarterback's reads because he does not have time to check off. Distort the receiver's coverage reads and linemen's count and gap control. Which gets you beat most, mental errors or physical ability? It is the mental error that gets you beat. Create confusion on the offense.

#13) *PERSONNEL GROUPINGS* - You have to have a plan to handle personnel grouping. How are you going to play four wide outs?

#14) *STOP THE RUN TO WIN.* Every game that we have lost at Florida or Marshall was because we couldn't run the ball, or we had trouble stopping the run. You have to stop the run, and you have to be able to run the ball to win big games. Three out of the last four years, we have lead the nation in touchdown passes. But, to throw the ball you have to be effective running it. Make the offense throw the ball. Understand the count, gap control, leverage, cut back run, and the alley player.

#15) Have your players understand the *HIDDEN YARDAGE IN FOOTBALL.* Those are the yards created in the kicking game, penalties, and turnovers.

#16) *STOP WHAT THEY DO BEST.* If they are a running team, make them throw. Make them play you left-handed.

Marshall is not far away from Cincinnati. It takes me about two-and-one-half hours to get home. I never close a practice. You are welcome to come down any time. You can get in the huddle. We don't hide what we are doing. I will share with you everything we do offensively, defensively, and special team-wise. You can stick you head in the huddle, and then turn around and ask me what that meant. I'll tell you to ask that coach over there, because I don't know. We would love to have you at our place. We really would. I think we have a good bunch of kids that work hard.

I promise you this. When we play, we are going to give great effort, and understand what we are trying to do. We want to play for a championship. I don't wear a championship ring. I have five of them from Marshall and two from Florida.

I'll tell you this story. The championship game in the MAC has been at Marshall the last four years. Some people claim that it is not fair to have the game at Marshall. The reason it is at Marshall is because no one else wanted it because they couldn't make any money. Marshall sells it out every year, and the conference makes money. We guarantee them 15,000 tickets because we sell them in our season-ticket package. We sell that many season tickets. That's not my fault. I would give the game to anyone who wants it. If they don't want to do it, they shouldn't bitch about us taking the game.

Since the game is at Marshall, we have had coverage from ESPN and for the first time in the conference's history, we have been on CBS. We are on national television four times a year. I'm proud of that, and I don't want to screw it up. We are going to exploit that and brag about that. We have great coaches and players in the MAC. It is a very competitive league. That is the way you have to approach this game. The meek will not survive in this sport. We are not trying to be cocky; we just go out and play. We don't down other schools. We praise them. But, we are going to do everything we can to win a championship, and our players expect it. The fans expect it, and I expect it. The bad thing about it is our Administration is beginning to expect it.

I've been on both sides. I've been at Florida where everyone expects you to win every year. That is better than the ones who just want to compete. The good Lord has been good to us. We have good players, and I think we will be good next year. You are welcome to come see us. Thank you.

PRESSURE DEFENSE

Lousiville Male High School, Kentucky

It is an honor to have the Nike Clinic people to ask me to speak. I want to talk about our pressure defense. I want to get to the defense as soon as possible. There is no way I can give you everything we do on defense in the time that I have been allotted. I could not do justice to the defense in a short time. If I give you an overall view of what we are doing and what we are trying to accomplish, it may give you some ideas of what we are doing.

I have to be the luckiest guy in the world. This year we won our third state championship at Male in the last 10 years. I have been lucky to have been able to coach some really great athletes in those years. I have been fortunate to get three rings with those championships.

We have another member of our family that got a championship ring this year. Our son, Chris, just completed his rookie year with the Baltimore Ravens. He was the third quarterback for the Ravens and did get in a few games this past year. He had a great career at the University of Louisville. We were excited about that, but to get on a NFL team and get to the Super Bowl and win and get a Super Bowl ring was just great.

My father and I were able to be a part of that experience. At the Super Bowl, we had to make the decision of our lifetime. Sunday morning, we were sitting in the lobby of the hotel. There were all kinds of people selling and buying tickets for the Super Bowl that morning. We were sitting there just watching everything. Several people offered us $1,000, $2,000 and even $2,500 for a ticket to the game. We had one man come up to us and offered us $5,000 per ticket. We had four lower-level tickets, but we held the course and turned him down. We went to the game and really enjoyed the results.

I watched the Ravens win the NFL. I watched the Oklahoma Sooners beat Florida State for the national championship. These three teams had one thing in common. That one common thing was a great defense. I have yet to see a team get to the championship without a great defense. I love offense, and I think we have a good offense. We throw the ball and have a lot of fun with our offense. But, we preach to our kids if we are going to get to the championship, we will have to have a great defense. Offense will help, but it will be the defense that puts us over the hump. In the three years we won the State, it was our defense that carried us, I assure you.

I am not going to stand up here and try to sell you a "save-all" defense. There is no such thing as the perfect defense. There is no defense that you cannot get behind, underneath, inside, outside, or score on. If there is such a defense, I would scrap this one and use it. In my opinion, there are only two concepts of defense. You can either drop seven players and play zone in the secondary and keep everything underneath, or you can bring seven men and apply pressure, and play man coverage in the secondary. I think either concept is sound, but you need to adopt one or the other.

Every story has a beginning. Every defense has a reason why teams play it. There is a reason why teams play certain defenses. This reason for us goes back about 25 years ago. I choose this particular style of pressure defense out of necessity. I was in a situation where I competed with the perennial state champions, Trinity High School, as a district opponent. We were neither physically strong enough, nor deep enough to line up in a base defense and play technique with them one-on-one. Yet, I had a strong desire to be competitive year in and year out. We accomplished this with our defense.

We felt we had to be able to take away what most high school football teams do best. We had to take away the run, which is, at the very least, seventy percent of the game.

This defense is not perfect, but we did make things interesting to say the least. Our defense may not be sound in all phases of the game of football. I am not really concerned about that. The only thing I am interested in is stopping the opponents on offense.

We accomplished this through sheer numbers to the strong or formation side by unbalancing the defense so as to appear to create a situation where there is a least one more person than can be physically blocked. To the weakside of a formation, we placed our three best football players, creating in my mind, an interesting choice for our opponents.

You either run where we have more bodies than the offense, or you attack the weakside of the formation where we have our best athletes, which is probably the short side of the field. We add to this a secondary that played man coverage exclusively and a position we cal Monster. This defense is designed to place our best athletes in a position on the field to cover any mistakes we make at the line of scrimmage.

I want to cover a few important concepts that form the basic philosophy of this defense. I hope this information is relevant and helpful.

PRESSURE DEFENSE PHILOSOPHY

PRESSURE: Like a full-court basketball press, this defense is designed to apply pressure and take the opponent out of their normal rhythm. Why should a coach cover fifty percent on the run, and fifty percent on the pass? Defense what most high school teams can do best, the run. Putting pressure on the offense produces turnovers and points.

NUMBERS: In applying pressure, we play a numbers game. We put more people on the strongside than the offensive can possible block. Then, we put our best athletes on the weakside. You either attack the strongside where we have more bodies than you can possible block, or you attack the weakside where we have our best football players.

We shut down the frontside at the Tackle with sheer numbers and run down the backside with our best athletes. We cover our defense with our best athlete at the monster back to cover any breakdown at the line of scrimmage. We use man coverage in the secondary. Man coverage will force the offense to quick outside routes under pressure.

COMMUNICATION: The object of the defense is to disrupt communication. The quarterback is the source of the offense. He is like a computer for a team. We bring pressure on the quarterback from front and back, forcing him out of his normal rhythm. We want to take out the computer.

GAME PLANS: This defense forces the opposition to beat you with something other than their best weapons. With quick penetration by the athletes, this defense creates confusion in the offensive-blocking schemes and backfield traffic. Striping and advancing the ball creates scoring opportunities, enthusiasm, and positive mental attitudes.

PLAYERS: This defense allows the quick, alert, and aggressive players to shine. As the defense is defined and grows, individual players recognize strengths, formations, and possibilities. The players then can check off the call and initiate the call as they see fit. Individual accomplishments build to a team concept. The players own this defense. Players have only one responsibility, and ownership of that responsibility aids in the improvement of the player and the team. Defensive players are given the opportunity to score by picking up loose balls. The players recognize the disruption the defense poses and thrive on it.

ABSOLUTE MUSTS FOR THE DEFENSE

Take away anything quick to the inside or in the middle; trap, slant In, and quarterback delays. The defensive players' first step must be to their responsibility. The second step is to find the ball and pursue. The players must not overrun the ball. The pursuit angles change with every step.

Fundamentals are practiced every day. These are the same as everyone teaches now. They can only enhance the skills of players in this defense. Pursuit drills are used every day. The players must step to their responsibility, and then pursue as a group to the ball.

Recognition of the players' responsibilities (who I have) can only be decided by the coach of the defense from the offensive side of the ball. Coaches have to be able to follow the players' eyes to be sure they step first to their responsibility and then to the ball and pursue.

Communication is critical to this defense. Players must call out their responsibility. Reverses, traps, passes, and other plays must be called out by the players. Calling out the plays helps with ball recognition and pursuit. The sideline can help by calling out run, pass, and ball when the ball is in the air.

The fundamentals of this defense must be worked on individually. Coaches should work with each of these groups. We want one coach with each group; down linemen (nose and tackle), ends, outside linebacker and monster, and secondary. Now, the nose, tackle, and end can be coached by one person.

The coaching of the defense is done on a team basis. Each coach has a part of the defense. We have one coach to watch the strongside corner, end, and tackle. We have one coach to watch the nose and middle linebacker. We have one to watch the weakside end, corner, and monster. We have another coach watch the secondary, which consist of the two halfbacks and a safety. Coaches need to watch their assigned players to be sure the stunts last one step and never go deeper than the ball.

CONSTRUCTION OF THE DEFENSE BY POSITION WITH BASIC RESPONSIBILITY

NOSE MAN

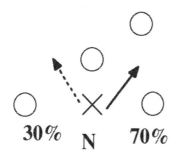

#1) Lines up nose on the center. Crowds the ball. #2) Will slant almost 100 percent of the time to the ear hole of the guard, either right or left. We say 70-30 percent to the weakside. We send him away from the unbalanced side just to try to even it up more. (Ex-

ception: sometimes he sits and read the screen or the draw play). #3)Responsibility: Near back inside to the side he slants to. #4) We will use the Nose as an extra person to load up on a particular back. #5) Fundamentals drills used are the slant, trap, and pass rush.

STRONG TACKLE (Normal Defensive End)

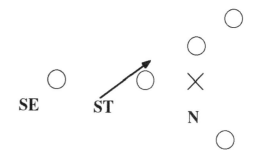

#1)Lines up nose on the offensive tackle. #2) Normal responsibility is the near back inside. #3) On an out-slant, his responsibility is the quarterback. #4) Fundamental drills used are the slant, pass rush and trap.

ENDS

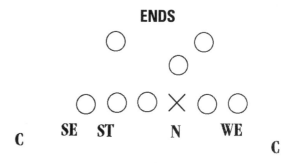

#1)Strongside end lines up nose on the offensive tight end. He treats a wing as a tight end; if no wing, outside shoulder of the tackle. #2)Weakside end lines up on the outside shoulder of the tackle. #3) Both ends' responsibilities are to put pressure on the quarterback both front- and backside. #4) Fundamental drills used are the angle drill, turnout drill, and man coverage.

CORNERS (OUTSIDE LINEBACKERS)

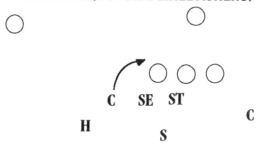

The corners line up on the outside shoulder of the tight end. If no tight end, the corners get as close to the defensive end as possible, slightly off the line of scrimmage, dropped for inside stunts. #2)Corner's responsibilities are near back on the outside (attacks the near back), covers screens, back out of the backfield, applies backside pressure, and checks and helps on reverse. #3) Fundamental drills used are veer drill (ends and corners together), man coverage, and backside pursuit drills.

MIDDLE LINEBACKER

#1) Lines up directly behind the nose, 3-to-5 yards deep. #2) Responsibility is near back inside (strongside). #3) Shed drill, scrape drill, and nose-on-ball drill are used.

MONSTER

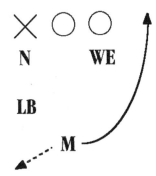

#1) Best athlete on the team; must stay in position to save all the time. #2) Lines up 5-to-7 yards deeps on the outside shoulder of the guard. #3) Responsibilities include near back inside, then cover the field; nose on at all times. Must get depth when ball flow is away. #4) Monster acts as linebacker when the flow comes his way. #5) Acts as free safety when flow goes away. 6) Fundamental drills used include linebacker, man coverage, zone Drill.

HALFBACK

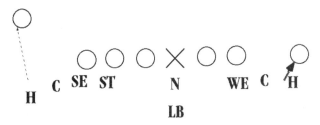

#1) Aligns where he can cover the widest receiver to his side. #2) Gets all the ball he can. #3) Forty-five percent of the time, keeps his eyes on the receiver's eyes. #4) Must take away the inside. #5) Must force pass routes to the outside. #6) In man-to-man coverage, the halfback looks back for the ball when the receiver looks back, hears "BALL" call, or runs three seconds without hearing anything. #7) Drills used are man coverage, fill the seam, react to ball, zone drill, adjust to ball, coverage on ball.

SAFETY

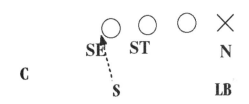

#1) Aligns on the second receiver on the strongside. #2) The safety acts more like a linebacker than any other secondary person.#3) Fills the seam as a linebacker would on a run. #4) Man-to-man pass coverage. #5) Safety acts as extra unblocked man. #6) Drills used are safety-oriented.

BASIC STUNTS AND RESPONSIBILITIES FROM THE 5-LOOK

IN-RED: The first call "IN" is the strongside call. The second call "RED" is the weakside call. The middle linebacker gives the nose a direction to slant. The secondary is always in man-to-man coverage. Note: red is probably seventy percent of the total calls made to the weakside. This allows the weakside to get into position to pressure.

Coaching point: When we stunt, which is basically every play, responsibilities change. It is important to call out these responsibility changes. Communication is essential to this defense. IN-RED is a tackle-to-tackle pinch stunt when the offense is attacking inside. We use this stunt when the offense closes down, or when their splits are toe-to-toe trying to prevent us from penetrating. This is when we use IN-RED to get pressure from the outside.

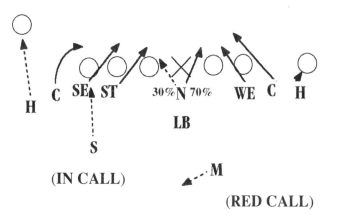

(IN CALL)

(RED CALL)

NOSE – Near back inside to the side he slants; 70% of weakside stunts.

STRONG TACKLE – Near back inside. First step to ear hole of near guard, second step to football.

STRONG END – Quarterback responsibility. First step to ear hole of near tackle. Put quick pressure on the quarterback. Attack the quarterback at the same angle he is attacking the line of scrimmage.

STRONG CORNER – Near back outside, pitch man on option. Man coverage if back releases outside or goes to a screen position outside.

MIDDLE LINEBACKER – Near back inside to the strongside. The first step is through the head of the near guard strongside. On second step, find ball and scrape to the flow.

WEAKSIDE END – Near back inside slants to ear hole of near guard. On second step, find ball and pursue.

WEAKSIDE CORNER – Quarterback responsibility.

The first step is through ear hole of near tackle. On second step apply backside pressure on the quarterback. Coaching point: We are trying at all times to put maximum frontside and backside pressure on the quarterback.

MONSTER – Near back. Outside to the weakside of formation. If flow comes towards the monster, he is responsible for the near back outside and must fly to that responsibility. Keep in mind that this is usually the shortside of the field and is not a difficult thing to reach.

Coaching point: If the weakside ends up on the wideside of the field, we change the stunt to "WHITE" automatically to cover the wideside. This will be covered in the next stunt which is our "OUT-WHITE."

If the flow goes away from the monster, he checks the outside responsibility then gets a depth of 7-to-10 yards, keeping everything in front of him and staying nose on the football in a position to save if there is a breakdown. It is a similar position of a normal free safety in a black board Zone Defense.

HALFBACKS – Widest receiver to their side of the field and play man coverage. Their first responsibility is pass. Their second responsibility is run support. If their receiver blocks they are to square up and find the football.

SAFETY – He has the second receiver to the strongside and plays man coverage. His first responsibility is pass. If the receiver blocks, he is to square up and fill the seam, similar to the linebacker.

Our next stunt is our OUT-WHITE. The first call "OUT" is the strongside call. The second call "WHITE" is the stunt we use to cover the outside, strongside when the offense is attacking the corner. On the wideside it provides pressure from the monster and allows us to cover the wideside when it becomes the weakside of the field.

Coaching point: No matter what the call on the weakside, we will audible to WHITE when the weakside is on the wideside of the field.

OUT-WHITE

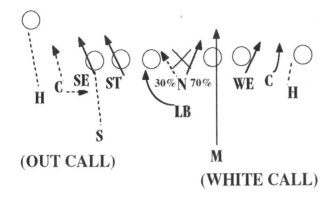

(OUT CALL)

(WHITE CALL)

NOSE – Near back to side he slants to. (Inside.)

STRONG TACKLE – Slants outside. The first step is to the ear hole of the tight end outside. On second step he is responsible for the quarterback.

STRONG END – Steps outside and assumes responsibility of the corner near back outside.

STRONG CORNER – Is free and reads flow. If flow is outside, he is free and attacks the near back outside. If flow is inside, he is free and can help inside on dive or wedge.

Coaching point: By dropping the corner slightly in his alignment, he can help inside or outside.

MIDDLE LINEBACKER – Steps to near back inside – strongside. He finds the ball and scrapes to it. (Always the same.)

WEAKSIDE END – Steps outside and has quarterback responsibility. The first step is outside, and then he attacks the quarterback at the same angle he is attacking the line of scrimmage. Do not overrun the stunt.

WEAKSIDE CORNER – Steps outside and is responsible for near back outside.

MONSTER – Stunts to near back inside. This is a total commitment by the monster. He has no responsibility deep. He should charge and break off stunt as the angle of the ball changes.

Coaching point: Remember, stunts last one step, then should be adjusted to the angle of the football.

HALFBACKS – Widest receiver to his side. Play man coverage.

SAFETY – Has second receiver to the strongside. Plays man coverage. He fills seam quickly if his man blocks.

We use the next stunt as a change-up stunt. It is our SPLIT-SPLIT.

SPLIT – SPLIT

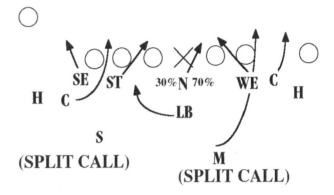

(SPLIT CALL)

(SPLIT CALL)

NOSE - Near back to side he slants to. (Inside)

STRONG TACKLE – Slants inside. Same as IN – near back inside.

STRONG END – Slants outside. Same as OUT – near back outside.

STRONG CORNER – Splits the seams between SE and ST. Responsibility is pressure on the quarterback.

MIDDLE LINEBACKER – Same, near back strongside and pursue.

WEAKSIDE END – Slants inside. Same as RED – near back outside.

WEAKSIDE CORNER – Slants outside. Same as WHITE – near back outside.

MONSTER – Splits the seam between weak end and weak corner. Responsible for the quarterback. This is an all out stunt for the monster. He has no pass responsibility, total commitment to run by the monster.

HALFBACKS – Widest receiver to their side. Play man coverage.

SAFETY – Has second receiver to strongside. Plays man coverage. He fills the seam quickly if his man blocks.

Our next stunt is what we call our STACK. If we call Stack, it is to the strongside. If we call DOUBLE STACK, it is a stack strong and weak. If we call TRIPLE STACK, it is a stack strong, weak, and middle.

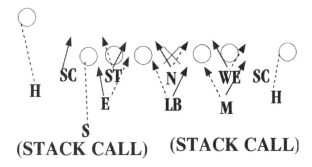

(STACK CALL)   (STACK CALL)

NOSE – Near back inside to direction he slants.

MIDDLE LINEBACKER – Opposite stunt of nose, near back inside.

STRONG TACKLE – Inside slant, near back inside; outside slant quarterback responsibility.

STRONG END – Stacked behind tackle, opposite slant of strong tackle, same responsibilities apply.

STRONG CORNER – Steps to near back outside.

WEAKSIDE END – Inside slant, near back inside; outside slant, quarterback responsibility.

MONSTER – Stacked behind weakside end, opposite slant of end. Same two responsibilities.

WEAK SIDE CORNER – Near back outside.

HALFBACKS – Widest receiver to their side. Play man coverage.

SAFETY – Has second receiver to strongside. Plays man coverage. He fills the seam quickly if his man blocks.

Our next stunt is SWING-RED. Basically it is a strongside stunt. To keep it simple, we have a "Red" call on the weakside. All of these calls are interchangeable to give us a variety of looks.

Coaching point: I love the outside-in stunts by the corners. How many guards do you know that check for an outside linebacker stunt in his blocking scheme?

SWING-RED

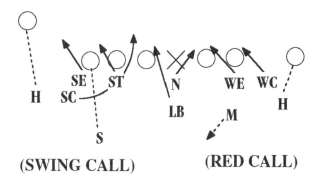

(SWING CALL)   (RED CALL)

NOSE - Near back inside to direction he slants.

MIDDLE LINEBACKER – Opposite stunt of nose, near back inside.

WEAKSIDE END – RED call.

WEAKSIDE CORNER – RED call.

MONSTER – RED call.

STRONG TACKLE – Slants outside, quarterback responsibility.

STRONG END – Slants outside, near back outside.

STRONG CORNER – Stunts to ear hole of near guard; Responsible for near back inside. Yes, I said near back inside. (Try it, you will love it.)

HALFBACKS – Widest receiver to their side. Play man coverage.

SAFETY – Has second receiver to strongside. Plays man coverage. He fills the seam quickly if his man blocks.

Our next stunt is called TRINITY-RED. This is an all-out slant or directional call based on a specific set or tendency we might pick up on a team. We are trying to totally eliminate the strongside of a set while being as sound as possible on the weakside of the formation.

TRINITY – RED

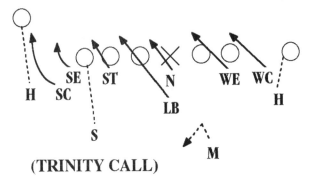

(TRINITY CALL)

NOSE – He will slant 100 percent to the strong side. Responsible for the near back inside to the strongside.

MIDDLE LINEBACKER – Slants to the ear hole of the offensive tackle, and he is responsible for near back inside with the nose.

STRONG TACKLE – Slants outside to ear hole of the tight end and has quarterback responsibility.

STRONG END – Slants outs outside and is responsible for the near back outside.

STRONG CORNER – Slants outside and is free (no responsibility); helps to totally eliminate the outside, quick-force flow back to the pursuit.

WEAKSIDE END – Slants inside to ear hole of guard and has near back inside and quick backside pursuit.

WEAKSIDE CORNER – Slants inside to ear hole of offensive tackle and has quarterback responsibility and quick backside pursuit.

MONSTER – Has near back outside if flow comes weakside. (Same as RED Call.) If flow goes away, he makes a slow read over weakside guard seam to check for counter or reverse. Then, he assumes free safety position as flow continues to move away. Should not fly out too quickly – slow read is important. The entire weakside is basically a Red call, with the exception of the slow read by the monster.

HALFBACKS – Widest receiver to his side. Play man coverage.

SAFETY – Has second receiver to strongside. Plays man coverage. He fills the seam quickly if his man blocks.

BASIC ADJUSTMENTS TO SETS

I want to go over some of our adjustments to different sets.

• ONE-MAN UNBALANCED – No adjustment to this set because the defense is already unbalanced. If unbalance creates a problem or we get out flanked on the corner, we will slant or "trinity" to the unbalance.

• TRIPS – Three receivers to one side.

TRIPS – FIRST ADJUSTMENT

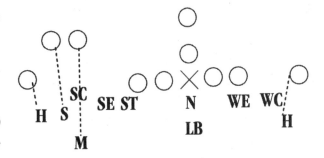

• TRIPS – Second adjustment.

TRIPS – SECOND ADJUSTMENT

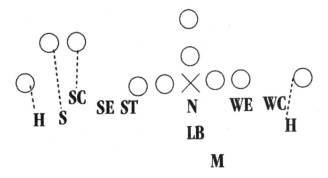

• DOUBLE SLOT – Strength is determined by wideside of he field. If the ball is placed in the middle of the field, the defense is strong left.

DOUBLE SLOT

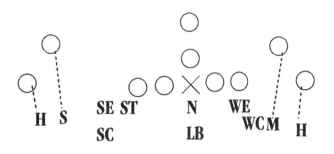

• POWER I, WISHBONE, DEAD-T – Same coaching points as on double slot (any three-back set). We automatically stunt safety to near back.

POWER I, WISHBONE, DEAD-T

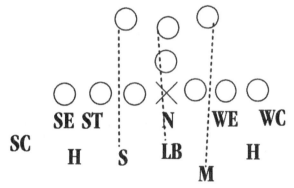

• DELAWARE WING-T – We use the same coaching points as we do on the wishbone.

DELAWARE WING-T

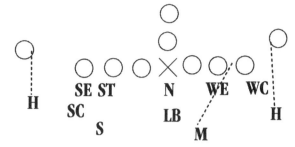

I do not want to stand up here and tell you we are doing these things on defense without showing you the defense on film. I have put together shots of our defense that covers each of these stunts. (FILM)

Thank you for your time. It has been my privilege to visit with you.

COACHING THE DEFENSIVE SECONDARY

University of Cincinnati

I have coached at this level for twenty years. The first nine years of my coaching career was spent in the panhandle of Florida at the high school level. I have been recruiting that area for about twenty years. Those first years of coaching were nine of the best years of my life. I started out as a head baseball coach and a JV football coach. I had one assistant coach to work with all 22 positions. After that, I coached the varsity for two years before I got a head-coaching position. I coached six years as a head coach at two different schools.

It was a lot of fun, and I really mean that. I probably will never be a head coach in college, but if I do become a head coach, I will not hire anyone who has not been a high school coach. I have cut grass and painted lockers like all of you have. It was fun being a high school coach. I have no secrets and everything I know, someone told me. I'll do anything I can to help you.

We are a 4-3 defense. But, we are a multiple defense. Multiple means more than one. We will try to do as much as we can, but we want to do it well. We aren't blessed with great players. I've had a lot of bad jobs. I've never been at a school where I've had as good of players as the opponent, except when I was at Alabama. But, even at Alabama, I was shocked at the bad players we had. We had players like Cornelius Bennett and Derrick Thomas.

What we try to do is to get our guys to believe they are as good as anybody they play against. It is not the team with the best players that win the game on Saturday. It is the players that play the best as a team. We really try to get our defensive guys to buy into that. Eleven people playing together hard will make good things happen.

The first thing we do on defense is run to the football. I have been blessed to work for some great defensive coordinators through the years. That was the big thing we stressed at Alabama. We wanted 11 guys running to the football. That will cover up many mistakes.

I'll never forget what a young man said to me one day. I was the defensive coordinator at the University of Kentucky. I was standing in the huddle, and one of my players said, "Damn coach, it's hard to get 11 guys to do it right every time." That struck me as important. It is hard to get 11 people to do what you want them to do exactly right every time. The most important thing is to try to get them to do it right.

If young men believe in themselves and each other, you have a chance to win. When I say believe in each other, they have to respect each other as people and players.

My topic tonight is secondary play. What I want to start with is some of the things we believe in at UC. We did the same things at Tulane and Kentucky. I will talk on those things, and then I will get into some techniques and schemes.

In this day and time, you have to tell your young men what is expected of them. At the first team meeting at all three places where I've been the coordinator, I've asked our guys "Who wants to be treated as men?" They all think they are men. I ask them if they want to be treated like men to stand up. They all stand up. I tell them if they want to be treated like men, they have to act like men. This is something they forget sometimes.

There are four things a man does. This is what our whole defense is built on. If I ever become a head coach, it will be what the whole program is built on.

First, you have to do what you are supposed to do, when you're supposed to do it, and how you are supposed to do it. If you don't, do what you are supposed to do, you must keep your mouth shut and take the consequences. What that tells those kids is this. In every decision they make in life, there are consequences they have to pay, good or bad. This is true if it is a good or bad decision. They could get on the interstate and drive at 100 miles an hour. If they get pulled over, they pay the $200 fine, because that was their decision.

When we talk about defensive philosophy we don't talk about schemes. In our philosophy, *conditioning* precedes anything else. The first 20 minutes of our practice our guys do nothing but run. We do about five to 10 minutes of agility drills. When they finish, they have to run five gassers on the clock. When they get through with the gassers, they have a 20-minute individual period. *Conditioning* precedes everything else. It gives you a chance to play hard. Physical conditioning precedes mental toughness. You can't be tough mentally if you are not in shape.

Don't sacrifice quickness and speed for size. I don't care how big they are if they can't run and are not in shape. I talk to my kids about being in great condition and being strong. Speed is everything at any position. I don't care about height. It they are tall, that is a plus.

We want *simplicity* in our defense. When players stop thinking, they can play. We never go to the next step until they understand what we are doing. We try to be real simple. If we call 50, we declare our front to the tight end. If we call 40, we declare it to the split end. The defense can be aggressive if they understand what they are doing.

We want to *play percentage football.* That is my job as the coordinator. I constantly break down films because I don't want to beat myself. The first thing I look at when I break down a film is field position. I am going to get down-and-distance tendencies. The next thing I break down is formations. The next thing is personnel packages.

We stress a sound kicking game, have a plan and believe in it, and control the sudden change. We talk to our guys about *turnovers.* I've been a coordinator for five years, and we have averaged 31.6 turnovers a season. Our goal is to get three turnovers per game. This year we got 36 turnovers. We were the only football team in Division I to be in the top ten in both fumble recoveries, and interceptions. In my first year at Tulane, we led the nation in interceptions. Why? We constantly talk to our team about turnovers, and we punish them if they don't get them in the game.

When practice is over, they know the first thing I'm going to ask, "How many turnovers did we get today?" They know if they didn't get at least three, they are going to run a ladder for everyone they did not get. A ladder is five yards and back, 10 yards and back, 15 yards and back, and 20 yards and back against the clock. They must get interceptions in passing drills, and recover fumbles in our inside drill. They MUST get turnovers.

Our goal every year is to be the best sudden-change defense in our conference. Sudden change means when our offense turns the ball over to the defense, we can't give up a touchdown. Our first year at Tulane, we were 96 percent at not giving up a touchdown after a turnover. Last year at UC, we were 89 percent. This year, we were 91 percent. Our offense turned the ball over 24 times, and we gave up three touchdowns. Sudden change is very important.

The most important statistics to a defensive coordinator are points given up, and number two is turnovers. You have to prepare your defense for turnovers. That is why we constantly talk about them. If you are on scholarship, and our offense turns the ball over, that is good for us. We get to go out on the field and play. That is why they are in school, to play. "Go out and stop the other team's offense and get the ball back."

You have to work on the intangibles in football. Discipline is extremely important to your defensive philosophy. We want to PLAY TO WIN. If a player is not going to class, he is not going to play. If a player doesn't go to weight training, he doesn't play. If you tell a guy to do something, he better do it. The first time you tell a guy something, and he doesn't do it, that is when your discipline starts to fall apart.

We preach togetherness and to be unselfish people. I don't believe you can be a football team with selfish people on your team. The game is played with your heart and mind. When I flip this film on, you'll see our kids running around and playing with a lot of heart.

You must have *incentives* in your program. We have three boards that we use. We have a GOAL, M-A-D, and a GREAT EFFORT board. We give very few trophies on defense at UC. The only way you can get a trophy at UC on defense is through *M-A-D plays*. M-A-D plays are plays that make a difference. Some examples of M-A-D plays would be sacks, tackles for loses, batted-down passes, tipped passes, or anything that is a negative play. We give a nice helmet award to the player who has the most M-A-D plays at his position. It is a game helmet mounted on a block of wood. It really looks nice. It is not a voted award. We keep track of it every week and post it on the M-A-D board. They really fight for that award. We do it by positions. The two ends and their backups have a chance to win one. The two tackles, the three linebackers, and the four defensive backs can win one at their position. We present these awards at our banquet.

On defense, we are a penetrating, gap-canceling team. We want our linebackers attacking downhill. They are two-gapping on direction and are very aggressive. They read the two backs for direction and run through the gaps they are responsible for. I'm not going to talk too much about our linebacker play because I'm supposed to be talking on secondary play.

Our secondary this year was about 49-percent zone and 51-percent man defense. We try to make everything look exactly the same and really mix up the coverages. When I talk about *zone-auto*, it means the zone we play will be determined by the offensive formation. It is getting hard to guess with people.

We have a *man-auto*, which looks exactly like zone-auto. You want your two-deep zone to look exactly like your two-deep man coverage. When you can do that people will start throwing the ball to you. Our zone-auto package is determined by the coverage formations. We call the zone-auto because most people think we are in the 4-3 defense, but we are really an eight-man front.

I don't think kids have changed as much as some people may think they have. If a young man knows what his boundaries are and what is expected of him, he can make good decisions. When he knows that if he breaks those rules, he is going to pay a price, I don't think they are a lot different than they used to be. In our play book on page two is a section titled "*What You Must Do To Play.*" I promise you men, if they don't do this, they don't play. They know I don't bend. They are going to do what they are supposed to do, or they are not going to play.

A man takes care of his business. They want to be treated like men, and this is what they live by. Players live and practice their way onto the field and take their shot in the game. If they don't do their alignment, assignment, and tackle, they will be on the bench.

We demand certain things from defensive players. The first thing is no loafing. I don't care if it is a defensive back loafing, the defensive line coach can dress him down if he sees it. All our defensive coaches are responsible for that team.

The second thing we demand is for them to be a competitor. We demand that they show in practice how far they can go. That means they have to bust their butts in practice. It is the coach's job to make the player do his assignment right every time. We accept nothing less than the player's best. We do not want any excuses — just results. If a player loses his position, he cannot blame us. He must come back to the practice field and win it back. We do not want them to make excuses about why they got beat out. I explain to them that I have been fired before and might be fired again, but I'm going to play the best football players. If he is one of the best players, he'll play.

We tell them, "It is not our job to please you. It is your job to please us." We stress to them to get better each day. A player either gets better each day, or he gets worse. We demand that they must accept responsibility for winning. We do not want them to take chances. We want them to make good decisions. Our last point that we demand is that they are not to show emotions after mistakes. We stress, "GET READY TO PLAY THE NEXT PLAY."

We expect the following things to be correct. They must align correctly. We want their feet in the proper places. We expect the ball to be contained on each play, if they have containment. We want the alleys filled properly on each play. We want them to tackle, plant and drive on the ball, and to have proper pursuit angles.

Players are always asking why they are not playing more or starting. We came up with an evaluation sheet about four years ago at Tulane to take care of this situation. We have categories that we keep track of. The first thing they have to do is take care of business. If I can't depend on the player, I'm not going to put him on the field. They have to complete their assignments with no mistakes. Their mental ability has to lead them to make correct decisions. They have to have athletic ability. They have to have the ability to be a great hitter. We want them to make big plays. We track the number of plays each player makes. Each position coach keeps up with the number of plays his players make. These are the M-A-D plays. When a player comes in to find out why he is not playing, we show him what he has done in practice.

Players have to be physically tough. They have to stay on the field. How can they be a tough guy if they are always in the training room? They have to play through little injuries they may get. They have to play and practice when they don't feel good.

I am not a big statistics guy. We talk to our players about trying to be the best defense in America. However, we do not play the same teams that Florida State and Michigan plays. The only statistic that interests me is W's and L's.

We have a GOAL BOARD with 12 points on it. We talk about these goal every Sunday at our meeting. These points are ways to help our team win. Sometimes your defensive goals are reflected on by how you're offensive team plays. Against Army, we accomplished only five out of 12 goals, but won the game. Against Wisconsin, we made four out of 12 goals and almost won that game in overtime.

The most important goal is three turnovers per game. We accomplished that nine times during the season. Another important goal is to not allow a score after your offensive team turns the ball over. We did that in nine games.

Lets look at our M-A-D board. M-A-D plays are those that make a difference. They are fumble recoveries, interceptions, knock down passes, tipped balls, tackles for losses, sacks, caused interception, scores by the defense, caused fumbles, and so on. We record those things from each game and put them on our board.

We try not to give up long passes or long runs, but sometimes those happen. We talk about negative plays. A negative play would be a 3rd-and-19 play, that the offense only got 18 on. On first down, if the offense runs the ball and gets no yards or loses yards, that is a negative play. An interception would be a negative play. If they throw a pass, and it is incomplete, that is a negative play. Those are examples of negative plays. Against Army, they had 63 total plays. Of those 63 plays, 30 of them were negative plays. That amounts to 47 percent of the time they snapped the ball. Against Louisville, they ran 75 plays and 30 of them were negative plays. That was a percentage rate of 40 percent, but we lost that game. We are shooting for 33 percent negative plays. For the year, we were 48 percent on negative plays. That is one reason why we went to a bowl game. We bend on defense, but we do not break.

This year we had 83 tackles for losses for 351 yards. We had quarterback sacks for 215 yards. That is the hidden yardage in football. Our defense accounted for almost a thousand yards. That all goes back to negative plays.

Let's get into secondary play and talk about our coverages. Every defensive front or coverage has a theory that goes with it. What I'm talking about is the number of people I'm going to rush, how many are covering under, and how many are covering deep. If I am talking about a two-deep zone, the theory is I'm going to rush four men. I'm going to put five into the six underneath zones, and I am going to play two-deep. You have to know the strength and weakness of that coverage. You have to know the adjustments and techniques. When we put in a coverage, we try to explain to our players that we are playing it for a reason.

If I call this coverage, and we execute, it cannot be defeated. If I call two-deep, and the offense runs four vertical pass patterns, the coverage will change to four-deep. If we call cover 3, which our two-deep coverage, the offense should never complete a 4-vertical pattern unless we screw up. The weakness of our two-deep is we give up a six-yard flat pattern. We pattern read in our coverages.

Because we do so much, there is a mental thought process that our defensive backs must go through. This came from Florida State when I played there in the early 70's. It is the mental thought process called CASFEB. The C stands for coverage, call, and concentration. The A stands for alignment, assignment, and adjustment. The S stands for stance, situation, and score. The F stands for field position, formation, and flow. The E stands for eyes, eligible receivers, and effort. The B stands for believe what you see.

I coach the safeties, but we try to get everybody on our defense to understand this because formations are so multiple today. Every formation in football has three characteristics. The first thing they have to understand about formations is WIDTH. They have to understand closed, single-width, and double-width formations. Are there any wide outs? If they do have wideouts, how many are there?

The next characteristic is the NUMBER OF BACKS IN THE BACKFIELD. There is a possibility of 3, 2, 1, or 0 backs in the backfield.

The last characteristic is the STRENGTH OF THE FORMATION. Every formation has a strength. The defense has to figure out where it is.

If the offense lines up with two tight ends and three backs in the backfield, our defense knows it is a balanced formation. They know it is balanced with three-and-a-half men to each side of the ball. How do we declare our front in a balanced set? If the ball is on the hashmark, we declare to the wideside of the field. If the ball is in the middle of the field, we declare to the left side.

If the offense came out in a one-back set with the H-back set in the slot to the split-end side, we know that is a double-width formation. With two receivers to each side, it is a balanced set. We would declare our front to the tight-end side and the secondary to the slot — split-end side.

Our secondary and linebackers have to understand the landmarks on the field. This is elementary, but essential. Our hashmarks in college are thirteen yards apart. From the hashmark to the sideline is 20 yards. From the bottom of the numbers to the sideline is seven yards. From the top of the numbers to the sideline is nine yards and from the top of the numbers to

the hashmark is 11 yards. Those landmarks are important when you are in zone coverage.

The first coverage I'm going to get into is COVER BLUE. This used to be our base coverage. It is our two-deep coverage. We are a 4-3 defense. We want to be a 4-3 defense with the ability to have one guy on our defense that can run deep, but also be the eighth man in the box. That takes a real special guy.

If there is a tight end-flanker back set in the game, we are going to play quarter-quarter halfs. If there are two receivers to the same side, we play two-deep. This is what we call our zone-auto. One side is playing quarter-quarter, and one side is playing two-deep.

In our two-deep coverage, we number the receivers from the outside in. The flanker in the pro set is number 1. The tight end is number 2, and the fullback to that side is number 3. The split end is number 1 weak, and the running back is number 2 weak.

BLUE TWO-DEEP

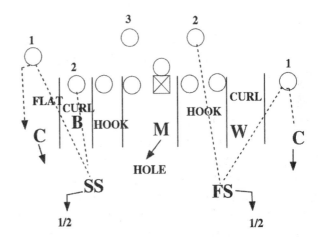

Our personnel consist of two corners, and a strong and free safety. The base alignment for the corners is 1-2 yards outside and 7-9 yards deep. Both corners take the same alignment. The safeties align halfway between the number 1 and 2 receivers to their side and 12 yards deep. The corners and two safeties are going to pattern read the same thing. The strong safety reads the triangle from the end man on the line of scrimmage through to the back to his side, and the quarterback. We try to see that triangle. We also want to see the blocking of the offensive linemen. We don't want him to have peripheral vision. He must have the same vision you need when you are driving a car. He has to see it all. The quarterback is his ultimate key, but the number two man is going to tell him how to position himself in his zone.

The safety's inside foot is up, and his outside foot is back with 90 percent of his weight on the inside foot. If the ball is in the middle of the field, he should be aligned a couple of yards outside the hashmark. If it is a pass, he wants to work for a width four yards wider than his original alignment and eight yards deeper. He always steps out and toward the boundary. He works for width. He has to cover the fade of #1 if #2 doesn't come deep. If #2 goes vertical, the strong safety plays quarter zone instead of half. He wants to be six yards outside the hashmark and 20 yards deep. He continues on that landmark drop until #2 tells him otherwise. If #2 is coming vertical, he wants to work back over the top of #2, read the quarterback, and break on the ball. Most vertical patterns will be released by the quarterback when the receiver is 11 yards deep.

The corner to that side is reading #2 to #1. When #2 goes vertical, the corner plays slow up the field. If #1 is not vertical, he settles at 15 yards and breaks on the ball. If #1 goes vertical, he turns and covers a quarter-deep zone to that side.

Another thing we talk about in zone coverage is this. This ball is going to travel so long in the air. That is what we call travel distance. We talk about flight time of the ball in zone coverage. The ball is going to travel so many yards in the air. If the ball travels 30 yards in the air, a good defense back should be able to travel one-third the distance the ball travels. For the offense to complete a fade route to the wide out against two-deep, the ball has to be caught about 25 yards from the line of scrimmage one yard inside the boundary. If the quarterback takes a 5-step drop, the ball travels 40 yards. The defensive back can break on the ball from 13 yards away and make the play. That is travel distance versus break distance.

I've got a drawing of a four-vertical pass pattern. If you study film, when the offense goes four verticals against any coverage, the ball will come out of the quarterback's hand when the receiver is between 11-12 yards deep. The receiver wants to catch the ball at 18-19 yards. If we have the proper cushion, there will be contact at 22 yards.

The corner shuffles back until he sees #2 going vertical. When that happens, he goes deep with #1. The strong safety is working for width until he sees #2 going vertical. He comes back over the top of #2.

FOUR VERTICALS VS. TWO-DEEP

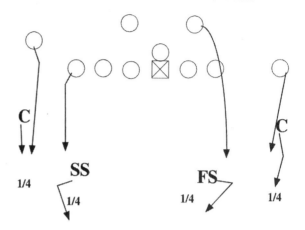

If the ball is on the hashmark, the throw into the boundary becomes a much shorter throw. Likewise, the throw into the wide field becomes a longer throw. We want to make the offense throw the longer throw. We use a zone adjustment in our coverage. We widen our safety to the wide side of the field and tighten to the short side. We tell our corners they can react back to short flat routes and make the tackle. We want him to respect the deep throw and react back to the short throw. It will take three of the six-yard patterns to make up for one corner of 22 yards. We want the corner to help on the corner throw and react back for the flat. A 22-yard fade thrown from the middle of the field means the ball has to be thrown 40 yards. With the ball on the hashmark, the ball has to be thrown 46 yards, which gives us two more yards of reaction time.

Let's look at this next situation. The strong safety is 12 yards deep. When he sees the ball off the line, he is looking at the triangle and pattern reading #2 to #1. If #2 releases flat or on a drag, he is no longer a deep threat. The safety forgets him. He now gets width and looks for #1. If #1 is squeezing to the hash, the safety has to work back to the inside of #1. The great safeties never have to look at #1 to get position on him. It is a constant weave with the defensive back and #1. He keeps his cushion and inside position on #1 at all times. If #1 runs across the field, I expect the safety to go with him, keeping his cushion and position.

CORNER/SAFETY VS POST/FLAT

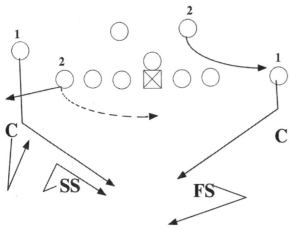

The corner starts shuffling back. If #2 is coming to him or going away, he has to settle at the bottom of the numbers, 15 yards deep, and key the quarterback. He is shuffling until he gets to that depth. He settles and prepares to break up or back on the ball. We tell him he is like a linebacker. We want him to cheat a half zone on the quarterback's shoulders. If the quarterback's shoulder is up and inside of the corner, he is thinking corner or fade route. When the shoulder crosses the quarterback's face, the corner has to react and break. He doesn't have to wait until the ball comes out, because he doesn't have deep responsibility.

CORNER/SAFETY VS CORNER

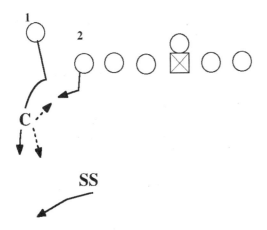

The next situation is the flat - fade pattern. The safety works for width and sees #2 go to the flat. He forgets about the tight end and works to the #1 receiver, getting width and going over the top of him. The corner doesn't have to jam the receiver, but he has to re-route his pattern. We don't want the receiver running straight down the field.

CORNER/SAFETY VS FADE

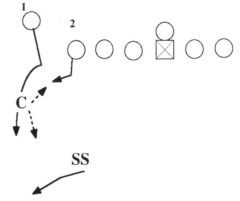

If we get a flat-and-up by the tight end or #2 receiver and a post by #1, the corner has to learn what to do. We tell the corner he has to cushion deep with the first guy through his zone. As #1 releases deep on the post, the corner has to cushion him deep until he leaves his zone. The safety takes over on #1 to the post, and the corner settles down for #2 running the flat. As #2 turns up his flat route, the corner reads the deep pattern and plays the deep quarter to his side.

CORNER/SAFETY VS FLAT AND UP/POST

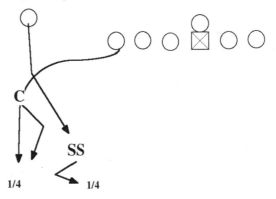

The next pattern is the corner-comeback. The safety and corner read #2 vertical. The corner is thinking 15 yards deep and to the bottom of the numbers. If #1 continues deep, the corner carries him deep. If #1 hitches for the comeback, he settles. He cannot give up the corner. The only way he can do that is be 15 yards deep. If he is 15 yards deep, and the corner route is going to be caught at 25 yards, he has to break at 10 yards. If the ball is thrown in front of him, he has to break seven yards to the ball. He can break the hitch or come back up and deter the quarterback from throwing the corner route. If the corner route is thrown, I expect that ball to be picked off. We have given up only one corner route in two years.

CORNER/SAFETY VS HITCH/CORNER ROUTE

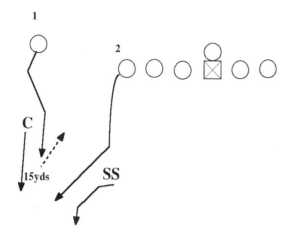

We work these combinations in practice every day. The hardest thing to get your guys to do is to key the quarterback. In zone coverage, you have to see the ball coming. If you don't, you're wrong. If the quarterback takes a 3-step drop, the safety who is working for width, sees the slant coming from #1. He has to drive on that pattern for a collision. The corner is going to shuffle in a little bit. On the 3-step drop, he changes jobs with the safety. He drives on the slant and shuffles over the top of #1 in case it is a skinny post. The safety's job is to knock down the #1 receiver. If he doesn't, and the route continues, he gets under him and trails him like a man under technique.

CORNER/SAFETY VS SLANT/SKINNY POST

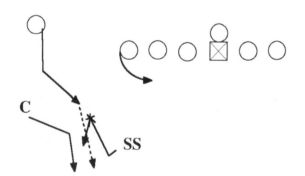

If we get a trips or three receivers to one side, we have to make some adjustments. To the one receiver side, there is a possibility of two out. We are in good shape on that side. We have three defenders on two receivers. To the trips side, we have four defenders on three receivers. If all three receivers go deep, we only have two guys deep. The Will linebacker has to be outside of #3 and inside of #2. If #3 goes deep, he runs with him. The Mike linebacker is walling #3 to the 3-man side. The corner has to be outside of #2 and inside of #1. If #3 goes vertical, the safety and corner play quarter coverage. If either of the inside slots go flat, they go back and play regular blue coverage.

CORNER/SAFETY VS TRIPS

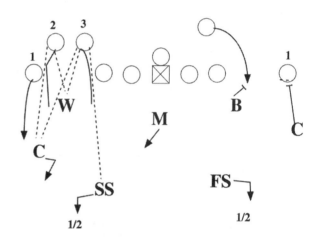

I want to show you some film now. You can ask questions when I'm done. Men, any time you want to come by UC and visit with our coaches; just give us a call. We are willing to help you in anyway we can. I'll stick around if you have any questions. Thank you.

LINEBACKER TECHNIQUES AND DRILLS

Purdue University

I appreciate the Nike Coach of the Year Clinic for the invitation to speak today. This is a great clinic. I spoke here nine or ten years ago. It is the best clinic I've ever been to. It is a privilege for me to be here. There are a lot of great coaches in the audience. I hope you learn something that can help you win a game or two.

I want to make sure we all understand what a positive influence a coach can have on a kid's life. All I ever wanted to be was a high school football coach because of my coach. But, I never became one. I played college and a pro ball. When I got cut, I went in college as a grad assistant in college and got into the rat race of Division I football.

My coach was real special in my life. I had good parents and grew up in a blue-collar industrial town in northern Illinois. Football was a big deal, and my parents wanted me to go to college. They wanted me to get an education. That kind of went in one ear and out the other. Fortunately, I had a guy who took me under his wing when I was fourteen. He showed me the way. He showed me I had to make my grades and be a student, as well as being a football player. He knew my goal was to some day play college football, and he was a huge influence on me.

When I signed my scholarship to go to Purdue, he pulled me aside, shook my hand, and made me promise to graduate in four years. I did that. He was a goal setter and a great motivator. The saddest day of my life was when he died. He was thirty-seven years old and developed cancer. He died the year I was a senior in college. That was a tough year for me. Because of that guy, I got into coaching. He changed my whole life as to the way I looked at academics and football.

We are a 4-3 defense. Your may not be a 4-3 type defense, but I'm going to talk about linebacker techniques in general. I'll give you some of the philosophy of why we do the things we do. Most of these ideas you can transfer over to any front or defense you play. I have a training tape to show you at the end.

The first point in our defensive philosophy is to be *AGGRESSIVE*. We want our front to create a new line of scrimmage. We are an up-the-field team. We key the football and take as much of the line of scrimmage as we can with our down four guys.

The second thing is to *DO WHAT THE PLAYERS CAN DO*. This year we were very young on defense. We started five freshmen in the Rose Bowl. We had nine freshmen on our two-deep depth chart. We didn't think we were going too win many games. We were hoping to get to six wins to qualify us for a bowl game. We were very fortunate to have some gifted players that came through for us. The freshman of the year in our conference was our free safety. But, we had to do what they could do. We have a lot of fancy zone-pressure schemes, we didn't use. We threw a lot of things at them in two-a-day practices to see what they could handle.

Physically, we could run. We were a fast team, and we set up the defense for speed. We are different than most of the teams in our league. We are fast and pretty undersized for the Big Ten. When you are thinking about schemes and techniques for your linebackers, make sure you do what they can do.

The third thing we want to do is to be *SIMPLE*. The more the offense does, the less we do. We play against one of the most complicated offenses in college football. We do it every day, in two-a-days, and in spring football. Our guys hate it, especially the linebackers, because they are playing out in space.

We live and die with *SPEED*. That is the fourth thing we talk about. That is critical for us, because we are playing with smaller players. We play with players who are fast or who play fast. Those things are different, but amount to the same thing. We tell our players, if they are not fast, they have to play fast. We made strides on defense this year because of that.

We want to *turn our players loose*. We don't try to bog them down with a lot of mental stuff. We keep it simple and turn them loose. We want our linebacker attacking the line of scrimmage and playing downhill.

We want the ball *to go east and west*. We don't want the ball going north and south on us. We try to spill the ball to the outside and run it down with speed.

We try to promote an environment for success. We do it with five things. I have a coach assigned for everyone of these points. I handle two of them.

The first point is *PURSUIT*. We grade them on it and talk about it every day. We tell them what they did good and bad. It is the first thing we talk about on defense every day. The second point is *ENTHUSIASM*. We coach it and grade them on it. We want to make sure our players are playing with a lot of emotion. The third thing is *TURNOVERS*. This year was our best year we've had on defense statistically since we've been here at Purdue. Our total defense was up, but our turnovers were down. Our first three years we either led the nation or were in the top ten in forcing turnovers. This year we weren't as good. I can't explain that.

We coach turnovers in practice and continually talk about it in practice. We work on tip drills, picking up fumbles, and all the drills relating to forcing turnovers.

The fourth thing in our philosophy is *TACKLING*. We tackle every day we are in full pads. That is critical. Our head coach is different than any head coach I've ever been around. During two-a-days practices, we have a live period every afternoon from ten to twenty minutes. A lot of teams in college don't tackle live because they are worried about injuries. Our quarterback is live in some of our drills and that includes Drew Brees. Coach Joe Tiller lets us play football, because that is the way it will be played on Saturday. We scrimmage live situations every day we are in pads. Tackling is critical to a football team.

The fifth thing we talk about with our players is *SOUNDNESS*. That to us is communication. It is alignment, assignment and communication. That converts to the soundness of our defense. We go over these five things at the end of practice every day and give them a grade. We are a 4-3 defense because it allows our players to be aggressive in attacking the line of scrimmage. We play with smaller players.

Our system is easy to learn and play. That allows us to play these young kids. It lets them get on the field quicker. I don't think there has ever been a year quite like this one. I would have never believed we could win the Big Ten playing that many young players. We feel the 4-3 increases our sacks, because we are an up-the-field team and are very aggressive with our down four and our linebackers.

There are certain things we look for in our linebackers. First and foremost is *SPEED*. If he is not fast, he won't play fast. A lot of our linebackers are former safeties. We have two linebackers who were former receivers. Our starting Sam linebacker is a true freshman. He came in as a receiver. He came to Purdue thinking he was going to catch the ball. We moved him to linebacker after the first day. We play the fastest guys we can find at linebacker. I can only remember two guys in the last two years that played linebacker for us, who were linebackers in high school.

I want guys who have *QUICK FEET*. When I evaluate a tape, I want to see a guy who has a great MOTOR. When I talk about a motor, I'm talking about great effort. That is critical to any linebacker. I am looking for guys to play linebacker who have *EXPLOSIVE POWER*.

Linebackers must have *GOOD FOOTBALL SENSE*. They have to be *TOUGH*. They have to have a great *WORK ETHIC*. I feel linebackers work harder than anyone else. They must be *TRUSTWORTHY*. I have to be able to trust them. They must have good *CHARACTER*.

We have a philosophy for our linebackers. We want them to be aggressive and play downhill. We want them to make plays on the offensive side of the line of scrimmage. We express that to them in our meetings. We want them playing downhill on forty-five degree angles. We want them to be big playmakers. That is critical for us to have our linebackers make big plays. We want them to play with great leverage and knee bend. A knee bender is a jaw breaker. We want our guys to bend their knees and strike on the rise. We want to keep it simple and create a language so we can communicate with them and make it easy for the player to understand.

What do we expect from our linebackers? We call it the "3 T's." The first T is tempo. We want them to play at a fast tempo. That is the *how* we play. In individual periods, we hustle and play the game fast. The second T is technique. That is the *way* we play. We want to play with great technique. The third T is toughness. That is *what* we are. These are three things we emphasize in our individual periods with all our guys.

In our individual period, we emphasis those three things. When you play with a 5.0 linebacker, he has to play fast. The first two years at Purdue, we had a couple of them. They played their butts off. They played fast and hustled all the time. We emphasis the tempo of our drills. I tell our coaches every day before we go out to practice, do not forget what we are trying to get done. We have to develop and train our players to play fast. In every drill we do, I want those guys running fast. I want them to hustle and bust their butts.

When we teach our techniques, we break them down. We cover every small detail involved. We want them to understand the way we play.

When we talk about toughness to our linebackers we challenge them. This morning for example, we ran eighteen, 180 yard conditioning intervals after we went through a forty-five minute training circuit. We get our players up at 6:00 a.m. We put them through a good training period for an hour. It is tough. Today, we went more than an hour because they didn't finish on the sprint. Instead of running six 180's, we ran about twenty. We want them perfect on sprinting.

We have a "thought progression" with our linebackers. If I put a new defense or stunt up on the board, I want them to go through this thought progression. The first thought should be "where is my stance going to be?" If I am an inside linebacker he is going to be in a two-point stance. If I'm a linebacker outside the box, his stance changes. He has to know the stance he is playing and how he gets out of the stance. When we talk defense, we constantly talk about "pads out." We want the player's pads over his toes. That is where we want them in a hitting position.

The second thing is "alignment." We have a very easy alignment system. We number our front alignments 0-7. If the alignment is off the line of scrimmage, we add a zero in front of the alignment. A linebacker aligned on the outside shoulder of the offensive guard would be in a "03" alignment.

The third thing is "footwork." That is getting out of our stance. I'll show you some tape in a minute that will demonstrate this. We have a thing we do, especially with young players. It is called popping our feet. This helps us eliminate false steps.

The fourth thing is "technique." We label all our techniques, especially for our linebackers. If our Will linebacker is playing in the B-gap, we call that a B-window technique. The Mike linebacker who has the A-gap, we call that a stack technique. The Sam linebacker playing in the C-gap, we call a C-window technique.

The fifth thing is "responsibility." Within every technique, there are responsibilities. On every play, there are three things the linebacker has to know. It is run to, run away, or pass. He has to know what he is going to do on each of those situations. It is pretty simple and easy. Obviously, it gets more complicated than that when we break it down. If I am a B-window player, our primary keys are the backs, and the secondary keys are the linemen. If I am a linebacker out of the box, my primary key becomes the uncovered linemen. That tells us if it is run or pass faster than a back would.

We have five things that are important in our individual drills. They are movement, defeating blocks, tackling, play recognition, and pass drops.

In our movement drills, we use bags and cones. We always incorporate some kind of football skill with those movement drills. We tackle coming off a bag drill. We defeat a cut blocker coming off a bag. We dip and rip with our outside arm coming off a bag. We plant the hands coming off the bag. We want to do some kind of football skill coming off a bag, dummy, or cone.

We take on blockers different ways. On direct blocks, we dip and rip taking them on with our forearms. On indirect blocks, we play with our hands. We tackle every day, and I'll show you some of these tackling drills later.

We use key drills for play recognition and pass drops. I break this down by technique. We are a pattern read defense as far as zone goes. We run pattern read drills every day in our individual drills.

The big question I get in most clinics is how we read and key. We have a simple system. I don't want a linebacker to be a robot. We have become multiple over the years. We can't just line up in a 4-3 and survive. We have to change up our fronts. Because of that, I went to this system. I stole this from the Jacksonville Jaguars. When you watch the tape this will make sense to you.

We label points on the defense as to where the linebacker should fit on flow. It relates to the angle of flow the linebacker's reads. The point over the ball is *the linside point*. The point between the guard and tackle is *the base point*. The point in the C-gap is *outside point*. The C-window technique has an outside fill or outside scrap.

POINTS ON DEFENSE

OUTSIDE   BASE   I/P   BASE   OUTSIDE

The reason we do this is to keep the linebacker from being a robot. I don't want the linebacker running to the B-gap just because the ball is run at him. If the ball is not in the B-gap, I don't want him in there. Understanding our key drill is critical to understanding these points on the defense.

There are four angles of flow by the offensive backs our linebackers must recognize. The first flow is a tight dive off the hip of the center. If the Will linebacker is getting a tight dive away he is a B-window player. His angle of flow on tight dive away is inside point, which is over the center. He is not flowing into the B-gap.

The Mike linebacker is mirroring the angle of the back. On the tight dive off the hip of the center, the Mike linebacker hits the A-gap like he is going to blitz. If he hits the A-gap, and the window closes, he scrapes over the top of his 3-technique.

TIGHT DIVE ANGLE

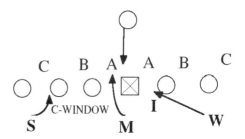

The next back flow is the dive angle. If the Mike linebacker reads the angle of the back toward the dive, his angle is a forty-five degree angle to clear the 3-technique. The Will linebacker on dive angle away still has inside point. The Sam linebacker reads dive angle toward him. He is the C-window player. He has to read the window and see whether it is opened or closed. If it is closed, he has the outside point scrape. If it is open, he attacks the back.

DIVE ANGLE

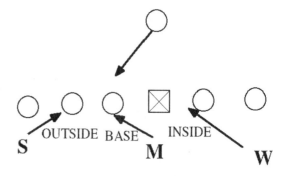

The next angle is the power angle flow. The Will linebacker has power angle away. He works for the inside point all the way to the opposite base point. His footwork will change somewhat. He stays flatter so he can clear the guard-center area. That is the area we call the hump. He checks the hump, then works downhill to the base point.

The Sam linebacker is keying the C-window. If the window opens, he fills right now on an outside fill point. If the window is closed, he outside scrapes off the butt of the defensive end.

The Mike linebacker mirrors the angle of the back. He is generally attacking at a forty-five degree angle. He attacks the base point to the outside fill point.

POWER ANGLE

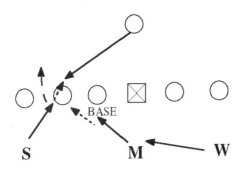

The next flow is sweep angle or what many people call fast flow. The Will linebacker on sweep angle away takes a flatter step and runs the hump. That means he is going to give a little ground. He works over the top of the inside point into to the guard-tackle box. When he reaches that point, he gets downhill.

The Mike linebacker clears the tackle and box, and gets downhill. The Sam linebacker plays off the offensive end. He is reading the flow of the tackle. If the tackle is fighting to reach, the Sam fills inside.

SWEEP ANGLE

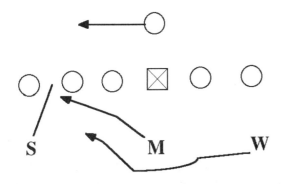

We create a language by using those points. This language makes it real easy for our linebacker to understand what you want them to do. This has been really good for us. When you play true freshmen who had never played the position, this made it easy for them.

Let's get into the tape now. We are a 4-3 alignment and our linebackers are quite deep. We play them with their heels at five yards from the line of scrimmage. The reason we play them so deep is to get them downhill with force.

There are things we look for in our stance. We want the pads out, which I talked about before. We want the chin up with a nice flat back. He has his toes slighted toed in and his heels slightly out. He has a slight bend in his knees with a good power angle in his knees and ankles. His feet should be flat on the ground but we want the weight on the inside. His elbows are tight inside. We put our hands on the thigh pads, but never on the knees. The reason we want the elbows inside is to create power. If you put your elbows outside, you can't push. That lets us dip and rip because the elbows are tight to the body.

This is a little drill we call "popping our feet." I got this from a high school coach in Texas. This keeps us from taking a false step. We play so fast downhill we want our linebackers to give a slight pop of the feet. Instead of wasting motion by jumping forward or backward, we pick the foot up and almost put it down in the same position. We can do this drill mirroring a back or lineman. In the dive angle, the linebacker pops his feet and then gets into his forty-five degree angle run.

FOOT POP

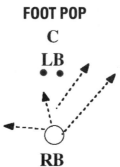

We want the shoulders down. We don't want to travel with our shoulders out of our stance. The critical part of a linebacker is getting out of his stance. I don't want him to raise or lower his shoulders as he moves. We always want his pads over his toes. We drill our angles without linemen to start with. They simple mirror the angle of the backs they are keying. They know their points by the angle of the backs.

When we teach our linebackers they have to know whether we are playing an eight or seven man structure defense. If it is seven man structure defense, the backside linebacker is shuffling. If it is an eight-man structure, he is running.

The Mike linebacker has inside point on the tight dive. He has the base point on a dive angle. He has out-

The Mike linebacker has inside point on the tight dive. He has the base point on a dive angle. He has outside point on the power angle. We don't use the term "wrong-arm." We call it "win inside." We want the defender to take on the block with his outside arm and kick the blocker's butt. On the dive angle, if the Sam linebacker reads the C-window open, he attacks the back in the hole. The Mike linebacker reads the base point and plays over top of the Sam linebacker who has closed the window.

On the next drill, we put linemen into the key drill. That gives the linebacker a cluttered picture. We are doing the same drill as we did without the line, but now they are seeing blocks. In every drill we do, we emphasize eyes up.

We do all kinds of ladder drills for footwork. We use form-tackling drills with a three-step movement. The approach is the first phase. The fit-up is the second phase. It is important in the fit-up position to squeeze your elbows together. He has to snap and roll his hips in the third phase of the drill. We approach the tackle under control, fit into a good position, and explode and lift to finish the tackle.

We use a drill that we call the "door drill." We put a cone in the middle and align a back and linebacker on either side five yards from the cone. The manager is the door. He stands over the cone in the middle. A lot of linebackers are not tall guys, and it is hard for them to see. The back takes two steps toward the door and breaks to one side or the other of the door. The linebacker takes two steps, reacts to the direction of the back, looking for the opposite colored jersey. Once he sees it, he lowers his pads, makes the hit, and drives him backwards.

A drill we like to run is our "drop and tackle" drill. We have the linebacker spot drop to an area on the field. He takes a good forty-five degree drop to a cone which is about eight-yards deep. We have a back standing next to the quarterback. Once the linebacker reaches the cone, the back can break into a flare pattern. The quarterback throws the ball and the linebacker reacts up to make the tackle. The linebacker works on driving on the ball and attacking from the inside out.

We use sleds and bags to work on playing off blocks. When you play off blocks, we want everything going forward. I don't want to see any body parts going out. We hit everything on a rise. We step with the inside arm and leg. If you are watching a boxing match, you never see a fighter throw a jab with his left hand without stepping with his left foot. We want to step and keep our leverage. We want our pad level under the level of the blocker. On contact, we want to roll the wrist out and swing the off hand through. I tell them it is like looking at your watch. At impact, we want the feet on the ground. We dip and rip and get underneath the blocker. We can do all these drills on a sled, as well with bags.

When we play with our hands, we want to play with our hands above our eyes. We strike and hit on a rise. When the backside linebacker is playing the inside point, he is playing with his hands. We want good fast hands with the elbows always inside. If he rolls his hips too much while he is playing with his hands, he has a tendency to get locked into the block. We want the hips to stay behind during this drill. We want their palms together with their thumbs up. Once we get on a block, we work on turning the blocker's shoulders. We want to push with one hand and pull with the other.

Gentlemen, I appreciate your time. Thank you.

COACHING AND TEACHING FOOTBALL

Willamette University

I have been coaching football for 23 years. I was a head coach in high school for 14 years, and an assistant for five years. Most of my time was spent in California. I have been at big schools, small schools, and medium schools. They are all similar. They have different problems but they are similar.

I have been in college coaching for six years. I was an assistant at Willamette University for three years, and I have been the head coach for the last three years. We have a great connection with Hawaii. ESPN did a special on our 1941 Willamette University team. They played the University of Hawaii on December 6, 1941. The attack on Pearl Harbor occurred on December 7, 1941. The entire team was conscripted into the army. It was a great group of guys.

One thing about Willamette University is that we are one of those academic schools. When I recruit, I need to know who the bright players are. We compete against the top academic schools.

I think there are some things offensively that we do better that gives us a chance to win. You have to hang your hat on something. You can not be an expert on everything. I have been coaching for 23 years, and I can not draw up the wing-T plays. But, I do know how to stop that offense.

One on the great things about football is it is one of the greatest teaching tools that we have. I am going to talk about some teaching techniques. Football lectures can be X's and O's, they can be philosophical, and they can be about teaching. I am going to go in that direction today with this part of the lecture.

When I grew up, we never traveled, and we never stayed in a hotel. Had it not been for football, I would never have ridden on an airplane. I would not have gone to college had it not been for football. I kept going to college because that was the only way to keep playing football. I was one of those guys that kind of hung around. I am thankful for all of the opportunities football has given me.

It is not always the X's and O's that are important in football. A lot of kids come back after football and tell me about all of the fun things we did while they were playing. All of those things are memories. It is the things people get fired up about. Football is memorable. It is an intense learning tool. I have a true story to illustrate what I am talking about. I saw this story in *Sports Illustrated* a long time ago.

"NORELCO PRESETS CLOSE SHAVES." The story was about a football game between LSU and Alabama in 1982. They were both nationally ranked teams, and the game came down to a field goal at the end of the game to win the game. LSU would win the game if they could make the field goal.

It was down to the kicker, holder, and the snapper to make good on the kick. The kicker was David Browndyke, the holder was Chris Moock. The regular snapper had left the team a few days before the game, and the first sub was inconsistent earlier in the game. The substitute snapper was Mike Hebert, a senior linebacker who had not snapped in a game since high school. The snap, the hold, and the kick were perfect. LSU won the game 19-18 and shocked 70,000 Alabama fans. After the game Hebert said, "it was one of the high points in my life."

I started thinking about that statement. In our lives, we have a lot of high points. We have children born, jobs, and a lot of other events. But when we look back at it, the memories in football become some of the high points of a kid's life. When you put these things in context, it means a lot. That is our job as coaches to put it to context.

I have come up with some basic thoughts on coaching. These are things that have meant a lot to me over the years.

TAKE CARE OF THE LITTLE THINGS AND THE BIG THINGS TAKE CARE OF THEMSELVES.

I got this from my junior college coach. I took over a program that was winless the year before I took the job. But, the next year we were 14-0. In 1990, we were selected as the team of the year in California. We won 41 of 42 games at one point. But, we never sat down as a staff and said, "we need to go 14-0." What we did was to sit down and come up with a plan to get as many kids out for the weight program. Then, we wanted to have as many kids as we could out for the summer program. Then, we wanted to win that first game. We knew we would have to work hard, and hopefully we could come up with a game plan to win the first game.

We will never do the big things unless we do the little things. We have to go to clinics, and do all of the things that are considered little things. It is not the big mistakes that make you lose games. It is the little things. We really buy into this theory.

THERE IS NO CAMELOT.

There is no perfect job in coaching. Everyone is looking for a better job. There is no better job. A lot of coaches want to coach in college. I am coaching in college. It is no better than coaching in high school. It is just a matter of having different problems. It is sad to me, but in this profession, most everyone is looking for that next job. They are looking for a better job. Sometimes you have the best job. There is no best job. If there were, we would know about it.

THERE ARE GROUPS TO WATCH OUT FOR.

This is especially true in high school. They are everywhere. There are roving tribes of trouble makers. You have to keep an eye out for them because they can destroy your program. The first groups I describe are DIPS. Those are doting, ignorant, parents. DIPS. I never understood DIPS, so I became a DIP. When my son became a freshman in high school, I immediately became a DIP. I wanted to know what the coaches were doing to my son. I knew, but I wanted to hear it from the coaches. Coaches do not need to spend a lot time with DIPS.

This next group are the FATS — fellowship of the angry teachers. They are teachers that hate athletics. They will disagree on anything you are in favor of. They must have been cut from every team they ever tried out for. They must have been last in PE class. They are angry at athletics. They do not understand the educational value of athletics. I used to tell them for educators they were not very educated. If they understood athletics, they would embrace athletics.

We had an english teacher that took pride in giving F's to athletes. If we had a freshman player get her as a teacher, he was in trouble. I told her if she was a heart surgeon she would be killing all of her patients. I asked her if she would take pride in doing that. She used to tell me one of my players was being bad in her class. "Your football players are disrupting my class." It was like I sired the players. I agreed to talk to the players. She would tell me "your football player did poorly on my test yesterday." I replied, "your english student fumbled on the 3-yard line Friday night. Would you do something about that for me?"

YA CANT'S - A GROUP TELLING YOU WHY SOMETHING IS IMPOSSIBLE.

These are the people always telling you that you can't do something. When I went to Merced High School, there was a lot of these people. "You can't do that with our kids. We tried that in 1974." I asked them if the water was different here. These three groups can make life miserable for the high school coach. They are the groups you must manage.

Another point I have learned about coaching is this. you must figure out a way to win. Don't waste time making excuses why your opponent has the advantage. I got caught up in doing that. "We can't do that. We only have 700 kids. We do not have any speed. We do not have any size." Everyone comes up with reasons why they can't win. That has to stop.

I hear it at our place now. Some people say if we start focusing on academics at Willamette, we are going to lose. We have to find a way to win. There are plenty of academic kids out there that can play for us. We just have to find them. That is our deal. Your deal is your deal. I find too many coaches that come up with too many excuses.

Another quote that used to drive me crazy was this statement. What you see on film you coached. I believe this. What you see on the film, you are responsible for. If players do not do it right in practice, they are not going to do it in a game. I think that is totally the responsibility of the coach. If you do not like what you see on the film, either replace him or coach him better.

IF YOU ARE GOOD ENOUGH – THEY ARE SMART ENOUGH.

Coaches used to tell me that we could not do something because it was too complicated. I would tell them if they were good enough as a teacher, they will get it. Some people talk about KISS: keep it simple stupid. I do not believe in this statement. To me simple is to run a dive left and a dive right. That is simple. Of course, it is simple for the defense as well. Simple would be one defense. But, that is simple for the defense. You have to make it complex for the opponent, but simple for your players.

IF YOU WANT TO GET GOOD AT SOMETHING – PRACTICE IT!

I had an assistant coach that used to tell me at the beginning of the year, we were going to be blocking a lot of punts each year. We never did block many punts. It was as if the coach made an edict, "we will now block punts. Let it be known through out the kingdom, we will now block punts." You can't get things done by edict. You have to practice something if you are going to be good at it. If you are going to block punts, you have to work on it.

You do not have to be great at everything. It may be you do not have players that can block punts. If that is the case, you may want to work on returning punts. There is nothing wrong with that. Whatever you decide, you must practice on it.

The secret in coaching is teaching. I think you have to teach kids everything. You can't assume anything. When kids come to us as freshmen, I am amazed at what they do not know. Football is hard to learn. You think about it. You have to teach them a language. You are bilingual. You are trilingual if you play both ways in football. You have all of the terminology to learn.

I went to Merced High School to coach, and I was told the team did not travel very well. They had a food fight and did a lot of damage to a Burger King the year before. I could not believe that. We went on short bus trips the first couple of games, and they acted as if they were going to a party. They did not have their minds on football. I decided to work on that problem.

I believe you can learn from films. Kids will watch film. I think you can teach more with film than by telling them. It was the fourth game, and we were going on a longer road trip. I told them I did not like the way they traveled the last couple of away games. I told them they acted as if they were going to a party. I told them we were going to a football game. I convinced them if they were to be great, they would have to learn to travel properly. This was varsity football, and I did not think I had to teach them how to travel. They were good kids that came from good homes. They did not throw food at their parents, but when they got together as a group, they were wild.

I showed the team a movie titled "*All the Right Moves*" with Tom Cruise. There is a great scene in the movie. These town kids were going to the suburbs to play a big game. The kids were in the bus, and it was silent in the bus. All you could hear was windshield wipers. Every kid on that bus had their "game face" on. One kid was saying the rosary. The other kids were concentrating. There was total silence on the bus. They were going to war!.

Last year I showed our team the film of "*Saving Private Ryan*." I talked about the scene when the troops were in the boat getting ready to invade the beaches. They were not asking each other what they were doing after the battle. They were totally focused. As football coaches we have to teach them to be focused. Once they get the hang of it, they like it. I showed those film clips and asked our players if they understood what it meant to get ready for a game. I showed the film clips over and over again. I just kept showing that film clip. The next time we got on that bus, those players were ready to play football.

One of the problems kids have today and especially in college is time management. We talk about time management a lot. Kids do not know how to study. That is the reason for ineligible players. They do not lift, or eat, or study properly. The reason is because they are not organized. They are not focused. I am going to show you what we go over with our kids related to this subject.

TIME MANAGEMENT – TIME IN A JAR

One day an expert in time management was speaking to a group of business students. To drive home a point, he used an illustration those students will never forget.

As he stood in front of the group of high-powered overachievers, he said, "Okay, time for a quiz." He pulled out a one-gallon Mason jar and set it on the table in front of him. He produced about a dozen fist-sized rocks and carefully placed them, one at a time, into the jar. When the jar was filled to the top, and no more rocks would fit inside the jar, he asked, "Is this jar full?" Everyone yelled out, "Yes." The time management expert replied, "Really?"

He reached under the table and pulled out a bucket of gravel. He dumped some gravel in the jar and shook the jar causing pieces of gravel to work themselves down into the spaces between the big rocks. He then asked the group once more, "Is the jar full?" By this time, the class was on to him. "Probably not," one of them answered. "Good" he replied.

He reached under the table and brought out a bucket of sand. He started dumping the sand into the jar, and it went into all of the spaces left between the rocks and gravel. Once more, he asked the question, "Is the jar full?" "No!" the class shouted. Once again he said, "Good." Then, he grabbed a pitcher of water and began to pour it in the jar until the jar was filled to the brim. Then he looked at the class and asked another question.

"What is the point of this illustration?" One eager beaver raised his hand and said, "The point is, no matter how full your schedule is, if you try really hard you can always fit some more things in!" "No," the speaker replied, "that is not the point. The truth this illustration teaches us is this. IF you don't put the big rocks in first, you will never get thme in at all. What are the 'big rocks' in your life — time with your loved ones, your faith, your education, your dreams, a worthy cause, teaching or working with others? Remember to put the big rocks in first or you will never get them in at all." So, when you are reflecting on this short story, ask yourself this question: What are the big rocks in your life. Then, put those rocks in your jar first.

We tell our players some of their big rocks had better be academics and football. Most kids have some spiritual side to them. It better be church. It better be nutrition. If their big rocks are hanging out, they are going to have problems. You have to know what the big rocks are. We talk about this with our players.

Excellence is balancing your life style. We are all pretty much unbalanced. But, it is healthy when you have your friends, church, fraternity, your family, school sports, and your social life together. Everything is balanced, and it is healthy if you can include all of those activities.

BALANCING YOUR LIFE

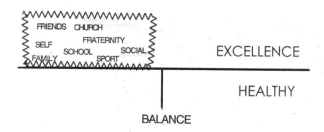

You get screwed up when you add things that are not healthy. These things include money, girl friends, partying, hanging out, video games, procrastination, not enough sleep, drugs and alcohol. This is when things get screwed up.

IMBALANCE IN YOUR LIFE

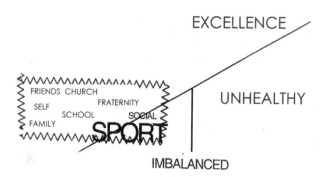

We have to teach our kids they are different. They must have a warrior mentality. They have to know they are a little different. They must know they can not do everything. They cannot be like Joe Normal. If they want to be great, they will have to give something up. You must keep balance. We talk to our kids about this balance idea. We give them the diagram so they can put it up in their room. It is a visual illustration of what balance is.

YOU GOT TO WORK BACKWARD!

When you think about a day, we have 24 hours. We tell our kids to work backwards. They have to list the big rocks first. Big rocks are: 1) family, church, and self; 2) school; 3) sport – in-season and out-of-season; 4) social life. Within a day, you count your hours backward. This is the way to count backward.

SLEEP = 8 hours minimum – self.

EAT = 2 hours – self.

SCHOOL = 6 hours — school.

HOMEWORK = 2 hours-school.

SPORT = 3 hours.

TOTAL = 21 hours.

Now, we are not talking about two hours of homework per semester. We are talking about two hours per day. That leaves the student about three hours for social life. They may select the activities. They may chose student government, fraternities, FCA, BSO, or any other activities on campus. The thing we stress is for them to use their time wisely.

Some students will tell you they only need four hours sleep per night. They say they eat real fast. They insist they do not need to spend two hours on studies. The ideal is that we are trying to teach time management. Kids do not understand time management. We have to help them with this problem at all levels. If you do not teach this, it is left to chance. If you do not take care of the little things, you will never take care of the big things.

I want to continue with this thought and talk about football practice. We talk about practice with a purpose. I think this is a critical statement; practice with a purpose. A lot of times, we just go through the motions. You have to learn how to practice. Here are some points that I think are important in talking about "PRACTICING WITH A PURPOSE."

What is the attitude of the drill? How do you want your players to act during the drill? I used to think you had to be a military type and a militant guy when you were on the field. We do not want to be serous for two and a half hours during practice. That is not any fun. There are times when our stretching period is really loose. We used to be in a line just like the military. We did have some rituals with the stretching, but it was a military-type drill. But, I have learned it is alright to have a little fun during the stretching drill. After we stretch, I bring the team up and tell them we are getting ready to focus on what we need to do for the day.

I have seen teams that were grab-ass at practice the entire session. You have to tell your kids how you want to practice. If you want them to move around slowly, take their helmet off when they want to, then you have to tell them. If you want them to be more focused, you have to tell them. I feel you can win both ways. I have never done a scientific study of this, but I prefer to be focused. I do know you have to teach kids how to act. You cannot kill each other in practice unless you have unlimited bodies. Most of us do not have that situation.

What is the tempo of the drill? How do you want the players to react? What is the speed of the drill? Is there to be contact? The lower the level of the teams, the more they want to go live. At the top level which is the pros, the less they go live in drills. I watched the Seahawks practice in shorts and helmets, and they were going hard. They are older, and they know how to do it.

When I first started coaching, I told the team we were going hard in practice everyday. I told them I want them to give 100 percent on every play. I think the players had a meeting a few days after that and decided they would only go 80 percent. I was not very smart to think our players would be able to go hard for that length of time. You can't go 100 percent for two hours.

We have a teaching speed. That is a chalk talk on the field. We call out, "ready go" and they walk through the drill. We have a one-half speed where they jog through the drill. We are not going to have contact during this time. Next, we have what we call THUD speed. Here, we are going live, but we are not taking the ball carrier to the ground. It is live, and the line is getting after each other, but we are not taking the ball carrier to the ground. It is hard to tell the difference between thud and full speed. In full speed, we cut; when we go thud, we stay up.

You must decide if a drill is to be an offensive drill or a defensive drill. You have to teach this to the kids. You do not want the defensive secondary to go home thinking they can't beat anyone. The seven-on-seven should be an offensive drill. Being the head coach, you must have a split personality. You have to be for both the offense and defense in practice. I tell our team is this. I want the offense to get inside the 10-yard line and then fumble. This way we all have some success.

What is the purpose of the drill? I remember my worst experience in football. I was in Pop Warner football. I was about 10 years old. Our coach asked me and another player to lie down on our back. He blew a whistle, and both of us had to get up as fast as we could. Then, the coach threw the other guy the football. He was on offense, and I was on defense. The ball carrier tried to run over me. I had to get the ball carrier to the ground. Now, in all of my experiences and in all of the films I have watched, I have never seen a game where this drill happened. I remember the ball carrier hit me so hard I thought I had broken everything in my body including my neck. I thought the game of football sucked. I did not want to go back to practice, but I did.

I do not believe in lining up and running sprints. All of our conditioning is game-related. If I want our players to run, I get our receivers and defensive backs and run the fade drill. If I want the line to work on something, I tell them to hit the sled. It is worth something. Now, if a player gets gassers, we make sure he does them. There is a toughness deal, and there is a camaraderie deal, and I understand that. But, the fact is we do not have time for drills that are not game-related. I worry about game carryover. If you have a drill that is not game-related, get rid of it.

I think the worst book on the market today is the book called "One Hundred and One Drills." What do they expect us to do? Do they want us to teach a new drill everyday? It takes five minutes to teach a drill and three minutes to set it up. Everyone can get one rep, and then the 10-minute period is over. We do the same drill everyday. Find three drills you like, stay with them and teach them. Find the best drills for the game. Ask the question "will it help our team win the game?"

Let me tell you what I did for spring practice when I was coaching high school football. I taught cover 3 so we would be able to play pass defense in the summer league. The rest of the time I taught the team pursuit drill. I taught it the way I wanted it. That is all we did. It helped us win in the fall.

We try to condition by position. Linebackers have to drop to the hook-curl area. We have them work on that phase of the game. We may have them do it twenty times in a row. We make it game-like. If you want to teach your team to play man coverage, teach that phase of the game to them. You can use those drills to condition the team. We spread out and get them doing football game-related drills.

I think the set-up of the drill is important. I went to visit Stanford's practice. I was so impressed with the way the drills were all laid out, and all the footballs were placed where they wanted them. They have the resources to get the job done the way it is supposed to be done. But, at our place and in high school, it is a different deal.

You call out "seven-on-seven drill," and everyone wants to know where to go. I design a map of our practice facility. Everyone knows where we are going to do each of the drills. If we want to change things around after a few practices, we can. I give each part of the field a name. When you tell players to go to a drill, it has to be fast. They need to know where to go before practice starts. We map out the practice area and give each area a name. I am big on squares. We have the squares painted and lined off. We do a lot of drills on the squares. You do not need cones when you have squares. There are a lot of drills you can do on squares. We do a lot of angle tackling in the five-yard squares. We do our offensive line drills in the squares. The box makes it a great teaching tool.

I have been to a lot of clinics, and the speakers get up and tell everyone if they can get one idea out of their lecture it will be worthwhile. I do not buy that. I want the playbook. I want the entire package.

Here is another point related to practice. How about having a whistle at practice? This is important to the defense. We tell them to play to the whistle. It is tough to coach defense with someone yelling at the defense to stop, or hold up, or calling out, "whoa." That is not what the ref is going to do. "Play to the whistle." I want every drill to stop with a whistle. I want each coach to have a whistle. If you want the players to stop, you blow the whistle. Teach them to play until the whistle blows.

I do not know how long a play is going last. In drills, it may go for a long time before we blow the whistle. Whistles are not expensive. You do not need to have a fund raiser to buy a whistle. Now, sleds are expensive. You have to sell a lot of candy bars to buy a sled.

We call the whistle situation neuromuscular patterning. It is when your muscles do what you want them to do. Think about the first time you drove a car. On my first time, I was focused on what I was doing. My brother wanted to turn on the radio, and I told him no because I could not concentrate. As I learned to drive later, I wanted the radio on when I was driving. It is neuromuscular patterning.

The number one goal in practice, in my opinion, should be reps. I do not care how long you practice. Count the number of times you snap the ball. The more reps, the better you are going to be. That is a mark of a good team. We are a no-huddle offense. The number one reason is because we can get more reps in practice We do not huddle. We do not practice coming out of the huddle. Our guys do not know how to get into a huddle. When the play is over, we get up and go back to the line. You get what you coach. What you see on film, you coach.

On Thursday, we have a checklist where we cover all the situations in a game. We cover all the kicking situations. We go over the overtime situations. You can make up your own checklist.

We want to get as many reps as possible in practice. We want to get as many players involved as possible. We want multiple groups, and we use circuits to accomplish this. I am a big fan of circuits. I do not want a group of players on a knee listening to a coach talk. That is not practice. That is a chalk talk. Don't do that on the field. Do that in the meeting room.

A good coach is one that coaches on the run. If you want good technique, you need to film the drills. If you are not happy with a drill, film it. Kids do a lot better on film. If you want to increase intensity, there are two things you can do. One is to get the stop watch out, and the second one is to film it. If you want your kickoff team to run, get a stop watch out. If we want to improve speed, we time them in the 40. Time them, and tell them their times. "The eye in the sky doesn't lie."

I think films are the best teaching tools in the world. I love films. Could you imagine if they filmed everyone at work. Coaches get hired and fired because of what people see on the film. Can you see someone filming a business person on a sale. "Did you meet the customer with a smile?" The boss tells the guy he is fired because he did not smile.

Good coaches do not get bored easy. You can use the same drill over and over again, and coach it up. If you are enthusiastic, they will be enthusiastic. If they buy into what you are teaching them, they will not get bored. Grant Teaff once asked a coach in Texas who had won more games than anyone what his secret to winning was. He replied, "I do not get bored easy."

I think you have to make practice tougher than a game. I am not talking about physically tougher. I am talking about putting them in a bad spot. If you know a blitz is going to hurt a certain running play, run it in practice. If you know a play that hurts your defense, then use the play in practice.

Another thing I am big on is trigger terms. Breakdown your drills into small bits and pieces. Use small words that mean something to everyone. You have to teach it "big" and then you coach it "small." Let me tell you what I mean. When we tackle, we use these terms: dip, hit, wrap, and drive.

The dip is this. It is the term we use to teach the player to get his shoulders square, his arms shoulder-width apart, and to get low enough to meet the ball carrier square. We take all of the verbiage and put it into one word. After a couple of days, all we have to say is we want to work on the dip.

The hit is how you want them to have the face on the impact, and what part of the body you want them to hit with. It is the contact part.

The wrap is right after the contact. It is what you want them to do with the arms. We talk about clubbing and grabbing cloth.

Then, we have the drive part. I have seen teams that did tackling practice by picking up the offensive man and putting him on his shoulder. I have never seen that in a game. In the drive, we want to run them over.

Now, we break this up into a tackling circuit. One station has a tackling sled. The coach at that station will do nothing but work on the dip in his drill on the sled. We coach that aspect of tackling on that drill.

The next station may be a square drill. That coach will work on the hit. He can work on tackling across the bow, or whatever he wants. You can teach tackling anyway you want to do it. But in this drill, all we are working on it the hit and wrap. That is why we say, "HIT – WRAP."

The last part is the drive part. We set up the drill where we have the ball carrier run through dummies. We have a defender make the tackle. We want the defender to drive the ball carrier back behind the bag or dummies. When we teach tackling, we are only critiquing one part of it. We may say, "good hit, no wrap; good wrap but no rrive."

Think about the drills you teach. As a coaching staff, go back and look at the way you are teaching your drills. Is it simple? Is it broken down in parts? I think this helps you get a lot of reps.

If I were smart, I would take all of the recruiting films from all over the country and put them into a highlight film. We see the funniest things. I should be sending them to that show called "*BLOOPERS.*" I could do a high school bloopers film and sell a bunch of them. It is hilarious what we see. I have learned that kids learn from other kids. When you get a great film clip of something you really like, you should make a copy of it. It may be a hit, a run, a catch, or whatever position you coach. It should be something that shows what you are trying to teach. It is better if it is not a NFL film. They do not react well to the NFL. They like it, but it is better if it is one of their guys.

On the day before the game, I show a highlight tape of the previous week. Before the games, I go around and tell the players to be sure they get in the highlight film for next week. It reinforces the things we want to teach. It is what we are trying to do, not what the NFL is doing.

I will show you a few plays on film. One is what we call SWARM. We put some highlights together of some of our players getting to the ball. This shows effort on the film. That is what we want. These are not great plays, but they are good plays. This is something you can do, and the kids will enjoy it.

Football is hard. I think the hardest part is language. You have some kids that are barely efficient at one language and may be struggling in another language. Then the kids have to learn football, and it is another language. You need to pay close attention to it. If you do not have a glossary of terms, you should think about it. That is an afternoon meeting for a coaching staff. "What are the words your are using to teach your players?" You have to teach kids your terminology. You do not have to call it what everyone else calls it. We think the players know all the terms, but they do not. Think about the terms you are using. You have to understand the terms before you go out and teach them.

You have to teach roles to football players. That is one of the fun things about coaching. You have a lot of players out for football who are not very good, but they love to be a part of the team. You cannot have everyone on the team starting. You have to cultivate the fact you need everyone on the team.

I think discipline is something that is misunderstood in football. Some coaches think discipline is yelling at the players. I think you can teach discipline. Discipline is doing the right things at the right time every time. I do not think it has anything to do with hair length.

I think being on time is a courtesy, and it is important. But, I have never heard a coach say they would have had a great year if their tackle had not been late for a lot of their meetings. I do not think it has ever cost us a game. You have to teach the kids what you want.

Discipline is getting your hand down, lining up on sides, and not getting stupid penalties. Those things to me are discipline.

Let me show you two drills we use in relationship to discipline. You are going to lose a lot of games on defense if they jump off sides. We put in the "bird drill" to teach the kids to stay on side. This is the way the drill works.

Coach #1 calls the cadence. All the players must be set with their hand behind the line. All players must get off on the snap count and stride past the next line 20-yards apart. All players immediately turn and get set again. As soon as coach #2 drops his arms, all players get off together and stride past the line. They immediately turn around, get set with their head up, and listen for coach #1 to give the snap count again. If all players can get off on the count, the coaches give a signal, and coach #1 announces it is a good or bad attempt. We try to go until we get two good tries. The drill is not full speed. We want them to jog from one end to the other. The bird man drops his arms to give the defense a chance to work on movement. The coaches give the thumbs up or thumbs down on the tries. The drill seems easy, but it is not. It helps them to go on the snap count. When the players do not get off on the snap count, the other players start yelling at each other. That is what happens when things start going badly in a game, right. This drill is not that easy, and it great when they get two trips correct. They go nuts.

THE BIRD DRILL

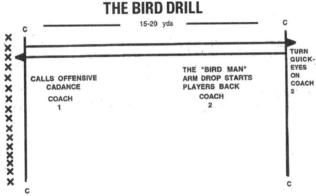

Another drill we do that is a lot of fun is the punt drill. It is a competitive drill, and it brings out a lot of character. We divide the teams into three groups, and we keep score. To get points everyone in the group must hustle to "down" the punt. Everyone must jog back to the 50-yard line, around cones and line up again. The punter is at the 50-yard line. I usually do the punting in this drill. Points are taken away for cutting corners, stopping early, or complaining about the drill.

THE PUNT DRILL

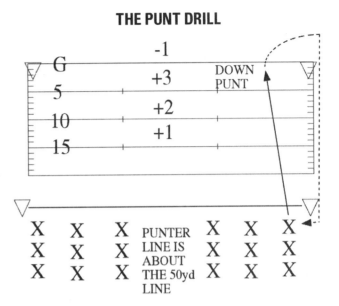

We divide the players by their positions. They start out from the 50-yard line. We have cones on the 15, 10, 5, and goal line. If they down the ball between the 15 and 10, they get one point. If they down the ball between the 10 and 5, they get two points. If they down it between the 5 and goal line, they get three points. If the ball goes in the end zone, they lose one point. We play to 12 points. A byproduct of the drill is that you get good at downing punts.

We may have them do a forward roll as the ball is punted. They sprint down to cover the ball. The first man downs the ball, and everyone comes around the ball. We count to three and call out "bears" three times. We were the bears, so we used that term.

If they complain about the drill, I may run with them down to the 20-yard line and then punt past the end zone. I tell them to shut up and run the drill. I tell them when they gripe, it is a crack. We tell our players to listen for the other team to crack. When they start griping, they will crack. We want them to develop the attitude that if they hustle, something good will happen. So, we do not want them complaining about any aspect of the drill.

I hope I have given you some ideas that will help you in your program. If I can do anything for you, let me hear from you. Thank you.

ESTABLISHING A CHAMPIONSHIP PROGRAM

University of Oklahoma

I want to start out by saying it is a privilege to speak to you today. I want to tell you first and foremost, that I respect everything you do as a coach regardless of the level you work. I respect football coaches and the people that you are. I am from a family of coaches. My father was a long-time high school coach for 28 years. He was the defensive coordinator for the same head coach for 28 years. I lost my father when he was 53 years old, 12 years ago. I believed he was the wealthiest man in the world because he did what he loved. Every day was a great day for him. He had a lot of influence on a lot of young people, and I know you have that same influence.

It does not matter what level of football you are involved with. It all gets down to relating to young men and helping them succeed. Again, I respect this profession, and I respect the job all of you do to help young people to succeed, regardless of the money situations. Never lose sight of what the job is all about. That is helping young people reach their dreams and goals and helping them to succeed. If you do that, certainly you are going to have a great career and a great life.

I was fortunate to be a young person that could be in the lockerrooms. I was fortunate to be the son of a coach that took me with him in the lockerroom. I would encourage all of you that have families and have children to include them in your profession. Take them to the school, take them to the games, and bring them in the lockerroom.

It is nothing to see young kids all over the halls at Oklahoma. I have a young staff, and they have children. You walk through our hallways, and you will run into one of them. It is nothing to have a coach sitting at the meeting with a child on his lap. We are smart enough, and we can concentrate well enough to get the job done without that being a distraction. I encourage you to include your family in your life. It is important for them to know what you do and why you are gone so much.

After the bowl game, I was getting ready to go recruiting. My four-year old daughter does not think she sees me enough. So, I was getting ready to hit the road for recruiting a week after the bowl game. She asked me where I was going and I replied, "recruiting." She turned to her mother and asked "what is recruiting?" My wife said that I was going to get more players for the football team. My daughter said, "doesn't daddy have enough players at Oklahoma already?" The point is this. Even at four years old, they start to understand about the game. I encourage you to include your family in your coaching career.

I am going to speak on our philosophy and how we approach our situation at Oklahoma. I have only been at Oklahoma two years, and our staff was fortunate enough to go 13-0 and win the National Championship. Winning a national championship is special. The more you down play it, and the more you think about it, the more you put into perspective the job we did in just two seasons. In coming from where we were in two years with a team that had not had a winning team in five years, and had not been to a bowl game in five years, to come back and win the championship in two years, some special things had to happen. I will be the first person to tell you it was not just me. I have an incredible group of assistant coaches. If I did one thing right as a head coach, it was the fact that I hired good people to work with me. Again, a note for all of you, surround yourself with good people. I believe I have the best coaching staff in the country.

On top of all of this, how we approached our game plan with our players was important. We walked in and went to work. A lot of times, a new coach will come in and make statements to the effect that it will take a few years to get things going and wait until we get our players that we recruit on the field. Some coaches will tell everyone they will need three or four years to build the program up. When you do that, you are talking to the players that are going to be playing for you that season. You are telling the players that you have that you do not expect to win for three or four years.

Once I walked into the door and accepted the head coaching position, everyone of those players were MY players now. I told them they were mine. I assured them I was going to find out how to learn all of the parents of the players and that I would find a way to get to know every player. "You are my players. I am committed to you to win." That is all they heard from me from the beginning. I went on to tell them, "the sooner you accept us and take to us, the faster we will win." There has to be a commitment in that situation.

People ask me if I were afraid to jump out and put the expectations of winning out there. I said no for two reasons. First, I am not afraid to say it, because if I told my players to wait three years to expect to win, it may take us three years to win." You do not want to convince your players that it will take them three years to win. The other thing is this. People are going to expect to win regardless of what the coach tells them. You might as well go ahead and admit that you are going to win. You want to win, so you might as well tell them you want to win as soon as possible.

Our staff has always tried to raise the expectations of our team right off the bat. It is easy to do in Oklahoma. It is a great job that expects championships. Here is a school that you walk into and they have six national championships, and 36 conference championships. Are you going to try to temper those people and tell them not to expect championships? If you do, you are wasting your time.

I believe the more you expect, the more you will get. If you expect an undefeated season, and you only win 10 of 11 games, it sure beats the heck out of being 5 and 6. Expect a lot, and you have a better opportunity to get it. We walked in to Oklahoma and raised the expectations.

The other thing we did was to change the perception that we had of our team. Again, a lot of it is mental. I believe in it. I believe in being positive, and I believe in being confident. I believe the more you talk to your players that way, the more it becomes a part of their nature. A confident and positive player on the field is better than one that isn't.

Our players did not perceive themselves as being very good. The media wrote how bad they were for five years. They were told they could not win and that they did not have any talent. We did not have this, and we did not have that. That is all they heard. Eventually, it soaked into them, and the administration around them talked to them the same way. The fans read the papers every day so they felt the same way. A big part for us to win was to change our perception.

We had to change the players' perception of themselves first, and then it starts to filter out to everyone else. You need for the team to think correctly. It was important for them to know who they were, and to know what they had to do. They had to learn to conduct themselves like a winner.

I am smart enough to know that just changing the perceptions and raising the expectations do not give you the opportunity to win. I talk to our players about the fact that everyone in the game of football meets with the squad and talks about raising the expectations and changing the perceptions but, they just talk. This is what I told our players in our first meeting. I told them we had a long way to go, and I told them I was being honest with them.

When we started our first winter workouts, we had 20 players that had to fall out of the drills the first day. They could not make through the first workout. They were throwing up in the trash cans, pulling up with pulled muscles, and all kind of excuses. They were in bad shape.

The next day, I had to give my staff a pep talk in the coaches office. They had come from some good schools and were not used to that. They were not sure what they had gotten into. I told them to visit with their players and to pep them up. I reminded the coaches that the players had not practiced since the end of the regular season which ended around Thanksgiving. They had been off a long time and had not been required to work out. I told our staff the players were not ready for the type of workout we were initiating. I told them to give the players some time. We went through the winter and made a lot of progress. We make a lot of strides.

Probably, the best person I hired was our strength and conditioning coach, Jerry Schmidt. He is the guy that spent seven years with Coach Lou Holtz at Notre Dame. They won a national championship while he was there. He spent four years at the University of Florida, and they won a national championship while he was there. He has been with us for the last two years, and we have won a national championship. So, I told Jerry that he was not that lucky. "That does not keep happening to you just because you are lucky." He is good at what he does. You watch us practice. You will never see any of our players with soft bellies. Our players are trained up and are ready to go. It is because of Jerry Schmidt. But, we did not start out that way.

I do not mean to jump around, but what I was getting around to is the fact that everyone talks about changing their perceptions and raising their expectations. Everyone does that. What we talk a lot about is "earning the right to win." We talk about earning the right to expect those expectations. You can expect to go 13-0. You can say that. But, you have to earn the right to put that expectation up on the board.

When we meet with our players in January, we did not talk about what we might or might not do as far as winning or losing. We never put up a goal. I told the players we were a long way from putting up any goals on the board. I told them the first thing we were going to do was to talk about earning the right to talk about winning. I told them we did not have the right to talk about anything.

We told them we were going to break things down into stages, we broke it down where we had a winner's stage, where we learn how to be an athlete. I told them we had to get to a stage where we looked and acted like a college athlete was supposed to act. That meant they had to be able to run, and to meet the run times Coach Schmidt put in front of them.

They had to be able to lift a certain amount. They had to be better than they were at that time.

Our linebacker coach, Brent Vanables, is a 28-year old man, and he went down and out lifted everyone of our players. That should not happen. So, the first thing we wanted to do was to get our players to look like football players in Division I and the Big Twelve were supposed to look like. That was all we were going to focus on and this was before spring practice.

We had some fights in the winter program. We had a player that came to the early workouts late. He was All-Conference and was a good player. We run our winter program at 6:15 am for three days a week. On one of those three days, we do speed work, and the other two days we do agilities. The way we work out is something to see. We really go hard.

That same player that had been late three times in the first two weeks came in late again. I had him take a seat in the complex. We went ahead and finished the drill we were doing. After the drills, I told everyone to get back in line and that we were going to start over and do the drill again because of the player that was late. He sat there and watched the other players do the exercise. Those players wanted to kill that guy on the way out of the dressing room. I told the team the late player was going to be on the team or he was going to quit, one of the other. Now, I did not want anyone to quit the team. Of course, you lose players. Because some kids do not want to work. I would never ask a player to do something that I did not ask others to do. You will lose some players. I had told our players at least four times that I did not want any of the players to leave the program. But, I assured them they were going to conduct themselves like a team. If one player is going to do something, then all of them would do it.

I sat the player that was late down in front of the team and told him it was his choice. I told him the team would start over every day that he was late, or he could quit. He was not late again after that session. He became an All-American and All Big Twelve, and he played in the Hula Bowl this year. He had to learn some responsibility and some accountability to his teammates if he was going to play for us.

I mean what I say, but I am not one to go get one of my coaches up at 5 am in the morning to get that one player that is late to the workout and have him work extra. That is hard on the assistant coaches. I do not want to do that. Why should I make one of my assistant coaches get up early? If the player does not have enough responsibility to get to practice, then we are not going to play that person. They have to be accountable and responsible to their team.

We wanted to learn how to be athletes. We broke it down into three stages. The first stage was our winter conditioning. We had to learn to be an athlete and to conduct ourselves like Big Twelve athletes should. We wanted to get stronger and faster.

Our second stage was our spring practice. Now, I did not want them looking ahead to spring practice. I did not want them looking ahead to the next season. We wanted to take it in stages. Now, we were at spring practice, and we had to learn to play football and to play it correctly. When we got to Oklahoma, everyone was bragging about how good our defense was. It was all the media talked about. They insisted that we had a great defense. Of the twelve schools in the Big Twelve, we were seventh in scoring defense. I asked them what in the world were they talking about. In the past, Oklahoma won six national championships, and they were use to leading the nation in about every category. Now, they were bragging about the defense that ranked 12th in the conference. I assured them that we were not going to accept that mentality. Last year, we were number one in the Big Twelve in scoring defense. That makes a big difference.

In the spring, we had to learn to play football. It took a while. I can recall one specific incident that was an example of what we needeed to learn. Coach Steve Spurrier, Jr. is our receivers coach. One of the players came up to Coach Spurrier after practice one day. He had been demoted to second team that week. He had been outplayed. The player walked up to Coach Spurrier and said, "Coach, I do not know if you know it or not, but I do not play very well on the second team." Coach Spurrier looked at him and replied, "I do not think you will play any better on the third team. Look, you are going to earn your way on the

field." We had to teach this to them. We told all of them this was the way it was going to be. That is the only fair way to do it. It does not matter what year in school they are, what religion they are, or anything else. We did not care about anything except production. Needless to say, that player quit at the end of the spring.

The media started to make an issue out of the fact that we had lost our second-leading receiver and would not be able to throw the football. I asked someone how many passes that receiver that quit caught the year before. They told me he caught eight passes for the entire year. I assured them we would have a replacement that would catch at least eight passes. I was not real concerned about it. In the first game, we had Brandon Davis catch ten passes. But, we had to learn to be a team on the field, and we had to learn to play football.

Spring practice went very fast. We made some strides. Now, we were ready for the summer. It was a big concern for me. What would our team be like for the summer.? Summer practice can be a major factor in setting the tone for the up-coming season in college football.

We had excellent participation in our summer workouts. We had 85 to 90 percent of the players there for the entire summer. In the second part of the summer, we had 95 percent of the players working out at school. We had great participation, and it made a difference. We were making progress, and we were committed to winning. We had great participation, and we were acting like a team. We had great two-a-day practices and were getting ready for the season.

Now that we were acting like a team, we could start talking about expectations. Now, the players had a lot invested in the program. Now, we could start talking about expectations. The week before the first game, we could get up and start talking about our goals with our captains and with the team. What have we earned the right to expect? In that first year, we were 7-4 and lost in the Independence Bowl on a last-second field goal. But, we led in every single game that year. We showed some signs that we could be pretty darn good. We played some very good games during the season. We beat Texas A & M 51-5 at our place, and they were a nationally ranked team at the time. We showed some spurts of being a very good team. However, we were not good enough to finish off some of those games, and we ended up losing a few games for a lot of reasons.

Our players came back this year, and they realized the fact that we had a chance to be good, but we did not have enough to finish off those games we lost. Players go along with the lead of the coaches. I hear a lot of coaches talk about the games they lost. "Boy, we should have won that game. That ref — that fumble — that bad snap — we should have won." You will never hear me tell the players that we should have won a game. You will never hear me quoted as saying, "we should have won." I do not believe in it. You either do or you don't. It is as simple as that.

You heard me say we were 7-4 and ended up losing the Independence Bowl, and our record was 7-5. We were not good enough to win at that time. We made too many mistakes to win the game. We did not make enough plays to win the game. The big quote associated with me is "no excuses!" To be frank, I have never heard a good excuse. They all amount to the same thing. They all amount to losing.

I hear a lot of coaches talk about how young their team is. "Wait until next year. We are really young." In our national championship team, we have 24 freshmen and sophomores that are on our two-deep roster. We are younger than all but one team in our league. If you give your players a reason as to why they did not win, or if you are quoted as to why you did not win, they are going to latch on to that. That is my excuse. That is my reason not to win or to be successful. They all amount to the same thing.

I never acknowledge injuries, and I am never going to acknowledge how young we are, or anything that has to do with losing. The reason for this is because I never want one of my players to have an excuse not to succeed or to win. In the end, no one cares. My fans do not care. You may convince them in the newspapers that you are too young this year and to wait until next year. But, you are still trying to justify why you did win this year. I do not want our team to have a crutch as to why they did not win.

The things we developed this year as opposed to that first year was this. We developed the work habits and the discipline to finish off the games when we were ahead in the games. We were a better football team, and we were better prepared. We were in better condition. We were stronger than we were a year ago after another year of training. We were more disciplined in our regiment and in our fundamentals to finish off those games. We were a tougher team, so we could finish off those games when we were ahead. We were able to build leads that were larger than they were the year before. It was not enough to talk about it. We had to develop work habits, the discipline, and the toughness to earn that right to have those expectations.

That has been engrained into our players. They know they have to earn the right to have the expectations. You earn it by the way you work, the way you prepare mentally, and the way you prepare your body physically. You had to have a toughness about you to be able to succeed.

I will give you some parts of the things we list on building a team. This is what I go over with the players in the summer when we get together. I talk to them on how we are going to build our team.

Establish trust. Players have to trust and believe in one and another. Look at the two Super Bowl teams. How many times did you hear them talk about how they cared about each other as individuals and as a team. You can not get away from this idea. You have to find different ways to get the players close.

When I first went to Oklahoma, if we had eight players in the dinning hall, we would have them sitting at seven different tables. Now, you walk in our training table you will see eight players at a table that only seats six people. You have to find ways to get the players to care about one and another.

Establish discipline. All players want to be disciplined. The coach has to be strong enough to give it to them. I do not believe that all players should be treated the same. You treat them the way they deserve to be treated. For example, the player that walked in to our winter practice late several times. Finally, I had enough, and this is what I decided to do. I set the discipline that I think will be best for that player. The next player comes in late, but he has been on time for twelve straight weeks. He has never been late. He tells me his car broke down. I am going to believe that player. I am not going to run the whole team for him. You have to be smart in your judgment. Sometimes, you have to make some tough calls. You do not treat them all the same. You treat them the way they deserve to be treated.

Establish a work ethic. You must give a good effort. To me the best compliment you can receive is when someone tells you, "Coach, it is fun to watch your team because of how hard they play." I value that comment more than any other. We grade effort. We watch the tape of the game. After we critique the film for assignment and fundamentals, we will go back and go through it quickly to see who is playing fast and who is not playing fast. We look to see who is playing hard and who is not playing hard.

Create team unity and establish trust.

Have a philosophy of offense, defense, and special teams. You must stick with the philosophy.

Understand who you are. Understand what you do. A year ago, we had Coach Mike Leach as our offensive coordinator. At the end of that first season, he got the head coaching job at Texas Tech in December. We were excited for Mike, and we are still great friends. It was good for him. I was really excited for his as a head coach, even though I was losing my offensive coordinator after only having him for one year.

We had a meeting set for the day of our first practice for the Independence Bowl game. It was our first bowl game in seven years at Oklahoma. Our seniors had not been to a bowl game in their years at Oklahoma. I expected to walk into that meeting and have everyone all excited about the bowl game. Now, that day the press had leaked the story that Mike Leach was going to be the new head coach at Texas Tech. It was not official, but everyone knew that Mike Leach was going to get the Tech job.

I was a few minutes late from a press conference. I walked into the meeting room, and you could hear a pin drop. Mike Leach was in the room. It was like I had walked into a funeral. I looked around and did not realize what was the problem. I saw Mike leaning on the wall. Then it hit me. I knew what this was. They were scared. They were thinking that we would stink again on offense.

I went to the front of the room and started talking to them. This is what I said, "Guys, you do not have this figured out yet, do you? You used to lose assistant coaches around here all of the time. You guys used to play so bad you got them fired." They laughed and showed a little humor. "Now, you have played so well you got an assistant a head coaching job in one year." They broke up laughing. I told them it was ok for Mike to get the head coaching job at Texas Tech. It was good for our program because we had been successful.

The players are going to follow the lead of the head coach. If they feel that I accepted the fact that Mike was leaving and that it was OK with me, it would be OK with them. Now, I did not want to lose Mike, but I was happy for him. I assured the players that I had four other assistant coaches that knew what was going on with the offense. If you build your team right, your assistants will be able to make the adjustments. I promoted an assistant from within. I made Mike Mangino the coordinator. He was a smart coach, and he understood what we were doing. I hired another quarterback coach in Chuck Long, who was an excellent quarterback coach and knew the offense in two weeks. We went on to get 580 yards in the bowl game. We did this, and we did not change the system. The players did not have to change anything.

Defensively, we are going to run the same thing each and every year, each and every week, and we are going to adjust it as we need to. We have always been able to adapt to what the offensive teams are doing. We continue to change and adjust. They are gradual changes. The big part of what I am saying is to stick with what you do. Do not make wholesale changes every year. Kids will not get a hold of it. We feel the repetition over the years will pay off. Some players catch on quicker than others.

Establish a system that goes along with your philosophy. It is the same thing with the offense, defense, and special teams.

Work within your system. Continue to brush up on the system. Keep it dusted. I see coaches at the college level that are so regimented, they never change.

They never expand their offense or defense. What I am saying is this. Stick with what you do, but continue to work on it and evolve with what the offenses are doing. You make slight changes as you grow. I do not believe anything stays the same. Offenses catch up with defenses. Defenses catch up with offenses. But, you will never see us make wholesale changes. We will adjust and make changes as necessary.

Be consistent in how you teach your system. We want to let players hear terms over and over.

Create a positive learning environment. Make sure the players have fun while they work. Talk confidently and positively to players. Eventually they will believe you. You want the guy that isn't so good to think he is great.

After we lost our first game in that first year, our staff was really mad at our Sunday staff meeting. They could not wait until Monday in the team meeting to get after the players. In our staff meeting on Monday morning, I told the staff I did not want anyone of them ripping into the players telling them how bad they were in the game the week before. I told them I did not want them to tell their players that they were crappy and that they stink. If you tell the players they are no good, that is what they will believe. I reminded them that we had to play with those same players the next six games. The point is that you have to be smart in how you teach and coach your players.

As hard as it is at time, we will never accept a losing performance. I will not tell a kid that his effort is not good enough. I will tell him here is how you should to do it. Even if the player can't do it, I will tell him how it should be done. Never tell a kid that he is lousy, or that he can't do something. Eventually he will believe you. Teach them in a manner where they will accept it and try to change.

Acknowledge performance and NOT potential. We are going to play players that play hard and make the most plays. We all have seen those unbelievable athletes. They look good, but when they get on the field, they do not make any plays. You have a little kid that no one pays any attention to and you put him on the field and he makes all of the plays. Play him. Don't play potential; play players.

If we play harder, smarter, and more aggressively than our opponent, we will win. It takes no talent to play smart, to play hard, and to be aggressive and to be tough. I preach this to our players all of the time. If we play a team that is more talented than we are, and they play harder and smarter and are more aggressive, they are probably going to win. Most of the time, a team is not going to do all three of those things in a game. Again, it takes no talent to do that.

Coaches must have great respect with one another and a great working relationship. Keep egos out of the office. Coaches must be willing to help each other, and they must be willing to help other coaches on the other side of the ball.

I read in a paper a comment that one of my assistant coaches had said about me. He was quoted as saying, "Bob Stoops has no ego." I thought about it and finally agreed with him. I appreciated that comment. If you are a coach, you have an ego. But, you have to be smart enough to control your ego and put it aside. I think I have as small an ego as possible.

I have no original ideas. Everything I do I have gotten from other people. I have been around a lot of great head coaches. I start with Hayden Fry to Bill Snyder, to Steve Spurrier. The person I identify with the most is Coach Spurrier who has been a great mentor to me. My point is that, as coaches, we steal everything from others. I have stolen a lot from all three of those guys. I do not claim to know anything. I go about my business the best I can like all of you. I am smart enough to use my assistant coaches. I do not get in their way. I use them in about every decision I make. I run it by them first. I will ask them what they think. I will go over our approach to the game each week. "What do you think of that?" They are not afraid to tell me what they think. They know I will not let my ego stand in the way. I am able to use my coaches. They know they can approach me about anything.

The same thing with our assistant coaches. They do not let their ego get in the way of the team. They will work with each side of the ball to help the team. If the defense needs work in one area, the offense will give the defense a good look at that phase of the game to help the defense. We do not get all caught up in who looks good. We want to make the team better. We help each other out to make sure the team is better.

Be sure the players take the responsibility of winning and losing with the coaches. As coaches, we always take the blame for our players. "It is my fault." I am not talking about the media. I am talking about in the meeting room and one-on-one. If we have worked on a certain play all week, and we have tested them on it on Friday before a game, and then the player blows the play in the game, when that player comes off the field and comes to me, he better look at me and tell me, "Coach I blew it." I tell him, "Your're right, we worked on that play all week." I do not want him to come to me and tell me that he has never seen that defense or that stunt. I want them to acknowledge to the coaches that they should have done better if we have covered what they need to do. That is being accountable for losing and winning.

A couple other things related to our philosophy relates to our offense and defense. Here are some of the things we list as our keys to success on defense. These things have not changed in several years. Be great hitters and tacklers. Work hard on tackling drills.

Since the national championship game, I have had a lot of coaches tell me how well we tackled. I appreciate that because we work on it. There is not a day in practice that we do not work on tackling. When we do our inside drill, we run up and butt the man. We make sure we get our body on the man. When we work in practice, it is the same thing. We do not run by them, or tag them. We are cautious. We do not go to the ground much, but we are going to get into position to lock up on all of our tackling.

Eight days before the Orange Bowl, we had a live scrimmage. It was an all-out scrimmage. I wanted to make sure our team was going to tackle well in that game. Also, I wanted our receivers and running backs to get the feel of being hit, so they would hold on to the ball when they got hit in the game. In the first quarter, we popped up two of them. But, it did make a big difference to our team in tackling. We actually scrimmaged two days in a row. We went live seven days before the game. We wanted good blocking and tackling and to be sharp in the game.

There are a lot of schemes. It gets down to fundamentals that win games. It takes good execution and playing hard to win games. Schemes are overrated.

We expect great effort on defense. Everyone must get to the ball. Again, we grade effort. Play physical and be aggressive. To me, there is no replacement for toughness.

Be disciplined with responsibility and technique. We must be able to depend on each other. To me, it is unacceptable not to know what to do. The two things that upset me the most is the player who does not know what to do, and the player who will not play hard.

Our defensive philosophy is to stop the offense immediately. We want to get three-and-out as much as we can get them. We want as many turnovers as we can get. We shoot for 50 percent of getting the three-and-outs. We want to give our offense field position. We have come close to that through the years.

First and foremost, our defense starts with dominating the run game. Going into the Orange Bowl, most talk was about Chris Wenke and the passing game. To us, the main focus for us was Travis Minor and the running game. First and foremost, we wanted to take away the running game. If a team can run and pass on your defense, you are in trouble. We want to force the offense to throw the ball. We want to get pressure to the quarterback and make it difficult for him to read coverages. Late in the third quarter, Florida State did not try to run the ball on us. When you do not have to worry about the run, you can change things up and give the offense problems.

We want to take away offensive strengths by playing percentages. I heard Bobby Bowden talking several years ago when I was coaching at Kansas State. Coach Bowden said, "if you try to take away everything the offense does, you end up taking away nothing." If you try to stop everything, you end up stopping nothing. That has always stuck with me. If you spend all of your time working on the crazy plays a team runs, and you do not work on their meat and potatoes, you are going to be in trouble. Everyone has some true offensive plays that they love to run. You have to take away what they like to do. Take away their best plays, and then react to the trick plays as best as you can prepare for with good fundamentals. The players need to know what they have to stop. You can not give them 15 plays to stop. Give them the most important

Be great in critical situations. This includes third down, the red zone, and goal line. We really gear into possession downs. Florida State was 1 for 17 on third and fourth downs. We stopped them 14 of 15 times on third down, and 2 of 2 on fourth down.

Our offense seems to be extremely complicated, but it isn't. It is fairly simple what we do. We are going to force the opponent to defend the entire field.

One of the best things we do on offense is to limit the number of plays we go into a game with. We go through our script on Monday. We adjust it on Tuesday. By Wednesday and Thursday, we go through the script in pass skeleton over and over again. Our guys are ready to run the plays. We do not have that many plays going into a game. If we add a play to our script, Coach Mangino will tell us to take one other play out. We want to be able to execute.

We want to force the defense to defense to defend the entire field. We have had as many as 12 to 14 players catch passes in a game. We get the ball to all of our backs. We do not want the defense to be able to zero in on us and say that this is the one guy we have to stop. We want to get the ball in the hands of several players, and we want to give them a chance to make a play when they get the ball.

We take what the defense gives us. A big part of our success this year was our ability to run the football. We spent a lot of time in the spring working on the running game. It was improved this year. We ended the year with 55-percent pass and 45-percent run. Our running back had 24 rushing touchdowns. The running game helped us be a more consistent offense. We want to be a balanced team.

We want to be able to audible to any play in our system. We want to use the run game to complement the pass. A big part of our success this year was the consistency of our running game.

We want to keep the defensive front seven on the run. We want to keep them out of their comfort zone. The big defensive linemen love to see that I-forma-

tion offense come right at them. That is what they are used to doing. Our system is going to force them to chase us play after play.

The offensive line's priority is to protect the quarterback. Our line only gave up 16 sacks this year. We do not hold on to the ball. We throw the ball by making quick decisions. We get it to a player and let him make the play.

We mix high-risk passes in with our high-percentage passes. We are not back there holding on to the ball. We mix the deep balls with the other passes. We want to get yards after the catch and yards after the hit.

I want to close with a couple of things. Our practices are open at any time. We may announce to the media that practice is closed for a certain period. That is not for the coaches. I want all the coaches to understand this. Our practice is never closed to high school coaches. The only thing we ask is that you let us know a few days ahead of time. We want to have a good relationship with all coaches. It is my feeling for coaches to share ideas with them any time. Let us hear from you, and we will find ways to work it out. Any way we can help you we are willing.

Our summer camp for juniors and seniors is June 3 through June 5. The camp for young players is June 5 through June 8.

I told you that I lost my father at 53 years old. That was 12 years ago. He looked as I do. Not that I look that good, but I am not overweight. He played fast-pitch softball at age 53. He could still beat out a bunt to first base. He looked great, and appeared to be in great health. He never had a health problem, and he never smoked, and never drank alcohol. He appeared to be in good health. I lost my dad at the end of a football game. It was a double-overtime game, and he suffered a heart attack and never lived to reach the hospital. I want to encourage all of you to get a physical exam before you start each season. You are around doctors during the season, and you can take time to get checked. Make sure all of your players and assistant coaches get checked. Make sure your wife and children get checked. The best thing you can do for your family is to take care of yourself. At age 40, I get checked every year. Make sure you are in good health.

There is too much good medicine out there not to take advantage of the situation. Don't wait until it is too late.

When I was at Florida, Coach Spurrier's wife started pushing for all of the people having anything to do with the football program to have a physical exam. We found a young GA that was only 23 years old had a form of cancer. Do you think that young man would have had that check up on his own? He is healthy today because he did get checked, and they found it early enough to do something about it. Again, it takes very little to do that. The best thing you can do for your family is to make sure you are in good health. I encourage you to do that.

I will open it up for questions now. I have enjoyed being here.

EAGLE DEFENSE AND ZONE BLITZ PACKAGE

University of Oklahoma

It is a pleasure to be here to share some thoughts on football. My father was a high school coach and teacher for twenty-eight years until he died. We have a long history in football coaching in my family. My brother, Bob, is the head coach at Oklahoma. My youngest brother, Mark, is at the University of Houston. We all were secondary coaches. We all enjoy the profession. I respect the profession and feel honored to be at the University of Oklahoma.

We run an eagle package and are a 50-front team for the most part. On normal situations and running downs, we are in a five-man front. We feel that is the best defense to be in to stop the running game. Against Florida State, we did some different things, because we had to protect ourselves against the passing game. We played a lot more two-deep and weren't as gap-sound as we would like to be.

We are going to use eight men in the box on every running-down situation. I'll show you how we integrate our safeties. Our safeties are the key players in our defense. Our defensive line has one-gap responsibility. We don't have any two-gap rules for the line. We fit everything to our safeties and our linebackers. Our strong and free safeties have to work with our Mike and Will linebackers on everything we do.

First, I want to show you some of our alignments to different formations. I know high school coaches see a variety of formations without a lot of personnel changes in the offenses. We make our calls according to the personnel we see on the field. But, you must be able to adjust to all formations. We'll start with some of the more basic formations and go on from there.

The first alignment is against a pro set, with two running backs, a tight end, and a wide receiver to either side. Our down linemen will shade to the tight end. We play our nose guard in a shade on the center

to the tight-end side in a square stance. The strong tackle and end, which we call Sam, play 5- and 9-techniques to the tight end side. To the split-end side we are in a 3- and 5-technique.

We play with a wide and shortside corner in our defense. We don't go left and right. We put our best cover guy into the field. That enables us to do some other things to the other side. Our safeties play strong and free. If the offense trades a tight end from one side to the other, our safeties will trade also. But the safeties are very similar. We could get away with staying where we are. What we ask them to do is pretty simple.

From this front we will play man-free coverage. We lock up man-to-man on the wide receivers with the corners, while the strong safety has the tight end. The free safety is free. The Sam backer goes to the flat to his side. The Mike backer goes to the strong-side curl area and the Will backer has the weakside flat.

The strong safety keys the tight end. If he comes vertical, he takes him deep. If he goes to the flat, he releases him to the Sam backer. If he comes underneath and crosses, the Will takes him. The strong safety on the cross or the flat route sits in the hole and watches.

The free safety is aligned at ten yards and reading the end man on the line of scrimmage to his side. Once the tackle shows pass, he is pushing to the middle right away. The only thing which will bring the free safety up to the weakside will be an option or an off tackle, where he reads the hard down block. If he reads that, he attacks downhill.

The strong safety is the eighth man in the box from this adjustment. He is the one who figures into the run support, which I'll get into later.

VS PRO SET

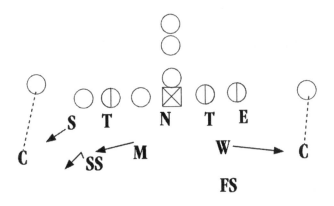

If the offense goes to a twin set with both wide receivers to the same side, we play it exactly the same. The strong safety stays on his side and reads the tight end. The linebacker's drops don't change. We bring both corners to the same side, because we want to look like we are always in man-free coverage.

VS TWINS

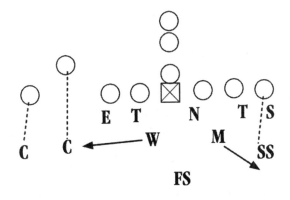

Our defensive line is not worried about getting their hands on defensive people to keep them off the linebackers. If we play a true veer team, that becomes a different story. But for normal offensives, we turn the D-line loose. We tilt our Sam backer so he can see inside. It is a slight tilt toward the ball. He looks at nothing but the tight end.

We work hard on the alignment of our safeties. We tell the high safety to align at ten yards. Where you align your low safety is very, very, important. What you tell your strong safety is tremendously important. If they get too wide or tight, they can take themselves right out of the play. We never tell him to get up tight to the line where he can't see and feel

his way around. He has to play off the people in front of him. We spend a lot of time with our safeties and linebackers getting to the football on time.

The safety has to be able to adjust inside if the linebacker gets too wide and doesn't bounce the ball outside. If the linebacker scrapes too wide, and the safety is outside him, it is the safety's fault. He has to play off what the linebacker does. The strong safety aligns at five yards.

He is watching the split of the wide receiver. If the wide receiver cracks back, the corner gives a warning and tightens down to play run support.

If we get long motion by their backs, we generally get out of the man free and into some sort of zone coverage. What they are trying to do is get a back up the sideline against a mismatch. In the man-free concept, if the wide receiver gets a tight split to the tight end, the corner should loosen up so he can see. If the wide receiver cracks, and the ball bounces, the corner can react to the ball. Up until that time, we are in a bump- and-run alignment.

If the offense comes out of the I formation and gets into a weak halfback set, we make an adjustment. They are trying to out gap us to the weakside. If we are in a defense where our strong safety is low, we make an ACE check. That means we are going to bring the strong safety high and the free safety low. We don't want people out-flanking us to the weakside. You could bump your linebackers over, but we do it with our secondary.

If we check to an ACE, Sam has the tight end man-to-man. The strong safety becomes the high safety and read the last man on the line of scrimmage, which is the tight end.

We align our corners head up to the outside eye on the wide receivers. We want to take away the fade route. We feel we can knock down slants. We play the splits for alignment. If they get wide, we move inside on our alignment. When we are playing this particular defense, all of the corner's help is to the middle of the field. We don't have help to the outside. That is why the fade and corners are hard to play.

ACE

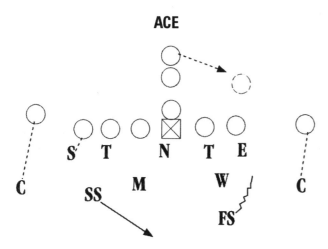

Our man coverage is color-coded. We call them brown, silver, and purple. Each color has a different technique. In brown coverage we never chase a receiver underneath the coverage. We teach the corner to read the crack back. If he sees the crack coming, his eyes open up immediately to the swing back coming on the swing route. We don't chase the receiver under. We focus on the next man to that side. That is a good coaching point in playing man free.

The next adjustment we make is called "EAGLE 43." That is quarter run support, with three deep behind it. Later, I will cover the options and I will show you why we call it "43." We do this because you can't play true quarter coverage any more. The way people are attacking the defense with the run makes it hard to get the eighth man in the box.

In this defense, the strong safety is low, and the free safety is high. Before the ball is snapped, our corner bails out and gets on the inside eye of the receiver to take away the post move. The corner is responsible for the deep third. The free safety is going to the middle third.

We want the free safety to set in the hole and give help on the dig routes. We want the corners to come off the dig routes and play the backside post routes.

The strong safety's read doesn't change. He reads the tight end. If the tight end blocks, he looks to fit up into the strongside B-gap.

The Sam, Mike, and Will linebackers' drops don't change. If the offense play-action passes and doesn't release the tight end, we still have three defenders to play their two receivers. If the tight end goes vertical and crosses, the strong safety is all over him. The linebackers drop into their areas, and we are three deep. If they motion the flanker to the split-end side, the corner goes with him and we end up in man free.

43-EAGLE

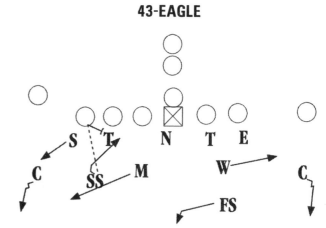

Those adjustments are good against great running teams. If we are playing a team with great wide outs, like Florida State, we have to change our coverages. They were a two-back running team, but had a great passing attack. You can't play the corners in man free and three deep. The corners can't match up with the wide outs, and you have to do something to help them. There are a couple of ways we like to do that.

The first thing we do is roll up and play quarter-quarter-half. We play the free safety in half coverage to the weakside. The strong safety is low, and the free safety is high, but he can't be involved in the running game. The strong safety is still reading the tight end. If the field corner sees action away, he is responsible for the post route. He has to get inside and stop the post.

Play action to the tight end, the Will backer has to give help on the fifteen yard dig route. That is how we give help to the boundary corner. We call it "43-CLOUD WEAK."

43 CLOUD

If we need help to the field side, we give a weak call. Every time we call weak, the safety run support has to change. It is a call we give to our linebackers. If we call weak, the free safety becomes the eighth man in the box. The strong safety has half coverage to the field. We show the same look each time and move late.

In the weak call, we bump our Linebacker half a step toward the tight end. They know they have help to the split-end side. They fast flow on anything to the weak side. We call this *WEAK-ROLL*. Our *CLOUD* call is weak and the *ROLL* call is strong. We are rolling to the tight-end side of the field. The field corner is playing a two-deep corner technique, with the strong safety in two-deep cover behind him. The Sam backer plays man-to-man on the tight end.

If the tight end goes vertical, the Sam backer is all over him. The Mike backer expands to the curl to flat, if the tight end goes vertical. If we get motion involved, we check to free man. We still feel we have them three-against-two.

WEAK-ROLL

We have four base coverages. We bring pressure out of these coverages. We have zone blitzes, as well as linebacker blitzes. But anytime we blitz a linebacker, we must change our run support. If we send the Will backer on a blitz, we have to bring the free safety down to replace him. If you bring Mike or Sam, the strong safety replaces them. We run zone blitzes in our package. That is the pass section of this defense. I will cover how the run defense coordinates with the pass coverage.

In our conference, we see teams that can run the ball as well as throw it. We played Nebraska. They are the best run offensive team in the country. I can show you how to defend it, but a lot of time, their guys are better than your guys. Against teams that run the ball that well, you have to go to some adjustments that can help you. I think what we run is the best run defense you can be in.

It doesn't matter which safety is high and which one is low. We play it the same. For the clinic talk, I'll talk about the strong safety in the low position. Our strong safety is a big guy. He is the player we like to get in the box.

On any lead play strong, most people try to scoop the nose guard. I'm going to show you some tape later. You are not going to believe what our strong safety does. Our strong safety is an incredible football player. If the offense runs a lead play strong, our strong safety is the eighth man in the box. As soon as the tight end base blocks, our strong safety is flying to the B-gap. The Mike backer fills the B-gap as big as he can. We want him to get on their side of the line of scrimmage. His job is to turn the ball into the safety. He does not let the ball come inside of him.

The reason we do that is because the Will backer is responsible for the backside flat. You can't have you Will backer fast flow to the strongside and be responsible for the weakside flat. Any play action away from leads him to step into the backside A-gap. If it is a play-action pass, he turns and runs out to pick up the tight end coming across or the arrow route to the flat. On a run, he is the cut-back player.

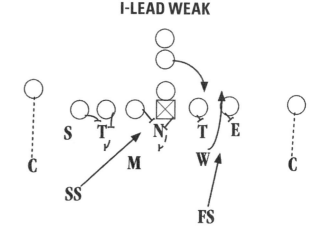

I-LEAD STRONG

I-LEAD WEAK

If the offense runs the lead play weak, they will combo the nose guard up to the Mike backer. We have the strong safety low. If the offense is not an option team, we play it this way. The Mike backer is fast flowing and filling downhill. He can beat the combo block because he is flying downhill. Everything we do with our linebackers is all by angles. All our linebackers attack the angle of the back. We don't attack the play.

When we teach our linebackers reads. We are going to get fast flow, an off-tackle read, a lead read, or split flow. Those are the four reads we teach our linebackers. The depth of our linebackers is five yards. They are very, very deep. They do a lot of faking up in the line, but to play the way we want to play, their heels are at five yards. That lets us attack at the right angle on the off-tackle play and downhill on the lead play.

The Mike backer is fast flowing because the strong safety is low taking the cut back run. Teams are now scooping through the backside for the safety so they can cut back to that side. If the safety is late filling, the offense can create a seam in the cut-back lane. We have to work hard on the strongside 5-technique closing down hard so the tackle can't get up on the safety. If the defensive tackle lets the blocker off on the safety, he has to close the cut-back lane off.

On the lead play weak, the free safety has to be aware of the play-action pass first and run second. He can't jump into the line and try to make a tackle. The Will backer keeps his outside arm free and spills the play back to the Mike backer.

Our defensive line is playing in shade techniques. We are not a reading team. We power step off and read on the run. We attack people. To the open side, we my be a slight bit wider in our alignment. Against a lead option team, if the tackle can pin your Will backer inside, you are in for a lot of trouble. Our alignment depends on the type of team we are playing.

The next play is the power G off-tackle play. We pretty much play this play the same on both sides. What we see is a double team on our strongside 5-technique, hoping to get off for the backside linebacker. We get a down block by the onside guard on the nose guard. The center blocks off for the pulling guard. The backside guard pulls for the front side Mike backer through the off-tackle hole. The fullback is kicking out the Sam backer.

Let me cover some coaching points here. The Mike backer cannot run through the B-gap. That gap is reserved for Will. If the fullback takes an off-tackle angle, Mike takes that angle also. The Will backer flies across the backside blocks and runs through the B-gap.

The Sam backer has to close the area as quickly as he can. He is not worried about keeping the down block off the tackle. He attacks the fullback through his crotch. We don't tell him to bounce or wrong arm, we tell him to attack it. We don't want to go too flat and let the fullback log him inside. That lets the ball bounce too quickly.

Our wide corner is our best cover man. We don't want him making all the tackles. Our safeties are much better tacklers.

The Mike backer is coming tight in a scrap outside the Sam backer. But, he can not let the ball get back inside of him. We want the ball to bounce. The strong safety is tight fitting outside the Mike backer. The strong safety can't be worried about getting cracked. We tell him to go straight ahead. Never go to the crack or through a crack. If the safety tries to cross face the crack and all that stuff, all that does is hurt the corner. The corner has to play the crack-and-go route of the receiver and play run support.

We run a drill in practice to help the corner recognize the crack-and-go route. We teach the corner to read the shoulders of the wide receiver. If our safety is doing what he is supposed to, the receiver has to get flatter to the line and get his shoulders parallel to the line to make the crack on him. If the shoulders of the receiver are pointed up field, the corner has to stay on top of him. They can't be too quick to react to the tackle.

We play it exactly the same way to the weakside. The only difference is the free safety is coming to make the tackle.

OFF-TACKLE G POWER

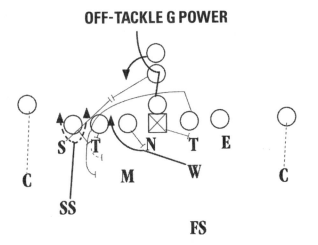

One thing we have tried to teach our safeties to do is to use their ears. We can let them stand back there with their eyes closed and tell whether it is a run or pass. If it is a run, they can hear the collision of bodies and hits in the line. A pass play doesn't have that type of hitting. That is a second-sense feeling that gives them an advantage.

We teach the counter the same way as we do the power play. It is the same play except different people are blocking it. But, we teach it the same way.

If both backs jab away or split flow, the linebackers start and pick up the guard's flow which should be right in front of them. We tell the end to make the second trapper go behind the pile. We want to disrupt the play.

Let's go to the option. We see every option known to man. The option we are seeing most is the lead option. On this play the Sam backer has the quarterback, and the strong safety has the pitch. The key to the way we play this play is our 5-technique. We tell our 5-technique, if the tight end spends time trying to help the tackle, get on him. The Mike backer better be outside on the inside half of the quarterback.

If the tight end goes straight up on the Mike backer, the 5-technique has the inside half of the quarterback, and the Sam backer is in the alley.

The Sam backer, 5-technique, and Mike backer all work together on this play. If the offense long times the 5-technique, the Mike and Sam backers have to be there. If they go straight up for the Mike backer, the 5-technique and Sam backer are there. The play is all based on how good you are at the 5-technique and how the offense tries to block it.

The Sam backer slow plays the quarterback. He never attacks the quarterback. We want our pursuit to get to the quarterback. He stays on the line of scrimmage and pursues down the line if the ball is pitched.

We play it exactly the same on the other side. The end is slow playing the quarterback, and the tackle or Will backer will be forcing from the inside. The free safety runs to the alley for the pitch.

LEAD OPTION

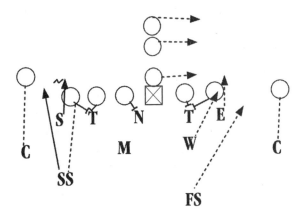

What we see from Nebraska is the G-pull scheme. They pull the guard around a down block by the tackle. What the offense has created is another gap for which the defense has to be responsible. They are running the fullback through the B-gap to get on the Will backer. They pull the guard to log the defensive end. If the defensive end stays outside the log block, and the linebacker stays inside the fullback, the offense has a gap to run the quarterback through. The safety is running for the alley.

We try to get help from the 3-technique to cross face the down block. We don't want the 5-technique to widen and create a big gap. The key coaching point to this play is the free safety. We tell him as he is on his way to the alley, he never runs by the quarterback. If the quarterback gets through the seam, he has to pull back and attack the quarterback. We play it the same way on the other side.

OPTION G-SCHEME

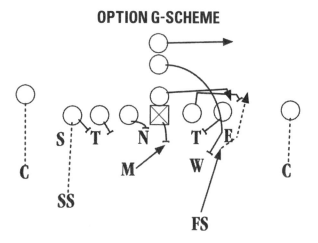

Let me show you what we do with a two-tight ends set with two backs. This kinds of fits in with our zone-blitz scheme. We want everything to look the same. We line up with a tight 9-technique to the second tight-end side. The rest of the alignment is like the regular eagle defense. The boundary corner aligns in the C-gap on the weakside at linebacker depth.

If the formation is with two tight ends and two wide receivers, we align with our 9-technique toward the second tight end. We look like a quarter coverage team in the secondary. Before the ball is snapped, we bring up our free safety into the C-gap. We always have a C-gap player in the secondary. We always set our strength into the field.

TWO TIGHTS/ONE BACK

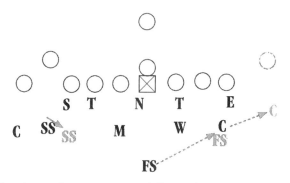

Let's get into our zone blitz schemes. This first blitz is called "RIP-DOGS." We are going to bring two dogs. We are going to blitz the Sam and Mike backers toward the weak 5-technique side. This is a first-and-ten call, when we are expecting a play-action pass. All these are field or strong calls. If it is in the middle of the field, we call strong calls. If the ball is on the hashmark, we call field calls. We flip-flop our D-line. The wide corner, strong safety, Sam backer, nose guard, and end always go to the field. The boundary corner, and 3- and 5-technique always go to the boundary.

On this blitz, the strong 5-technique is ripping flat all the way down into the A-gap. The Mike backer starts up field and comes tight off the 5-technique through the B-gap. If they run the lead play, he has to bounce it outside. The strong safety does not do anything differently. He cheats up into the C-gap and is in position to make the tackle. If it is a play-action pass, the strong safety sits over the top of the tight end and works out underneath the number one receiver. The Will backer goes to the number two receiver to the strongside. The weakside end goes under the number one receiver to the weakside, and we are three deep behind them.

The Will backer is fast flowing behind the Mike backer. We don't tell him to flow over the Mike backer, because he may get too wide. If the Mike backer gets too wide, the Will backer has to slow down and cover the bend back if it is a run. We want a guy under and over the receivers. The backs are not getting out. If they do, we have a sack. The tight end may stay in, but they can't release and block at the same time. Either the backs or the tight-end have to stay in and block.

RIP DOG

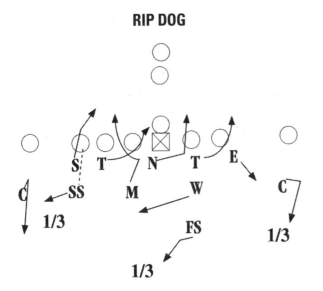

If there is a tight end away from the call, we get an automatic *CHEAT* call. If we have a tight end away from the call, we are in a 4i and tight 9-technique. The Sam backer walks out and cheats back. Everything else is the same. We are over and under all receivers and bring five rushers. It is a good defense versus the run, but it is not great against the option.

RIP DOG VS TWINS

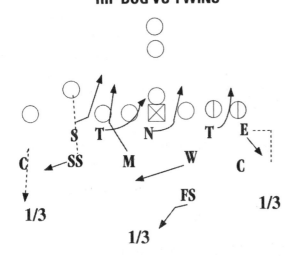

We have to make adjustments to handle things the offense may do. If the offense motions to a one-back set away from our call, we bump the Will backer out to the motion. If they line up in that spread, the Will backer would line up out there. The Will backer is used to playing pass coverage so we give him the flat cover. We give an *EDDIE* call to the zone-blitz end. That means, he drops into the middle, instead of outside. Anytime the offense has two speed receivers into the boundary, that is how we make the adjustment.

EDDIE

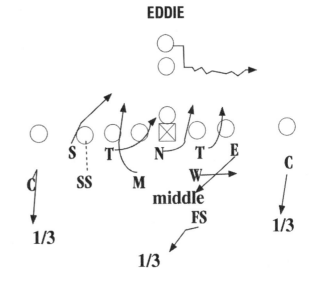

Anytime we play a one back-set, the flat-cover man always plays seam to flat. He never runs to the flat. We are going to be off the line five to six yards and disrupting routes. The flat player plays the seam and never goes to the flat until someone takes him there.

If the offense sets up in a one-back trips set, we get a *CHEAT* call to the backside. We walk the Sam backer out on the trips set. The strong safety is on the number two receiver that way. The corner is on the number one receiver who is wide. The free safety cheats over the ball. The Will backer has to cheat toward the strongside slightly. He has to get under the number three receiver in the trips set. The strong safety sits on number two and carries him deep if he goes vertical. The Will backer does the same thing with the number three receiver. The corner is on the number one receiver and is in the deep zone. To the backside, it is played the same as any tight end.

VS TRIPS

If the offense gets into a twin set strong and a tight end and split back weak with one back, we have a coaching point for the drop end. We are still coming with the zone blitz, but now, the drop end can't run to the flat. If he does, he gives the tight end the seam. He has to ride him up the seam. If we are getting hurt weak by the wide receiver and tight end, we adjust the Will backer to the weakside, cushion the strong safety in the strong seam, and get the drop end into the flat.

SPREAD ADJUSTMENT

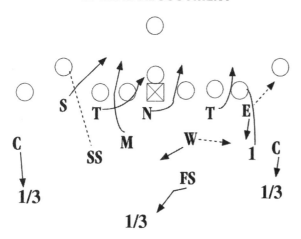

Against two tight ends and a double flanker, there are some similar adjustments to make. We use our two-tight ends adjustment. We bring the Will backer to the middle of the field. The strong safety aligns in a four-deep position and cheats to the line before the snap. He sits over the tight end and reads. The strong safety and drop end have the flats, but they don't run there until someone takes them there. We are three deep behind it. If they brought four vertical patterns, we would play the two corner and two safeties like four-over-four.

TWO TIGHTS/TWO FLANKERS

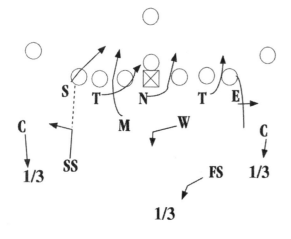

The other zone blitz we run a lot is called OPPOSITE CROSS FIRE. That means we are going to the middle third with our strong safety. The free safety is a hole player in the middle and the Mike and Will are blitzing to the strongside in a crossing stunt. Mike goes first and fires through the strongside A-gap and Will fires through the strong B-gap with the nose going through the weakside A-gap. The free safety checks for the lead play and takes the tight end.

OPPOSITE CROSS FIRE

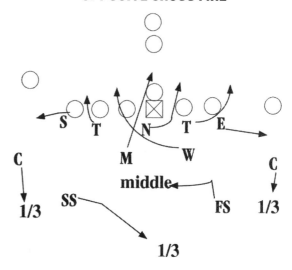

There are a number of cross charges we use with our linebackers. We can send the nose through the strong side B-gap, with the Mike and Will backers crossing in the strong and weakside A-gaps.

OPPOSITE CROSS FIRE

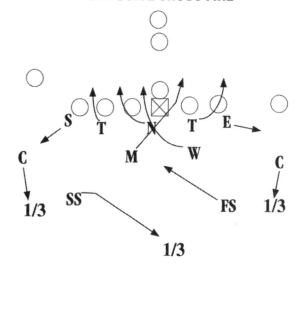

If the offense puts two speed receivers into the boundary, we make a different adjustment. The Will backer is running a blitz, so he can't adjust outside. The free safety moves out and gives the EDDIE call to the drop end. The drop end drops to the middle and plays the free safety's position. The end is never going to drop to the flat with two speed receivers that way. He is going to the middle.

CROSS EDDIE

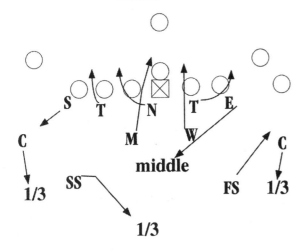

The other zone blitz we like is our "G-BLOOD-CRASH." We bring the weak corner on a blitz and run an inside stunt with the 3- and 5-techniques.

G-BLOOD-CRASH

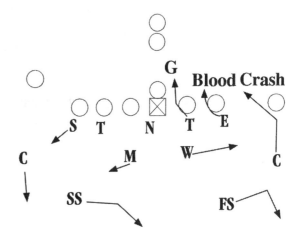

This scheme has been good for us. I know it doesn't fit everyone's program. It is really good against the two-backs running game. But, you have to have a system. You have to stick with it and believe in it. That is one thing we did. It took us two years to get our system in place for our kids to understand. This was one of those years when everything went right for us. We have a great coaching staff and great players. We had great team chemistry. If there is one thing that made our team, that was it. They played for the guys next to them. You don't get that in a lot of places. We were fortunate to get in that position. To play as well as we did down the stretch is a credit to a lot of people.

I really appreciate you being here. Thanks.

WHY AND HOW THE ONE BACK OFFENSE

Purdue University

I did grow up here in the midwest. Louisville is in the midwest, I guess. I had a brother that lived in Louisville for about six years, and I did serve time at Purdue as an assistant coach from 1983 to 1986. We came down to Louisville during that time and it was an easy trip for us. Anyway, I grew up in the midwest.

I wanted to play football in the Big 10 but was not good enough. I went out west where I could play college football. You learn a lot of things by getting involved with a different culture and a different part of the country. I went to school at Montana State. In Montana, they say "men are men, and sheep are nervous."

I will never forget the time I spent in Wyoming. While I was in Wyoming, I learned what the three biggest lies of a Wyoming cowboy are. If you have been west you will certainly appreciate this. The three biggest lies of a Wyoming cowboy are interesting. These three guys are sitting at the bar. The first cowboy states "the pickup truck is paid for." The second cowboy said "I won this belt buckle at the rodeo." The third cowboy said "I was just trying to help that sheep across the fence." Those are some of the things you learn by coaching in the west.

I am going to talk football now. I want to thank all of the coaches for the job you do with young people. All of you are in a leadership position in one way or another. As a college coach, I can appreciate the influence you have on young people. I guess I am a dinosaur because I am very concerned about our game of football. I am concerned about the moral decay, if you will, that is taking place in the sports world. I am very concerned about the direction our young people are going in. Young people need a lot of help today. Any help you can give them will be appreciated. We seem to be spending more and more time with young players. We recruit the cream of the crop. Any help you can give in social skills and anger control is very im-

portant to us. We did not have to deal with those issues a few years ago. But today, it is a changing landscape. We appreciate the effort of coaches of young players.

I have been fortunate at Purdue. I have been there four years, and we have had some degree of success. We have played in four bowl games during those four years.

People have asked me how did we accomplish that feat. I tell them I will show you how we did it. Then, I pick up my brief case and open it up. They think something magic is going to come out of the brief case that has allowed us to be successful. But, you know that is not the way it works. We have been successful for a number of reasons. One reason has been our coaching staff. When we came to Purdue, we changed the staff intact. At the college level, you have a head coach and nine assistants. You get to have two GA's. Actually, when we came to Purdue 11 of those 12 were new. We only had to hire one coach. We hit the ground running. We all knew what each other was doing.

We did have a little bit of a honeymoon on the schedule. That is something you may not be able to arrange on your level. We can't arrange a favorable schedule very often, although I wish I could, at least every other year. We did not play Ohio State or Michigan our first two years at Purdue. I am no fool, I know we had a favorable schedule those first two years.

We had some players that stepped up and played very well. Also, we had an element of surprise going for us. We were a mystery for some of the teams on our schedule. That was the one-back offense. That is what I am going to talk about tonight. It is no mystery to me. We have spent the last 14 years with this offense. We feel we are still learning about the offense. We are going to tweak it and change it some. We are doing that because we are losing a very good quarterback. He was a Heisman Trophy candidate the last couple of years. Obviously, we do not have the talent level to replace him at this time, although we do like our young quarterbacks that are coming up. We will tweak the offense a little, but my point is that we have finished 14 years with the one-back offense.

People continually ask me if I think the defense is catching up with the one-back offense. My response is to show them the stats for the past four years. We finished 4th in the nation in total offense. We were 8th in the nation in passing offense. We were 18th in the nation in scoring offense. They may be catching up with us, but we are still very productive with this offense. I do not think the offense is a trendy thing. I think it is real, and there is a lot of flexibility in the offense. It provides a lot of flexibility, and there are opportunities, and it certainly levels out the playing field. That is the single, biggest point about the offense.

I do not know how blessed you are with big, strong, physical linemen. This offense does not require big, strong, physical linemen. Having been a line coach the majority of my life, I like this. It allows us to put a lot of players on the field. When I was coaching at the high school level, I thought this was real important. We were always trying to find a place for the school superintendent's kid to play. We came up with some formations where we could put those type players on the field. We never threw them a pass. The point is that we can get a lot of players involved. It has been a fun offense for us. It is an offense that anyone can take advantage of.

I want to show you where we start the offense, and what we are looking to accomplish with the offense. Why are we going with this offense? Number one, it has enabled us to spread the field with speed. The last four years, we have been able to play a small kid at wide out that was only 5'7" and only weighed 160 pounds. We were able to put him on the field and get some productivity out of him. The reason I am telling you this is this. If you have any resemblance of speed, you can get them on the field with three or four players at a time.

The second point about this offense is that it creates minimal looks for the offensive line. Another important thing for us is the quarterback. As I said, I am a former offensive line coach. The fewer looks you face as a blocker the better chance you have of being successful. When we spread the field, we take another defender out of the box. It makes it a lot easier for the linemen on their blocks. It also makes it easier for the quarterback. That was particularly important for me because at one time, my son played quarterback. I told everyone that we had to keep things simple for him. I told the coaches it was a hereditary problem with him.

With this offense, we see fewer coverages. We see a lot of man-free coverage, but we only see two or three different coverages. We are not seeing the multiple coverages we used to see with conventional offenses. We know this certainly helps the quarterback because he does not have to read all of those coverages.

With this offense, we work to create mismatches with our personnel. We try to do this by formation, by motion, and by substitution. We are always looking for physical mismatches, particularly in the underneath coverage.

Another aspect of the offense is that we are going to eliminate one successful blocker needed in the running game. That means we have to block one less man in the box. I continue to watch other offenses and what is required of them to be successful. Again, as a former offensive line coach, the less you have to work on with the linemen the better chance you have of being successful. We like to spread the defense out where we do not have to block as many defenders in the box.

In talking about this offense it is a recruiting tool. As high school coaches, it is a recruiting tool for those that run this type of offense. It is a popular offense for all levels. High school coaches are recruiting within your building. It is a easier to find small, fast players, than it is to find big, tough fullbacks, or big tough linemen.

One of the great testimonials to this offense is not something we can take credit for, but rather something that Dennis Erickson can take credit for. As most of you know, Dennis Erickson won a national championship at Miami with this offense. He later went on to the Seattle Seahawks, and is now at

Oregon State. He has been running a one-back offense for his entire coaching career.

Prior to going to Miami, Coach Erickson took Wyoming to a bowl game. I went to Wyoming after Coach Erickson left. They left their playbook behind. We picked the playbook up and continued to run the offense. That was the first time I had been introduced to the one-back offense.

Another factor to indicate the difference in the type of linemen needed in the one-back offense is this. Dennis Erickson, by the way, is a graduate of the great citadel of learning, Montana State, my alma mater. Before Dennis went to Wyoming to coach, they ran the wishbone offense. Dennis changed the offense and used the same personnel that had previously run the wishbone. That tells you something about the transition and flexibility of the offense. The one back is much easier to run than most offenses.

Also, when we went to Purdue in 1997, we found a similar situation with the personnel. Purdue is the home of Mike Alstott of the Tampa Bay Bucs, and was a member of the team. All of the personnel there at the time had been recruited for the two-back offense by Jim Colletta and his staff. They were dedicated to running the football. We came in and passed the lights out of the football. We were pretty good offensively that first year with our one-back offense with the same personnel. Again, being a line coach, you do not have to be as good in the offensive line. I like the heck out of that.

Teaching the quick-passing game over the power-running game can negate the lack of athletic talent at the line of scrimmage. We do a lot of that by zone blocking. If you are allowed to cut block, this is a great offense. In high school, some of the states will not allow you to cut block. In our running game, we eliminate most of the power blocking. We do zone blocking, to me it is the finest type of sissy blocking that I know. You really do not have to block anyone. All you have to do is to get in the way of the defenders and screen them off. We do a lot of cut blocking. Our line coach is Danny Hope, a graduate of Eastern Kentucky University. He played on their national championship team at EKU. He does a great job with our front line. He uses a term of "butter them up" to describe the cut block. He tells our linemen it is like a hot knife going through butter. We cut the defensive linemen in our offense.

Another factor in favor of the one-back offense is the fact that it fatigues the defense late in the game. I use the term "extended lateral" in our bubble-screen play. All we are doing is to take the ball and throwing it outside behind the line of scrimmage. It forces the defensive linemen to run outside if they want to be involved in the tackle. If the defensive man does chase outside throughout the game, we find that late in the game, we control the line of scrimmage.

We do such a good job of pass protection, it is hard to believe. I will throw a statistic at you that will illustrate my point. This past year we had 489 pass attempts to lead the Big Ten. Iowa was the second leading passing team in the Big Ten behind us. We threw the ball 85 more times than Iowa did. With the quick-passing game and cut blocking, we only had eight sacks. Iowa threw 404 passes and gave up 57 sacks. I am not saying Iowa was not a good pass-blocking team. I am saying that the quick-passing game and cut blocking cuts down on the number of sacks. To throw the ball 489 times and only give up eight sacks is phenomenal to me. I am selling this offense, and I am sticking to it.

We have multiple formations which create a lot of misalignments. We find that teams that usually like to blitz a lot, do not blitz as much against us. They are more concerned about leaving receivers uncovered. They have to make so many adjustments, and it takes a lot of time to make all of these adjustments.

We will run a play in a game to get it on tape that we have no intention of running again. In each game, we will do that at least one time because we want the next opponent to practice on that play the next week. We have learned over the years that the more the next opponent has to work on, the more time it will take and the less prepared they are when we play them on Saturday.

Those are the reasons why we use the one-back offense. If you are interested in this "basketball on grass" as we call it, come see us. If you are going to be playing against this type of offense, these are the things you should be aware of.

The first point is this. The defense must cover all of the receivers. If they leave a receiver uncovered, we will throw the ball to him. I can recall when I first started coaching back 30 years ago. We were getting ready to play our rival at Montana State. We ran two tight ends and two backs in our base offense. We decided to put a something tricky against them that year. We did not have any great receivers, so we took our fourth-string quarterback and split him out wide. I was really shocked. The defense actually sent someone wide with him on each play. I thought that was amazing. I thought it was revolutionary. But, I found out you have to be willing to throw the ball to someone out there if they leave him uncovered.

I will guarantee you if you put two wide receivers to the same side the defense will cover the widest receiver. The secondary coaches all coach to get as deep as the deepest and wide as the widest offensive man. So, the first rule is that the defense must cover all receivers.

The second principle is this. If the defense has too many men in the box, you have to throw the ball. You can't force the ball on the run. We try to throw high-percentage type passes. We have a high completion average. You need to know if you have a tight end in the game, and the defense has seven or more in the box, you must throw the ball. If you do not have a tight end in the formation, and they have six or more in the box you have to throw the ball. The reason for that is simple. They have you out numbered.

You have to be committed. You must be sound in your play selection. You must be mathematically sound in your principles.

Let's say you may be interested in this offense. How do you get to it? How do you line the offense up? Our biggest problem was how to get the right guys on the field. Who do you want on the field? About six or seven years ago, we went to what we call grouping. I will show you these groupings, and you can take a look at it. You can see how quickly you can substitute and how quickly you can get the personnel on and off the field.

This is how we call out our groups. We call out the grouping on the sideline. As soon as we call out the

group, those guys hit the field. Then, we signal the formation on the field and send the play in the game.

Let's say we wanted to get into a double formation, trips, spread, twin, or fox. Any of those formations are a normal grouping for us. On the sideline, our assistant coaches call out "normal – normal." We all know what players are involved in the "normal" grouping. In our normal grouping our tailback, and our Y-end (which is our tight end), our A-back, (which is our Slot man), our X-end, (which is our split end), and our Z- back are all on the field. We do not have to yell out the formation. All we do is to call out the personnel. We call "normal – normal", and the kids know who will be on the field. We can very quickly communicate on the sideline.

The next grouping is our "heavy" unit. When we call "heavy – heavy" on the sideline this is what we get. We get a tight-end and our "H-back" in the game. The "H-back" is the slot that is really another tight end. We use this with a motion man.

If we call out "jumbo" grouping, which we will do on goal-line situations. Now, we have our tight end, and the "U" who is our second tight end, and our "H-back" which is another tight end-type player. You can use a lot of different type players at this position. He can be a good blocker or a pass receiver. He is not fast enough to play the wide receiver, so you play him inside. That is how we do grouping.

GROUPING

Normal = A – X – Z
Heavy = "H"
Jumbo / goal line = TE – UE – "H"

That is how we got to the groupings. I am not going to wear you out with it. That is how we communicated on the sideline. But, I want you to know that was a problem for us. It was difficult to get to our grouping and to communicate on the sideline.

Why did we have to go to groupings instead of trying to yell out the formations. The reasons are simple. Number one, we create confusion for the defense by sending a group on the field. The defense has no idea what the formation will be. Often, we find defensive teams that try to match up with us. It tends to be more difficult for the defense to do this as time goes by.

It is very easy to substitute on game day, and that is very important to us. I know Purdue is an engineer school, and we have a lot of smart players, but that is not enough. Some players are too damn smart.

Another reason we went to groupings is the fact that it allows more players the chance to play. We have plays where we will call out "number two normal." When we do that we may sub our third-string flanker. The reason he is our number 3 flanker is simple. He can't run very fast, but he is a good blocker. When we put him in the game, there is a fifty-percent chance we are going to run the football. We can really get a lot of different players in the game. We can keep a lot of players happy this way.

This is how it works on game day. A sideline coach is going to yell out the grouping. A signal is made to the players on the field. As the subs come on the field, they are yelling for the other group to come off the field. Then the formation is signaled in to our quarterback. Then, motion is signaled in to the quarterback. The sub brings the play to the quarterback from the sideline.

We have to be smart in this situation. When we first started doing the groupings, we treated it as a "two minute drill." We tried to send in the plays with some of the players that were not so smart. They were not very attentive, and we would get the play screwed up. We learned the hard way to use the smart players to take the play on the field. We do not treat it as a "two minute drill" now. In our two minute drill, we send in groupings while we are on the line of scrimmage.

I am going to go through our formations. I will cover what the advantages of the formations are. We start out with twins. This is a formation we like to use in our two-minute game because of what it avails us on the field. We have a lite grouping. We put more speed on the field, because we obvious have two receivers to both sides. We find that 90 percent of the time one of the two inside receivers will be covered by a linebacker. The dime package on defense is the only way

to keep you out of this formation. We like the formation particularly in the two-minute game.

TWINS

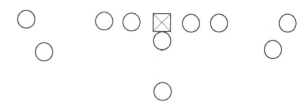

Another formation out of our normal grouping is our double set. It allows us to keep the field spread. It is very good against the seven-man front. It is very good to our strongside running game.

DOUBLES

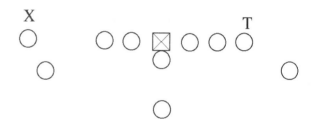

I spoke at the American Coaches Association Convention in 1988. The title of that lecture was "A Two-Back Attack In A One-Back Offense." The reason I bring this up is this. At that time we ran a lot of doubles formation. The difference was that we ran the doubles out of heavy group with the H-back in the formation. We would put the H-back in motion and pull the backside guard and run the counter play to the strongside. We would bring him back inside and run it like a basic isolation play. We ran it like a two-back attack out of what was considered a one-back set. I bring this up because we feel this formation based on the personnel is very good for the strongside running game.

Our next formation is our trio. It is a trips set with the tight end open to the call side. In your lite grouping, you can sub a lighter, faster, and less physical player to play the Y-end but he really is not a tight end. The match ups on A and Z, with an empty set by motioning the back outside, are usually in favor of the offense. I am not suggesting that you do this in terms of running crossing routes and picking the defense, but you can cross these two receivers and get some good yardage. If the defensive backs run into each other, one of them will be open. It is a good formation to work the short passing game. It is a good formation to work what we refer to as "rubs". We throw a lot of 5-yard routes. We make a lot of first downs in this formation.

TRIO

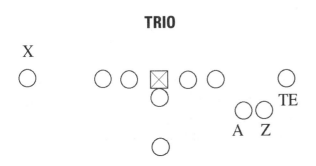

With speed on the field, the defense keeps a corner outside instead of bringing the corner inside to defend the inside receivers. As a result, it is a more attractive formation.

Our trey formation has two receivers on the same side with our tight end. The X-end is split to the other side. This is another formation where the strongside running game is very good because of the way the defense chooses to defend the formation. We end up getting a cover #3 look on this, and the safety rolls down inside. We end up running the ball inside.

TREY

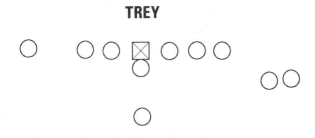

It is very difficult to bracket the backside receiver. We were getting a lot of bracket coverage at one time. We went to this formation and pretty much eliminated bracket coverage by the defense.

Next is our triple formation. This is a formation with two tight ends on the field that allows us to run the counter either way. We can run lead play either way with motion inside. It has a lot of flexibility, and it is particularly good for running the football.

TRIPLE

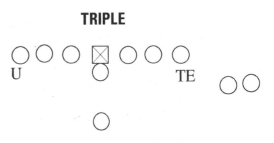

We had a tight end that was good. We have a good end now who won the John Mackey Award. He is an exceptional tight end. But out of this triple formation one year, we had one end that caught 69 passes, and the other end caught 67 passes. This past year, our tight end caught 59 passes, and most of them were out of this formation. It is an excellent formation if you have a good tight end. You can move the tight end around to any position you want him in.

Next is our trips formation. This is a basic formation for any team in the one-back formation. It is a great formation to empty out the backs by motion, or you can have the running back go outside and line up. You have a lot of possibilities with this formation.

TRIPS

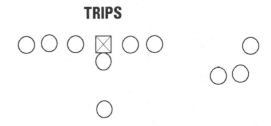

I want to talk briefly about the empty package. I will cover the things we are looking for in our empty set. A lot of coaches have to defend this set. We have some thoughts on this set in regard to the way we coach our quarterback in terms of his reads.

This is the progression we want the quarterback to follow. The first thing he does is to check the adjustments to motion. This is out of the empty set. This will create his first read. If anyone is uncovered is the second thing we check. This is on the pre-snap read or when they adjust to motion. If the defense leaves a receiver open, then that is the man we want to throw the ball to. If the defense slides or bounces the coverage, and everyone is covered up on the pre-snap read, then the quarterback is going to his called route. It would be whatever the combination route was called. If he did not like the called route based on the defensive coverage, then we are always running a backside dig route or a similar backside route.

I do not know how many of you saw our Ohio State game this year. We had to win the game twice. We took the lead with about three minutes to go in the game. We held Ohio State on the next possession. Then, we threw a real ugly interception that allowed Ohio State to go down and score. We came back with 1:12 left on the clock, and hit a backside receiver with a pass for a touchdown. We sent a man in motion and then our quarterback went through this progression. He came back to the backside route and found the end open for a touchdown.

Here are our called routes. This is about 90 percent of our offense. You may have asked what our called route was on the third read in the progression. First, are the option routes run by the receivers based on the coverages. The second called routes are the crossing routes with adjacent receivers on the opposite side of the ball. We are just crisscrossing the receivers. The third called routes are the delayed routes. The fourth called routes are the follow routes particularly on the goal line. Here, we line up three receivers to one side and have all three receivers break in the same direction. This has been effective for us in goal-line situations.

So, having said all of that, I want to go back to my statement on why the one-back offense. I want to wrap this up and show you some tape on the offense and answer any questions about things you may be interested in. I will put the tape on now and point out some of these things to you that we have covered. If there is something you want me to cover or run back, just let me know.

The things that we have done have been good for us. They have been very effective. When I go out to speak, I am always in a dilemma where to start. I make the assumption that you have not been in the one-back, and you have not run it before. I try to explain how we get into the one-back. If I don't, all of a sudden no one understands anything about it. This is basically how we start it. If you want to study it at Purdue, you need to come and spend some time with us. We are always open to high school coaches throughout our spring practice. We are actually open to colleges every other year. During odd years, our staff goes to other colleges to study their systems and practices. I have enjoyed being with you. Best of luck, and win them all. Thank you.

THE AUBURN 4-3 DEFENSIVE PACKAGE

Auburn University

Good morning. I'm going to get right into my topic. I'm glad to be here. This is my first clinic of the year. I usually do about ten or fifteen of these a year. I enjoy the opportunity to speak at clinics. I was fortunate to start in the high school ranks. I had success and worked my way up. I was one of you, and I know what it is all about.

I have been fortunate in my life to have been around some pretty good coaches. I have worked with R. C. Slocum, Dennis Erickson, and others. The guy that taught me the most about defense was Jimmy Johnson. Jimmy is an excellent coach, but particularly on the defensive side. That is what I've always been. When I think back to 1983, he really revolutionized the way we are playing defense today in college.

Having been a high school and college coach, I think without a doubt, this is one of the best defenses you can teach. It is good for high school because of time limitations and personnel. I coached at a small AA school. We didn't have a lot of linemen, and I think this defense would fit into that category. Everyone thinks you have to have big players to win. In 1989, we won the national championship at Miami and didn't have a defensive lineman over 240 pounds. This whole defense is predicated on speed. It is based on a philosophy of simplicity and being able to adjust to all the sets we see today. You can play it against the wing-T. It is great against the option. You can run the defense each week and not have to worry about changing for different offenses.

I was a 50 defensive man in the early 80's with a guy named Larry Lacefield, who was the defensive coordinator at Oklahoma in their hay days. He kind of started the eagle defense, because of the I formation. But by the middle of the 80's, people started to get away from that because of the adjustments they had to make. The preferred defense became the 4-3 with three linebackers off the line of scrimmage. It is easy to adjust and is a pressure defense.

People think pressure defense means you blitz. That is not the case. I have heard guys talk, who have tried to copy what we did in Miami in the mid-eighties. We started running this defense in 1984, and people started to copy it and run it. By 1987, Florida State was running it. Notre Dame and Kansas State went to this defense. They all started doing what we were doing because we were doing it with speed.

In 1988, Jimmy Johnson went to the Dallas Cowboys. There were 28 NFL teams. Two teams were running a four-man front. He put this defense in at Dallas and went 1-15. People laughed at him. Head Coaches and offensive coordinators in the league said he couldn't run that college and high school defense in the NFL. Two years later, they won two Super Bowls back-to-back. They didn't make any changes in the defense. Now, almost every NFL team is runs it. They run this defense because it is simple, aggressive, and it makes things happen, and it is easy to coach.

If you have fewer coaches or smaller linemen, this is the kind of defense you need to run. You can put people on the field and not substitute for different kinds of defenses. In a goal-line situation, you may have to substitute one guy.

The first thing we are going to talk about is the defensive line. From there, we will go to the linebackers. At the end, I'll try to get into the most popular coverage for this defense. The most important thing you need to understand if you are going to run this defense is the line.

We play with two defensive tackles and two defensive ends. You only need two defensive linemen. The tackles should be a little bigger personnel. They are there to create double teams because this is a gap-control defense. They are never head up and always attacking the shoulder of an offensive lineman.

I'll tell you a little about the personnel. Probably, the best defensive linemen I've coached are guys in the 6-0 to 6-1 range and are athletic. I don't like these 6-5 guys. When we won the national championship, we took our back-up defensive ends and moved them inside. They were 240. We didn't have anybody up front who weighed more than 240, and we won the national championship.

We play two defensive tackles. We always call our strength to the tight-end side. We play our tackles in a 3-technique to the tight end and a 1-technique to the split end. The defensive ends play a shade alignment also. They play a 9-technique to the tight end side and a 5-technique to the split-end side. We letter our gaps when we talk about responsibility. The defensive ends we play are basically linebackers. We like them a little taller because of the pass rush. This defense is based on five linebackers and two defensive linemen, when you are picking out personnel.

4-3 DOWN LINEMEN

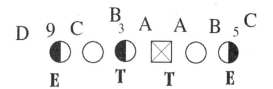

We play a shade defense in a three-point stance. I think it important as far as consistency to play in a three-point stance and not change it. When we bring guys in and put them in this defense, we either play them on the right or left side. We don't flip guys from one side to the other. The most important thing about this defense is the first step the defensive lineman makes. We don't want a lineman one time stepping with his right foot and the next time stepping with his left foot. The only way to be consistent is to have a right and left side.

The right side of the line will always have their inside foot back and their inside hand down on the ground. The left side does the same thing. The stance is really predicated on down-and-distance. But, as a normal rule, we like a heel-toe relationship. We don't

want a big stagger in their stances. The first step taken by the tackles is a small step. We align as tight to the ball as we can get. When we started teaching this, our guys were worried about being offsides. I told them during the course of a game if we don't have two penalties for lining up offsides, we are not close enough to the ball.

As a result, the offensive line started moving back off the ball as far as they legally could. We felt that was an advantage for the defense. As we taught them to crowd the line of scrimmage, we had to come up with some technique to keep them from lining up offsides. The biggest problem we had was the helmet getting in the neutral zone. What we did was to put them down on one knee. They looked at the ball, put their hand down, and then got into their stance after the hand went down. We told them not to get their helmet in front of their hand.

If you are going to play an aggressive defense, you have to crowd the ball. You have to get across the line of scrimmage when the ball is snapped. If the defensive lineman takes his first step and is not across the line of scrimmage, he is playing a read defense. That is not what we are teaching. We want to play on their side of the line of scrimmage. We want the butt a little higher in the stance. When they take the first step, their back will be flat if they start with the tail a little higher. The first step normally brings the butt down. If you start out with a flat back and take your first step, the pads start to come up. When the pads come up, we start to play too high and not under the pads of the blockers. We want 60 to 70 percent of their weight on the hands in this stance. We are going forward, not laterally.

The stance of the defensive ends is a little different. They have their inside hand down and inside foot back, but their stagger is more like a track stance. The height of the player dictates the stagger in the stance. The taller they are, the more stagger they need.

We play gap control. The strongside tackle has the B-gap to his side. The splitside tackle has the A-gap to his side. The ends play the D-gap strong and the C-gap weak. Our base alignment is inside foot of the defense on the outside foot of the offense. That is where we start out.

We adjust our alignment from there, depending on who we are playing, how close they are to the line of scrimmage, or how big the splits are. The closer the offense is to the line of scrimmage, the tighter we line up to the ball. If they are an option team and take as much of the ball as they can, we get as tight as we can. If they are a zone team back as far as the rule allows, we get wider.

When the ball is snapped, we want to create a new line of scrimmage. We are looking at the guy in front of us, but we don't move when he does. We move when the ball moves. To do that, you have to work hard in practice. You can just give it lip service. When you start working on ball movement in practice, you will be amazed. We want to be on their side of the ball before they can get out of their stance. We are looking at the ball out of the corner of our eye. When the ball moves, we're gone. We are moving on the movement of the ball. The offensive linemen, particularly in college, a lot of time can't hear the snap count and end up moving when the defense moves. In our practices, anytime the defensive line has to come out of a stance we are going to use a ball. We are not going to use a sound or cadence.

If you are going to play this defense, you have to work on getting off on the ball. We don't move when the guy moves in front of us. We move when the ball moves. It is easier for the tackles to do this because they are closer to the ball. They don't have to turn their head to see the ball move. If you look at all the teams playing this, you will find that all of the defensive linemen, except for the ones on the ball, are turned slightly toward the ball in their stance. I am not talking about cocking the stance to the inside. The stance is slightly out of square to the line of scrimmage. We turn our shoulders in our stance so we can see the ball.

We want them to get in a comfortable stance with their shoulders turned so they can see the ball. When they get those shoulders turned, that is the direction they are going. We don't want them to turn their shoulder, and, on the snap of the ball, turn up the field. An aggressive defense is not an up-the-field defense. We are attacking the line of scrimmage and attacking the ball. The guy with the toughest scenario is the defensive end aligned on the tight end. He has to get in a big tilt with the tight end to his side.

When we bring in players to play this defense, we start them all out on the right side. A lot of guys can't put their left hand down and left foot back, and get out of the stance. We start everyone in a right-handed stance, until we can find the guys that can play in those left-handed stances. If you force a guy to play from a left-handed stance, he will be a lot less productive.

If the offensive line widen their splits, we have a one-yard rule. Up to one yard, we stay on the outside shoulder. If a split is wider than a yard, we move back inside to our gap. We play the area, not the alignment. The entire defense is predicated on forcing double teams and making the ball go wide.

The attacking part of this defense is playing with our hands. We don't play with our forearms. We do a lot of drills on the one- and two-man sleds. One of them recoils, and our players hate it. We want a sled that they can grab. Some of the sleds we install with a lot of foam and a jersey over the top of it. They have to use their hands. When Butch Davis was with us, he bought a ton of racket balls. He had his defensive players squeeze those balls to strength their hands. We have had a number of hand injuries over the years by getting them caught in jerseys and face masks. But, that is just part of football.

We are going to play with hands as we step. We attack the line of scrimmage. The biggest fallacy is attacking upfield. We are reading, but we are reading on their side of the ball on the run. We are not standing on our side of the ball, trying to make heroes out of the linebackers. We tell our defensive line they are in there to make plays. We don't worry about the guys behind us. We don't squeeze a lot of blocks. If there is a lineman who gets in our way, we may hit him as we are going down the line. But if he runs from us, we don't chase him to get a piece of him.

The guy who should be your leading tackler in this defense should be your middle linebacker. He is over the center and has opportunities to make plays on both sides of the line. The next guys who are going to be your leading tacklers are the defensive ends. That is because of the way we turn them loose and let them play.

Let's say we are in a right call with the 3- and 9-techniques to the right and the 1- and 5-techniques to the left. The first step we take is with our back foot. We are turned in our stance, not square. That is so we can see the ball, and it takes us to the "V" of the neck of the offensive lineman. Our aiming point is the "V" in the neck of the offensive lineman we are attacking. We are not going upfield, we are going at an angle. We however, will attack up the field in a pass-rush technique. If we think the offense is going to run the ball, we are coming off at an angle trying to get one-yard deep in the backfield. We step, but not over-step. People think since you are an aggressive team, you take off running. That is not what we want. We want to bring our back foot up to parallel or slightly in front of our up foot. From there, we play football.

Over the years we have named some of the things we think are important. We call that first step a POWER STEP. That lets us communicate a coaching point. When we tell a lineman he didn't get his power step, he knows what we are talking about. What we try to do is step with our back foot, keep our head to the outside, shoot our hands under the pads, grab cloth, and get our thumbs up. In a perfect world, all those things happen. We teach this on the sled, not on people. When you hit the sled and get separation, you have to grab something. You just can't push on the sled. When you are doing sled work, make sure there is someone snapping a ball, so you can work on getting off on the ball. The best thing to do when you teach this, is to film it from all angles and let them see what they are doing.

STEPPING OFF THE BALL

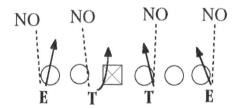

Let me talk about blocks that we encounter and how we should play them. Let's talk about a base block. The offensive lineman explodes, and the defensive lineman explodes. The thing that we don't want to do it stay on the block for more than a second. We teach this on the sled. We come off, get our hands under the pads, and drive the sled back. After we get penetration in the first and second step, we use a rip

move. Most people want to stay on the block and squeeze until they see the ball. We want to get off the block.

If we get an inside release by the blocker, we are going to do the same thing if the ball is coming at us or going away. The first thing we tell our players when they get an inside block is the ball is going away from him. His thoughts should be to catch the ball from behind. If it is an isolation or sweep away, he is thinking catch the ball. He reads the inside release and adjusts his path. He doesn't continue upfield. He comes down the line. As he attacks the "V," and it goes inside. If he can hit him, he does. He is not going to chase the man inside to make contact. He gets into a chase mode on the ball away. He turns his shoulders and runs. Ends will make more plays on the ball away than coming to them. They are not responsible for the bootleg or reverse. If you make him responsible for that, you destroy his aggressiveness.

There are a lot of things that can happen on an inside release besides the ball going away. That is the first thing we think. If the defensive end gets an inside release, and it is a veer play, the defensive end takes the fullback. The next thing is someone coming to block the defensive end who has read inside release. He has his shoulders turned and is coming hard down the line. If he encounters a block, he comes underneath the block and makes the ball go outside. We call it trapping the trapper. A lot of people think they have done the job once they bounce the ball outside. We don't want to just give ourselves up. We want them to make contact, get under the block, and work upfield. The cardinal sin is to miss the blocker. If he doesn't take out the blocker, he continues on and blocks the next guy.

INSIDE RELEASE

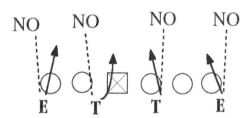

The next thing is a double team. That is what we hope we can create with our 3-technique or 1-technique. We attack the "V" of the neck and get the double team. The biggest mistake is to try to take on both blockers. You can't beat both of them. You have to defeat one of them. We try to beat the guy in front of us. We fight back into the down block, but we want to give him a small target. We try to turn our backs to the guy who is double teaming us. We want to get small, and get up the field. We don't want to fall. We want to create as much penetration as possible. If you get off the ball, you have a chance to get upfield. If you don't get off the ball, and the center gets a good post on you, we are in trouble. You will see our guys fall down and create a pile. That is the last thing we want them to do.

The next block is a reach or hook block. If you are playing this defense and stepping with your inside foot, you are going to get reached. If I am aligned with my inside foot on his outside foot, I'm going to get reached. But, the whole objective is to get into him before he gets into you. For a tight end to hook or zone block, he steps laterally and up the field. If they do that, and you are coming off the ball, you can get them back on their heels. We are not worried what the blocker does. I am responsible for an area. That is my domain. Where I start from is where my domain is. It doesn't exist anywhere else. If the defensive end goes outside or widens out of his domain, he creates inside running lanes. We want the ball outside.

I don't care that the offensive blocker has taken an outside release. I am into the "V" of his neck and ripping up the field. People don't try to reach block much on this defense any more. Instead of reaching, they base block and try to take the defender where he wants to go and let the back break into seams. What we see are zone schemes. They are not trying to reach. They are stepping laterally and trying to read your charge or get you to widen.

That is basically all the blocks you will see. The inside or outside release, zone block, base block, or trap block. We play them all just about the same. We get off the ball, make contact if possible, protect our gap, get penetration, and chase the ball. Everyone has to make the ball go to the sidelines.

If the offense comes up with a no-tight end set, we game plan to declare our direction. The end to the side of the direction is playing on a GHOST TIGHT END. Since the end has a 3-technique tackle to his side, there is no reason for him to align tight on the offensive tackle. If the tackle is going to block anyone, it better be the defensive tackle. The defensive end can not keep the tackle from double teaming, so why should he align tight on him? The defensive end takes his alignment on the GHOST END as if he were there. He will be slightly tighter than normal, will turn his shoulders, and will attack the line of scrimmage. He gets into a tilt inside and comes off hard. He is not worried about hitting the tackle or end, he hits the first thing to show inside.

His path is off the hip of the offensive tackle. If the tackle turns outside, the end has to make sure he stays outside. The aiming point becomes the butt of the offensive tackle. He reads the back in the backfield. That becomes his key as to ball toward or away. His responsibility on an option is to hit the guy with the ball. If it is a speed option, he has the quarterback. If it is a dive option, he has the fullback. He doesn't have a responsibility other than to hit the first thing that shows.

GHOST TIGHT END

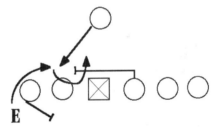

Let's look at the three linebackers. Actually, they are our Mike linebacker and the two defensive ends. We have two guys who are supposed to be linebackers, but they are actually strong safeties. They are defensive backs who can run and make plays. They have to be aggressive players who can run. The Sam linebacker has to be a little tougher, because we aren't squeezing too many blocks off him. They are playing with their heels at five yards from the ball. If they get too tight they are going to get killed. That is important. You don't have to tell them that too many times. If the Mike linebacker starts to creep up, and the tight end "ear-holes" him, he'll back up. They do not move laterally like a read defense. They play downhill toward the line of scrimmage.

The Sam linebacker has the C-gap strong. The Mike linebacker has the strong A-gap. The Will linebacker is responsible for the B-gap to the weakside. Their alignment is not cut in stone. They are going to be in the area of their responsibility. They play with their hands, unless we get one thing. If we get a double team and a two-back isolation, we tell him to get a hold and hang on. It becomes a tackling drill on the fullback as deep in the backfield as we can get. Their keys are generally the first back to their side or the fullback in the two-back set.

I have seen coaches over the years that really get into stances. To me it doesn't make a hill of beans as long as it is comfortable, and he can move out of it. We don't work laterally unless both backs go lateral. If they run a toss sweep, the linebackers may take a lateral step. After that they attack their gaps on the line of scrimmage. They are mirroring the running backs.

If the ball goes to the tight end side, the backside linebacker has to slow down. The backside end is chasing everything going away from him. That means the backside linebacker has to slow down and cover some things. We tell him to keep his shoulders square. That lets him react to the ball if it comes back. The thing you don't want to do is over-coach. Don't give them a lot of things to read. Turn them loose, and let them play. Remember there are not a lot of squeezing by the defensive line. We want them to be athletes and run to the ball.

If the Sam linebacker plays into the C-gap, and the defensive end has closed up the C-gap with a trap blocker, the linebacker moves one gap wider and plays football. If the end has picked off the guard, and the fullback is running in front of the tailback, Sam does the same thing. He is going to take on the fullback and bounce the ball outside.

OFF TACKLE POWER

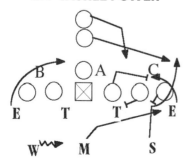

Let me cover a two-tight end set. We play personnel against personnel. It is crazy to line up against two tight ends and two backs with a 4-3 defense. There are too many running seams, because you have only four down linemen. We make a personnel adjustment. We take a corner or free safety out of the game and replace him with a defensive linemen. He plays a loose 3-technique away from the Sam linebacker. Everyone else plays the same defense. We game plan the direction of our front. It is a good adjustment. It is also our short-yardage defense.

TWO TIGHT ENDS

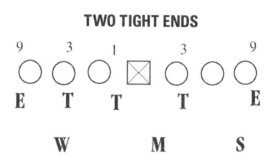

There is one thing you want to remember about defense. Defense is about ninety-percent desire. Don't over-coach. Let them play, and keep it simple. Always remember you can't play a different defense every week. If you are going to play, it may work. But remember those kids are the ones who are going to line up. They have to be comfortable and confident that they know what they are doing. If you can get them lined up, they will play.

We can play a two-tight end set with the normal 4-3. Toward the second tight end, we move the tackle from a 1-technique to what we call a *G-scheme*. We move the tackle into a 2i technique on the guard. The weakside end moves into a 7-technique, or inside shoulder alignment on the second tight end. That would be our adjustment if we didn't see the second tight end come into the game, or if they moved the fullback into the second tight-end position. We would have a corner up outside the second tight end also. You don't want to play a 1-technique with a 7-technique. It give the Mike and Will linebackers too much to cover. Everyone still plays the same gaps and the stances don't change. The 2i player is in the same stance, but he is attacking the gap and not the "V" in the neck. We are going to force the guard to block him. The same is true with the 7-technique. He is attacking the gap, not the man.

G-SCHEME

If the offense used two tight ends and two wide-outs, we would play situation. If it were a running

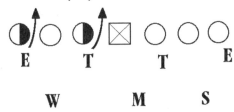

situation, we would substitute the down lineman and play run. If it were a passing situation, we moved our linebackers over and played more for the passing game. The Will linebacker assumed the role of a strong safety.

2 TIGHT ENDS-2 WIDE OUTS

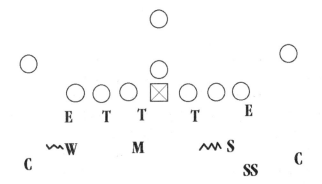

We run a couple of stunts to try to break the monotony of the defense. You don't want to do run them every down. But, if someone is running bootlegs and reverses on us, we run this stunt. Probably every three or four plays we will run a stunt. The most effective one we have used is to bring our weakside defensive end on an inside charge and bring the Will linebacker on the outside blitz. We can do it to the other side with the Sam linebacker and defensive end. We can also blitz the Mike linebacker by calling "base Mike." All he does is to blitz through his A-gap. Anytime you blitz the Mike linebacker, the tackles have to rip straight up the field. That creates a seam for the Mike linebacker. Anytime you bring the Mike linebacker, it is a three-man stunt.

STUNTS

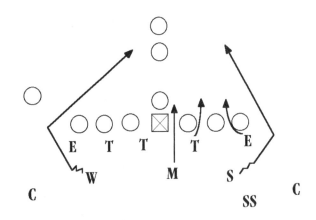

The thing you have to remember is we are coaching a technique every day that is probably the most under-coached technique in football. We are coaching every day in this defense the pass-rush technique. The main key to an effective pass rush is going back to what we do every down. We get in a good alignment and key the ball. If we are playing against a shotgun formation, we may widen our defensive ends somewhat. Anytime a Sam or Will linebacker has more than one back outside of him, he has to move out. The farther we go out, the deeper we get. I don't have time to cover our pass coverage, but we would be four across, zone with a four-man rush.

SHOTGUN FORMATION

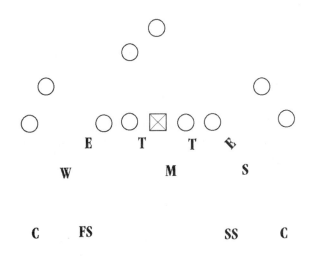

The next thing I want to look at before I quit is the wing-T. To start with, let's look at how we play a wing set. It doesn't matter whether we have a tight end or open end, we do not play an even technique. If we get the wing set, we put our end in a GHOST technique. He gets wider and runs his hip technique. His main objective is to get the wing back to block down on him. He gets in the cocked stance and comes down on the hip of the tight end. There have been times when we have brought the end on a path toward the inside shoulder of the wing, to make sure he blocks him. The Sam and Will linebackers are deep enough to beat the block of the tight end. But, they can't beat the block of the wing back. That is why we take him out with our defensive end.

Every time you have a wing, you have to force the double team, and you have to determine which blocker you want to take out. We have found out that the hip scheme is the best way for us to play that formation.

WING-T

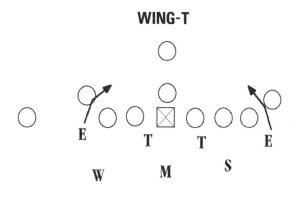

Let me briefly talk about what we do in the secondary. Most of the teams in college and the NFL are running this. Previously, people played a two-deep coverage. Some people still play that coverage. But because we need more run support from the secondary, we have gone to a quarter coverage. That helps with the four vertical patterns that so many people are running now. You line up and make it look like two-deep and play four quarters.

To the tight-end side, the corner keys the number one receiver to his side. He is keying number one to number two. He is responsible for outside and one quarter of the field. The strong safety keys number two and has one quarter of the field. The free safety keys number two to his side, whether he is in the slot

or backfield, and has one quarter of the field. The weakside corner has the same responsibility as the strong corner. The linebackers work off the backs to their side. We give up the weakside flat in this scheme. The linebackers are playing curl-to-flat depending on the patterns. The Mike linebacker is playing the number three receiver most of the time. We don't drop much because we are already five-yards deep.

The strong safety keys number two to his side. If he goes vertical, he takes him and plays one quarter of the field. The corner is keying number one-to-two. If number one goes vertical, he carries him deep as long as the number two is running vertical. If the number two receiver runs to the flat, the strong safety works for depth and width and plays over the top of the number one receiver running the flag or post. The Sam linebacker keys the number two receiver. If he goes flat, he works under the curl of number one. The Mike linebacker takes the number three receiver to either side. If number three blocks, he works into the hook zone.

QUARTER COVERAGE

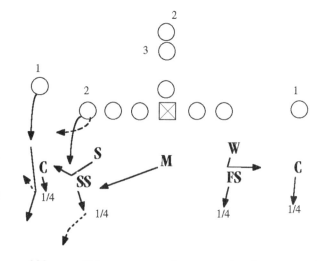

We run this coverage because it gives you the chance to get the safeties involved in run support. It allows you to get the eighth and ninth man in the box. It is a good disguise coverage that forces the offense to do something they don't want to do.

Guys, I enjoyed it and appreciate your attention. If you have any questions just send them to Auburn and I'll be glad to answer them. If I can help you in any way, just come see us. Thank you very much.

INSTALLING THE JET SERIES

Marysville High School, Ohio

First I want to thank the SWOFCA for giving me this opportunity to talk today. This talk will be different than the lectures on the wide open, spread, throw-the-ball-down-the-field-type offense. This is a different mentality as far as the offense goes. We are basically a wing-T offense. We are eighty percent a one-back offense.

The last couple of years, we were looking at ways to attack the split-end side, and we have evolved into the Jet series. We did not have a great option quarterback, but we wanted to be able to attack the split-end side. We decided to incorporate another series that would give us the ability to go to both sides of the offense.

We are not limited to a tight-end offense. We do use two wideouts in our offense. We make personnel adjustments the same way most of other teams do.

This is our base wing-T set. It is a one-back set. The reason we went to the Jet series is because it is a good series for any offense that runs the one-back set. You could run the wing-T, the midline, run and shoot, or double wing. You could run it anytime you line up in two wings, or when you are in the spread set and motion one of the wings back You can run the Jet series from all of these sets.

BASIC FORMATION

Let me give you some of the positive things about the Jet Series:

• It can easily be incorporated into any one-back offense.

• It is a series within itself.

• It is a four-back attack. It balances up the defense.

• We can attack the entire defensive front. We run four plays that all look very similar in action, both to the split-end side and the tight-end side with the quick sweep series. We come back with the trap inside. Next, we have a misdirection off our counter play that we call our scissors play. Finally, the fourth thing is our bootleg pass off the series. If you run any wing-T or triple option, you have your series oriented. We put the series in relatively easy, and it is easy to teach the series. We do not have a hard time at all of picking up the adjustments on the blocking assignments of the four plays.

• The blocking schemes are relatively simple. It is series-oriented. When we tell our kids we are going to work on the Jet series, the kids know what we are talking about.

• The two wingbacks are potential ball carriers. The fullback and quarterback are potential ball carriers. The bootleg pass is a run-pass option.

• You can utilize a variety of formations to outflank defenses. When you line up, you can look at the defense and see what they are giving you. You can put in an audible system and get out of the formation. We just call "opposite", and it takes us out of the formation, because it is a four-back attack.

The thing we like about this is the fact that we had a lot of kids in the wing positions that had equal ability. They were all between 175 and 200 pounds, and their speed was comparable. Some of the wingbacks were a little better at catching the football. Some of them had a little more speed than the others.

Our one-back was our fullback. Out of the wing-T, he had a lot of experience running the trap. It was a natural position for him. We moved the tailback up to the slot or wing position, depending on where we wanted to attack, and how we wanted to attack.

The blocking schemes are very simple. The trap series may present a little more teaching in the Jet series in that you must decide who you are going to trap, and how you are going to block the other defenders. When we talk about running the sweep, we are talking about an outside zone play. The play is the same from different formations. We teach a reach-and-run technique.

Another favorable point of the Jet series is the fact you can take advantage of your speed and quickness. You do not need to be a big team to run this series. You can play smaller and quicker linemen because there is a lot of misdirection, a lot of reach/run techniques used, and zone blocking techniques involved. When we run the scissors play, it is just a down-blocking scheme. Most of this is already a part of our system. It is just angle blocking in our system.

The fact that we are going to put the wingback in motion and hand him the ball on the run full speed has a tendency to improve his 40-yard time. If he is a 4.8 man, and you hand him the ball going full speed, to the defense he appears to be a 4.7 man. He is moving while the defense is reading. This gives the offense a slight advantage. We have a few backs that can run a 4.6 or 4.7. We do not have a big tailback or a big, powerful fullback. That is one reason we implemented the Jet series with our wing-T. It has been a fun series for us. Our kids like to run it.

I want to start with our plays in the Jet series. First is the Jet Sweep. It is an ugly 6-to-8 yard play. I will show you the play against the 50 defense first. We saw this in the playoff games.

JET SWEEP VS. 50 DEFENSE

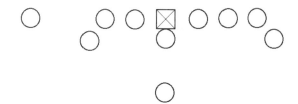

The first thing we want to check is how they support the edge. If the defense is in this look, we would run to our tight-end side. If they overload to our wing side and are in man coverage, we would come back to the split end side at times.

The first thing we want to do is to secure the edge. What we like to do is to run to the tight-end side. Our blocking for our lineman is real simple. We give our linemen the blocking techniques when we call the play. If we call 48 Reach, it means we are going to reach to the 8-side, or the even side. Our linemen know we are going to take a 45-degree step, and we are going to run. We call it reach and run. If the slant tackle on the playside comes down inside, our onside guard will reach block him. This play is good against stunting defenses. It has also worked out well against teams that walk everyone up inside and stunt. When we are going to attack the perimeter, that is the defense we like to see. The tighter the defense plays to the line of scrimmage, the better. That means we can get to the edge quicker if they are tight on the line of scrimmage. You will find out when that wingback takes his running start, he is on the corner before the linebacker can take his first step. So, the thing we are going to do is to try to secure the edge.

Our blocking on the play is our outside zone technique. It is reach – step – and run. Once our linemen take that outside step, we are going to run. We try to reach the defender's outside number. We do that all along the line of scrimmage. We reach and continue to run downfield.

We hand the ball to the motion back, and he is going to run full speed and run as hard as he can to gain as many yards as he can We want to gain six-to-eight yards on the play. We call it an ugly 6-to-8 yards gain.

The wingback on the callside takes an outside release and tries to work through the outside number of the outside support defender. It is an arc course against the outside defender. If the defender tries to work him inside, the wingback pins him inside. If the wingback feels a blitz coming from the corner, he battles him on the line of scrimmage. He wants to keep him on the line of scrimmage. We want to secure the edge even if they are running some type of stunt.

The quarterback comes up to the center and gets set. He gives the signal to the motion back with a nod of the head when he wants him to start in motion. You can use different ways to set the man in motion. You can use "Red – Set – Go," and have the motion start on the Red. You can start him on the nod of the head, movement of the heel, or whatever you want to use.

The motion back takes the handoff full speed. He is working on the outside for six-to-eight yards outside. He is running hard. If the defender wants to move outside wide, the ball carrier wants to skim the defender's hip and move back into his running lane. It is not a cutback play. We do not want them cutting back inside. The reason we do not want him cutting back is because it goes against the principles of the outside-zone play. If he has to run out of bounds, then we tell him to go ahead and run out of bounds. We tell him to come back to the huddle, and we will try something else. We do not want him to cut back where it will stop his momentum. We never want him to stop his momentum. We want him to read on the run with the ball. If the defender widens, then the running back is going to try to come up inside the hip of that man and then skim back outside. We call that skimming the hip.

The steps for the quarterback are important. He starts the backs in motion, and the ball is snapped over the outside leg of the guard. After the handoff, he goes to the midline read for the fullback. He fakes the trap to the fullback and then fakes the bootleg pass away from the play. The fullback fakes the trap.

Again, we have the quarterback give the nod to the motion back, and the ball is snapped when the back is over the outside leg of the guard next to the wingback. The quarterback takes the snap, hands the ball to the wingback, and steps to the midline to fake to the fullback. Then the quarterback runs the bootleg-pass fake to the opposite side. The quarterback takes a complete pivot on the play. It makes the transition smooth for the quarterback. His complete motion keeps the play moving. His feet keep moving all of the time. All fakes are run at full speed to set up the series action.

You may get a play that breaks for long yardage, but we are just trying to sell out kids on the six-to-eight yard gain and to get the first down. We want the defenders to chase the ball carrier from behind. Once we get them chasing from behind, we are gone. We do not want them to cross our face. If the defense crosses our face, they are just going to keep us running wide.

On the sweep play, we tighten the linemen down to one-foot splits. When we run this series we line to come up to the line and get down and go without a lot of delay. We do not want to let the defense get set. We want to get the back moving in motion and get him into the void and go. We use our splits just like most other wing-T teams do as far as the trap, and down play. To us, our scissors is our down play. There are different ways to adjust your splits depending on where the ball is going to hit.

On the sweep, we want to tighten down on our splits especially against the eight-man fronts. Against teams that like to blitz a lot, we like to tighten down and seal them inside and get to the corner very quickly. As I said, we are basically a running team. We may throw the ball 15 times per game if we need to. A lot of the things we do are based on speed, quickness, misdirection, getting up to the line, and getting off the ball.

Against the 4-3 defense, we like to run the Jet sweep back to the split-end side. It is important for our split end and wingback to practice on the stalk block. They must work on staying on their defensive man. The bottom line is for our blockers to stay in contact with their man throughout the play. The defenders cannot make the tackle if our blockers are in their face.

JET SWEEP VS. 4-3 DEFENSE

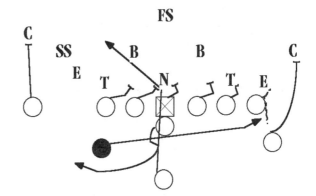

We are going to reach and run on the line. The onside guard will pick up the linebacker that is running the scrape technique on that side. The backside guard will pick up the Sam linebacker on the backside. We teach our linemen to take that reach step and when he sees the opposite color jersey come, he wants to make contact and continue upfield. We want to lock on to the defenders and force them to run behind us. We want to get secured and get "people-on-people." That is the key—people on people." If we can do that, the back can get the six-to-eight yard gains.

We send the wingback in motion full speed. I have seen teams that pulled the backside guard and had him lead the wingback on the play. That is not the idea on our play. The idea of this play for us is to get on the corner quickly. When our back sees the nod, he is on a dead sprint. You have to work on the timing on the play.

The next phase in our Jet series offense is our Jet trap. The fullback has his toes lined up at four yards. All of our backs use a stand-up stance. We are all in a two-point stance. It fits into our wing-T offense. Our wingbacks line up looking straight downfield, but they will peek inside to get the signal to start in motion. Some teams like to tilt the wingbacks inside, but we do not. We like to keep them flat so they can release on passes and get out quickly on the blocks where they can see the defense better.

Our trap is our number one play. Against the 50 defense, we trap the 5-technique defensive man.

TRAP VS. 50 DEFENSE

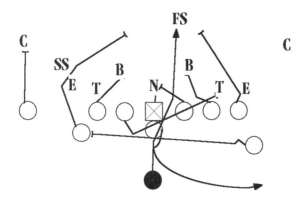

As soon as the wingback goes in motion on the play, he has to sell the play to the defense. The reason we call this a Series is because every play starts out the same. All four of the plays basically look the same. We sprint the wingback on the motion just like we did in the sweep. We funnel the wingback and the tight end into the middle to pick up the defensive secondary.

Our quarterback is giving up the midline. He fakes to the motion man going full speed. We can trap both sides of the line against the 50 defense with this play. After the quarterback fakes the ball to the wingback in motion, he hands the ball to the fullback, and then fakes the bootleg pass to the outside. We hope the bootleg action will hold the two outside men on the defense. That is why we the quarterback must run the bootleg action full speed every time. The quarterback cannot hand the ball off and then turn around and watch the play to see if it is going to be successful. When we snap that ball, each of the backs must run their assignment full speed. If they do not run full speed, it takes away the effectiveness of the play.

Our offensive line uses one- or two-hole trap rules. We like to trap the 3-technique against the 4-3, 4-4, or 50 shade defenses. We trap the 5-technique defender on the 40 defense, but we do not like to trap long. We like to look inside to the 3-technique defender.

JET TRAP VS. 4-3 DEFENSE

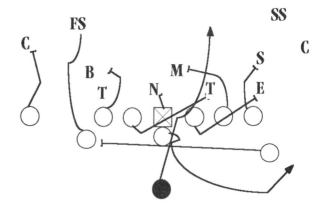

The reason we like to trap the 3-technique is because when we pull our onside guard, it widens the hole because the defensive man goes wide with the onside guard. This gives us a little more of a seam inside. It is a good play against any inside even-front defense.

Our guards make all of our calls on the traps. If we make a long call, it means we are going to trap the 5-technique man. But, we like to trap the 3-technique man. We may have the quarterback find the 3- technique man and change the play. We can also "BLACK" the call. For example, we wanted to change the call and we called BLACK, we would run the two trap. For us, we may use black or white as live colors. We run a lot of different schemes inside.

Next, I want to go over the scissors play. The scissors play is a quick play. Basically, it is run just like the other plays. The motion back on the playside lines up a step deeper. He starts the play by going in motion. The ball is snapped in the same way, when the wingback is over the outside leg of the guard. He must make a good fake on the play. He goes in motion and runs all out. The fullback kicks out the frontside defensive end. The backside guard pulls and blocks the frontside linebacker. The line gap blocks the playside and scoop blocks the backside. The quarterback turns 360 degrees and hands to the second wingback inside. After the handoff, he must carry out the bootleg pass fake to hold the outside corner on the playside.

SCISSORS VS. 50 DEFENSE

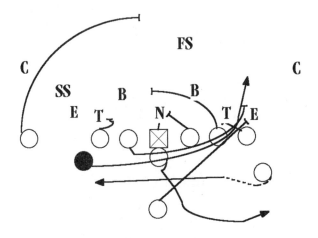

We can run the play to both sides. We can run it against the 4-3 defense as well. It is a down scheme. We will not run this play too often if the defense is blitzing a lot. We just go ahead and run the sweep if they are blitzing. This is how we run the play against the 4-3 scheme.

SCISSORS VS. 4-3 DEFENSE

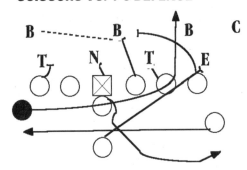

Against the 4-4 look, we have our onside tight end influence block on the outside backer. The reason we added this series is because it has given us a different way to block on our overall schemes to attack the edge. We just call it 58 or 59 scissors. It is a part of the 50 series for us. We like to give the defensive ends a lot of different looks. They do not know if they are going to be kicked out, or if they are getting down blocked. This causes the ends a lot of problems against our sets.

SCISSORS VS. 4-4 DEFENSE

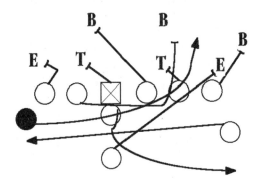

The last play in the series is our Jet boot pass. We still want the wingback to start in motion. We base block on the frontside and hinge block on the backside. We want to make as easy as possible for the front guys.

The fullback uses an overthrow block on the front-side defensive end. He tries to pin his outside number. The motion back fakes the Jet and blocks the backside end. The tight end or the number one receiver runs a corner route. It is an inside release for the tight end. The backside halfback drags to the open area on the playside.

The quarterback looks to break contain. He has a run/pass option. This is a good play on early downs.

JET BOOT PASS VS. 50 DEFENSE

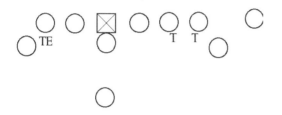

You can run the tight end on different patterns. You can have him run an arrow, a corner, or a regular out cut. You can run him on any route you want, based on the defensive coverage you face each week.

Now, you can take that wingback that goes in motion and fakes the Jet, and send him down the far sideline like South Carolina did against Ohio State. That is a nice gain from that play. We call that play boot throwback.

JET BOOT PASS VS. 4-3 DEFENSE

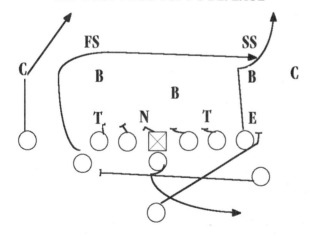

You can take the offside wingback and bring him across into the hole in the open area. He is an athlete, and he is going to find that open area.

We can tell the line that we want the quarterback to run the ball. All of the line and backs block, and the quarterback will keep the ball on the boot run.

We do like to use a lot of different formations. One formation we like to use is the unbalanced formation. We move the tight end over to the short side. We bring the left tackle over to the right side on the outside of the right tackle. We can still run the same four plays. This is especially true when the defense plays the shade defense. We can run wing-T plays out of this set as well. Our Jet play looks good to both sides from this formation.

UNBALANCED FORMATION

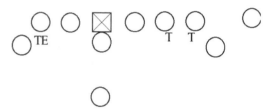

We can bring our tight end over to the split-end side and line him up inside and on the line of scrimmage.

DOUBLE SPLIT

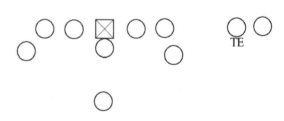

A lot of teams run these four plays out of the regular gangster set. It is a double slot with two split ends. Now, we have the defense balanced up. We can run what ever we want to run to both sides from this set.

GANGSTER SET

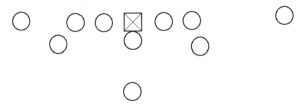

EMPTY SET

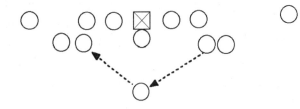

You can run the boot play out of the empty set. You move the fullback up to the wing on either side and come up and snap the ball. That is our empty set.

We have a 15-minute walk through daily. Our backs work on blocking he edge and reading the blocks. The line work on blocking schemes for the Jet series.

My time is up. Thanks guys.

INNOVATIVE SHOTGUN RUNNING GAME

Northwestern University

It's always good to be back in Cincinnati. You get to see a lot of coaches you've known for sometime. I'm representing Coach Randy Walker and all the staff from Northwestern. We have a great group of guys. This is our second year up there, and we made some nice strides this year. Tonight, I'm going to talk about some of the things we are doing.

I think we are running the ball effectively out of our shotgun. We did a good job of changing the attitude of the kids at Northwestern. We really played hard this year. Maybe because we went to a no-huddle and shotgun offense, that helped a little. But ultimately, our team played real hard. We were really physical and fast. The four games that we lost, we didn't do that as well.

It is a simple game. We kind of window-dress it, and it looks a little different. I think there is a flavor of some single-wing in some of the stuff we do. The only difference is we do it from a spread set.

The reason we evolved this way was because we didn't have a fullback. Also, we didn't have an every-down tight end. Our tight end was a converted quarterback. In the spring, when this young man was a second year quarterback, he didn't throw a very good ball. I played center and guard in college and threw the ball better than he did. He was 6-5 and 235. He had never been in a stance in his life. We taught him how to bend his knees, and how to get into a stance, and this year he became our tight end.

We are in a shotgun with three and four wide receivers all the time. We were second in the Big Ten in rushing. We averaged 258 yards a game. Our tailback led the Big Ten in rushing with 177 yards per game. He rushed for an average of 194 yards a game in the Big Ten games. The best thing about him is the fact he had no fumbles.

We are in shotgun. We sprint out, quick throw, drop back, and use play-action passes. What I am going to do tonight is show you how we take an I-back and one-back concept and run our attack out of the shotgun.

The first thing you have to consider in the shotgun is the snap. The quarterback's toes are five yards from the line of scrimmage. The tailback has the same alignment as far as depth. That can change a little if we want to deepen the tailback or cheat him wider. But typically, he is five-yards deep, aligned behind the offensive tackle. That is what works for us.

I'm not going into a lot of detail about how we do our no-huddle. It is not hard. We signal formations and concepts, and our quarterback verbalizes to the line what we are doing. Everyone else goes off the signals. The signals are quick, and the communication is fast. The more you signal from the sideline, the slower it goes on the field. We want it fast. Because they are simple and quick, we are not concerned about what the defense hears. They have to get their own information. If they are going to try to steal our signals, they'll be in one defense all night. The defense has problems with their communication. Quite honestly, the only way the defense can get on to what we do is if we check a play over and over one certain way.

We work quickly with our automatics and signals so the defense doesn't get too much help by watching what we are doing signal-wise. Of course, it helps to have guys who are scoring 1400 and 1500 on their SAT's. We have some talent, but all our kids are pretty smart.

The other thing I want to share with you, before I go any further, is our conditioning. If you saw us practice when we were at Miami of Ohio, I think you would know we work hard. I think Coach Walker's record to date with the lead going in to the fourth quarter is 56-2. We are a well-conditioned, hard-working football team. We are trying to use conditioning as a factor.

With this scheme, we think we can wear some teams out. In our last four games, we had 95 plays against Minnesota, 90 against Michigan, 95 against Iowa, and 102 against Illinois. If you get 90-plus snaps a game you can fatigue the defense. Working at that quick pace forces them to line up so you can start picking and choosing some plays that are good for you.

To be a shotgun team, the first thing you have to do is execute the snap. We are in the shotgun 85 percent of the time. The only time we came under center was short-yardage or goal-line situations when we were running an I formation play. If we had a tight end and fullback, we probably would be in more I formation and under the center more on snaps.

At Miami, we spent two years doing the Bengal's version of the no-huddle. We used the sugar huddle and all that stuff. That was too slow for us. If you saw our Michigan game, you probably thought it was poor clock management on our part. But, if we had slowed down and milked the tempo, we wouldn't have scored. We are best when we play at full tilt. In basketball, if you are an athletic team, you play as fast as you can. If you are not athletic, you slow the game down. It is just the opposite in football. If you are pretty good, you line up and mash the other team. We are just the opposite. We don't know — if physically we're that good. We are trying to be unusual to gain the advantage.

The center has a square stance. We want his feet slightly flatfooted. The reason is we don't want his butt coming up. If it does, the ball sails high. We have an excellent center who is just a sophomore. The quarterback needs to be in a relaxed position. He can't be stiff. We don't want him totally focused on the ball. He has to see things that are going on around him. It is like dribbling a basketball. You don't have to look at it to dribble. He can't be looking all over the place. He sees the center's butt and the snap, but he has to have some awareness. He needs to feel the blitz coming off the end or the rotation of the secondary.

If he calls ready and gets glued in on the ball, the defense will move around after he calls ready. That is why we want him relaxed and comfortable in his stance.

Next, let's go to snap mechanics. We want the center to get the V of the thumb and forefinger facing the target. If the center cups his hand to the side, you get a curved action and the ball comes out sideways. The ball comes out like a loaf of bread instead of front-to-back. The snap is like a fisherman casting a rod. It is a short snap of the wrist with a dart-throwing action. The center takes the laces. We do not want him to cock the ball a lot. If he does, he will throw it into the ground. We want him to try to keep the ball flat. He uses a straight-line motion, and the ball comes out straight. He snaps the ball back with some steam on it. It is not a floating snap.

The next thing we talk about is the ball placement in the center-quarterback time up. Our quarterback is like a shortstop or second baseman. He is not like a pitcher. The shortstop catches and throws. The pitcher winds up and throws. We want the ball placement around the numbers. We want the ball up. In the quick-passing game, all the quarterback does is catch the snap and make the throw.

Every day in practice, we do what we call run game time-up. I bring the quarterbacks and centers out 15 minutes early. The first 8-10 minutes we do a warm up. The last 5-7 minutes, the centers and quarterbacks do run game time-up in pre-practice. We have four centers, quarterbacks, and tailbacks. They all go at the same time.

The first thing we do is practice an under-the-center play. The first play we run is the fullback belly play. We actually ran that play twice this year. They all go at once with the tailback running 20 yards. While he is on the way back, the quarterbacks and centers are taking two more snaps.

The next thing we do is the zone play. Each time while the tailback is running back, the centers and quarterbacks are getting two more reps at the snap. In that 7-minute period, we get 40 snaps. From there, we go to shotgun and do the same thing.

RUN GAME TIME-UP

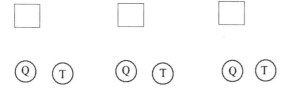

ROUTES ON AIR

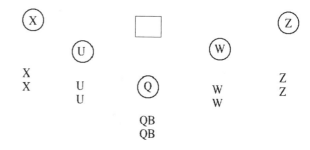

If you are going to be a quick shotgun team you have to learn to catch and throw. During the warm-up period, the quarterback works on catching the ball and getting his hands set on the laces quickly. He catches, gets the laces, and throws the ball back to the other quarterback.

In the off-season, we do a lot of basketball drills with the quarterback. He rotates the ball around his head, through his legs, and around his waist. We do all kinds of drills to improve his hand-eye coordination. That is important to a quarterback, particularly to one in the shotgun. Part of the warm-up is what we call machine-gun throws. All we do is have the quarterback catch and throw the ball in rapid secession.

We have another drill we call rapid fire. We put the receiver five yards down the field. We snap the ball, and the quarterback throws as fast as he can. We want to decrease the time it takes to get off the throw. I think we are too slow at this right now. I don't think we throw enough hitches, because my quarterback doesn't have a great arm, and I'm afraid of people setting on the outs and hitches. The nice thing about being in shotgun is that we have a 6-foot quarterback. He doesn't have to worry about getting back. All he has to do is catch it, get the laces, and throw.

After we go through this, we go to routes on air. Our receivers are labeled with letters. The tight end is Y. We have two receivers, U and W. They are generally slot receivers. The split ends are X and Z. We line up in position and run routes on no defense. The quarterback throws hitches to begin with as rapidly as possible to all the receivers. We are going one at a time, but that is because of lack of numbers. If I had two quarterbacks, I would go two at a time. During this drill he is constantly catching and handling the ball. That is the whole purpose of this drill.

We want to run the ball, but if you are going to spread the field and use a shotgun, you have to be able to throw the ball. If the defense doesn't spread out when you do, you are wasting you time. You have to be effective throwing the ball. We threw it 58 percent of the time this year.

I'm going to talk about a few of our base running plays. I'm going to talk about the zone play, G-scheme sweep/zone, trap, counter, and counter flip. I'm going to go fast and try to get to all of them. The only other plays we run are draw and speed option. That are all the running plays we have.

The first play is the inside zone play. Typically, we like to run this toward a 1i or 2i technique. We do a lot of bootlegs with our quarterback. That tells us who the defense is going to assign to the quarterback on the bootleg. That ties into our zone scheme, because we don't need a tight end in the game. On the back-side, we are not going to block one man. The defensive end or linebacker has to be responsible for our quarterback. We have a one-back play with two backs in the backfield. This is also good against blitzes because the quarterback can see them coming. He doesn't have his back turned, he is facing them.

In the zone play, we are using combo blocks with our linemen blocking zone. Against a 4-2 defense, with a 1-3 stack left, we like to run left. We shift the tailback right and run left. The center and left guard combo on the 1-stack. The left tackle reaches to the outside. The backside guard and tackle combo on the 3-stack. We don't block the backside end. He has to be responsible for the quarterback.

ZONE PLAY VS 42

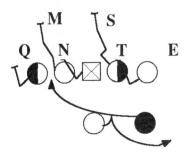

Against a shade weak, we combo the backside and reach the call side. The center reaches the shade, the guard lateral steps, and goes up on the linebacker. The tackle reaches outside.

ZONE PLAY VS SHADE

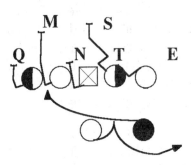

Against a 50 defense, we combo with the center and backside guard on the nose guard. The onside guard steps out at the tackle and up on the linebacker. The onside tackle reaches outside. The backside tackle cuts off the backside.

ZONE PLAY VS 50

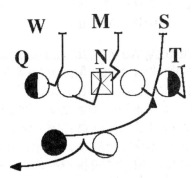

The backside blocking scheme will either be reach, base, or cut off. We decide each week on how the defense is going to cover the quarterback on the bootleg. If they chase down with the end and let the linebacker take the bootleg, we base block the tackle and end. If the end has the quarterback, the tackle and guard combo or cut off the backside tackle and linebacker.

Against the double eagle, man free Bear look, the defense can't have two linebacker in the box. If there are two linebackers in the box, that means they are playing zero coverage, and we are throwing the ball. Everyone reaches, with the center and backside guard working a combo on the nose and backside linebacker. The tailback runs the play the same way against all defenses.

ZONE VS BEAR

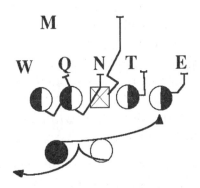

The tailback is reading the playside A gap player. If he bounces the play, he is on his own, and he has to be right. The aiming point is the inside leg of the tackle. The quarterback catches the ball, opens his hip up, and rides the tailback. The tailback drop steps, opens, and gets his eyes on the A gap. If he doesn't know what to do, he crams the ball into the A gap.

The next play is still called zone, but is run with a tight end and a G-scheme block with it. The tackle toward the tight end blocks down. The tight end base blocks the 6- or 7-technique. The guard pulls around the tight end's block. The backside is blocking the zone play. The action is the same for the tailback and quarterback except the tailback is thinking more sweep play than a zone play. He has a pulling guard in front of him. His aiming point is the butt of the tight end, instead the inside leg of the tackle. You can read this play if you want to and sometimes we do. We don't read zone plays as much as we do our counters. This play goes so fast we worry about fumbles if we read it. We don't read the defensive end so much because we want the back to be smoking to the playside.

If the tight end has a 9-technique on him, the pull will probably be up inside. He has to stay on his block. He doesn't have to kill the guy. The ball will go inside or outside of him. The tackle is the one who has the tough block. He has to know if he has a tackle that is penetrating or playing soft.

G-SCHEME SWEEP

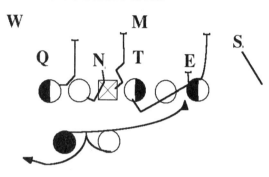

The next play I want to show you is guard-trap. The playside guard pulls like the G-scheme. The playside tackle influences down to the linebacker. The center blocks back unless he has a 1i or 2i technique to the playside. In that case, the center pulls and traps the first man outside the guard. The guard blocks down on the 1i or 2i technique. The backside guard stays in and combo blocks the 2- or 3-technique on him with the tackle. In most cases, the center blocks back for the cut off. The backside guard pulls and traps the first man past the center. The backside tackle cuts off the backside linebacker.

TRAP-CENTER PULL

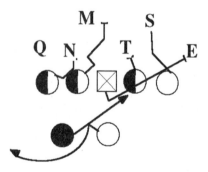

The quarterback-tailback mesh point is different from the zone play. The quarterback catches the snap and steps up. The tailback is coming right now like he is shot out of a cannon. It hits so fast that it would be hard to read. Seldom do we read this play, but you could. If the defensive end can close fast enough to stop this play, we should be doing some-

thing else. We like to run this play against a 6-man front. If they are playing seven, we throw the ball or run the option.

TRAP-GUARD PULL

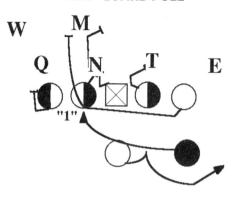

Against the bear look, we block down with the playside guard on the nose guard instead of influence pulling. The center blocks back on the backside defensive tackle and the backside guard traps the 3-technique. The tackles are on the linebackers.

TRAP VS BEAR

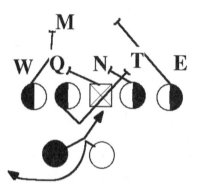

We pull with all our linemen. We pull the guard and center on the trap and the tackles on the tackle trap. Our linemen are pretty big. We have three kids over 300 pounds. The center was 280, and the right guard was 295. We are no pencil-neck team.

We run a tackle-pull counter. On the tackle trap, we are trapping the first man past the guard. It is the same hand-off as the zone play for the quarterback and tailback. The tailback is going to jab step to the right and come back left. Our tailback is responsible for the ball. The quarterback is responsible for the end. Since the tailback is looking for the ball, it slows him down a bit. That gives the fat guy time to get in front of him.

If we have a shade 1i or 2 i techniques, we are going to combo block with the center and playside guard. The playside tackle can pass set and drive the 5-technique like a draw play. He can stretch him outside like a sweep, or he can drive block him like the zone play. He can do whatever he wants, or he can use them all and mix them up. If the 5-technique slants inside, the tackle has to redirect and block him down. He is responsible for the 5-technique.

TACKLE TRAP-COUNTER VS SHADE

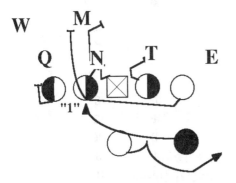

If there is a 3i or 4i technique, the playside guard and tackle set and drive the 3- and 5-technique outside. The backside tackle pulls inside the guard's block and turns up on the linebacker. The center and backside guard combo block on the backside shade, 1i or 2i defensive tackle, and the linebacker. If we get a slant inside by the 3- or 5-techniques, the tackle has to go around the down blocks. We tell the pulling tackle we would like to capture the outside breastplate of the linebacker and run to green grass.

TACKLE TRAP-COUNTER VS 3 TECHNIQUE

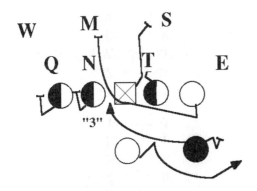

We could pull the backside guard and tackle, but that gives the defense a good chance to penetrate.

If someone penetrates off the backside, that knocks someone off their coarse. We would rather not have that. We also get a lot of wrong-arm techniques which spills the play. Doing it this way, we get north and south yardage most of the time.

Here is a good play you guys will like. It is a curve ball. There are a lot of teams that like to play an alley player. We went to a two-back set in the gun. We ran the same counter, and put a lead back on the alley player. We can run the same counter play and run a triple option from it. Instead of being in four wideouts, we are in a split-back shotgun. We can get an option going and only practice it five minutes a day. We want the end chasing from the backside. He is easy to read, and we have a heck of an option play.

2-BACK GUN

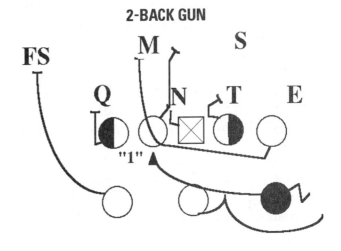

The last thing I want to show you is not a different play. It is called counter flip. This play mirrors the zone play or G-scheme. We use the same counter blocking, but instead of having the tailback on the side of the pulling tackle, he is on the other side. Everything is the same except he aligns opposite the pulling tackle. He takes three steps toward the quarterback, receives the ball, and breaks it back the other way. For the offensive line, the blocking is the same. In fact, we have run six different looks, and the fat guys are still blocking the same scheme. That is simple. This play averaged 8.2 yards this year. According to the statistics, this was our best running play. However, in the games we lost, this play sucked.

COUNTER FLIP

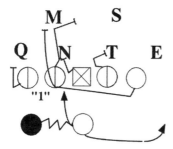

We read this play a lot. If the defensive end is closing, we pull the ball back, and the quarterback is free on the corner.

We threw for 220 yards a game. Our passing attack was not that bad, but we ran it better. The point of our success was that our guys played hard. We had some nice passing games because we spread the defense out. Our running game was excellent.

Before I quit, I've got to tell you this story. The Catholic Coaches League in Cincinnati was having a meeting. One of the coaches asked the group what the fastest thing on earth was? The first coach to reply said, "The mind, the human brain. Just think how fast the human brain translates all the responses to the muscles and organs of the body."

He asked another coach what he thought. The second coach thought about it for a minute and said, "The blink of the eye." He said he blinked all the time and didn't even know it.

He asked a third coach and that coach said, "Electricity. You can flip a switch, and the lights come on instantly."

Finally, he asked the last coach what he thought was the fastest thing on earth. The coach thought for a minute and then said, "Diarrhea." Everyone looked at each other shaking their head. They all wanted to know why he thought that. He said, "I woke up this morning and before I had a chance to think about it, blink an eye, or turn on a light, I messed in my pants."

I'll leave you with that. You are welcome to come to Northwestern to see us. It is always a pleasure to come to Cincinnati. I look forward to seeing you later. Thank you.

Notes

Notes

Notes

Notes

Notes